Library of
Davidson College

The Mythographic Art

Theseus and Ariadne, from John Gower's *Confessio Amantis*. Courtesy The Pierpont Morgan Library, New York, M. 126 f. 120.

The Mythographic Art

Classical Fable and the Rise of the Vernacular in

Early France and England

❧

Edited by
Jane Chance

University of Florida Press

Gainesville

The University of Florida Press is a member of University Presses of Florida, the scholarly publishing agency of the State University System of Florida. Books are selected for publication by faculty editorial committees at each of Florida's nine public universities: Florida A&M University (Tallahassee), Florida Atlantic University (Boca Raton), Florida International University (Miami), Florida State University (Tallahassee), University of Central Florida (Orlando), University of Florida (Gainesville), University of North Florida (Jacksonville), University of South Florida (Tampa), University of West Florida (Pensacola).

Orders for books published by all member presses should be addressed to University Presses of Florida, 15 NW 15th Street, Gainesville, Florida 32603.

Copyright © 1990 by the Board of Regents of the State of Florida

Printed in the U.S.A. on acid-free paper ∞

Library of Congress Cataloging-in-Publication Data

The Mythographic art : classical fable and the rise of the vernacular in early France and England / edited by Jane Chance.
    p. cm.
    Includes bibliographical references.
    ISBN 0-8130-0974-X (alk. paper).—ISBN 0-8130-0984-7 (pbk.: alk. paper)
    1. English literature—Classical influences.   2. Mythology, Classical, in literature.   3. French literature—To 1500—Classical influences.   4. Fables, Classical—Appreciation—England. 5. Fables, Classical—Appreciation—France.   6. Chaucer, Geoffrey, d. 1400—Knowledge—Folklore, mythology.   7. Shakespeare, William, 1564–1616—Knowledge—Folklore, mythology.   8. Christine, de Pisan, ca. 1364–ca. 1431—Knowledge—Folklore, mythology.   9. Green, Richard Hamilton.   I. Chance, Jane, 1945– .   II. Green, Richard Hamilton.
PR149.M95M98   1990
820.9′15—dc20   89-20422
                CIP

For Richard Hamilton Green

Contents

Preface   ix

Introduction
The Medieval "Apology for Poetry": Fabulous Narrative and Stories of the Gods   3   Jane Chance

I. Early France: The Mythographer and the Poet

From Mirror to Metamorphosis: Echoes of Ovid's Narcissus in Chrétien's *Erec et Enide*   47   Jeanne A. Nightingale

Sources, Nature, and Influence of the *Ovidius Moralizatus* of Pierre Bersuire   83   William D. Reynolds

Christine de Pizan as Chivalric Mythographer: *L'Epistre Othea*   100   Judith L. Kellogg

Christine de Pizan and the Judgment of Paris: A Court Poet's Use of Mythographic Tradition   125   Margaret J. Ehrhart

II. Early England: Chaucer and the Mythographers

Pallas Athena and the Threefold Choice in Chaucer's *Troilus and Criseyde*   159   Patricia R. Orr

Chaucer's Zephirus: Dante's Zefiro, St. Dominic, and the Idea of the *General Prologue*   177   Jane Chance

Mercury in the Garden: Mythographical Methods in the *Merchant's Tale* and *Decameron* 7.9   199   Janet Levarie Smarr

From Knossos to Knight's Tale: The Changing Face of Chaucer's Theseus   215   Melvin Storm

III. Renaissance England: Shakespeare and the Mythographers

The Comedy of Love: The Medieval Venus and Shakespeare's *Venus and Adonis*   235   Theodore L. Steinberg

Hercules in the Mind: Mythographic Tradition and the References in *Hamlet*   246   George D. Economou

Sandys, Ovid, and Female Chastity: The Encyclopedic Mythographer as Moralist   257   Deborah D. Rubin

IV. Bibliographic Epilogue

Eleven Unpublished Commentaries on Ovid's Judson Boyce Allen
Metamorphoses and Two Other Texts of
Mythographic Interest: Some Comments
on a Bibliography   281

Bibliography   291
Contributors   317
Index   321

Preface

Mythography, the explanation of classical mythology that often involves moralization or allegorization, remains unfamiliar even to most medievalists, unless they have worked specifically in the field. And yet it is impossible to forget that many medieval poets must have had at least some access to that tradition in the Middle Ages, given the plethora of mythological images in their poems and the prevalence of schoolbook commentaries incorporating mythographic glosses. Indeed, Richard Hamilton Green ends his influential essay, "Classical Fable and English Poetry in the Fourteenth Century" (presented initially to the English Institute in 1959 and published a year later in a volume edited by Dorothy Bethurum for Columbia University Press, *Critical Approaches to Medieval Literature*), with a challenge to the modern reader of medieval literature. His challenge consists of two parts. First, How exactly does the medieval poet—for example, Chaucer—use mythological images? And second, What kinds of answers to this question can be found in fourteenth-century mythological treatises and the mythographic tradition from which they derive?

One reason for the importance of this question remains only implicit rather than explicit in Green's statement: the incongruity of a Christian poet's use of pagan myths matches the incongruity of a moral poet's use of immoral and scandalous stories, as were many of the tales of the Roman gods. To look for resolutions of such apparent incongruities in the "olde bokes" of the fourteenth-century mythological tradition, as Professor Green suggests that we do, attempts both a historical *and* a literary reconstruction of the poetic process at that moment. What we should look for are reasons that poets might safely ignore both the lack of belief and lack of morality in the classical myths they used.

Exactly where—from what "olde bokes"—did Chaucer and other poets of the vernacular derive these classical fables and how much original interpretation did these poets themselves offer? If they substituted their own interpretations for earlier interpretations of these myths, then how, and why? What will their successors make of their treatment?

To begin answering some of these questions, we need first to understand more about the source material for much of their poetic fabulizing—the mythographers and commentators. Then, in response to the second and third questions, while it will not be possible in this book to explain how all medieval and Renaissance writers specifically used the mythographic tradition, nevertheless we can at least suggest why some of them did and the ways in which many of the most important figures united vernacular forms with Latin scholarship. The particular essays gathered in this volume reflect the interests of scholars currently at work on mythography in selected poets and mythographers. The field is large, important, and to a great extent untapped. We are hopeful that these essays will catalyze further exploration of the many medieval and Renaissance writers who drew upon the mythographic tradition.

This volume has been collected to honor Richard Hamilton Green on the eve of his retirement. Through his teaching, his administration of English departments and graduate programs in English, and his seminal articles on medieval poetics he has shaped modern scholars' understanding of the Middle Ages—he has presented the appropriate questions necessary to answer before we read Chaucer and other medieval and Renaissance poets. For this reason the title of this volume reflects a variation of Professor Green's own English Institute lecture. For this reason, too, the volume is dedicated, with much appreciation, to him.

Thanks are due especially to the National Endowment for the Humanities, from whose 1985 Summer Seminar for College Teachers on "Chaucer and Mythography," which I was fortunate enough to direct, the impetus for several of the essays contained in this volume emerged. In addition, research for material contained in my Introduction and on the whole of the mythographic tradition, which has shaped this volume, was completed in part in Italy in 1980–81 because of released time granted by a John Simon Guggenheim Memorial Foundation Fellowship, for which I am most grateful. Also, my own Introduction was recast during a visit to the Institute for Advanced Study in Princeton, 1988–89, to work on the longer study of medieval mythography, for which released time from teaching I am indebted both to the Institute and to Rice University. Finally, funds for travel relating to this volume were in part supplied by a Rice University research grant for 1984–86; the dean of humanities, Allen Matusow, has also supplied funds for rechecking of bibliographic references and for an index.

In collecting and editing this volume I have been aided by the sage advice in particular of David Anderson, Jackson J. Campbell, Margaret Ehrhart, R. Allen Shoaf, Melvin Storm, and Julian Wasserman. Marcia Carey at the Historical Library of the Institute for Advanced Study very kindly checked medieval names against the Name Authority File and helped check documentation, as did Deborah Thompson of the English Department at Rice University.

Although none of the essays in this collection has previously appeared in print, several have been delivered in shortened and altered form as conference papers. Theodore L. Steinberg delivered a portion of his essay previously as a paper, "*Venus and Adonis*: Immortality or Immorality?," at the Fourth Ohio Conference on Mediaeval Studies, John Carroll University, Cleveland, Ohio, October 9, 1977. Janet Smarr presented her essay originally as "Chaucer and the *Decameron*: Some New Connections?" in a session on Boccaccio and Chaucer at Kalamazoo, May 8, 1981. My essay, "Chaucer's Zephirus and the Idea of the *General Prologue*," was delivered as a paper in a May 1985 session on "Chaucer and Mythography," which I organized for the Twentieth International Conference on Medieval Studies, Kalamazoo, Michigan. Judith Kellogg's paper, written for the NEH Summer Seminar on "Chaucer and Mythography," was presented at the Twenty-first International Conference on Medieval Studies, The Medieval Institute, Western Michigan University, Kalamazoo, Michigan, in May 1986, in a session I organized on "The End of Medieval Mythography" and was entitled, "Christine de Pisan's *Epistle of Othéa* as Mythographic Text." The essay by Melvin Storm was delivered as a paper in a session I organized for the Twentieth CEMERS Conference on Medieval Studies, "The Classics in the Middle Ages," State University of New York, Binghamton, New York, on October 19, 1986. Finally, Margaret Ehrhart's shortened version of the essay on Christine de Pizan, "Christine de Pizan and the Judgment of Paris: A Court Poet's Use of Mythographic Tradition," was delivered on February 20, 1988, at the Fifth Annual Conference of the Illinois Medieval Association, in Quincy, Illinois.

Introduction

The Medieval "Apology for Poetry"
Fabulous Narrative and Stories of the Gods

Jane Chance

At the end of the pilgrimage in the fourteenth-century masterpiece of *The Canterbury Tales*, just before the last (and longest, most moralistic) "tale," the Host turns to the Parson and cries, " 'Telle us a fable anon, for cokkes bones!' " (*Parsons's Prologue*, line 29, ed. Benson). It is a strange request: parsons normally deliver sermons, although they may use "fables" to illustrate and elucidate their texts. And indeed, Chaucer's Parson responds indignantly:

> Thou getest fable noon ytoold for me,
> For Paul, that writeth unto Thymothee,
> Repreveth hem that weyven soothfastnesse
> And tellen fables and swich wrecchednesse.
> Why sholde I sowen draf out of my fest,
> Whan I may sowen whete, if that me lest? (31–36)

The antipathy of Chaucer's solemn and moral Parson to "fable" attests to the *wrecchednesse* of *draf*—meaning pejorative lies associated with the fables of the pagans. The Parson prefers instead *soothfastnesse*, or *whete*—the truth of God as expressed in the moral lessons of the seven deadly sins delineated in his own homily. In the context of the *Canterbury Tales*, he reacts so vehemently to the Host's suggestion that he tell a fable because of a desire to dissociate himself from the scandalous tale just retold by the Manciple. That tale was scandalous because it invoked the god Apollo's murder of the pregnant Coronis in response to the news of her adultery delivered by the tattletale crow. What is interesting about this moment in the masterpiece is what it tells us about late medieval literary theory and the secular use of classical myth in vernacular poetic.

Despite the Parson's rejection of classical fable, or *fabula*, medieval poets frequently adapted apparently immoral or unseemly stories of the gods to their own moral, satiric, and political purposes in the manner of Chaucer's Manciple. Such major medieval poets begin as early as the twelfth-century allegorist, the French Alanus de Insulis, and continue in the vernacular in succeeding periods with Guillaume de Lorris, Jean de

Meun, Guillaume de Machaut, Jean Froissart, Eustace Deschamps, and Christine de Pizan. In Italy, the major poets using such fable include the fourteenth-century Dante, Petrarch, and Boccaccio; in England of the fourteenth and fifteenth centuries, such poets include Chaucer, John Gower, John Lydgate, William Dunbar, Robert Henryson, and Thomas Hoccleve.

What kinds of mythological fables do these poets find attractive? They frequently center on love, sexual relationships, immorality. In Chaucer alone, to use one example, in addition to the supposed adultery of Coronis in the *Manciple's Tale*, in the *Complaint of Mars* the sun exposes Venus's adultery with Mars so that she flees to refuge with Mercury. In the *Parlement of Foules* Venus lies undressed, lasciviously desporting with her porter Richesse, and prominently placed Priapus boasts a large virile member. In *Book of the Duchess* Morpheus as god of sleep acts buffoonishly when he himself is awakened from sleep and is implored for help by a sleepless lover. In the *Merchant's Tale*, Pluto and Proserpina, fairy king and queen, first allow the old blind January to see his young fresh wife May cuckolding him in the crotch of the pear tree and then grant her the rationalizing explanation that convinces him she was trying only to help him—indeed, successfully at this moment—restore his sight. In the *Knight's Tale* the gods and planets Venus, Mars, and Diana, to whom the principal characters build altars, remain responsible for human suffering whether found in courtly love, murderous combat, or childbirth. Even though most of these poems soften the gods' immorality with humor and irony, thereby mitigating the harshness denoted, say, by son Jupiter's castration of his father Saturn (depicted as chief god by Chaucer in the *Knight's Tale*), nevertheless the immoral activities remain disreputable. Of course Chaucer's use of these mythological gods was by no means unconventional in the Middle Ages—his friend "moral Gower" in the *Confessio Amantis* (*Confession of Amans*) uses the Roman god Genius as a priest of love who confesses the lover Amans by reciting classical tales of heroic and divine love, and Lydgate in a poem of the same name describes a "Temple of Glass" inscribed with stories of distraught lovers taken from Ovid and other classical writers and devoted to Venus.

These medieval poets frequently cast as characters in their poems Greco-Roman gods whose roles or decisions affect or reflect the complexity and idiosyncracy of human behavior, particularly of a sexual or moral nature. To an audience that has accepted the theocentricity of the Middle Ages, this practice may bewilder. But the medieval poets who used them did so for two reasons. First, imitation and convention—other poets had done so, implicitly drawing on the codification of literary theory found in the fourth-century Macrobius's commentary on the *Somnium Scipionis* (*Dream of Scipio*). This important work rationalized the use of the pagan gods in certain kinds of narrative and constituted the wellspring of much late medieval poetry. Second, literacy, by which is meant Latin literacy—as educated men, they were all familiar with the school commentaries on the great classical epic poems of Virgil and Ovid, the *Aeneid* and the *Metamorphoses*, and with handbooks of medieval mythography, or the rationalizing of classical myth through moralization and allegorization. These texts had been used initially in the medieval schools—from postclassical times—for students studying grammar and rhetoric; the commentaries and handbooks developed because of the difficulty, in time, in understanding ancient poets such as Virgil and Ovid and their (by then) puzzling or obscure references to mythology (in addition to geography, rhetoric and grammar, history, religious ritual, among others). Let us briefly explore each reason in greater detail.

In relation to the conventionality of poetic practice, the most important theoretical justification for the use of classical myth in medieval poetry derived from its moral validation, as a means of cloaking base or ignoble truths, and the viability of this means over a period of several centuries in the later Middle Ages. Macrobius followed in the footsteps of Plato in preferring philosophy to the fables of the poets in his commentary on Cicero's *Somnium Scipionis*, itself a "commentary" on the tenth book of Plato's *Republic*. Influencing medieval literary theory primarily through its categorization of dreams and its analysis of fiction,[1] Macrobius's commentary explains, first, that the kind of fable that enhances virtue has a true setting and plot—is truthful—but is written in a fictitious style, acceptable to philosophy. Second, such fable is called *narratio fabulosa*, "fabulous narrative." Third, it is used "cum veritas argumento subest solaque fit narratio fabulosa"—when "the argument is real but is presented in the form of a fable" (1.2.10). Such a narrative is appropriate only for sacred matters, defined by Macrobius as the performance of sacred rites; the stories of Hesiod and Orpheus that "de deorum progenie actuve narrantur," "treat of the ancestry and deeds of the gods"; the mystic concepts of the Pythagoreans; and discourses about the soul, or the powers of the lower or upper air (1.2.9, 14). In addition, for fabulous narrative to be formally appropriate, "sacrarum rerum notio sub pio figmentorum velamine honestis et tecta rebus et vestita nominibus enuntiatur," a "decent and dignified conception of holy truths, with respectable events and characters, is presented beneath a modest veil of allegory" (1.2.11). This *velamen figmentorum*, or "veil of images, allegory," is necessary because, when a philosopher imprudently reveals these *arcana*, or "secrets of Nature," as did Numenius when he interpreted the Eleusinian mysteries, he debases and offends the gods (1.2.19) and allows base men to see Nature "apertam nudamque," "openly naked" (1.2.17).

This particular fourth- (or fifth-) century tract became especially important in the twelfth century, in part because of the interest of Parisian philosophers like William of Conches, who wrote a commentary on it; from him the contemporary theologian and writer Alanus de Insulis obtained his practice in the Latin visionary allegory of *De planctu Naturae* (*The Complaint of Nature*), as did Bernard Silvestris in his *Cosmographia*. And thus the terminology and concept of *fabula* and fabulous narrative entered the literary conventions which so influenced poets of the medieval romance languages. We know that as late as the fourteenth century Chaucer was familiar with Macrobius and the theory of dreams because of his reference to him in several of his dream visions and the *Nun's Priest's Tale*.

In relation to the second reason, Latin literacy, because the preservation of the classics in the Middle Ages has ensured the existence of modern editions, their concomitant preservation of classical mythology has revealed a fascinating conundrum. Despite the monotheism of Christianity, monastery and cathedral schools developed in which learned Christian commentators and their scribes worked to transmit classical culture in written form. From these transmitters and rationalizers of classical mythology, called "mythographers," whose commentaries on the classics depended upon moralizations and allegorizations our scientific age would regard as eccentric, bizarre, the later medieval poets primarily drew their allegorized classical gods and goddesses.

Why certain works were chosen for such glossation and then commentary, and *how* classicism—or specifically pagan literature containing stories of the gods, often licentious—was allowed to coexist with Christianity and the study of scripture becomes clearer with an examination of the evolution of the schools, their types and curricula, and their geographical distribution in the Middle Ages, although there has been no complete and systematic study of the mythographic tradition or the transmission and moralization of classical mythology in the Middle Ages. As long ago as 1947, Elliott and Elder hoped in print that "Someday . . . someone will give us the full and fascinating story of classical mythology in mediaeval poetry, much as Professor Bush has done—and one hopes with nearly as much skill—for two periods of English poetry" (p. 190). Unfortunately, despite various more specialized studies of individual mythographers, historical periods, or gods in the Middle Ages, no such study has appeared. General definitions of medieval allegoresis have been supplied in studies by Curtius; de Lubac; Tuve, *Allegorical Imagery*; Robertson, *A Preface*; and Chydenius; as have general overviews of the literary or artistic survival of the pagan gods in the Middle Ages, in works by von Bezold, Panofsky and Saxl, and Pépin. Others have traced the moralization of a single classical god or hero through the literature and art of the Middle Ages—Saturn (Panofsky, *Studies*; Klibansky, Panofsky, and Saxl), Venus and Cupid (Lynn F. Williams, Twycross, Schreiber), Nature (Economou), Fortune (Patch), and Genius (Chance, *The Genius Figure*), Hercules (Panofsky, *Hercules*; Tate, Gaeta, Jung), Orpheus (Heitmann, Freidman, Warden), Aeneas and Dido (Hall, Lord) and the Argonauts (Roseberg), Pandora (Dora and Erwin Panofsky), Cerberus (Savage), and Paris (Chance, "Medieval," Ehrhart). Still others have analyzed the mythographic or allegoric process within a single century, the twelfth century in works by Jeauneau, "L'Usage," Stock, Wetherbee, and Dronke; the fourteenth and fifteenth centuries in works by Green, "Classical Fable"; Smalley; Judson B. Allen, *The Friar as Critic*; Minnis, *Chaucer*; and the sixteenth century in works by Bush; Seznec; Tuve, *Elizabethan and Metaphysical Imagery*; Wind; D. C. Allen; and Moss. Scholars have also focused on the range of commentators on a particular classical or medieval author, but often without much attention to mythography per se—those commentators on Virgil (Comparetti, Baswell), Ovid (Battaglia, Demats, Munari, Robson, Hexter), Boethius (Courcelle, "Etude critique," *La Consolation*; Bolton, *varia*; Gibson), the *Ecloga Theoduli* (Guthrie), and Dante (Rocca; Sandkühler; Hollander, "Dante Project"). Finally, research on individual mythographers, with some exceptions, has centered mostly on the establishing of texts. Clearly a longer study is needed, to probe the provenance, history, and influence of each mythographer within the tradition as it was inherited from an earlier age, ultimately deriving from classical poetry, philosophy, and mythography[2]—a direction reflected in the work of the late Judson B. Allen (*Ethical Poetic*).

Jean Seznec and D. C. Allen in their work on the sixteenth century argued that the Middle Ages and the Renaissance formed a more or less continuous tradition in which the ancient gods were preserved in historical (euhemeristic), physical (natural), and moral (or else etymological) interpretations drawn from classical tradition and, with the exception of the historical, frequently allegorical in character. They did differentiate the Renaissance from the earlier traditions in one respect—in its approach to mythological evidence. Seznec specifically assumed the pagan gods were transmitted to the Renaissance not alone through texts but especially through manuscript illustrations and monumental art, and D. C. Allen assumed that, of the commentaries, those on Ovid in the later Middle Ages were most influential in the development of the mythographic handbook of the Renaissance.

To shape their conclusions to reflect more accurately the nature of medieval mythography, the premise of this collection concerns the differences between the tradition in the Middle Ages and in both the classical and Renaissance traditions, although one may see clearly how the entire tradition, from antiquity to the Renaissance, developed in one continuous and interwoven network of written sources and influences, interrelated media, and meshed kinds of writing, Latin and vernacular, scholastic and courtly. Because medieval mythography was a product of the schools and universities—emerging out of the glosses of grammarian and philosopher preserved in schoolbooks or written down by their students—the interpretation of myth changed as educational forms and systems changed, and in accord with the shaping of external political and ecclesiastical forces. When the schools shifted from monastery and court school to the cathedral and then to the university, so also the texts studied in those schools changed; dialectic and then philosophy—Neoplatonism followed by Aristotelianism—were preferred over grammar. Because Ovid was a schoolbook author only very late in the Middle Ages, the commentaries on the *Metamorphoses* and his other poems really began very late, in the twelfth century, and attained a vogue only in the fourteenth and fifteenth centuries. It was also in this period that medieval poets like Chaucer and Gower used these earlier commentaries and handbooks of mythography to understand the antique poets and to create their own classicized and mythological poems.

The Mythographic Commentaries, Glosses, and Handbooks of the Schools

In these commentaries and glosses medieval "literary critics"—the grammarians, schoolmasters, university teachers, and philosophers—attempted to perceive the natural truth underlying the artificial integument or "cover" supplied by the literal or historical level of the *narratio fabulosa*, "fabulous narrative," and thus justify the study of the classics by Christian exegetes. This process of uncovering, we should note, is the mirror (obverse) image of the poet's act of covering up secrets, or truths, with integuments.

Most of these classical myths originally appeared in the epics of Homer and Hesiod and were rationalized by mythographers (Greek schoolmasters and philosophers) as early as the sixth century BC. Medieval mythographic commentaries tended to center on a few seminal classical epics—those of Virgil (70–19 BC), Ovid (43 BC–17? AD), Lucan (39–65

AD), Statius (45–96 AD)—and a late medieval epic, what might itself be termed a "commentary" on Virgil's *Aeneid*, at least the sixth book thereof with its descent into the Underworld, the *Divina commedia* of Dante (ca. 1307). They also focused on popular schoolbooks whose mythological allusions required exegesis, such as *De nuptiis Philologiae et Mercurii* (*The Marriage of Philology and Mercury*) of Martianus Capella (ca. 410–439 AD), a *chantefable* or *prosimetrum* like its imitator, the *De consolatione Philosophiae* (*The Consolation of Philosophy*) of Boethius (?480–?524 AD), and the ninth- or tenth-century imitation of Virgil's *Eclogues*, the *Ecloga Theoduli* (*Eclogue of Theodulus*). In addition there were dictionaries and encyclopedias that helped to explain puzzling classical and mythological allusions, often set within the frame of the seven liberal arts of the schools—that by Isidore perhaps of greatest importance, but also by Papias the Lombard, Osbern of Gloucester, Hugutio of Pisa, Giovanni Balbi, and other compilers—and actual handbooks of mythography heavily influenced by Fulgentius known as the three Vatican mythographies and the Digby mythography. Finally, very late in the Middle Ages—in the fourteenth and fifteenth centuries—there appeared commentaries on Seneca's tragedies and Augustine's *De civitate Dei* (*The City of God*). The former were especially influential in England and Italy, having an effect on the humanism of the English Renaissance that spawned Shakespeare and Elizabethan and Jacobean drama.

For the Middle Ages, commentaries on Virgil by Servius and Fulgentius were the most influential, supplemented by the Neoplatonic glosses on Virgil in Macrobius's commentary on the *Somnium Scipionis* and the *Saturnalia*. Two traditions developed from these commentaries: first, an *Eclogue* tradition, through the Merovingian scholia on the *Eclogues* and *Georgics* by the Berne Scholiast (Adanan the Scot?), and the ninth- (tenth-) century Virgilian imitation, the *Ecloga Theoduli*; and second, an *Aeneid* tradition, through the Carolingian commentary on the sixth book of the *Aeneid* (possibly by Remigius of Auxerre), the long twelfth-century commentary on the first six books supposedly by Bernard Silvestris, glosses on Macrobius's commentary on the *Somnium Scipionis* by William of Conches (which no doubt influenced the work of Bernard, in Dronke), and later moralizations of the *Aeneid* by John of Salisbury (in the *Policraticus*) and Alexander Neckam in *De naturis rerum* (*On the Natures of Things*), both of which depend for their interpretations upon Bernard's commentary.

In addition to these early Virgil commentaries there also were grammatical glosses, frequently etymological when coupled with explanations of the gods, on Statius. These appeared in the sixth-century scholia on

Statius's *Thebaid* by Lactantius Placidus and the "commentary" by Fulgentius—and continued to be used in dictionaries and epitomes such as the tenth-century scholia on the *Achilleid*, as well as in the encyclopedic *Etymologiae* of Isidore in the seventh century and the *Epitome* of Festus by Paulus Diaconus in the eighth and ninth centuries. The technique also appears in tenth-, eleventh-, and twelfth-century scholia on Lucan (ed. Endt and Usener), including those of Arnulf of Orleans. The tradition culminates, in the eleventh and twelfth centuries, with the *Derivationes* of Papias the Lombard and of Osbern of Gloucester, whose works were used rather heavily by Hugutio of Pisa and Giovanni Balbi of Genoa in the twelfth and thirteenth centuries.

Martianus Capella commentaries had an enormous impact on the rest of the Middle Ages. They began with the Irish scholars Martin of Laon, the author of the Anonymous Cambridge, and John Scot, and eventually reached the continent with the influential Remigius of Auxerre. The latter's commentry (and revisions and translations by Rather of Verona, Notker Labeo, and the Anonymous Barberinus) remained current until the twelfth century, when it was driven out by the Florentine commentary (perhaps by William of Conches) and commentaries by Bernard Silvestris and Alexander Neckam.

Similar in importance and impact was the Carolingian emphasis on Boethius—specifically, scattered mythological allusions in the *Consolatio*—beginning with the glosses of the Anonymous of St. Gall, the supposed commentary of Asser (MS Vat Lat. 3363), and the translation by King Alfred into Old English. The late Carolingian Remigius of Auxerre's very important commentary, like his Martianus Capella commentary, drove out the earlier ones and reigned through revisions and translations (by the K reviser, Notker Labeo, the Pseudo-John Scot or Erfurt commentary and the Vatican commentaries), until the twelfth century, when the glosses of William of Conches, who also wrote a commentary on the *Timaeus*, superseded it.

Handbooks similar to the fifth-sixth-century Fulgentius's *Mitologiae* (*Mythologies*) summarize the myths found in Hyginus (especially *Fabulae*), Servius, Lactantius Placidus on the *Thebaid*, and other texts, and moralize them primarily by using ideas taken from Fulgentius, or indirectly from Fulgentius through the Boethius and Martianus Capella commentaries. They begin with the first Vatican mythographer (possibly Adanan the Scot), continue with the Carolingian second Vatican mythographer (possibly Remigius of Auxerre, or someone of his school), and conclude with the twelfth-century Fulgentian plagiarist Baudri de Bourgueil, the English Digby mythographer, and the influential third

Vatican mythographer (possibly Albericus of London, or Alexander Neckam).

Engendered by the translation of Aristotle into Arabic and then into Latin, the Ovid commentary was heavily affected by all the preceding commentaries, especially the Fulgentian handbooks. In embryonic form it first appears in the sixth-century epitome of the *Metamorphoses* by Lactantius Placidus, the Carolingian comments on various Ovidian stories in a mythological poem by Theodulf of Orleans, and grammatical notes on Ovid's *Metamorphoses* by the tenth-century Manegold von Lautenbach and the twelfth-century Ralph of Beauvais. The moralizing of Ovid is fostered by the eleventh-, twelfth-, and thirteenth-century glosses on the *Fasti*, and by twelfth-century commentaries on both the *Fasti* and the *Metamorphoses* by Arnulf of Orleans. It is the transitional John of Garland in the thirteenth century who bridges the gap between the grammatical and moral glosses of the earlier scholiasts and the full-scale commentaries of the later allegorists.

Nonepic works contributed to the growth of the mythographic tradition—for example, two late eleventh-twelfth-century commentaries by Bernard d'Utrecht and Alexander Neckam on the *Ecloga Theoduli*, that Carolingian imitation of Virgil's *Eclogues*. This schoolbook became important for the later Middle Ages because it juxtaposed classical myths with Old Testament legends and thus signaled the development of a new kind of allegorical exegesis of classical myth that would flourish in later centuries. But in the earlier Middle Ages its commentaries were also important, in their glosses on classical myths, because of their incorporation of material drawn from all the various commentaries, especially the Boethius and Martianus Capella commentaries and the Fulgentian handbooks.

It should be made clear that not all the classical epics and medieval schoolbooks were equally important as sources of mythological material in the Middle Ages. The Fulgentian manuals and the commentaries on Ovid's *Metamorphoses* provide the richest and most influential mythographic material, and the *Ecloga Theoduli*, Lucan, and Statius the least, either because of the paucity of fable within the work (Statius), or because of the relatively few commentators (all three). The Virgil, Martianus Capella, Boethius, and Dante commentaries provide a middle ground, largely because the original works offer a smaller proportion of mythological material than the Ovidian.

Further, the distinction between poem as school text and its prose commentary blurred as the scholastic tradition developed. That is, the mythographic tradition in the Middle Ages may have begun with commentaries on the classical epic whose myths were later collected into mythographies, but there were also late antique and medieval works which did not fit the epic definition that were also used as texts in the grammar schools and commented on by monks, such as the *prosimetra* of Martianus and Boethius, just as there were medieval poems written in imitation of classical forms—"epics" and "eclogues"—heavily indebted to the commentary tradition and used as schoolbooks. The relatively late schoolbook of the *Ecloga Theoduli* is not epic at all but eclogue, modeled on those of the epic-writer and great "magister" Virgil; but as a poem it draws heavily on the Virgil commentaries of Servius.

Interestingly enough, in the fourteenth century, especially in Italy, the close relationship between epic and mythographic commentary is revealed in the mixing of two forms. Dante's epic can be seen as a "commentary" on Virgil's *Aeneid*, especially the sixth book with its descent into the underworld. Similarly Petrarch's Latin epic *Africa* (which includes a long catalogue of gods in its third book) can be viewed as a "gloss" on Macrobius's commentary on the *Somnium Scipionis* in that it relates the story of Scipio's conquest of Carthage at the end of the second Punic War. Further, the mythographic manuals of Giovanni Boccaccio and Coluccio Salutati borrow epic themes or structures to unify their material. Boccaccio's *Genealogie deorum gentilium (Genealogy of the Gentile Gods)* begins with an "epic hero" similar to Augustus, descendant of the gods in the *Metamorphoses*, only he is the progenitor of the gods—Demogorgon, a figure who first appears in the second Vatican mythography.

If, as we have just observed, the lines of demarcation between school commentary and poem blurred and softened, and even interchanged (as they did in the ninth-tenth-century *Ecloga Theoduli*), why did they do so? And at what point did the mythographic and vernacular literary traditions converge?

The Vernacular Poets and the Latin Mythographic Tradition

The Carolingian *Ecloga Theoduli*, written as it is in paired quatrains of leonine hexameter alternating classical myth with Old Testament legend organized by the chronology of Scripture, may very well have been designed as a mnemonic text for schoolboys to recall the important figures of two necessary scholastic traditions. A mythological rather than a mythographic work—there is no glossation per se—it obeys Macrobian dicta concerning the veiling of secrets and truths. While it differs from the *Metamorphoses* in that it does not relay whole fables but instead merely summarizes them succinctly, it differs also from most other school texts of mythographic interest, like Martianus's *De nuptiis* or Boethius's *Consolatio*, because it also weaves into the summary information drawn from Servius's commentary. It is also modest and decorous in its treatment of what might have been regarded as "ignoble" material—for example, Jupiter expels his father Saturn, but there is no mention of the severing of his testicles. If it were intended for the school boys it was later used to educate, such veiling seems not only appropriate for pedagogical reasons but also for Macrobian and literary ones. Indeed, in outlining fabulous narrative as a form, Macrobius took care to exclude as inappropriate the philosopher's use of bawdy and immoral stories of the gods. In such a case, "contextio narrationis per turpia et indigna numinibus ac monstro similia componitur ut di adulteri, Saturnus pudenda Caeli patris abscidens et ipse rursus a filio regni potito in vincla coniectus," the "presentation of the plot involves matters that are base and unworthy of divinities and are monstrosities of some sort (as, for example, gods caught in adultery, Saturn cutting off the privy parts of his father Caelus and himself thrown into chains by his son and successor)" (1.2.11).

By the twelfth century, however, the French Alanus de Insulis in his *De planctu* laments the homosexuality and other deviant sexual practices of his contemporary ecclesiastics; his use of graphic metaphor and symbol for the reproductive organs (hammer and anvil, pen and parchment) governed by Venus does veil the literal truth—but barely. His thirteenth-century French imitator Jean de Meun, in continuing the visionary *Roman de la Rose* (*Romance of the Rose*) written some forty years earlier by Guillaume de Lorris (1230–35?), even more graphically depicts the sexual organs, as plow and furrowed earth, and ends his sequel with what seems to be the lover plucking and violating a rosebud (the lady), but that act in the way it is described—mythologically compared to the confrontation of Hercules with Cacus in his cave—leaves nothing to the imagination.

Late medieval poets may have disregarded Macrobius's prohibition against the use of scandalous stories of the gods because of the influential literary theories of the University of Paris, which encouraged the use of classical fable as a vehicle for Neoplatonic philosophy.[3] Among such theories were the specifically Macrobian comments of William of Conches, who, with his contemporaries, argued that the pagan gods represented projections of the World Soul or Natura. According to William, the pagans mistakenly apotheosized this world, and all its earthy and earthly processes and products, into divine figures, in contrast to the Christians, who believed in the Other World as the source of the divine, and in contrast to the Neoplatonists, who envisioned the immanence of

Idea in this world. The processes of nature, therefore, for William manifested the World Soul, Spiritus Sanctus, *anima mundi*. Frequently identified in the twelfth century with the concept of Natura, these processes were depicted so in literary and allegorical form, as in Alanus de Insulis's *De planctu Naturae* and *Anticlaudianus* (Chenu, *Nature*, 20–21).

The most important reinterpretation of Macrobius in the Middle Ages belongs to William, whose commentary primarily glosses the second chapter of the first book, that section dealing with fiction, to justify descriptions of immoral activities by the gods through an explanation of their reflection of natural or physical laws. When, for example, Macrobius denigrates stories about the "di adulteri," "gods who are adulterers," in 1.2.11, William responds, "*Ut dii adulteri*: hec verba sunt turpia, sed tamen per illud adulterium aliquod honestum et pulcrum revera habet significari, utpote de adulterio Iovis legitur cum Cybele, Semele, et huiusmodi alliis [sic] que in loco suo exponentur" (7a, Dronke, 71; "the words are base, and yet by that adultery something honorable and beautiful must indeed be meant: as can be read in the case of Jupiter's adulteries with Cybele, and Semele, and other things of this kind which will be expounded in due course").[4] Indeed, William rationalizes (makes "honorable and beautiful") through the philosophical truths of Nature all the gods mentioned in Macrobius as behaving scandalously and thus unsuitably for mention in fabulous narratives. For example, the literal myth of Semele's impregnation by Jupiter, which resulted in the birth of Bacchus, William naturally explains as the earth impregnated by aether in winter to produce the vines in summer.[5] The castration of Saturn by his son Jupiter, from which act Venus was born, is explained in the Macrobius commentary as, first, the ripening of fruits by the warmth of the upper element, which makes them ready for harvesting, and second, the casting of the fruits into the sea—that is, the human belly, from which Venus or *luxuria* (sensual delight) is born.[6] He also explains the adultery of Mars and Venus, the relationship of Ceres and Bacchus, and Pluto's rape of Proserpina in similarly moralized fashion.[7]

The conventional twelfth-century literary term to describe this "cloak" of immoral secrets is literally *involucrum*, or *integumentum*, "cover" (used for plates of food).[8] Because it is used by poets to cover up an immoral or unfortunate trait ascribed to some worthy person or god, it follows Macrobius's second, improper, kind of fabulous narrative.[9] William's concept of *integumentum* apparently covers both scriptural and classical texts (although his follower Bernard Silvestris distinguished between *integumentum*—which applied to mythology—and *allegoria*—which applied to the Bible). That William's rationalizations of immoral fable endured and influenced other poets is clear from the influential words of the fourteenth-century Jean de Meun in his continuation of the unfinished *Roman de la Rose*. His character Raison justifies to the lover Amaunt her use of the indelicate word *coilles* ("cullions") by contrasting its truth, its natural reality, with the covert and hidden—"Les integumenz aus poetes" ("integuments of the poets," 7168):

> Si dist l'en bien noz escoles
> Maintes choses par paraboles
> Qui mout sont beles a entendre;
> Si ne deit l'en mie tout prendre
> A la letre quanque l'en ot.
> En ma parole autre sen ot,
> Au meins quant de coilles palaie,
> Don si briement paler voulaie,
> Que celui que tu i veauz metre;
> E qui bien entendrait la letre,
> Le sen verrait en l'escriture
> Qui esclarcist la fable ocure;
> La verité dedenz reposte
> Serait clere s'ele iert esposte;
> Bien l'entendras se bien repetes
> Les integumenz aus poetes:
> La verras une grant partie
> Des secrez de philosophie,
> Ou mout te voudras deliter,
> E si pourras mout profiter;
> En delitant profiteras,
> En profitant deliteras,
> Car en leur jeus e en leur fables
> Gisent deliz mout profitables,
> Souz cui leur pensees couvrirent
> Quant le veir des fables vestirent;
> Si te couvendrait a ce tendre,
> Se bien vequz la parole entendre.
> Mais puis t'ai teus deus moz renduz,
> E tu les as bien entenduz,
> Qui pris deivent estre a la letre
> Tout proprement, senz glose metre.   (7153–84, Langlois 3:32–33)

["In our schools indeed they say many things in parables that are very beautiful to hear; however, one should not take whatever one hears according to the letter. In my speech there is another sense, at least when I was speaking of testicles, which I wanted to speak briefly here, than that which you want to give to the word. He who understands the letter would see in the writing the sense which clarifies the obscure fable. The truth hidden within would be clear if it were explained. You will understand it well if you review the integuments of the poets. There you will see a large part of the secrets of philosophy. There you will want to take your great delight, and you will thus be able to profit a great deal. You will profit in delight and delight in profit, for in the playful fables of the poets lie very profitable delights beneath which they cover their thoughts when they clothe the truth in fables. If you want to understand my saying well, you would have to stretch your mind in this direction.

"But afterward I pronounced these two words—and you understood them well—which should be taken quite strictly according to the letter, without gloss."   (7153–83, Dahlberg, p. 136)

Reason means that some words do not require gloss because they are not hidden—they represent the thing itself, uncovered, natural. The advent of Aristotelian philosophy has altered not only Macrobius's, but even William of Conches' Neoplatonist theory of fiction. This loosening of the bonds of literary theory and classical fable accompanies other changes in the way the Latin mythographic tradition and the vernacular intersect.

If later poets like Chaucer were not as interested as William in Neoplatonic concepts of the World Soul and Nature, or as Jean de Meun in Aristotelian concepts of Nature and generation, nevertheless their poems suggest that they were equally if not more interested in the use of pagan gods in "fabulous narrative." It is at this point that we must ask, what mythographic forms were inherited by the vernacular poets from the earlier Middle Ages in that period? How did the changes in the mythographic tradition affect the rise of vernacular literature? How did the poet writing in the vernacular adapt the mythographic Latin tradition to his or her own purposes? How did mythography in other vernacular poems influence individual poets? Did the Renaissance really discard the wealth of mythographic and poetic material inherited from scholars and the poets of the Middle Ages and instead return to the classical text itself?

Although we cannot begin to answer specifically all these questions in the limited space of one volume, nevertheless it is possible to isolate one turning point within the evolution of the mythographic tradition. As Richard Hamilton Green implicitly noted in his English Institute lecture of 1959, the fourteenth century played a pivotal role in this evolution, although this role has not generally been recognized (in Bethurum, *Critical Approaches*, 110–33). What we shall find is that the fourteenth century reclaimed and absorbed from the mass of mythographic materials a specific interest in Ovid and other mythographers—it can be seen in practice to have mixed mythography and poetry vitally so as to establish a true "Renaissance" that harkens backward to the classical humanism of the twelfth-century University of Paris and forward to the sixteenth-century English Renaissance.

This collection will raise general questions about the French and English writer's use of the mythographic tradition in the fourteenth century, leaving aside for the moment the vexed question of the Italian Renaissance as a literary repudiation of the commentary tradition of the Middle Ages (although the mythological poems of Dante, Petrarch, and Boccaccio certainly influence the French and English poets we shall consider here). To understand the pivotal role of the fourteenth century, what we need to do first is to define the specific mythographic conventions of the twelfth to the fourteenth century and the tradition from which they derive, on which they depend, and which they continue; second, to examine in greater detail the use of the tradition and sources by Chaucer and other French and English poets; and third, to examine the influence of Chaucerian (and fourteenth-century) practice on the later period, culminating in Shakespeare and the sixteenth-century English Renaissance.

The premise of this volume depends upon the convergence of the learned Latin tradition associated with medieval schools and universities and the rise of the vernacular in poems and dramatic works associated with the courts and then the theater. As the essays herein will show, poets borrowed mythographic glosses from the schoolmasters and innovative adaptations of those glosses from each other; schoolmasters imbued the tradition with their own idiosyncratic and individual biases. For example, Chrétien de Troyes borrowed from moralized Ovid and the allegorical explanation of Narcissus and Echo provided by the commentators in structuring the relationship of his characters in *Erec et Enide*. So also Chaucer borrowed from these commentators, from his own treatment of classical figures in other, earlier, poems, and from his French and Italian contemporaries writing in the vernacular, Guillaume de Lorris and Jean de Meun in the *Roman de la Rose*, and Dante and Boccaccio. And Christine de Pizan borrowed from herself and from English, French, and Italian poets, including Chaucer, Machaut, and Boccaccio, as William Shakespeare borrowed from Chaucer and contemporary scholars and sources in constructing characters in poems and plays.

Whereas these creative writers bend to their own purpose the mythographic tradition—from the Latin commentary or the vernacular poem—

often with ironic or humorous intent, mythographers of the same period similarly inject their own biases into their adaptation. The French mythographer Pierre Bersuire is motivated by ecclesiastical reform; Christine de Pizan as the first woman mythographer reflects feminist concerns; the Renaissance mythographer George Sandys alters the medieval tradition through his misogyny.

All the late medieval writers and scholars, however, share a need to veil harsh truths while educating their audiences. The court poet Chrétien uses a common mythological image to deepen his audience's understanding of a character, whereas Chaucer, de Pizan, and the popular dramatist Shakespeare cloak their occasionally scandalous secrets under guise of classical fable, just as the mythographers Bersuire, de Pizan, and Sandys openly reveal, rationalize, and moralize those secrets. Innovative writers, whether poet or scholar, continental or insular, medieval or Renaissance, all exemplify the influence of the mythological tradition, and hence assimilate Latin scholarship within vernacular poem or play.

The relationship between the vernacular and the Latin tradition is complex, whether we are addressing the problem of the medieval poet writing in the vernacular but using Latin mythographic handbooks as a source for his mythological characters, or whether we are discussing the impingement of vernacular and marginal glosses in Latin commentaries on classical mythological poems. It is the task of this collection to address this vexed problem, and to reveal the intercourse between traditions (mythographic and learned, poetic and courtly), and genres and forms (poem, commentary), or between national cultures, or between historical literary periods like the Middle Ages and the Renaissance. At the same time it is important to distinguish how different cultures, different periods, different traditions, and different writers handled this dis-semination.

Let us speak first of the advent of the vernacular in the Latin mythographic commentary tradition, to pinpoint the time at which convergence first occurred. There exist marginal glosses in Welsh in several ninth-century insular commentaries on Martianus Capella, and in Old High German in several ninth-century continental commentaries on Boethius. Most probably the impetus for such glossation in England grew out of the Alfredian reforms in education in Wessex, and the drive toward literacy in Anglo-Saxon in the ninth and tenth centuries, which resulted in vernacular translations of works like Boethius's *Consolatio*. On the continent the Carolingian pursuit of education as an ideal and the previous gathering of scholars from throughout Europe at Charlemagne's court no doubt enhanced this cross-fertilization of vernacular and Latin.

Thereafter, it was in Germany that vernacular glosses continued, most noticeably in the commentaries of Notker Labeo on Boethius and Martianus during the tenth and eleventh centuries, simultaneously with the advent of the earliest (and German) Latin glosses on Ovid (by Manegold von Lautenbach). The vernacular in Notker's case allowed for translation and reinterpretation into a more familiar and native cultural mode, which of course enhanced the assimilation of that which was alien and different into that which was like, known, and therefore acceptable.

From such models the twelfth-century renaissance of the University of Paris drew for its Neoplatonic works, whether learned and scholastic (as in the case of Boethius, Martianus, and Ovid glosses), or allegorical and fictional (prosimetric, as in the case of Alanus de Insulis's *De planctu* and *Anticlaudianus*). To adapt the mythographic tradition to the writing of an allegorical complaint of Nature, from which Alanus derived his characters Venus, Hymen, Cupid, Genius, and others, in the *De planctu*, is to marry two seemingly diverse modes in a splendid flourish. Also in twelfth-century France, a poet like Chrétien de Troyes will pollinate his courtly and aristocratic vernacular romances with material from the learned mythographic tradition, specifically relating to Ovid, but also Macrobius and Martianus. The convergence of the traditions and forms is perhaps best illustrated through a thirteenth-century phenomenon, the *Roman de la Rose* created by Guillaume de Lorris as a highly artificial, allegorical and courtly, love romance, continued some years later in very different form by Jean de Meun. Jean de Meun adds to the allegory of the rose satire and Aristotelian philosophy to undercut ironically what must have seemed at the time and in comparison old-fashioned Neoplatonic allegorization. From our point of view, the significant event is the intersection of the vernacular and fictional poetic with the scholastic and learned *Weltanschauung*. The revolution in the schools—the arrival of the New Philosophy of Aristotle—did indeed call all in doubt, specifically the archaic commentary tradition and the moral allegory of the mythographers. To use the myth of Hercules battling Cacus in his cave, as Jean de Meun did at the end of his sequel when the lover seduces the rose, as appropriate for the phallus deflowering a virgin is to mock and invert the mythographic tradition. Or rather, it is to harness it for ironic and subtle ends. Is this misuse of mythography merely another metaphor for the errant lover's misuse of his sexual desire, in the practice of courtly love, outside marriage?

Accompanying the scholastic revolution caused by the introduction of Aristotle was the new emphasis on empiricism. In relation to mythography, a tradition long dominated by Stoic and Neoplatonic ideas, commentators turned to Ovid and his book of changes entitled *Meta-*

morphoses to document their interest in generation, transformation, corruption. From the mid-thirteenth century, the glossators on Ovid will dominate mythography, beginning with John of Garland and continuing into the fourteenth century with Giovanni del Virgilio, the *Ovide moralisé (Ovid moralized)*, and then Pierre Bersuire. These commentators are accompanied by the mythographic compilers of the fourteenth and fifteenth centuries such as John Ridewall, Giovanni Boccaccio, and Christine de Pizan. Their attention to a text full of seductions, rapes, and love affairs adds to their attractiveness for courtly poets whose chief interest, in many cases, lay in the relationships of the nobility and in piquing the interest of, and continuing, royal patronage. It is no accident, then, that an English poet like Geoffrey Chaucer or a French poet like Christine de Pizan will use Ovidian glosses to frame and structure the dramatic narrative involving mythological characters and allegorical personifications. The marriage—to continue our metaphor—has been fully consummated. The vernacular is informed by the Latin learned tradition so completely that the resultant web appears seamless. Dante's *Commedia*, as early as the turn of the fourteenth century, perhaps most sensationally witnesses the turning inside out of the Latin and classical mythographic tradition, in a vernacular Italian allegorical and mythological poem whose central characters are the modern poet Dante and the object of the medieval commentary tradition, Virgil himself. The underworld they tour in the *Inferno* is peopled with an amazing amalgam of contemporary and classical, real and fictional, mythological and historical.

And, accordingly, in the thirteenth to the fifteenth centuries, the commentary tradition, which continues to use Latin for the most part, interjects the approaches of vernacular poetics. The thirteenth-century English mythography of John of Garland is written in Latin, but in Latin poetry rather than the commentator's prose. The fourteenth-century Giovanni del Virgilio, following the twelfth-century commentator Arnulf of Orleans, weds mythological poetic text and prose explication, in his commentary on Ovid, mirroring the *prosimetrum* form of the allegorical fictional works of Alanus de Insulis. The fourteenth-century friar John Ridewall will even gloss a glossator, Fulgentius, in his *Fulgentius metaforalis*, unifying his comments by means of Augustinian psychology. The fifteenth-century Christine de Pizan will write a chivalric and vernacular "commentary" on Ovid in the *Epistre Othea*. And later in that century Cristoforo Landino will structure a portion of his commentary on Cicero's *Tusculan Disputations* by means of a poetic narrative—the journey of Aeneas from Troy to Italy. It is no accident that poet and scholar, in the late fourteenth and fifteenth century, are the same person, whether Chaucer, writing a treatise on the Astrolabe; Boccaccio, writing in the vernacular tales like those of the *Decameron* but also glossing the first few cantos of Dante's *Inferno* in Latin and collecting myths into a Latin "Genealogy of the Gentile Gods"; or Christine de Pizan, writing a variety of poems and scholarly treatises in the vernacular. Let us first examine medieval French poets and mythographers to see how this intermarriage of Latin and vernacular, poetic and scholastic, differs from later English examples.

French Poets and Mythographers

Is there a particularly French ambience for mythographers and fabulizing poets? Certainly the examples we have in this collection suggest a French interest in manners, decorum, the courtly idiom and the chivalric mode. This interest permeates both the romances of Chrétien and the poems and mythography of Christine, two French poets who deliberately invoked the mythographic tradition (indeed, Christine is unusual in that, like Boccaccio, she was both poet *and* mythographer). There may be other poets writing in the vernacular in this period, like the Anglo-Norman Marie de France, who used fable and mythological allusion within a text, but not necessarily as extensively or with attention to the mythographic tradition. And much more so than in the later English poets (for whom for so long the dominant court language was in fact Norman French), the courtly, if not the scholastic and ecclesiastic, trend is toward the vernacular. The two examples we have provide chronological poles: Chrétien wrote in French because it was the language of the court; Christine wrote in French not only because it was the language of the court but also because, whatever her self-schooling, she was not allowed to learn Latin formally and apparently never wrote in that language.

These mythographizers and mythographers, nevertheless, share with later poets and scholars a desire to innovate, to transform, to breathe life into stale schoolroom exercises. Myth is a vehicle here, as for others writing in other periods, other lands. In its earliest incarnation—Chrétien—it serves ultimately as a vehicle for philosophy, Neoplatonism, but used ironically and dramatically in relation to character. In its later incarnation, in Christine's poetry, it will be used for political and moral purposes. And both poet and mythographer will now, as later, conflate two forms, romance and commentary, or *balade* and gloss, or even two media, as in Bersuire, literary gloss and iconographic description. There is, in Chrétien and Christine, as in Chaucer and Shakespeare, also a strong political bent—their works are written by courtiers for patrons, and with Dante-like messages intended to warn, help, educate, or entertain rulers.

In the first section of this book, then, we will first turn to the French poet and mythographer. Jeanne A. Nightingale, in a ground-breaking essay, "From Mirror to Metamorphosis: Echoes of Ovid's Narcissus in Chrétien's *Erec et Enide*," explores Chrétien's Macrobian use of Ovid, specifically, of the figure Narcissus from *Metamorphoses*, in *Erec et Enide*. Her arguments reveal how the court poet's awareness of the learned Latin tradition of mythography informs his chivalric romance and the levels of its irony. From the allegorical signification of the figure as representative of self-knowledge through love, Chrétien turns to the impossible debate issue of courtly love within marriage, with Narcissus as the prototype for Erec. When he gazes into the "mirror" of Enide's beauty, he narcissistically sees himself reflected back as Arthurian Hero, a self-centered mistake which brings about his "death" in courtly society. During the couple's *avanture*, because of Enide's role as a catalytic agent, Erec "metamorphoses" into the true image of the ideal knight, to allow for a harmonious union of hearts and minds. Their new "union" mirrors the *conjointure* of the courtly and chivalric poetic with the scholastic mythographic tradition—or, put another way, of the mythological *matière* of Celtic fable and the new *sens*, or poetic meaning, derived from Chrétien's adaptation of the mythographic technique. As in Guillaume de Lorris, the Narcissus *exemplum* guides the reading of the love fiction, warning us of the dangers of reading too literally (as Erec misreads Enide's mirror). The Ovidian elements of hunt, fountain, thirst—the passionate thirst for carnal satisfaction—recur in the poem, while the reference to the philosophical *Aeneid* acts as a mirror image or analogue of the narrative sequence of the romance.

But the vernacular can also influence the Latin tradition, and not only within national boundaries: a French scholar can use the poetry of an Italian to brilliant advantage. The blending of two different kinds of mythologizing—mythography and iconography—according to William D. Reynolds in "Sources, Nature, and Influences of the *Ovidius Moralizatus* of Pierre Bersuire," occurs in the hands of Pierre Bersuire in his mythographic (literary iconographic) cosmology of the gods. Wishing to describe how the gods should appear in painting, Bersuire combined Ovid commentary with the poetic description of the gods found in Petrarch's *Africa*, a vernacular (Italian) national epic. Much of his inspiration also came from the desire to aid preachers, and so his tract is full of Christianized allegorical interpretations of Ovid intended to enhance faith, as in the example of Io, changed by faith in Christ from a sinner to a just woman. Thereafter Bersuire's mythographies influenced other mythographers—most significantly, Thomas Walsingham—other preachers, and art and manuscript illumination for some time, affecting iconographic descriptions in Gower and Chaucer.

"Christine de Pizan as Chivalric Mythographer: *L'Epistre Othea*" presents this fifteenth-century mythographer as Bersuire-like in combining two traditions in her *Epistre Othea*, the chivalric (romance) tradition that Chrétien made so famous, used as a fictional frame, and the mythographic allegorical tradition that Bersuire made so famous in the fourteenth century. Just as the most famous and masterful exemplars of each tradition, poetic and scholastic, blend and synthesize tense and conflicting ideas and forms, so also does the vernacularizing of Latin mythography produce a tertium quid. Although Christine very likely drew upon the *Ovide moralisé* rather than the *Ovidius moralizatus* for her allegories, it is also clear that Bersuire may also have used much of the earlier commentary in compiling his own. What is especially French about Christine (as opposed to the more English Chaucer in the next section) is her use of Hector, who was understood to be related to the present line of French kings through his nephew; the *Epistre* (*Epistle*) is addressed to Hector by the goddess of wisdom, Othea. Christine's intent here, according to Judith L. Kellogg, is therefore to revitalize myth as a living part of the Christian world: "As Christine brings her mythic layer into Christian time at the end, that moment of crossing gives additional resonance to the allegorical level she has described throughout. That moment becomes a reminder that the chivalric and Christian levels have never really been separate, though the lessons in each can certainly be contemplated separately and distinctly." As a result, this synthesis of chivalric and Christian provides a kind of "universal history."

In her role as a court poet rather than just as mythographer, Christine, according to Margaret J. Ehrhart in her essay "Christine de Pizan and the Judgment of Paris: A Court Poet's Use of Mythographic Tradition," also provides a mirror for magistrates in her moral and political use of myth. Specifically, Christine uses the fabulous version of the Judgment of Paris in the Trojan saga to instruct and educate the court, in a *balade*, in the *Epistre Othea* (*Letter of Othea*, 1400), and the *Livre du chemin de long estude* (*Book of the Road of Long Study*, 1402–3). In these cases her sources for the myth vary, not always learned and Latin but often courtly and vernacular—she used Guillaume de Machaut's *Dit de la fonteinne amoureuse* (*Poem of the Amorous Fountain*) in all three of these works, but the mythographic and vernacular *Ovide moralisé* in the *Epistre* and *Chemin*. In the early *balade*, in which Christine argues that the poet-clerk should search for wisdom rather than for love, Machaut's poem most informs its mythography. But in the later two poems, Christine's use of the myth of the Judgment changes.

Like Chaucer after her, she is so prolific that, whatever her initial sources in her versions of a myth in various poems, she will eventually draw on those same earlier versions in writing the later ones: her impression of a myth develops as her literary career develops and she becomes more influential. Thus, later, in the *Chemin*, she cannibalizes her earlier self as poet, using material from the *balade*, but also cannibalizes herself as mythographer and scholar, in the *Epistre*. In the *Epistre* the Greek goddess Pallas offers wisdom predicated upon spiritual chivalry; Christine understands Pallas not from Latin mythographies but from vernacular poems by contemporaries, and once she defines the deity, she continues to appropriate that vision from herself. Further, Christine at least supervised the manuscript illuminations in her own work, which in the *Epistre* accompany a mythographic text; thus presented, side by side, the mythographies of iconography and textual commentary illustrate Christine's twofold importance in the mythographic tradition. In *Le Livre du chemin de long estude* she turns to a more astrological and planetary association of deity in her interpretation of the myth, with the goddesses as planets, suggesting the force of destiny, but Paris as individual, the freedom of will to choose. The choice goes beyond wisdom and sexual pleasure at the beginning, in the *balade*, echoed in the *Epistre*, but in the *Chemin* only between wisdom, chivalry, riches, and power. Her audience —somewhat dissolute princes, we recall—might react somewhat more positively to this dilemma. As always, wisdom is the ideal Christine most celebrates and most urges on her reader. At the end, then, Christine "invents her own fable," in Ehrhart's words.

Chaucer and the Mythographers

Poets writing in the vernacular in medieval England treated pagan gods in their poems because they had read other poets in France or Italy—and later in the fourteenth and fifteenth centuries, in England itself—who had done the same. John Lydgate's *Temple of Glass* and *The Assembly of Gods*, John Gower's *Confessio Amantis, Sir Orfeo*, Robert Henryson's *Testament of Cresseid*, William Dunbar's *Thrissil and the Rois*, or *The Golden Targe*, all rehearsed classical myths or employed a mythographic understanding of them in depicting mythological figures. And of course Chaucer himself used them, an excellent example because his mythological poems were so many in number and because he influenced so many other poets, both in his own country and elsewhere.

The major Latin mythographers of England in the fourteenth century were for the most part "classicizing" friars, as Beryl Smalley and Judson Allen have described them. As such Robert Holkot and John Ridewall combined iconography with comment on the Bible in their mythographic works. Nicholas Trivet glossed Boethius—but he also commented on Augustine's *De civitate Dei* (*City of God*) and on Senecan tragedies, creating new trends for the mythographic tradition. The use of classical mythological materials for preaching drew popular as well as scholarly attention. The iconographic support—verbal pictures of the gods, as in John Ridewall—interrelated the text with manuscript illumination, and his adaptation of the literary iconography so prevalent in late medieval mythography may be seen as parallel to the "stories" depicted in stained glass windows and cathedral sculptures and friezes. Indeed, the collection of moralized myths in Thomas Walsingham's *Archana deorum* attempts to assimilate in one orderly grouping all the mythological fables from frequently different commentary traditions—Mercury in one tradition a positive (*in bono*) figure, but in another, negative (*in malo*). The attempt to find order, to reduce tensions, to come to a scholarly synthesis, if not consensus, is one motivated by the turbulence of the outside world in fourteenth- and fifteenth-century Europe.

But English poets did differ from their French counterparts, Chrétien before Chaucer, and Christine after, by also borrowing framing materials and methods from French and Italian poets who had already incorporated deities within their poems. In his use of the Judgment of Paris myth to structure the "contrapuntal" movement of Troilus's love for Criseyde in the psychological romance of *Troilus and Criseyde*, Chaucer highlights the importance of choice, volition, both within a philosophical and Boethian framework and psychologically within a love relationship. Patricia R. Orr, in "Pallas Athena and the Threefold Choice in Chaucer's *Troilus and Criseyde*," argues that he may have drawn on Latin passages by Fulgentius, the second Vatican mythographer, and Bernard Silvestris in his commentary on the *Aeneid* to relate Paris's choice of the three goddesses, and therefore also to Troilus's, to Aeneas's decision to leave Troy, to leave Carthage, and to found Italy. The mythography and its moralization had also appeared in Pierre Bersuire's *Ovidius moralizatus* and in Boccaccio's *Genealogie*. But Chaucer combines his particular understanding of a god in a myth (drawn from Latin learned materials) with a narrative frame—the love story of Troilus found in Boccaccio's *Il Filostrato*, and Petrarch's Sonnet 88 (for Troilus's first song). There are also thirteenth-century French romances of Troy that linked Paris's judgment with Troilus's love story and the *Ovide moralisé*. Chaucer's purpose may also have been political—if Aeneas of Troy was the ancestor of Brutus of Britain, the failure of Trojan leadership might well prove telling to English royalty. Unlike Christine, whose main focus falls on the *choice* of Paris, with the ideal of Pallas Athena preferred over the others, Chaucer shows Troilus as a second Paris in choosing Venus.

In Jane Chance's "Chaucer's Zephirus: Dante's Zefiro, St. Dominic, and the Idea of the *General Prologue*," from Dante's *Paradiso* comes an explanation for Chaucer's specific use of the figure Zephirus in the *General Prologue* to the *Canterbury Tales*. Chaucer borrows the image and idea of Zephirus tied to the birth of St. Dominic, used by Dante, to anglicize the hagiographical principle that structures the pilgrimage in the *Canterbury Tales*. Unlike Dante, however, whose interest remains in portraying an orderly Christian hierarchy of spiritual being, Chaucer wishes to depict ecclesiastical, social, and political satire—the failure of hierarchy. St. Thomas à Beckett, like St. Dominic, becomes a national "deity" arousing dormant pilgrims as the sun makes the buds bloom in the spring. Both Chaucer and Dante were probably aware of the earlier Latin glosses on Zephirus found in various commentaries and mythographic manuals—Isidore, the first two Vatican mythographers, thirteenth-century dictionaries, John of Garland, Pierre Bersuire, the *Ovide moralisé*, Boccaccio's *Genealogie*. But the image also refracts throughout Middle English poems Chaucer may have known—*Sir Gawain and the Green Knight*, and his own poems, including *Book of the Duchess*, *Troilus and Criseyde*, and the *Legend of Hypermnestra* as well as the *Prologue* to the *Legend of Good Women*.

Scholars who have debated Chaucer's use of another Italian work, Boccaccio's *Decameron*, have compared plot outlines and narrative details without analyzing Chaucer's purpose in borrowing this material. Janet Levarie Smarr, in the next essay, "Mercury in the Garden: Mythographical Methods in the *Merchant's Tale* and *Decameron* 7.9," acknowledges that the *Merchant's Tale* is closer in plot to sources other than *Decameron* 7.9, yet also notes that these other sources manifest none of the symbolic and thematic developments in Boccaccio and Chaucer, such as the symbolic garden and pear tree, the system of mythographic and astrological associations with Mercury and Saturn, and the more figurative sense of blindness. That is, while Boccaccio and Chaucer may have borrowed the garden they share from the *Roman de la Rose*, and while Chaucer may have taken from the Italian mythographer's *Genealogie* significations for the figure of Mercury that color the imagery and symbolism of his tale, nevertheless, the resulting masterpieces transcend mere echoing of source materials. Smarr concludes that Chaucer may be "the English Boccaccio," then, not because of his borrowing of a few plots from the Italian, but because both writers sought to develop in a similar and sophisticated way the symbolic and mythographic potentials of elements from simple popular comic tales.

Finally, as a vernacular poet with a literary career spanning thirty years, Chaucer, like other medieval and modern writers, will borrow one idea or image from an old poem when writing another. Often the diverse portraits of a deity within the mythographic tradition (a diversity dictated by point of view) will inspire Chaucer to use those different views diversely. Hence, Melvin Storm in "From Knossos to Knight's Tale: The Changing Face of Chaucer's Theseus," traces the metamorphoses of the figure Theseus as Chaucer uses him again and again in differing ways, in different poems. Theseus begins this evolution as a slight figure who betrays women (in particular, Ariadne) in the earliest poem, the *House of Fame*, changing to a more sympathetic traitor in the *Legend of Ariadne*, where Chaucer adds Phaedra as his salvation: the poet takes liberties with the mythographic tradition by granting Phaedra, rather than Theseus, prominence in the responsibility for the betrayal of her sister. Chaucer apparently conflated his sources to arrive at a new and original treatment of the story of Ariadne and Theseus. Here the Ariadne story is lifted out of a variety of sources—Ovid, Plutarch, Hyginus, Virgil, the *Ovide moralisé*, and Boccaccio (although Ovid ignores Phaedra in the version of Ariadne's story in *Fasti, Metamorphoses*, and the *Heroides*; only in *Fasti*, 3.8, does Bacchus, rather than Theseus, leave Ariadne for another woman; and there is a letter from Phaedra to Hippolytus in Ovid's *Heroides* wherein she accuses her husband of faithlessness to her as he has to Ariadne). Thereafter, Phaedra is a supplanter in the *Genealogie* and the *Ovide moralisé*, a treatment preferred by Gower as well as Chaucer; and indeed in Chaucer, Ariadne's *Ovide moralisé* soliloquy is given to Phaedra to form the plan itself. But Chaucer also borrows from himself: when Ariadne cannot find the departed Theseus (2185-7), Chaucer uses similar language from the context of the *Reeve's Tale* and his miller's wife, who nearly enters what she thinks is the wrong bed because the crafty clerks have moved the marking cradle. Finally, in the *Knight's Tale*, Chaucer turns to Boccaccio's *Teseida* as a source, but he probably also had *Ariadne* in mind when he composed it. Because Chaucer had a different point of view in the *Knight's Tale*—the martial Knight as speaker—and because the narrative demands were more complex, his Theseus also had to reflect the "conflicting claims of martial and courtly chivalry."

The Renaissance: Shakespeare and the Mythographers

In the Renaissance, the situation changes for a master writer like Shakespeare. Like Chaucer, Shakespeare went behind minor changes in his source material—he "manipulated" the source so as to create a new poem. But the new poem he created—according to Theodore L. Steinberg in "The Comedy of Love: The Medieval Venus and Shakespeare's *Venus and Adonis*"—had little to do with political, social, or ecclesiastical satire. From Boccaccio's *Genealogie* he took the mythographies for two

Venuses, and from the *Parlement of Foules* the late medieval tension between different kinds of love, heavenly and carnal. Shakespeare fuses the two Venuses into a single figure of comic proportion, reflecting complex developments of Renaissance mythography. In *Venus and Adonis* he adds the image of Adonis's horse to reflect the pull of the carnal—between sexuality and psychology at puberty. That is, Adonis's desire for chastity perverts natural law and renders as comic what can be seen as heavenly love. This Renaissance theme—chastity witnessed in married life, characteristic of Spenser—and procreation as a moral necessity, found in Shakespeare's chastisement of the young man in the sonnets for sexual abstinence, is finally played out in the dramatic entanglement of Adonis facing the boar (death) and Venus (life-giving procreation). The tragedy in the poem suggests the ambiguities inherent in love and sexuality; there are no solutions, for the natural sex is both frightening and desirable. Shakespeare's Venus, finally, is a goddess who as a character fully dramatizes and experiences what Chaucer can indicate only through discordant allegorical images.

Shakespeare's use of Hercules is Erasmusan, George D. Economou notes, in "Hercules in the Mind: Mythographic Tradition and the References in *Hamlet*." Shakespeare in *Hamlet* borrows not from Chaucer or from the mythographic tradition so much as from a contemporary and highly idiosyncratic treatment of what had been an idealized figure, for the most part, in the Middle Ages. Economou acknowledges Chaucer's somewhat negative treatment of Hercules as trusting too much in Fortune in the *Monk's Tale*. And also in the *Legend of Hypsipyle*, in the *Legend of Good Women*, Hercules is portrayed as a conspirator and go-between of the nefarious and deceitful Jason. Other literary models portray him equally negatively—he is the "braggart soldier" and "sham" of the New Comedy, and he represents the phallus in Jean de Meun's *Roman*. Mostly, however, like Chaucer before him, Shakespeare draws on his contemporaries' reinterpretations of mythological figures to invest his own characters, or images, with an original signification. From the sixteenth-century Gallic Hercules—taken from Lucian's *Heracles* and the new primary awareness of other Greek and Latin models—comes a humanistic interpretation of Hercules. If, for the French, Hercules was a patron of their culture and language, used to suggest that the kings of France fit into the tradition of ancient heroism, as he was from Francis I to Henry IV, then in England Hercules becomes ludicrous, a comic figure, as he was in *Midsummer Night's Dream* and the use by Nick Bottom. In *Hamlet*, Hercules is used for similar dramatic (but more subtle psychological) effect as a foil for Claudius as understood by Hamlet: any ass can wear a lion's skin.

The complex psychological usages to which mythography is put in creating a poetic (or dramatic) aesthetic are balanced in the Renaissance with complex scholarly mythography, especially when we turn for one last look at the Ovid commentary—in this case, of George Sandys, in the essay by Deborah D. Rubin, "Sandys, Ovid, and Female Chastity: The Encyclopedic Mythographer as Moralist." How Renaissance mythography differs from medieval mythography can be seen in its refreshment by means by rereadings of Latin and Greek original texts as models. And the desire for encyclopedic knowledge is also expressed in the mythographic manual, as it was in historiography. The chief mythographers are now Italian—Giraldus, Natalis Comes. The chief Ovidian commentators are Sabinus, Jacobus Pontanus, Ficino, Vives, Scaliger, Bacon, and Bolzani.

But the approaches are different, more secularized than the medieval: in addition to the historical-euhemeristic, physical, and ethical "undermeanings" of classical fable, we have many more political readings of myth (hinted at, even in Shakespeare's more popular adaptation), as in Francis Bacon's *De sapientia veterum*. The Renaissance vogue for hieroglyphics and emblems gave impetus to fragmented readings, often in a potpourri of Christian and enlightened pagan wisdom. One misogynistic example occurs in the use of the myths of Actaeon and Callisto. Despite Sandys's restraint in using his sources, his concision, there is a stronger critical voice, even within the Renaissance. Unlike the endless philological variants of Giraldi, the moral summations and resummations of Comes, and the line-by-line explications of Latin prosody by Pontanus, Sandys creates a "smoothly seamed commentary" on Ovid, with unified focus within episodes and a distinct thesis. For Callisto he elaborates sexual ethics, and for Actaeon, a political ethic. But under this smooth cover he masks misogyny.

We have journeyed, then, from the Macrobian desire to ignore or veil scandalous and unsuitable sexual escapades of the gods, to the twelfth-century attempt to justify them by means of natural (physical) allegories, or moral allegories, to the fourteenth-century attempt to depict them in allegorical poems whose theme is philosophical or psychological, to the Renaissance dramatic poem and drama, whose humorous or political use reflects the full ambiguity of gods depicted as mirror images for human beings, frail, mortal, mistaken.

And to return to the scholarly mythography, from the earliest commentary intent on justifying the pagan because of its underlying truth, we have inverted the approach, to use the pagan precisely because it is suspect, an emblem of the fallen. For this reason, the world of the court, of the courtier and the poet, the dramatist, the scholar, is a Machiavellian world, and even the scholarship—no matter how resonant of the knowledge of the world—reflects bias and idiosyncrasy, misogyny, subjective misinterpretation. The classical fable is a lens through which we perceive the world, and ourselves, but the image we see is a mirror of our own original sin, our own mortality, our human weakness.

These essays, then, reveal the extent to which the classical gods and heroes reappeared in medieval guise. The gods Venus, Juno, Pallas Athena, Mercury, Ceres, Triptolomous, Zephirus the West Wind, Pluto and Proserpina, the heroes Theseus, Hercules, Hector, and Paris, and human victims like Ariadne, Phaedra, Adonis, Callisto, and Actaeon all receive their share of mythological and mythographic attention. In addition, the mythographers—and the commentary traditions to which they refer—include Macrobius, Fulgentius, Remigius of Auxerre, the three Vatican mythographers, Ralph of Beauvais, Arnulf of Orleans, William of Conches, the author of the *Ovide moralisé*, Pierre Bersuire, Boccaccio, Robert Holkot, John Ridewall, Thomas Walsingham, Christine de Pizan, Natalis Comes, and George Sandys. These scholars either comment on the *Timaeus, Aeneid*, Ovid, Juvenal, Statius, Macrobius, or Martianus Capella, among others, or they collect in handbooks moralized tales of the gods, or combine biblical exegesis with allegorization of classical fable.

What remains for us as scholars to investigate? In addition to the full-scale history of the mythographic tradition requested by Elliott and Elder, Judson B. Allen, in a bibliographical epilogue to this collection, "Eleven Unpublished Commentaries on Ovid's *Metamorphoses* and Two Other Texts of Mythographic Interest: Some Comments on a Bibliography," first reveals the existence of eleven unpublished commentaries on Ovid's *Metamorphoses* and other mythographic texts requiring re-editing, and then stresses the need for care in evaluating the "Ovidian influence" until such time that the plethora of manuscripts and glosses can be edited and published. But he also suggests that we move ahead now to a more specific analysis of "Chaucer's mythography, or Dante's, or even John Calderia's." This volume, then, constitutes only a beginning, and a sampler of possible approaches.

After reading the essays in this collection, we might conclude that those readers of medieval poets like Chaucer who revel in his lascivious but humorous (or allegorical) portrayal of the gods have only to thank mythographers like William of Conches. Rather surprisingly, by the end of the Middle Ages, the mythographic tradition did not so much exhaust itself as divert to different—unusual, fresh—forms, as forecast by these essays in their different ways. The return to literalism, as expressed in natural history and euhemerism, and Protestantism, also signaled a return to humor, to satire, to this world, as suggested by the essays of Theodore Steinberg, George Economou, and Deborah Rubin, a return anticipated in part by the powerful comic use of mythography by Chaucer. Indeed, Chaucer and Christine de Pizan flourished between the flowering of mythography in the renaissance of classical humanism—the Neoplatonism of the twelfth century—and the renaissance of classical humanism in the new worlds of the sixteenth century. Classical fable, then, throughout early France and England continued to provide a vehicle for mythographic use in literature in the vernacular, even though the poet's purpose in such use changed, even though poetry blended with scholarship, the learned Latin tradition converged with the rise of the vernacular: mythography survived, and with it the preservation of classical mythology and the allegorical impulse.

Notes

1. Macrobius's analysis of dreams occurs in Book 1, chapter 3, and of fiction in Book 1, chapter 2. It is clear that Macrobius, like Plato, applauds and prefers the truths of the philosophers rather than the lying fictions of the poets. He declares in 1.2.14, "ceterum cum ad summum et principem omnium deum, qui apud Graecos *tagathon*, qui *proton aiton* nuncupatur, tractatus se audet attollere, vel ad mentem, quem Graeci *nous* appellant, originales rerum species, quae *ideai* dictae sunt, continentem, ex summo natam et profectam deo: cum de his inquam loquuntur summo deo et mente, nihil fabulosum penitus attingunt," Willis, 6–7 ("But when the discussion aspires to treat of the Highest and Supreme of all gods, called by the Greeks the Good [*tagathon*] and the First Cause [*proton aition*], or to treat of Mind or Intellect, which the Greeks call *nous*, born from and originating in the Supreme God and embracing the original concepts of things, which are called Ideas [*Ideai*], when, I repeat, philosophers speak about these, the Supreme God and Mind, they shun the use of fabulous narratives," Stahl, 85–86).
2. I am at present working on a two-volume study of the mythographic tradition in the Middle Ages from which the summary presented in this introduction comes. This study has been described in two essays: "Chaucer and Mythology" and "Origins."
3. See the various recent studies of literature and literary theory in the twelfth century, including Wetherbee, Stock, and Dronke. William of Conches in a gloss on the *Timaeus* points to a higher authority on poetic integument than Macrobius—Plato. William reasons that, *because* Plato knew and used the immoral stories of the gods—as can be detected in later philosophers' revealing glosses on the *Timaeus*—*therefore* those stories must be suitable for use by modern philosophers. In a gloss on Plato's discussion of myth-interpretation in *Timaeus* 41de, he mentions those ignorant of Plato's mode of speaking about philosophy

through *integumenta*. For excerpts from these glosses, see *Glosae super Platonem*, ed. Jeauneau.

4. On the Macrobius glosses see Jeauneau, "La lecture des auteurs classiques," 95–102. Selections from Macrobius (1.1–16) also appear in Dronke, 68–78.

5. 7b, Dronke, 71: "Cuius fabule hec est veritas: Iupiter dicitur ether, Iuno inferior aer, que dicitur uxor Iovis, quia inferior aer subditus est superiori, et coniunctus; dicitur etiam eius soror, quia inter quatuor elementa nullum est simile ei ita ut aer. Sed superior eter [*sic*] concubuit cum Semele, id est cum terra, quia superior inde nascuntur; sed mediante Iunone, quia per calorem celestium arbores et fructus generantur. *Quod vero Bachus dicitur bis fuisse natus, primo scilicet a Semele, postea ad tempus nativitatis a femore Iovis, hoc in se veritatis tantum continet quod vinee, quas per hunc intelligimus, quia deus earum, inpregnate per calorem solis revirescunt, per quod prima Bachi intelligitur nativitas, postea crescentes usque in estate botrum emittunt, et hec est secunda Bachi nativitas*" (trans. Dronke, 29: "The truth of the fable is this. Jupiter is the name for the ether, Juno for the lower air, called wife of Jupiter because the lower air is subject to the aether and conjoined with it. She is also called his sister, because among the four elements none is so like the ether as the lower air. But the upper air slept with Semele, that is with earth, for it impregnates the earth in winter, and thus Bacchus is born, for from this union come the vines—but through Juno's mediation, for through the heavenly heat trees and fruits are generated. That Bacchus is said to be twice born, first of Semele, then of Jupiter's thigh at the time of his nativity, contains so much of truth that the vines [which we understand by Bacchus, for he is their god], impregnated by the sun's heat, become green—this is what Bacchus' first birth refers to—and later they grow, until in summer they put forth grapes—and this is Bacchus' second birth").

6. No. 6, in Dronke, 70 (Latin) and 26 (trans.), on Macrobius 1.2.10. A rationalization for this cruel act can be found in part in the Juvenal glosses, which identify Saturn with Wisdom because of a mistaken identification of Charon with Chronos, or time, but a mistake that explains William's earlier use of Saturn. That is, William confuses Charon, who transports the dead to the underworld, with Cronos, time, understood through "the old man and son" (clearly meant to be Chronos and Saturn) as *sapientia* or *prudentia* because old men are and were understood to be wise. "Coron est tempus quasi cronorum quod interpretatur tempus, unde senex et filius p . . . lidemi [*sic*] qui interpretatur multa sapientia. Dicitur quia in senibus auget sapientia et a antiquis prudentia" (Dronke, 162).

7. These myths are glossed as follows: the conjunction of Venus as benevolent star and Mars as malevolent star involves him corrupting her through his "malice": "Quia eius benivolentiam sua malitia corrumpit," 7c, Dronke, 72, taken in part from Fulgentius, *Mitologiae*, 2.7. The true role of Ceres involves "terre naturalis potentia crescendi in segetes et eas multiplicandi," "earth's natural power of growing into crops and multiplying them," just as Bacchus is "terre naturalis potencia crescendi in vineas," "earth's natural power of growing into vines" (13a, Dronke, 75). William justifies Numenius's naked revelation of the

Eleusinian mystery (Macrobius 1.2.19)—that is, the myth of Pluto's rape of Proserpina and her mother Ceres's search for her—as astronomical allegory, with Ceres as the earth, Proserpina the moon, and Pluto the shadow that obstructs it (16a, Dronke, 75–76): "Quod non est aliud, nisi quod Ceres ponitur in designatione terre, et dicitur Ceres quasi 'crees', quia ex ipsa creantur universa, Proserpina pro luna ponitur, et dicitur *sic quasi 'prope serpens', quia propinquius terre movetur quam reliqui planete*. Dicitur filia terre, quia magis contrahit ex terrena substantia quam alterius elementi. Pluto in designatione umbre ponitur, que quandoque impedit lunam" ("This is nothing but that the name Ceres is used to mean the earth, called Ceres on analogy with 'crees' [you may create], for all things are created from her. By Proserpina is meant the moon, and her name is on analogy with 'prope serpens' [creeping near], for she is moved nearer to the earth than the other planets. She is called earth's daughter, because her substance has more of earth in it than of the other elements. By Pluto is meant the shadow that sometimes obstructs the moon," Dronke, 54; compare William's etymology of Ceres in *Glosae*, ed. Jeauneau, 197; see also Servius, *Georgics* 1.39, and this passage in Bernard's commentary on the *Aeneid* 6.59). William also identifies the search of Ceres as the heat of summer which longs most for the moon's moisture to help the fruits increase, especially at night when the moon is near; the results of Jupiter's decision mean that half the month Proserpina remains in the upper hemisphere, half in the lower, beneath the earth.

8. For the concept of *involucrum* and *integumentum* in the twelfth century, see especially Robertson, "Some Medieval Literary Terminology"; Chenu, "*Involucrum*"; Jeauneau, "L'Usage"; and Brinkmann.

9. For discussions of William's use of *integumentum*, see Jeauneau, "L'Usage," 35–100, and of his allegorical method in general, Hatinguais, 417–29. For the use of *integumentum* to mask an imperial flaw, see *Glosae in Iuvenalem*, ed. Wilson, 91, 108.

A Chronological List of Major Medieval Mythographers

4th–7th centuries

Servius (ca. 389), Commentaries on Virgil's *Eclogues, Georgics*, and *Aeneid*
Macrobius (ca. 433), *Saturnalia*; Commentary on the *Somnium Scipionis*
Fulgentius (fl. 468–533), *Mitologiae; Expositio continentiae Virgilii; Super Thebaiden*
Isidore (fl. 602–636) *Etymologiae* (8.11.1–104, "De diis gentium")

8th–11th centuries

Theodulf of Orleans (ca. 786), "De libris quos legere solebam et qualiter fabulae poetarum a philosophus mystice pertractentur"
Rabanus Maurus (776?–856), "De diis gentium" of Isidore copied in *De universo*
First Vatican mythographer (8th–9th c.?), Mythography
Remigius of Auxerre (ca. 841–908), Commentaries on Boethius, the *Aeneid*, and Martianus Capella

Second Vatican mythographer (9th–10th c.?), Mythography
Ecloga Theoduli (9th–10th c.)
Notker Labeo (d. 1022), Glossed Translations of Boethius and Martianus
Bernard d'Utrecht (11th c.), Commentary on *Ecloga Theoduli*
Baudri de Bourgueil (1046–1130), Poem 216: Fragment of a Moralized Mythology

12th–13th centuries

William of Conches (1090–1145), Commentaries on Boethius, Macrobius, Martianus Capella, Juvenal, Plato's *Timaeus*
Bernard Silvestris (1085–1178), Commentaries on the *Aeneid* and Martianus Capella
Third Vatican mythographer (12th c.), *De diis gentium et illorum allegoriis*
Arnulf of Orleans (fl. 1175), Glosses on Lucan, Ovid's *Metamorphoses*, and Ovid's *Fasti*
Alexander Neckam (1157–1217), Glosses on *Ecloga Theoduli*, Martianus Capella; *De naturis rerum*
John of Garland (1180–1252), *Integumenta Ovidii*

14th–15th centuries

Nicholas Trivet (ca. 1314), Commentaries on Boethius, St. Augustine's *City of God*, Seneca's *Tragedies*
Ovide moralisé (14th c.)
John Ridewall (fl. 1331), *Fulgentius metaforalis*, Commentary on *City of God*, 1–3, 6–7
Giovanni del Virgilio (fl. 1332–33), *Allegorie librorum Ovidii Metamorphoseos*
Robert Holkot (fl. 1332–34, d. 1349?), Commentaries on the Book of Wisdom, the Twelve Prophets, Ecclesiastes
Pietro Alighieri (ca. 1340–41), Commentary on Dante
Pierre Bersuire (ca. 1342), *Ovidius moralizatus*
Giovanni Boccaccio (fl. 1313–75), *Genealogie gentilium deorum*, Commentary on the *Inferno*
Coluccio Salutati (1331–1406), *De laboribus Herculis*
Thomas Walsingham (d. 1422?), *Archana deorum*
Christine de Pizan (ca. 1399), *Epistre Othea*
Cristoforo Landino (fl. 1481), Commentaries on Virgil and Dante

Medieval Mythographers, Mythographic Commentaries, and Dictionaries

Please see the select bibliography at the end of the volume for a more comprehensive listing containing primary and secondary works cited in this collection as well as other mythographic works from the Middle Ages and Renaissance.

Albericus, of London (third Vatican mythographer). *See* Mythographi Vaticani.
Alfred, King. *King Alfred's Old English Version of Boethius: De consolatione Philosophiae*. Edited by Walter John Sedgefield. Oxford, 1899.
———. *King Alfred's Version of the Consolation of Boethius*. Translated by Walter John Sedgefield. Oxford: Clarendon Press, 1900.
Alighieri, Jacopo. *Chiose alla cantica dell'Inferno di Dante Allighieri atribuite a Iacopo suo figlio*. Florence, 1848.

———. *Chiose di Dante le quali fece el figiuolo co le sue mani: Messe in luce da F. D. Luiso.* Vol. 2: *Purgatorio.* Florence: G. Carnesecchi and Sons, 1904.

Alighieri, Pietro. *Petri Allegherii super Dantis ipsius genitoris Comoediam commentarium nunc primum in lucem editum.* Edited by Vincentio Nannucci. Florence, 1845.

Anonymous Barberinus. In "Barberini Manuscripts 57–66 and 121–130," edited by Ann Rose Raia. Ph.D. diss. Fordham University, 1965.

Anonymous Florentine. *Commento alla Divina Commedia d'Anonimo Fiorentino del secolo XVI.* Edited by Pietro Fanfani. 3 vols. Bologna, 1866–74.

Anonymous of St. Gall. Commentary on Boethius. The shorter. Naples. MS IV G 68. Fols. 1r–92r. The longer: St. Gall. MS 845. Fols. 3–240.

Anonymous Selmiano. *Chiose anonime alla prima cantica della Divina Commedia di un contemporaneo del poeta pubblicate per la prima volta a celebrare il sesto anno secolare della nascita di Dante da Francesco Selmi con riscontri di altri antichi commenti editi ed inediti e note filoligiche.* Edited by Francesco Selmi. Turin, 1865.

Anonymous Teutonicus. *Commentum in Theoduli eclogam e codice Utrecht, U.B. 292 editum (1).* Edited by Arpád P. Orbán. *Vivarium,* 11:1 (1973): 1–42; 12 (1974): 133–45; 13 (1975): 77–88; 14 (1976): 50–61; 15 (1977): 143–58.

Arnulf, of Orleans. *Allegoriae super Ovidii Metamorphoses.* In "Arnolfo d'Orléans, un cultore di Ovidio nel seculo XII," edited by Fausto Ghisalberti. *Memorie del Reale Instituto Lombardo di Scienze e Lettere* 24 (1932): 157–234.

———. Commentary on Ovid's *Fasti.* Rome, Vatican Library. MS Reg. 1548.

———. *Glosule super Lucanus.* Edited by Berthe M. Marti. Rome: American Academy in Rome, 1958.

Asser. Commentary on Boethius. In the Appendix to *Tradizioni Perdute: L'Antica "Fortuna" della "Consolatio Philosophiae,"* edited by Fabio Troncarelli, 141–201. Padua: Editrice Antenore, 1980.

Augustine, St. *De civitate Dei contra paganos libri.* Edited and translated William M. Green. 7 vols. Loeb Classical Library. London and Cambridge, MA.: Harvard University Press, 1963.

———. *De civitate Dei libri XXII.* Rev. Bernhard Dombart and Alfonsus Kalb. Bibliotheca Scriptorum Graecorum et Romanorum Teubneriana. 5th ed. Stuttgart: B.G. Teubner, 1981.

Balbi, Giovanni (Joannes Balbus). *Catholicon.* 1460. Reprint facsimile. Westmead, Farnsborough, Hants, England: Gregg International Publishers, 1971.

Bambaglioli, Graziolo. *Il commento Dantesco di Graziolo de' Bambaglioli dal "Colombino" di Siviglia con altri codici raffrontato.* Edited by Antonio Fiammazzo. Savona: D. Bertolotto, 1915.

Bargigi, Guiniforto delli. *Lo Inferno della Commedia di Dante Alighieri col comento di Guiniforto delli Bargigi.* Edited by G. Zacheroni. Marseilles: Leopoldo Mossy; Florence, 1838.

Baudri, de Bourgueil. Poem no. 216, "Fragment of a Moralized Mythology." In *Les oeuvres poétiques de Baudri de Bourgueil (1046–1139),* edited by Phyllis Abrahams, 273–316. Paris: Librairie Ancienne Honoré Champion, 1926.

Bernard Silvestris. *The Commentary on the First Six Books of the Aeneid Commonly Attributed to Bernardus Silvestris.* Edited by Julian Ward Jones and Elizabeth Frances Jones. Lincoln and London: University of Nebraska Press, 1977.

———. *Commentary on the First Six Books of Virgil's Aeneid.* Translated by Earl G. Schreiber and Thomas E. Maresca. Lincoln and London: University of Nebraska Press, 1979.

———. *The Commentary on Martianus Capella's De nuptiis Philologiae et Mercurii At-*

tributed to *Bernardus Silvestris*. Edited by Haijo Jan Westra. Studies and Texts, 80. Toronto: Pontifical Institute of Mediaeval Studies, 1986.

Bernard d'Utrecht. "Bernard's *Commentum in Theodulum: Editio Princeps*." Edited by Morton Yale Jacobs. Ph.D. diss., University of North Carolina–Chapel Hill, 1963.

———. *Commentum in Theodolum*. Edited by R. B. C. Huygens. Biblioteca degli "Studi medievali." Spoleto: Centro italiano di studi sull'alto medioevo, 1977.

Berne Scholia. *Scholia Bernensia ad Vergilii Bucolica atque Georgica*. Edited by Hermann Hagen. Jahrbücher für classische Philol. Suppl. vol. 4, pt. 5 Leipzig, 1867.

Bersuire, Pierre. *De formis figurisque deorum*. Cap. 1 of *Reductorium morale, liber XV: Ovidius moralizatus*. Edited by Joseph Engels. Utrecht: Instituut voor Laat Latijn der Rijksuniversiteit, 1966.

———. *Reductorium morale, liber XV, cap. ii–xv: Ovidius moralizatus*. Edited by Joseph Engels. Utrecht: Instituut voor Laat Latijn der Rijksuniversiteit, 1962.

———. "The *Ovidius Moralizatus* of Petrus Berchorius: An Introduction and Translation." Translated by William Reynolds. Ph.D. diss., University of Illinois–Urbana, 1971.

Boccaccio, Giovanni. *Genealogie deorum gentilium libri*. Edited by Vincenzo Romano. 2 vols. *Opere*, vols. 10–11. Scrittori d'Italia, no. 200–201. Bari: Giuseppe Laterza and Sons, 1951.

———. *On Poetry*. Translated by Charles G. Osgood, 1930. Reprint. Indianapolis: Bobbs-Merrill, 1956.

Boccaccio (False), of Roveta. *Chiose sopra Dante testo inedito ora per la prima volta pubblicato*. Edited by William Warren Vernon. Florence, 1846.

Bode, Georgius Henricus. *See* Mythographi Vaticani.

Buti, Francesco di Bartolo da. *Commento di Francesco da Buti sopra de Divina Comedia di Dante Allighieri*. Edited by Crescentino. 3 vols. Pisa, 1858–62.

Christine de Pizan. *L'Epistre Othea*. In Halina D. Loukopoulos. "Classical Mythology in the Works of Christine de Pisan, with an Edition of 'L'Epistre Othea' from the Manuscript Harley 4431." Ph.D. diss., Wayne State University 1977.

———. *The Epistle of Othea*. Translated into Middle English by Stephen Scrope. Edited by Curt F. Bühler. Early English Text Society. London, New York, Toronto: Oxford University Press, 1970.

———. *The Letter of Othea to Hector, Translated, with Introduction and Interpretive Essay*. Translated by Jane Chance. Cambridge, MA: Focus Information Group, 1990.

Dante Alighieri. *La Divina Commedia*. Edited by C. H. Grandgent. Revised by Charles S. Singleton. Cambridge, MA: Harvard University Press, 1972.

———. *The Divine Comedy*. Translated by John Sinclair. 3 vols. 1939. Reprint. New York: Oxford University Press, 1981.

De Boer, C. *See Ovide moralisé*.

De Foxton, John. *Liber Cosmographiae: An Edition and Codicological Study*. Edited by John Block Friedman. Brill's Studies in Intellectual History, vol. 5. Leiden and New York: E. J. Brill, 1988.

Digby Mythographer. "An Edition of an Anonymous Twelfth-Century *Liber de natura deorum*." Edited by Virginia Brown. *Mediaeval Studies* 34 (1972): 1–70.

Duemmler, Ernest, ed. *Poetae Latini Aevi Carolini. Poetarum Latinorum Medii Aevii*. Vol. 1, *Monumenta Germaniae Historica*. Berlin, 1881.

Ecloga Theoduli. Edited by John Gottlob Samuel Schwabe. Altenburg, 1773.

———. *Theoduli eclogam recensuit et prolegomenis instruxit Joannes Osternacher*. In *Fünfter Jahresbericht des bischöflichen Privat-Gymnasiums am Kollegium Petrinum in Urfahr für das Schuljahr 1901/02*. Urfahr prope Lentiam: programmate Collegii Petrini, 1902.

———. *See also* Bernard d'Utrecht.
Endt, Johann, ed. *Adnotationes super Lucanum.* Leipzig: B. G. Teubner, 1909.
Erfurt Commentator [Pseudo-John Scot]. *Saeculi noni Auctoris in Boetii Consolationem Philosophiae Commentarius.* Edited by Edmund Taite Silk. Papers and Monographs of the American Academy in Rome, vol. 9. Rome: American Academy in Rome, 1935.
Florentine Commentary on Martianus Capella. Florence, Biblioteca Nazionale Centrale. MS Conventi Soppr. J. 1. 28. Fols. 50r–64 v.
——— [Selections]. Edited by Peter Dronke. In *Fabula: Explorations into the Uses of Myth in Medieval Platonism,* 114–18, 167–83. Mittellateinische Studien und Texte, vol. 9. Leiden and Cologne: E. J. Brill, 1974.
Fulgentius, Fabius Planciades. *Mitologiae.* In *Opera,* edited by Rudolf Helm. 1898. Reprint. Stuttgart: B.G. Teubner, 1970.
———. *Fulgentius the Mythographer.* Trans. Leslie George Whitbread. Columbus: Ohio State University Press, 1971.
Giovanni, del Virgilio. *Allegorie librorum Ovidii Metamorphoseos a magistro Johanne de Virgilio prosaice ac metrice compilate.* Edited by Fausto Ghisalberti. In "Giovanni del Virgilio espositore delle 'Metamorfose.'" *Il Giornale Dantesco* n.s., 4, 34 (1933): 3–110.
Godman, Peter, ed. *Poetry of the Carolingian Renaissance.* Norman: University of Oklahoma Press, 1985.
Guido, da Pisa. *Expositiones et glose super Comediam Dantis or Commentary on Dante's Inferno.* Edited by Vincenzo Cioffari. Albany: State University of New York Press, 1974.
Holkot [Holcot], Robert. *In librum duodecim prophetas.* Oxford, MS Bodleian 722.
———. *Liber moralizationum historiarum.* In *M. Roberti Holkoth . . . In librum Sapientiae Regis Salomonis Praelectiones CCXIII,* 705–50. Bale, 1586.
———. *Moralitates.* Venice, 1514, 1586.
———. *Super librum Ecclesiastici.* Venice, 1509.
Hugutio [Huguitio; Uguccione] da Pisa. *Liber derivationum* or *Magnae derivationes.* Oxford, Bodleian Library. MS 376. Florence, Biblioteca Medicea Laurenziana. MS Pluteus XXVII Sinister, Codex 1. Fols. 1r–453v.
Hyginus. *Astronomica.* Edited by Bernard Bunte. Leipzig, 1875.
———. *Fabulae.* Edited by H. J. Rose. Leiden: A. W. Sijthoff, 1934.
———. *The Myths.* Translated and edited by Mary Grant. University of Kansas Publications: Humanistic Studies, no. 34. Lawrence: University of Kansas Publications, 1960.
Isidore, of Seville. *Etymologiarum libri XX.* Edited by W. M. Lindsay Scriptorum Classicorum Bibliotheca Oxoniensis. 2 vols. Oxford: Clarendon Press, 1911.
John, of Garland. *Integumenta Ovidii: Poemetto inedito del secolo XIII.* Edited by Fausto Ghisalberti. Testi e documenti inediti o rari, 2. Messina and Milan: Giuseppe Principato, 1933.
———. *Integumenta Ovidii.* Translated by Lester Kruger Born. In "The Integumenta on the Metamorphoses of Ovid by John of Garland—First cited with Introduction and Translation." Ph.D. diss., University of Chicago, 1929.
John, Scot [Joannes Scottus]. *Annotationes in Marcianum.* Edited by Cora Lutz. 1939. Reprint. New York: Kraus Reprint Co., 1970.
Lactantius Placidus. *Commentarii in Statii Thebaida et commentarius in Achilleida.* Edited by Richard Jahnke. Vol. 3 of *P. Papinius Statius.* Leipzig, 1898.
———. *Narrationes fabularum Ovidianarum.* Edited by Hugo Magnus. In *P. Ovidii Nasonis Metamorphoseon libri XV et Lactantii Placidi qui dicitur Narrationes fabularum Ovidianarum.* Berlin: Weidmann's, 1914.
Lana Bolognese, Jacopo della. *Comedia de Dante degli Allagherii col commento di Jacopo della Lana Bolognese.* Edited by Luciano Scarabelli. 3 vols. Bologna, 1866–67.

Landino, Cristoforo. *Dante con l'espositione di Cristoforo Landino, e di Alessandro Vellutelli*. Venice, 1564.

———. *Disputationes Camaldulenses*. Edited by Peter Lohe. Instituto Nazionale di Studi sul Rinascimento, Studi e Testi 6. Florence: Sansoni, 1980.

———. *Disputationes Camaldulenses*, Books 3 and 4. Translated by Thomas H. Stahel. In "Cristoforo Landino's Allegorization of the *Aeneid*: Books III and IV of the *Camaldolese Disputations*." Ph.D. diss., Johns Hopkins University, 1968.

Lucan. *See* Endt; Usener.

Macrobius, Ambrosius Theodosius. *Macrobius*. 2 vols. Edited by James Willis. Leipzig: B. G. Teubner, 1963.

———. *Commentary on the Dream of Scipio*. Translated by William Harris Stahl. Records of Civilization: Sources and Studies, no. 48. 1952. Reprint. New York and London: Columbia University, 1966.

———. *Saturnalia*. In *Macrobius*, translated by Percival Vaughan Davies. Records of Civilization: Sources and Studies, no. 79. New York and London: Columbia University Press, 1969.

Manegold, von Lautenbach [Lutterbach]. "Explicationes Metamorphoseon Ovidii." Munich, Staatsbibliothek. MS Monacensis Latinus 4610, 144872, 14809.

———. "Explicationes Metamorphosen Ovidii." Edited by Meiser. In "Ueber einen Commentar zu den Metamorphoseon des Ovid," 47–89. *Sitzungsberichte der philosphisch-philologischen und historischen Classe der Königliche-Bayerische Akademie der Wissenschaften zu München*. Munich, 1885.

Martianus Capella. *Martianus Capella*. Edited by Adolf Dick. Corr. Jean Préaux. Bibliotheca Scriptorum Graecorum et Romanorum Teubneriana. Stuttgart: B. G. Teubner, 1969.

———. *Martianus Capella and the Seven Liberal Arts*. Vol. 2: *The Marriage of Philology and Mercury*. Translated by William Harris Stahl and Richard Johnson with E. L. Burge. New York: Columbia University Press, 1977.

Martianus Capella, Anonymous Commentary on. Cambridge, Corpus Christi Library. MSS 153, 330.

Martin, of Laon (Dunchad). *Glossae in Martianum*. Edited by Cora E. Lutz, Philological Monographs no. 12. Lancaster, PA: American Philological Association, 1944.

Mythographi Vaticani. *Mythographi Vaticani I et II*. Edited by Péter Kulcsár. Corpus Christianorum, Series Latina, 91C. Turnholt: Brepols, 1987.

———. *Scriptores Rerum Mythicarum Latini Tres Romae Nuper Reperti*. Edited by Georgius Henricus Bode. 2 vols. 1834. Reprint in 1 vol., Hildesheim: Georg Olms, 1968.

———. "Text, Authorship, and Use of the First Vatican Mythographer." Edited by Kathleen Overmeyer. Ph.D. diss., Radcliffe College, 1942.

Neckam, Alexander. Commentary on the *Theodoli Ecloga*. Rome, Vatican Library. MS 1479. Fols. 15v–25r.

———. *De naturis rerum; De laudibus divinae sapientiae*. Edited by Thomas Wright. Rolls Series, 34. London, 1863.

———. *Super Marcianum de nupciis Mercurii et Philologie* (Books 1 and 2). Oxford, Bodleian Library. MS Digby 211. Fols. 34b–88.

Notker, Labeo. *Notker's Des teutschen Werke*. Edited by Heinrich Hattemer. In *Denkmahle des Mittelalters. St. Gallens altteutsche Sprachschätze*, vol. 3. St. Gall, 1846.

———. Boethius, "De consolatione Philosophiae," Buch 1 / II–III. Edited by Petrus W. Tax. Vols. 1–2, Die Werke Notkers des Deutschen. Tübingen: Max Niemeyer, 1986, 1988.

———, trans. *Boethius de consolatione Philosophiae*. In *Notkers des deutschen Werke*, edited by E. H. Sehrt and Taylor Starck. Vol. 1, pts. 1–3. Altdeutsche Textbibliothek nos. 32–34. Halle and Saale: Max Niemeyer, 1933–34.

———, trans. *De nuptiis Philologiae et Mercurii*. In *Notkers des deutschen Werke*. Edited by E. H. Sehrt and Taylor Starck. Vol. 2. Altdeutsche Textbibliothek no. 37. Halle and Saale: Max Niemeyer, 1935.

Odo, Picardus. *Liber Theodoli cum commento noviter impressus*. London, 1508.

Osbern, of Gloucester (*Glossarium Osberi*). *Thesaurus novus latinitatis, sive lexicon vetus e membranis nunc primum erutum*. Edited by Angelo Mai. In *Classicorum Auctorum e Vaticanis codicibus editorum*, vol. 8. Rome, 1836.

Ottimo Commentary on the *Divine Comedy*. *L'Ottimo Commento della Divina Commedia testo inedito d'un contemporaneo di Dante citato dagli accademici della Crusca*. Edited by Alessandro Torri. 3 vols. Pisa, 1827–29.

Ovid [Publius Ovidius Nasonis]. *Fastorum libri sex: The Fasti of Ovid*. Edited and translated by Sir James George Frazer. 5 vols. London: W. Heinemann; New York: G. P. Putnam's Sons, 1931.

———. *Metamorphoses*. Edited and translated by Frank Justus Miller. 2 vols. Loeb Classical Library. 3d ed. Cambridge, MA: Harvard University Press; London: W. Heinemann, 1977.

———. *Metamorphoses*. Translated by Rolfe Humphries. Bloomington and London: Indiana University Press, 1955, 1972.

Ovide moralisé: Poème du commencement du quatorzième siècle. Edited by C. de Boer et al. *Verhandelingen der Koninklijke Akademie van Wetenschappen te Amsterdam. Afdeeling Letterkunde*. Nieuwe Reeks 15 (1915): 1–374; 21 (1920): 1–394; 30 (1931): 1–303; 37 (1936): 1–478; 43 (1938): 1–429. Reprint in 5 vols. Wiesbaden: Martin Sändig, 1966–68.

Papias, the Lombard. *Vocabulista*. Turin: Bottega d'Erasmo, 1966.

Paulus Diaconus. *Excerpta ex libris Pompeii Festi de significatione verborum*. In *Sexti Pompeii Festi de verborum significatu quae supersunt cum Pauli epitome*, edited by Wallace M. Lindsay. 1913. Reprint. Hildesheim: Teubner, 1965.

Petrarcha, Francesco. *L'Africa*. Edited by Nicola Festa. *Edizione nazionale delle opere di Francesco Petrarcha*, Vol. 1. Florence: G. C. Sansoni, 1926.

———. *Africa*. Translated by Thomas G. Bergin and Alice S. Wilson. New Haven and London: Yale University Press, 1977.

Rabanus Maurus. *De diis gentium*. In *De universo libri XXII*, 15.6. In *Opera omnia PL* 111: 426–36.

Ralph, of Beauvais. *Liber Titan*. London, British Library. MS Add. 16380. Fols. 111r–19v.

Rambaldi da Imola, Benvenuto. *Benevenuti de Rambaldis de Imola Commentum super Dantis Aldigherij Comoediam nunc primum integre in lucem editum*. Edited by William Warren Vernon. Revised by Jacopo Philippo Lacaita. 5 vols. Florence, 1887.

Remigius, of Auxerre. *Commentum in Martianum Capellam libri I–II, and II–IX*. Edited by Cora E. Lutz. 2 vols. Leiden: E. J. Brill, 1962, 1965.

———. Mythological Glosses from the Commentary on Boethius. In "The Study of the Consolation of Philosophy in Anglo-Saxon England," edited by Diane K. Bolton. *Archives d'histoire doctrinale et littéraire du Moyen Âge*, 44 (1977): 61–78.

———. See also Savage.

Ridewall [Ridevall], John. *Fulgentius metaforalis*. Edited by Hans Liebeschütz. In *Fulgentius metaforalis, ein Beitrag zur Geschichte der antiken Mythologie im Mittelalter*. Studien der Bibliothek Warburg, no. 4. Leipzig and Berlin: B.G. Teubner, 1926.

———. Commentary on *De civitate Dei*, books 1–2, 6–7. Oxford, Corpus Christi Library. MS 186–87.

Salutati, Coluccio. *De laboribus Herculis*. Edited by B. L. Ullmann. 2 vols. Zurich: Editrice Antenore, 1951.

Savage, John Joseph H. "Mediaeval Notes on the Sixth *Aeneid* in *Parisinus 7930.*" *Speculum* 9 (1934): 204–12.

Serravalle, Giovanni da. *Fratris Iohannis de Serravalle translatio et comentum totius libri Dantis Aldigherii cum textu italico*. Edited by Fratris Bartholomaei A. Colle. Prato, 1891.

Servius, Grammaticus. *Servii Grammatici qui feruntur in Vergilii carmina commentarii*. 3 vols. Edited by Georg Thilo and Hermann Hagen. 1881–87. Reprint. Hildesheim: G. Olms, 1961.

———. *Servianorum in Vergilii carmina commentariorum*. Edited by Edward K. Rand et al. 2 vols. Lancaster, PA: Lancaster Press, 1946.

Statius, P. Papinus. *The Medieval Archilleid of Statius*. Edited by Paul M. Clogan. Leiden: E. J. Brill, 1968.

Theodulf, of Orleans. "De libris quos legere solebam." *PL* 105:331–33.

———. *See* Duemmler; Godman.

Trivet [Trevet], Nicholas. Commentary on Augustine's *De civitate Dei* (Books 11–23) and on Seneca. Oxford, Bodleian Library. MS 292.

———. *Exposicio super librum Boecii consolatione*. Oxford, Bodleian. MS Rawlinson G. 187. Fols. 46rff; Rome, Vatican Library. 562 and 563; Reg. lat. 1066; Rossian 358; Ottob. lat. 1671 and 2026.

———. Commentary on Boethius (excerpts). Edited by Charles Jourdain. In "Des Commentaires inédits de Guillaume de Conches et de Nicolas Triveth sur la Consolation de la philosophie de Bòece." *Notices et extraits des manuscrits de la Bibliothèque Impériale et autres bibliothèques*, 20.2 (1862): 40–82.

———. *Commento alle "Troades" di Seneca*. Edited by Marco Palma. Temi e Testi, vol. 22. Rome: Edizioni di Storia e Letteratura, 1977.

Usener, Hermann, ed. *Scholia in Lucani Bellum civile*. Part I; *M. Annaei Lucani Bernensia*. Leipzig, 1869.

Vatican Mythographers. *See* Mythographi Vaticani.

Villena, Enrique de [Henry of Arágon]. *Los doze trabajos de Hércules*. Edited by Margherita Morreale. Madrid: Real Academia Española Biblioteca Selecta de Clásicos Españoles, 1958.

Walleys, Thomas [Waleys; "of Wales"]. Commentary on *De civitate Dei*, books 1–10. Oxford, Bodleian Library. MS 292.

Walsingham, Thomas. *Archana Deorum*. Edited by Robert A. van Kluyve. Durham, NC: Duke University Press, 1968.

William, of Conches. Glosses on Boethius. Excerpts in Édouard Jeauneau. "L'Usage de la notion d'*integumentum* à travers les gloses de Guillaume de Conches." *Archives d'histoire doctrinale et littéraire du Moyen Âge* 32 (1957): 35–100.

———. Glosses on Boethius [excerpts]. Edited by J. M. Parent. In *La Doctrine de la Création dans l'École de Chartres: Étude et Textes Publications de l'Institute de'Études Médiévales d'Ottawa*, 115–21. Vol. 8. Paris: J. Vrin; Ottawa: Inst. d'Études Médiévales, 1938.

———. *Glosae in Iuvenalem*. Edited by Bradford Wilson. Textes philosophiques du Moyen Âge, 18. Paris: J. Vrin, 1980.

———. *Glosses on the Timaeus*. In *Glosae super Platonem: Texte critique avec introduction, notes et tables*. Edited by Édouard Jeauneau. Textes Philosophiques du Moyen Âge, no. 13. Paris: J. Vrin, 1965.

Works Cited

Allen, Don Cameron. *Mysteriously Meant: The Rediscovery of Pagan Symbolism and Allegorical Interpretation in the Renaissance.* Baltimore and London: Johns Hopkins University Press, 1970.

Allen, Judson Boyce. *The Ethical Poetic of the Later Middle Ages: A Decorum of Convenient Distinction.* Toronto, Buffalo, and London: University of Toronto Press, 1982.

———. *The Friar as Critic: Literary Attitudes in the Later Middle Ages.* Nashville, TN: Vanderbilt University Press, 1971.

Baswell, Christopher. "The Medieval Allegorization of the *Aeneid*: Ms. Cambridge, Peterhouse 158." *Traditio* 41 (1985): 181–237.

Battaglia, Salvatore. "La tradizione di Ovidio nel Medioevo." *Filologia romanza* 6 (1959): 185–224.

Boethius, Anicius Manlius Severinus. *De consolatione Philosophiae.* Edited by L. Biehler. Corpus Christianorum, vol. 164. Turnhout: Brepols, 1957.

———. *The Consolation of Philosophy.* Translated by Richard H. Green. Indianapolis and New York: Bobbs-Merrill, 1962.

Bolton, Diane K. "Manuscripts and Commentaries on Boethius, *De consolatione Philosophiae* in England in the Middle Ages." B. Litt. thesis, Oxford, 1965.

———. "Remigian Commentaries on the 'Consolation of Philosophy' and their Sources." *Traditio* 33 (1977): 381–94.

———. "The Study of the Consolation of Philosophy in Anglo-Saxon England." *Archives d'histoire doctrinale et littéraire du Moyen Âge* 44 (1977): 33–78.

Brinkmann, Hennig. "Verhüllung ('integumentum') als literarische Darstellungsform im Mittelalter." In *Der Begriff der Repraesentatio in Mittelalter: Stellvertretung, Symbol, Zeichen, Bild.* Miscellanea Mediaevalia, vol. 8. Berlin and New York: Walter de Gruyter, 1971.

Bush, Douglas. *Mythology and the Renaissance Tradition in English Poetry.* 1932. Rev. ed.: New York: W. W. Norton, 1963.

Chance [Nitzsche], Jane. "Chaucer and Mythology." *The Chaucer Newsletter* 6:2 (Fall 1984); 1, 2.

———. "The Medieval Sources of Cristoforo Landino's Allegorization of the Judgment of Paris." *Studies in Philology* 81:2 (1984): 45–60.

———. *The Mythographic Tradition in the Middle Ages.* Vol. 1, complete.

———. "The Origins and Development of Medieval Mythography: From Homer to Dante." In *Mapping the Cosmos*, edited by Jane Chance and R. O. Wells, Jr., 35–64, 151–59. Houston, TX: Rice University, 1985.

Chaucer, Geoffrey. *The Riverside Chaucer.* Edited by Larry D. Benson. 3d ed. rev. from Fred C. Robinson. Boston: Houghton Mifflin, 1987.

Chenu, M.-D. "*Involucrum*: Le mythe selon les théologiens médiévaux." *Archives d'histoire doctrinale et littéraire du Moyen Âge* 30 (1955): 75–79.

———. *Nature, Man, and Society in the Twelfth Century: Essays on New Theological Perspectives in the Latin West.* Selected, edited, and translated by Jerome Taylor and Lester K. Little. Chicago and London: University of Chicago Press, 1968.

Chydenius, Johan. *The Theory of Medieval Symbolism.* Commentationes Humanarum Litterarum, 27.2. Helsinki: Societas Scientiarum Fennica, 1960.

Comparetti, Domenico. *Vergil in the Middle Ages.* Translated from the 2d ed. by E. F. M. Benecke. 1895. Reprint. New York, Leipzig, Paris, London: G. E. Stechert and Co. (Alfred Hafner), 1929.

Courcelle, Pierre. *La Consolation de Philosophie dans la tradition littéraire: Antécédents et postérité de Boèce.* Paris: Études Augustiniennes, 1967.

———. "Étude critique sur les commentaires de la Consolation de Boèce (IXe–XVe siècles)." *Archives d'histoire doctrinale et littéraire du Moyen Âge* 14 (1939): 5–140.
Curtius, Ernst Robert. *European Literature and the Latin Middle Ages*. 1948. Translated by Willard Trask. 1953. Reprint. New York and Evanston: Harper and Row, 1963.
Demats, Paule. *Fabula: Trois études de mythographie antique et médiévale*. Publications Romanes et Françaises, no. 122. Geneva: Droz, 1973.
Dronke, Peter. *Fabula: Explorations into the Uses of Myth in Medieval Platonism*. Mittellateinische Studien und Texte, vol. 9. Leiden and Cologne: E. J. Brill, 1974.
Economou, George D. *The Goddess Natura in the Middle Ages*. Cambridge, MA: Harvard University Press, 1972.
Ehrhart, Margaret J. *The Judgment of the Trojan Prince Paris in Medieval Literature*. Philadelphia: University of Pennsylvania Press, 1987.
Elliott, Kathleen O., and J. P. Elder. "A Critical Edition of the Vatican Mythographers." *Transactions of the American Philological Association* 78 (1947): 189–207.
Friedman, John Block. *Orpheus in the Middle Ages*. Cambridge, MA: Harvard University Press, 1970.
Fulgentius, Fabius Planciades. *Mitologiae*. In *Opera*, edited by Rudolf Helm. 1898. Reprint. Stuttgart: B.G. Teubner, 1970.
———. *Fulgentius the Mythographer*. Translated by Leslie George Whitbread. Columbus: Ohio State University Press, 1971.
Gaeta, Franco. "L'avventura di Ercole." *Rinascimento* 5 (1954): 227–60.
Gibson, Margaret, ed. *Boethius: His Life, Thought, and Influence*. Oxford: Basil Blackwell, 1981.
Green, Richard Hamilton. "Classical Fable and English Poetry in the Fourteenth Century." In *Critical Approaches to Medieval Literature: Selected Papers from the English Institute, 1958–59*, edited by Dorothy Bethurum, 110–33. New York: Columbia University Press, 1960.
Guillaume, de Lorris, and Jean de Meun. *Le Roman de la Rose par Guillaume de Lorris et Jean de Meun*. Edited by Ernest Langlois. 5 vols. Société des Anciens Textes Français, vols. 117–21. Paris: Librairie ancienne Honoré Champion, 1914–24.
———. Translated by Charles Dahlberg. Princeton: Princeton University Press, 1971.
Guthrie, Shirley Law. "The *Ecloga Theoduli* in the Middle Ages." Ph.D. diss., Indiana University, 1973.
Hall, Louis Brewer, "The Story of Dido and Aeneas in the Middle Ages." *Dissertation Abtracts* 14 (1954), 2339 (University of Pittsburgh).
Hatinguais, Jacqueline. "Points de vue sur la volunté et le jugement dans l'oeuvre d'un humaniste chartrain (Guillaume de Conches, XIIe siècle)." In *L'Homme et son destin d'après les penseurs du Moyen Âge. Actes du premier Congrès international de philosophie médiévale*, 417–29. Louvain: Éditions Nawelaerts; Paris: Beatrice-Nawelaerts, 1960.
Heitmann, Klaus. "Typen der Deformierung antiker Mythen im Mittelalter: Am Beispiel der Orpheussage." *Romanistisches Jahrbuch* 14 (1963): 45–77.
Hexter, Ralph J. *Ovid and Medieval Schooling. Studies in Medieval School Commentaries on Ovid's Ars Amatoria, Epistulae ex Ponto, and Epistulae Heriodum*. Münchener Beiträge zur Mediävistik und Renaissance-Forschung. Munich: Arbeo-Gesellschaft, 1986.
Hollander, Robert. *The Dartmouth Project on Dante Commentaries: A Data Base*. Dartmouth: Dartmouth College, forthcoming.
Jeauneau, Édouard. "La Lecture des auteurs classiques à l'école de Chartres durant la première moitié du XIIe siècle. Un témoin privilégié: Les 'Glosae super Macrobium' de

Guillaume de Conches." In *Classical Influences on European Culture A.D. 500–1500*, edited by R. R. Bolgar, 95–102. Cambridge: Cambridge University Press, 1971.

———. "L'Usage de la notion d'*integumentum* à travers les gloses du Guillaume de Conches." *Archives d'histoire doctrinale et littéraire du Moyen Âge* 32 (1957): 35–100.

Jung, Marc-René. *Hercule dans la littérature française du XVIe siècle: De l'Hercule courtois à l'Hercule baroque*. Travaux d'humanisme et Renaissance, no. 79. Geneva: Droz, 1966.

Klibansky, Raymond, Erwin Panofsky, and Fritz Saxl. *Saturn and Melancholy: Studies in the History of Natural Philosophy, Religion, and Art*. London: Thomas Nelson and Sons, 1964.

Lord, Mary Louise. "Dido as an Example of Chastity: The Influence of Example Literature." *Harvard Library Bulletin* 17:1–2 (1969): 22–44, 216–32.

Lubac, Henri de. *Exégèse médiévale*. Paris: Aubier, 1959–64.

Macrobius, Ambrosius Theodosius. *Commentarii in Somnium Scipionis*. Vol. 2 of *Macrobius*. 2 vols. Edited by James Willis. Leipzig: B. G. Teubner, 1963.

———. *Commentary on the Dream of Scipio*. Translated by William Harris Stahl. Records of Civilization: Sources and Studies, no. 48. 1952. Reprint. New York and London: Columbia University, 1966.

Minnis, Alastair J. *Chaucer and Pagan Antiquity*. Woodbridge, Suffolk: D.S. Brewer; Totowa, NJ: Rowman and Littlefield, 1982.

Moss, Ann. *Poetry and Fable: Studies in Mythological Narrative in Sixteenth-Century France*. Cambridge and New York: Cambridge University Press, 1984.

Munari, Franco. *Ovid im Mittelalter*. Zurich and Stuttgart: Artemis, 1960.

Panofsky, Dora, and Erwin Panofsky. *Pandora's Box: The Changing Aspects of a Mythical Symbol*. London: Routledge and Kegan Paul, 1956.

Panofsky, Erwin. *Hercules am Scheidewege und andere antike Bildstoffe in der neueren Kunst*. Studien der Bibliothek Warburg, 18. Leipzig and Berlin: B. G. Teubner, 1930.

———. *Studies in Iconology: Humanistic Themes in the Art of the Renaissance*. 1939. Reprint. New York: Harper and Row, 1967.

Panofsky, Erwin, and Fritz Saxl. "Classical Mythology in Mediaeval Art." *Metropolitan Museum Studies* 4 (1932–33): 228–80.

Patch, Howard Rollins. *The Goddess Fortuna in Mediaeval Literature*. 1927 Reprint. New York: Octagon Books, 1967.

Pépin, Jean. *Mythe et allégorie: Les Origines grecques et les contestations Judéo-Chrétiennes*. Paris: Aubier, Editions Montaigne, 1958.

Robertson, D. W., Jr. *A Preface to Chaucer: Studies in Medieval Perspectives*. Princeton: Princeton University Press, 1962.

———. "Some Medieval Literary Terminology, with Special Reference to Chrétien." *Studies in Philology* 48 (1951): 669–92.

Robson, C. A. "Dante's Use in the *Divina Commedia* of the Medieval Allegories on Ovid." In *Centenary Essays on Dante*, by Members of the Oxford University Dante Society, 1–38. Oxford: Clarendon Press, 1965.

Rocca, Luigi. *Di alcuni commenti della Divina Commedia composti nei primi vent'anni dopo la morte di Dante*. Florence: G. C. Sansoni, 1981.

Roseberg, Nathan Francis. "A Literary History of the Legend of the Argonautic Expedition through the Middle Ages." *Dissertation Abstracts* 14 (1954): 2339 (University of Pittsburgh).

Sandkühler, Bruno. *Die frühen Dantekommentare und ihr Verhältnis zur mittelalterlichen Kommentartradition*. Münchener romanistische Arbeiten, no. 19. Munich: Max Hueber, 1967.

Savage, John Joseph H. "The Medieval Tradition of Cerberus." *Traditio* 7 (1949–51): 405–10.

Schreiber, Earl G. "Venus in the Mythographic Tradition." *JEGP* 74 (1975): 519–35.

Seznec, Jean. *The Survival of the Pagan Gods: The Mythological Tradition and its Place in Renaissance Humanism and Art*. Translated by Barbara F. Sessions from the 1940 ed. New York: Harper and Row, 1953.

Smalley, Beryl. *English Friars and Antiquity in the Early Fourteenth Century*. Oxford: Basil Blackwell; New York: Barnes and Noble, 1960.

Statius, P. Papinus. *Statius*. Translated by J. H. Mozley. 2 vols. 1928. Reprint. London: W. Heinemann; Cambridge, MA: Harvard University Press, 1969.

Stock, Brian. *Myth and Science in the Twelfth Century: A Study of Bernard Silvester*. Princeton: Princeton University Press, 1972.

Tate, Robert B. "Mythology in Spanish Historiography of the Middle Ages and Renaissance." *Hispanic Review*, 22 (1954): 1–18.

Tuve, Rosemond. *Allegorical Imagery: Some Medieval Books and Their Posterity*. Princeton: Princeton University Press, 1966.

———. *Elizabethan and Metaphysical Imagery*. Princeton: Princeton University Press, 1947.

von Bezold, Friedrich. *Das Fortleben der antiken Götter im mittelalterlichen Humanismus*. 1922. Reprint. Otto Zeller Verlagsbuchhändlung, 1962.

Warden, John, ed. *Orpheus: The Metamorphosis of a Myth*. Toronto and London: University of Toronto Press, 1982.

Wetherbee, Winthrop. *Platonism and Poetry in the Twelfth Century: The Literary Influence of the School of Chartres*. Princeton: Princeton University Press, 1972.

Wilkins, Ernest Hatch. "Descriptions of Pagan Divinities from Petrarch to Chaucer." *Speculum* 32 (1957): 511–22.

William, of Conches. *Glosae in Iuvenalem*. Edited by Bradford Wilson. Textes philosophiques du Moyen Âge, 18. Paris: J. Vrin, 1980.

———. *Glosses on the Timaeus*. In *Glosae super Platonem: Texte critique avec introduction, notes et tables*, edited by Édouard Jeauneau. Textes Philosophiques du Moyen Âge, no. 13. Paris: J. Vrin, 1965.

Williams, Lynn Flickinger. "The Gods of Love in Ancient and Medieval Literature as Background of John Gower's *Confessio Amantis*." Ph.D. diss., Columbia University, 1967.

Wind, Edgar. *Pagan Mysteries in the Renaissance*. 1958. Rev. ed.: London: Faber and Faber, 1967.

Part I. Early France

The Mythographer and the Poet

From Mirror to Metamorphosis

Echoes of Ovid's Narcissus in Chrétien's *Erec et Enide*

Jeanne A. Nightingale

> Peut-être [Chrétien] fut en quelque mesure, l'Ovide de la mythologie celtique ou de ses reflets.
>
> Jean Frappier[1]

The art of transforming a favorite old story into a new, more aesthetically pleasing and more thought-provoking version of that tale—a skill that Chrétien de Troyes claimed to have perfected when he transformed the popular *Conte d'Erec* into what he knew would be a French "classic"—was a practice that had been refined before him by one of Chrétien's classical mentors, the poet Ovid. "If the historical Ovid took Paris and Helen from Homeric epic and metamorphosed them into figures for his comedy of love," Edward Rand reasons, "the posthumous Ovid assisted Chrétien in a similar abstraction of Lancelot and Guenevere from Celtic fairy legend, and a similar adaptation of their characters to his romance" (125). Indeed, the epic form of Ovid's *Metamorphoses* may conceivably have provided Chrétien with a working model of a narrative, which—like his own "molt bele conjointure"—had been composed of mythological fragments of varying sources, arranged to fit a unified and historically ordered plan, and designed to breathe new life and purpose into the old bones of obsolete myth, the "inventions of lying bards," *materiem vatum falsique*.

In the prologue to his *Metamorphoses*, Ovid implores the gods, the original authors of changing forms (*mutatas formas*), to make his narrative flow in one unbroken song (*carmen perpetuum*) from the very creation of the world down to his own times. Metamorphosis thus provides the poet with a unifying theme and a working metaphor for the organization of his material as he proceeds, in imitation of the creative forces in the cosmos (including "kindlier Nature," *melior natura*,[2] the "Great Renewer" of the material universe) to transmute the chaos of ancient mythical forms into a "cosmos of poetic reality" (Rand, 56). While Ovid begins his work by commemorating the triumph of "melior natura" over primal chaos, he ends it in a celebration of his own artistic achievement, his "melior pars," which he believes will guarantee him an immortal place above the stars as he continues to be read throughout the ages. It is this authorial boast that Chrétien de Troyes echoes centuries later in the prologue to his first romance, *Erec et Enide*. His version of the *estoire*, he tells his courtly audience, represents, with God's grace, the very best of himself—his talent, his intellect, and his learning—and promises to be a work of lasting value throughout the history of Christendom: "qui toz jorz mes iert an mimoire tant con durra crestïantez."

A similar *translatio* of fame is seen in a commentary on Ovid's *Metamorphoses* written in Chrétien's century by Arnulf of Orleans, a leading exponent of Ovid.[3] Arnulf glosses the new heavenly star, into which Ovid had transmuted Julius Caesar's deified soul at the end of his work, as the same star that guided the wise men to Christ ("who will live and reign for ever and ever, Amen"). Arnulf expresses his fervent hope, moreover, that by reading Ovid's tales as adumbrations of Christian morality, he—like Ovid—would immortalize his own name as well: "vivam cum Ovidio," he proclaims, "I will live with Ovid."[4] Both Arnulf and Chrétien shared with Ovid a belief in the underlying universality of myth and the duty of each successive generation of poets to adapt its antiquated forms to the idiom of their own times, and to revive and transmit its eternal message. As Rand expressed it, "The past is plastic in the author's hands. It is the same process that ran rigorous course in the Hellenistic age of Greek literature and culminated in Ovid himself. He was the first of the medieval romancers. He would have enjoyed seeing his stories of Pyramus, Narcissus, Byblis, and Phaethon extracted from their context and retold in what to the Medieval author seemed a modern way" (124).

This interpretive approach to mythical narrative belongs, in fact, to the larger tradition of poetry and commentary that we now have identified as the "mythographical tradition." Just as the Romans used the "lying myths" of the ancient Greeks to illuminate the beauty of Roman truth, so the Christians found divine moral teachings typologically prefigured in the pagan tales of the Roman gods. The process of *translatio* was a kind of continuous *revelatio*. Mythographers from Homer to Dante were driven by a desire to discern and expose the abiding truths adumbrated in the ancient narratives of gods and heros, as if these constituted some archetypal language or divine pedagogy. While many of the works included in the corpus of this tradition are ponderously didactic in their handbook-style exposition of moral truths, others are meticulously crafted epics of the human spirit, into which countless narratives of ancient myths were woven. The comprehensive design of these encyclopedic works (a kind of verbally ordered universe) was strategically devised so as to become progressively revealed as the reader—scanning forward and backward along the surface of the fiction—perceived the elaborate network of internal resonances and allusions. By the twelfth century, this widespread adaptation of myth had become what Brian Stock calls "a consistent and systematic literary theory," one that featured both a "demythologization of ancient fables and myths to elicit their hidden meanings and the making of new myths, the actual creation of structures that sought to symbolize the true nature of reality" (49).

The conventional authority for this interpretive, or "integumental," approach to myth in the Middle Ages was the late classical *auctor* Macrobius who, in his commentary on Cicero's *Dream of Scipio*, justified the use of myth and dream narrative as a valid mode of truth (2.18, 19). To meet the objection that fiction had no place with those who profess to tell the truth, and that poets were but tale-mongers and liars, he argued that it was precisely the false nature of mythical fictions that made them useful as a "cover" for truth and as an educative tool. If myth were conceived as a fabulous disguise, then its function would be twofold: to challenge worthy minds to "*dis*-cover" the profound insights under the surfaces of fiction, and to conceal sacred mysteries from less worthy minds. To sanction this double function of myth, Macrobius drew upon the analogy he saw between poetic imagery and the "vestment" of *visibilia* with which the goddess Natura protects her most arcane secrets from common sensibilities. For Macrobius, as for Ovid, literature ideally imitates the creative processes of nature. Whenever commentators and poets spoke of *integumenta* or *involucra*—terms used to indicate the twofold nature of mythical narratives, *fabula* and *veritas*, the story and its concealed meaning—it was invariably in reference to Macrobius's theories on the use of dream and myth fictions ("*narratio fabulosa*") as veiled descriptions of philosophical truth.

The reference that Chrétien de Troyes makes to Macrobius at the end of his first romance, acknowledging the Latin *auctor* as a teacher and mentor, is most often dismissed by romance scholars as "out of place" in an Arthurian romance, or discredited as a careless—and once more erroneous—source-reference for his scholarly iconography (the four quadrivial arts sewn into the Celtic hero's coronation gown). As I have argued elsewhere, however, this reference—together with a number of other explicit allusions to the Latin commentary tradition found in the romance—provides us with a significant link between the textual universes of courtly and cosmic epic—both conscious adaptations of *fabula* to the purposes of *veritas*, "*matière*" to "*san*"—which demand further study (Nightingale, "Chrétien" and "Court"). If, by invoking Macrobius's authority at the end of his first romance, Chrétien was declaring his indebtedness to Macrobius's teachings on the adaptation of mythical narrative, then he was purposefully and mindfully recognizing Macrobius as the founder of the literary tradition to which he intended his retelling of the Erec story to belong.

From the list of Chrétien's earlier works found in the preface of his romance *Cligès*—a listing that includes the translations "an romanz" of four of Ovid's pieces[5]—and from the many reflections of Ovid's poetry throughout his romances, we can infer that Ovid's work provided Chrétien with the inspiration and a major source from which, in the spirit of *translatio studii*, he freely borrowed and adapted to the requirements of his own poetic vision. Jean Frappier imagines that Chrétien most likely learned to write by translating Ovid before yielding to the charms of the Breton tales (*Chrétien*, 11). Once he learned to master Ovid's strategies and techniques of creative translation, he applied them in turn to the mythological themes of Celtic as well as classical origin.

While Chrétien's indebtedness to the poetry of Ovid has long been acknowledged, it is only recently, with the advent of intertextual readings, that research has devoted attention to the complexities of the poetic process by which these Ovidian-inspired transmutations take place in Chrétien's romances (Freeman, 158–68; Dornbusch 34–43). The focus of the present study will be on Chrétien's first major work, *Erec et Enide*, the title of which heads Chrétien's list of predominantly Ovidian adaptations written prior to his *Cligès*, but which, as most scholars continue to maintain, contains the least number of recognizable Ovidian elements of all his romances.[6] Although there are no explicit references to Ovid in *Erec et Enide*, I have discovered a number of textual quotations from Ovid's tale of Narcissus that appear to be intentional, but which have been so ingeniously camouflaged in the text that they have escaped notice. The aim of this essay will be to show how these hidden allusions to the Ovidian myth can elucidate some of the more puzzling moments in Chrétien's narrative and, further, how Chrétien's application of Ovid's poetics of reflection and metamorphosis can lead us to a new understanding of the creative processes implied in what he calls his "molt bele conjointure."

As we discuss the implications of these Ovidian borrowings, it will be important to remember that in the twelfth century, often characterized as an *aetas ovidiana*, Ovid's works had become included in the standard curriculum of the schools and were regarded as an essential element in a liberal arts education (Rand, 119). As one of the major classical *auc-*

tores, Ovid rivaled Virgil in popularity; while Virgil stood for conservative tastes in literature, Ovid came to represent the new interest in poetic innovation.[7] His *Metamorphoses*, the most popular of these works, was studied by some as a model of Latin style and by others as a compilation of cautionary fables whose purpose it was to teach various ethical truths. For the Goliards and for the lyric and romance poets, of course, Ovid was exalted as *praeceptor amoris*, the authority on the art of romantic love and master of the language of the heart. For humanist educators like Hildebert de Lavardin and John of Salisbury, for mystics like Bernard de Clairvaux and Hugh of St. Victor, and for philosopher-theologians such as Peter Abelard and Alanus de Insulis, Ovid was an authority on moral conduct (Battaglia, 132). The Neoplatonist poets of Chartres, discovering timelessly valued truths underneath the frivolous surface of his fictions, mined Ovid's epic, as they did Virgil's, for its rich store of philosophical integuments, which they integrated into their allegorical cosmologies.

Working within this commentary tradition, Arnulf of Orleans used Ovid's philosophy of cosmic metamorphosis as an interpretive key to the intrinsic *utilitas* of each of his fables. "Ovid's intention," Arnulf explained, "was to describe mutability so that we may understand by it not simply those changes which take place outside us affecting material things in good or bad ways, but also those which take place inwardly in the soul. In this way, Ovid sought to recall us from error toward a recognition of the true Creator."[8] By depicting stories of amatory mutations, Ovid sought to transform our irrational love of mutable temporal things into a rational love of that which is eternal.[9] His poems provide a way for the mind to ascend to a vision of the divine truth *per creaturas ad creatorem*.

The Narcissus story lent itself particularly well to this kind of interpretation. Narcissus, Arnulf tells us, was changed into an ephemeral flower because he loved his shadow and placed his own excellence above all other things. Gazing into the "faulz mireoirs de cest monde," he was unable to discern the true object of his love, that transcendant Ideal of which his image was but a fatal mockery. His shadow (*umbra*) and the flower into which he was transformed (*flos sine fructu*) became emblems of the emptiness (*vanitas*) and transience of life and the evanescence of earthly beauty. It is within this medieval tradition of *Integumenta Ovidii* that the Narcissus figure came to exemplify those souls who seek vain and fluctuating glory only to lose true lasting joy: "qui pour tel vain bien et muable / pert la grant Joie pardurable."[10]

The tale of Narcissus was thus read in the twelfth century not only as a tragic adventure of two futile loves; the myth provided moralists, philosophers, and poets alike with an admonitory exemplum that exposed the peril of falling victim to such sins as hardened pride ("tam dura superbia"), *vanitas, arrogancia, inanis gloria,* the confusion between appearances and reality, the idolatrous attachment to worldly images, obstinate self-delusion, disdainful self-absorption. In an age when the inner life of the individual was being subjected to scrutiny both inside and outside the monastery, the experience of Narcissus stood as the paradigm of the problematic quest for self-knowledge through love.[11] "No mirror," says Frappier, "equaled the fabled prestige of that luminous spring in which the beauty of Narcissus was reflected. If the remarkably fluid narrative of the tale charmed our old poets, nothing proved it more than the many ingenious ways in which they translated it" (*Variations,* 14, my trans.).

In order to show how Chrétien has appropriated the Narcissus figure—as it was depicted in Ovid's text as well as it was portrayed in the many "mirrors" of medieval commentary—and how he has woven it into the thematic fabric of the Breton narrative, I will first give a brief sketch of the plot:

> Chrétien's tale begins, as does Ovid's *Metamorphoses,* with a celebration of nature's renewal. King Arthur resolves to re-enact the ancient custom of the White Stag, according to which tradition the knight who kills the faerie beast will bestow a kiss[12] upon the most beautiful maiden. The purpose of this communal rite is to restore the ideals of order, justice, truth, and reason that his dynasty represents. The proposal backfires, however, and provokes a crisis at court which reveals the deep-seated rivalry that threatens the stability of the kingdom. The beauty of each maiden, each claimed to be more lovely than the next, is believed to mirror the heroic capacities of each of the 500 male contestants. The crisis is resolved when Erec—paragon of Arthurian knighthood—discovers his counterpart in beauty in the forest.
>
> Enide is described as having been created as the epitome of all worldly perfection by the goddess Natura. "Bel a demesure," her luminous beauty is made to be gazed upon and reflected into as if it were a mirror: "ausi com an un mireor" (441). Moreover, her beauty doubles as a mirror of Providence, for, as Nature says, it resembles most perfectly the divine *"essamplaire"* from which she copied her and from which all earthly beauty is derived. Enide thus provides the absolute standard by which the worth of all who behold her can be measured. It is her superior beauty and the universal esteem in which she is held that mediates the crisis and restores order at court, for she embodies that very ideal that Arthur sought

to restore. The newlyweds are celebrated as an exemplary pair, yet the nature of their bond is revealed to be unsound.

In the subsequent series of adventures, Chrétien examines the problem at its "heart" and sets out to correct its inherent flaw. The romance ends with the restoration of order and the coronation of the couple. The emblematic Quadrivium that four fairies have woven into his robe and the shining emerald *speculum naturae* that Erec bears as scepter stand as final commentary on the nature of his achievement. Yet it is through the mediating role of his bride (Nature's supreme achievement) that the laws that govern the human heart have become adjusted to harmonize with the laws that regulate the cosmos.

Prior to the hero's final victory in the garden of "joie," the romance landscape of *Erec et Enide* is populated with estranged couples whose love relationships deviate in various degrees from the ideal of chivalric love. The mutually reinforcing bonds between male and female members of the courtly society, meant ideally to function as an impulse toward moral virtue and service to others, have degenerated into self-serving devices by which to legitimize personal claims to power and recognition and egocentric detachment from the public sphere: in short, a narcissistic cult of the self-image.[13] Human desire, ideally obedient to reason and virtue, has become subordinated to the logic of lust, an inversion of the moral order that manifests itself throughout the romance with increasingly precise focus. The succession of covetous thieves, lascivious counts, and sadistic giants that line adventure's path and the series of *têtes coupées* that encircle love's garden are but repeated testimony to the corruption and anarchy that have befallen this *Terre Gaste* of human love like a fatal curse, a curse that must necessarily make its mark upon the designated protagonists of the story. The fairy couple entrapped in the hapless Celtic Elysium of the "joie de la Cort" adventure distills into metaphor the situation in which the five hundred courtly couples find themselves in the opening scenario of the romance. Like Mabonagrin and his *amie*, each pair of lovers has become yoked in the paralyzing symmetry of a specular relationship: perfectly matched and matchless, their exemplarity cannot be contested without risking perpetual bloodshed and without destroying the structural bonds of the community.

This portrayal of the fallen world of human love is in many ways comparable to the fallen state of the allegorical universe depicted in a contemporary Latin work, Alanus de Insulis's *Liber de planctu Naturae*. The entire "fabric" of Arthurian society—not unlike the *textura* of the goddess Natura's integumental tunic, which allegorically mirrors the created order—has been torn apart by the unbridled quest for erotic fulfillment. In the abuse of the laws of human love, the goddess laments that humankind has brutalized its own nature and, in so doing, has violated the basic coordinating principle that once gave unity and coherence to the earthly order.

The comparison with Alanus's *De planctu* is worth pursuing here, for it is a mythographical work that reflects many of the concerns held by imaginative thinkers of Chrétien's century and can offer insights into this reading of Chrétien's romance. In Alanus's allegory, the goddess Natura is depicted as the personification of the visible universe (*imago mundi*) as well as the literary artist responsible for its composition. She is at once the speaking text and the figural representation of the natural world, the shining "mirror to mortality" (*speculum caducis*), as it is revealed to the dreaming poet (he tells us) in the "mirror" of dream allegory. The universal harmony of this literary cosmos is expressed using metaphors of wedlock. Terms denoting the connubial embrace and the act of marital union—*copula maritalis, nuptiali complexu, oscula conjugatis*—appear again and again as figures for the sacramental gesture by which Natura in her office as *pronuba* and *procreatrix* mediates and joins together all the opposing elements in her integument—heaven and earth, body and soul, male and female, idea and representation, subject and predicate—into a coherent and harmonious design, *textura matrimonii*. Natura laments that the world—that is, her integumental tunic—has become a barren cosmos, a syntactical maze of error, for instead of observing the natural laws of marital coitus, humankind has committed monstrous acts in the union of genders and has thus violated her "grammar of love." Citing mythological examples, such as Helen of Troy, Medea, and Narcissus ("and many other *juvenes* like him" [*PL* 210:150]), she regrets that she has adorned human nature with too many privileges and beauty, for he has abused these honors and distorted the logic of love. As a result, the *textura matrimonii* of her integument suffers division in that part of her garment where the fancies of art give the image of humankind ("hoc ergo integumentum per hanc scissuram depingitur"; *PL* 210: 296).

The lapse perceived in human nature is thus seen by Natura to have also pervaded the art of expression and distorted the figural capacities of language. It is because of fallen human nature that the allegorical mode of discourse that Natura must use to relate her hidden mysteries to dreaming poets is obscure and cannot be immediately transparent. The inadequacy of figurative expression thus becomes metaphorically associated with the fallen condition of the poet himself.

To correct the ways of poets who have "stripped Nature of her dress and reduced her to the disgrace of a harlot"—an image that alludes to

Macrobius's comparison between Nature's *visibilia* and mythological *involucra*—Natura paraphrases Macrobius's validation of mendacious fables as a figurative mode of truth:

> In the shallow exterior of literature, the poetic lyre sounds a false note, but within speaks to its hearers of the mystery of a loftier understanding, so that, the waste of outer falsity cast aside, the reader finds, in secret within, the sweeter kernel of truth. Sometimes poets combine historical events and imaginative fancies, as it were in a splendid structure to the end that from the harmonious joining of diverse things [*ex divisorum competenti conjunctura*] a finer picture of the story may result. (Trans. Moffat)

Alanus uses the term *conjunctura* here—the only known instance of this word to appear in medieval Latin literature—to suggest the difficult "marriage" between fiction and truth, the two essential ingredients of poetic allegory.

The French variant of this word does occur, however, in the prologue of Chrétien de Troyes's *Erec et Enide*. Chrétien resolves to salvage the popular version of the *Conte d'Erec*, which profit-seeking bards have consistently mangled and degraded ("depecier et corronpre suelent"), and, to fulfill what he proclaims to be his dual mission as poet and teacher of moral truth (*bien dire* and *bien aprandre*), he will transform the adventure story into a more significant work of literature, "une molt bele conjointure."

> Por ce dist Chrestïens de Troies
> que reisons est totevoies
> doit chascuns panser et antandre
> a bien dire et a bien aprandre;
> *et tret d'un conte d'avanture*
> *une molt bele conjointure.*   (vv. 9–14, my italics)

[So Chrétien de Troyes maintains that one ought always to study and strive to speak well and teach the right; and he derives from a story of adventure a very pleasing argument.]

In the romance, as in the allegory, moral crisis manifests itself in both the tale and in the telling. For Chrétien, the creative task of restoring the lost coherence and harmony in the fictional world of Arthur becomes one that demands a working synthesis between the resources of both hero and poet—that is, between those of *chevalerie* and *clergie*, between the figurative potentialities of the fragmented *conte* and the *sens* of Chrétien's new poetic vision (or, to use Macrobius's terms, between the mutually enriching *fabula* of the Arthurian "estoire" and the *veritas* derived from Chrétien's "escience" and "estuide"). The romance can be read as a written record of a parallel metamorphosis: Erec's heroic perfection of the imperfect kingdom through a redefinition of chivalric love, and Chrétien's literary creation of a new aesthetic order by adapting the ruined fragments of earlier storytelling to the *sententia* of his poetic vision. At the end of the romance, the Arthurian hero takes on the demeanor of a philosopher-king as the clerkly narrator takes his bows as a philosopher-poet. The wedding and coronation of the couple celebrates the restitution of social and moral order in the Arthurian community, as it commemorates the *cohaerentia artium*, the harmonious "marriage" between the arts of the *trivium* and the sciences of the *quadrivium*. Erec's robe is embroidered with the four quadrivial arts, and, as a complement to Erec's achievement, Enide's adventure dramatizes the development of the skills of the *trivium* (Musseter, 147–66).

Romance scholars have long assumed that, since Chrétien was the only author to use the term *conjointure* in vernacular literature, the word was either his own invention or it was derived from Horace's neologism, *junctura*, which he used in his *Ars poetica* to explain the way poets join words together to express an idea. "*Con*-junctura," however, emphasizes the reciprocity of the union, a mutual *con*-joining to form a new structural whole. Since Chrétien's romance is a story of the love adventure of a married couple, it is quite likely that Chrétien meant it in the same way his contemporary Alanus de Insulis meant it: as a synthetic pun, a double-entendre suggesting an analogy between the two human creative activities that are in jeopardy: love and art. (If Chrétien's term were derived from Alanus's, his romance might well have been intended as a literary response in the vernacular to Natura's complaint.) "Conjointure"—like "avanture" with which it is rimed in Chrétien's prologue—is formed from the Latin future participle, and refers perhaps less to the romance composition as a completed and formal arrangement (the usual understanding of the term) than it does to a unifying and perfecting process. Chrétien's readers are invited to witness the *event* of a *conjointure*, a *texte en devenir*: as love redefines itself, the old *conte* becomes a new aesthetically coherent work of literature.

To understand the dynamics of this parallel process, we must understand the mediating role of the female protagonist. Neither poet nor hero can accomplish his "bele conjointure" without the *persona* and the *parole* of Enide, Nature's "criature," whose torn garments, like Natura's integument, emblematically reflect the corruption of values that characterize the condition of the *conte*.[14] The mirror figure that Chrétien has used to portray Enide's unparalleled beauty is cleverly complex in function and central to the reading of the romance. On the one hand, it is made to signify the specular relation between man and woman: the beauty of Enide's countenance ideally reflects, illuminates, and inspires Erec's exemplary qualities. On the other, her beauty mirrors the archetype of Beauty itself, which Nature, God's artisan,[15] claims she has copied from the divine template, or *"essamplaire,"* in order to fashion her earthly *chef-d'oeuvre* (and which Chrétien will then emulate as he transforms his fictional hero into a *homo microcosmos*, man as mirror of the universe).

Using the mirror image, Chrétien has fused together the figural schemes from two very different yet strangely analogous traditions of imaginative thought: the courtly love lyric and the Latin cosmographical fable. Each of these traditions uses the mirror metaphor and its association with the figure of Narcissus—to problematize the quest of self-realization through the mediation of representative forms.[16]

The expression *se mirar en* is a figure commonly used in love poetry to mean "to use as a model." Looking into the mirror of his lady, the courtly lover perceives the task and the promise of his perfection (Goldin, 14). Her perfect beauty is seen to reflect his idealized image as he consecrates himself to her service—in song or in deed—in his struggle to become one with the vision of his ideal. The Lady becomes the representation and custodian of this ideal, as well as the mediating force (*mulier mediatrix*) between the courtier and his highest aspirations. The love he feels toward this lady, be she real or abstract, functions as a creative force within him, for it impels him to give expression to that which is most noble within himself. Yet the idealizing mirror of the Lady can also serve as a standard by which he is judged and measured. Her look has the power to condemn as well as to sanction, to invalidate as well as to realize. He must constantly look into the mirror, as Goldin points out, that external agent of his conscience, to verify his progress and to ratify his very existence. Regarded in this way, courtly man is the psychic heir of Narcissus, for like Narcissus, he requires a mirror to know himself.[17]

The second use of the mirror metaphor stems from the Neoplatonic conception of Creation as a fall into an unreal world of mirrors. The material universe, compared to the reflecting surface of a mirror, was said to receive copies of the celestial Forms that reside in the intelligible order. Narcissus's infatuation with his self-image became a *topos* in this kind of speculation. In the Hermetic text *Poimandres*, for example, the temporal world of matter was seen to result from a faulty union between archetypal man and Nature, in whose mirror he sees a reflection of himself. Plotinus rejected the role of narcissistic love in the cosmic process and considered the material world born of cosmic mirror-play as essentially good. In this scheme, Narcissus represented only a temporary disorder of the soul that needed to be corrected (Hadot, 100). For Plotinus, Nature was the creative intermediary between the ideal and material worlds, a force that generated images of herself and communicated life to all she illuminated "just as a single face in several mirrors" (*Enneads*, 1.1.8, trans. Guthrie). This image of infinitesimally multiple reflections became a model for the hierarchical gradation of the Cosmos, the great Chain of Being, which Macrobius perceived as a chain of mirrors.

Conversely (by "reflection"), love (the Platonic *eros*) was the force that drove souls to ascend the scale of Being and perfect their resemblance to their origin. Attraction to the inferior levels of Being was thus continually corrected by an opposite movement, a conversion back to the center from which it emanated. While the presence of Eros in any being was a sign of the deficiency in its nature, it also signified its capacity to transcend this imperfection and participate in the eternal drama of return. Carnal love and contemplation of earthly beauty were good if they kindled a vague recollection of the love once felt in the presence of transcendent Beauty, enabling it to be perceived as "through a glass dimly" (an idea expressed in Plato's *Phaedrus*; interestingly for this study, Plato warns us that this same glass can blind the lover and delude him into perceiving the image of himself in the "mirror" of his beloved, *Phaedrus*, 250, 255). Macrobius, pursuing his analogy between nature and literature, classified myth and dream narratives according to their degree of fidelity to the truth, an ordering that mirrors the descending degrees of the Neoplatonic cosmos. The function of the myths he called *narratio fabulosa* was to provide the soul with a series of *imagines*, or figurative stepping stones, which would guide it in its ascent from the earthly shadows to a vision of the *splendor veritatis*, the light of truth and virtue.

In Plotinus's scheme, the figure of Narcissus illustrates the type of deviant soul who became so distracted by the visible spectacle of beauty he saw mirrored in the pool that he failed to recognize it as the *imago* or adumbration of the true object of his love. "Whoever would let himself be misled by the pursuit of those vain shadowed, mistaking them for realities," Plotinus says, "would grasp only an image as fugitive as the fluctuating form reflected by the waters and would resemble that senseless Narcissus, who wishing to grasp the image of himself disappeared and was carried away by the current. He who would embrace corporal beauties and not release them," he goes on to say, "would likewise plunge, not in body but in soul, into the gloomy abyss, there to be condemned to total blindness and see naught by mendacious shades."[18]

As a mythological antitype to Narcissus, who lost himself in the watery elements and pleasures of the senses, Plotinus proposed the epic figure of Ulysses, who, according to the Homeric "allegory," escaped the waters and eluded the temptations of the sirens by averting his eyes, reversing his perspective, and returning homeward toward his true goal. The two myths share the same thematic elements of illusion, death, and recognition of error, but whereas Narcissus emphasizes a descent, Ulysses emphasizes an ascent. The Narcissistic soul can thus be corrected, Plotinus says, by imitating the Ulyssian soul, by training his inner vision, and, like the artist who shapes and polishes his statue according to lofty aesthetic principles, by perfecting himself and restructuring his destiny. The process of conversion from Narcissus to Ulysses is described in terms of an inner metamorphosis motivated by love. This involves, in Pierre Hadot's words, a dissolution of a "faux moi" (a false self), or bodily reflection, and the birth of the "vrai moi" (the true self), the soul raised to the level of the Intellect. This *vrai moi* must transcend the common notion of the self and reach an understanding based on the more global perspective of the Intellect (Hadot, 106).

By bringing together two figural schemes that share the image of mirror as a governing metaphor, Chrétien de Troyes has, in effect, conflated two ethical systems. Both schemes share the belief that primal erotic impulses can be oriented toward a higher moral purpose. Yet, while the troubadors admitted illicit love as a noble and ennobling passion, the Neoplatonists exalted the conjugal bond as the only worthy form of human love. The lawful union between a man and a woman was seen as a living metaphor for the basic principle of harmony in the universe and within the individual. It was only through the sacred bond of marriage, in which passion is properly subordinated to reason, that lovers can participate in the eternal plan of the cosmos. (Chrétien's characterization of Enide as both lover and wife thus participates in both schemes.)

In both traditions—the courtly and the cosmic—the mirror figure is used to represent the division between two worlds or two states of being, but since these two worlds appear identical, the mirror represents the locus of deception as often as it serves as a bridge to a higher level of reality. Ever preserving its essential ambivalence, the mirror can invite transgression or transcendence. Thus, it can stand both as a test for him who would be a true lover and a trap for fools like Narcissus. The Narcissus *exemplum* is cited in both figural schemes as a tragic misuse of the mirror, a perilous confusion of the heart. Courtly love may be born in the eyes of the Lady, but if the lover becomes seduced by the image of perfection he finds there and fails to perceive it as a dim reflection of that ideal toward which he must aspire, he will only alienate himself further from the true object of his longing and share Narcissus's fate. For the Neoplatonists, the mirror was a mode of vision reflecting life the way art does and furnished indirect knowledge of the intelligible order. The discovery of one's image can be the first step to self knowledge. Yet, once enlightened, one must study how to go beyond the deceptive surface of the mirror and approach the ideal it reflects.

Let us now go back to the romance and take a closer look at Chrétien's portrait of Enide, the one whose face was meant to be gazed upon as if in a mirror. The countenance that Erec beholds in speechless wonder, as we shall see, bears a remarkable likeness, feature for feature, to the reflected image that Ovid's Narcissus discovers as he kneels down to the water's edge:

De ceste tesmoigne Nature
c'onques si bele criature
ne fu veüe an tot le monde.
Por voir vos di qu' Isolz la
   blonde
n'ot les *crins* tant sors ne luisanz
que a cesti ne fust neanz.
Plus ot que n'est *la flors de lis*
cler et blanc le front et le vis;
sor la color, par grant mervoille,
d'une *fresche color vermoille*,
que Nature li ot donee,
estoit *sa face anluminee*.
Si oel se grant clarté randoient
que *deus estoiles* ressanbloient
onques Dex ne sot fere mialz
le nes, la boche ne les ialz.
Que diroie de sa biauté?
Ce fu cele por verité
qui fu fete por esgarder,
qu'an se poïst an li mirer
ausi com an un mireor . . .
Erec d'autre part s'esbahi,
quant an li si grant biaute vit.

    (*EE*, vv. 421–41, my italics)

[Nature bears witness concerning her that never was so fair a

Adstupet ipse sibi vultuque inmotus eodem
haeret, ut e Pario formatum
   marmore signum
spectat humi positus *geminum*,
   sua lumina, sidus
et dignos Baccho, dignos et Apolline *crines*
inpubesque genas et eburnea
   colla decusque
oris et in niveo mixtum *candore*
   ruborem
cunctaque miratur, quibus est
   mirabilis ipse.

    (*Met.* 3. 415–24)

[He looks in wonder charmed
   by himself
Spellbound, and no more
   moving
Than any marble statue, Lying
   prone
He sees his eyes, twin stars, and
   locks as comely
As those of Bacchus or the god
   Apollo,
Smooth cheeks, and ivory neck,
   and the bright beauty rising

creature seen in all the world. In truth I say that never did Iseut the Fair have such radiant golden tresses that she could be compared to this maiden. The complexion of her forehead and face was clearer and more delicate than the lily. But with wondrous art her face with all its delicate pallor was suffused with a fresh crimson which Nature had bestowed on her. Her eyes were so bright that they seemed like two stars. God never formed better nose, mouth, and eyes. What shall I say of her beauty? In sooth, she was made to be looked at; for in her one could have seen himself as in a mirror... Erec, for his part, was amazed when he beheld such beauty.][19]

in the fair whiteness. Everything attracts him That makes him so attractive.][20]

In both passages, we read of eyes like twin stars (*"geminum, sua lumina, sidus"*; "si oel . . . que deus estoiles ressanbloient"), of splendid locks (*"dignos crines"*; "crins tant sors ne luisanz"). Ovid compares them to those of Bacchus and Apollo from classical mythology and Chrétien compares them to those of Isolde from the *matière bretonne*.[21] Both poets speak of the wondrous way (*quibus est mirabilis*; "par grant mervoille") in which the blushing red color of the cheeks heightens the dazzling whiteness of the complexion. (Chrétien, not unwittingly, compares the "cler et blanc" of the face to that of a lily, "flor de lis.") True, the details and comparisons in Ovid's diction are almost clichés in Augustan love poetry. Likewise, various combinations of these traits—the splendor of the hair, the bright eyes, the red and white tones of the skin—are common in the portraits of beautiful men and women in Old French texts (Colby).

Yet this particular medley of traits, with minor modifications, seems to be associated specifically with the portrait of Narcissus. The only Old French texts in which this portrait occurs are the twelfth-century *Lai of Narcisus* and in Guillaume de Lorris's portrait of Narcissus in the

Romance of the Rose, which Michelle Freeman has shown to be a "creative *translatio*" of Ovid's text via the blood-drops-on-the-snow scene in Chrétien's *Perceval* (158-68). In both the *Romance of the Rose* and *Perceval*, as well as in *Erec et Enide*, the radiant glow of the face, suggested in Ovid's choice of "rubor" and "candor," has been rendered in Old French by the word "anluminee," an image that Alice Colby says is highly unusual if not unique: "As far as we know," she says, "no writer of the period mentions the way in which the rosiness of a woman's complexion illumines her face." In the *Lai*, the colors are described as "meslement blanche et vermeille" (compare Ovid's *mixtum candore ruborem*). It is the face itself that shines as if by reflected light: "Cler plus que cristaux ne glace" (v. 78, cf. Ovid's *in niveo mixtum*). Chrétien's comparison of Enide's beauty to a mirror ("qu'an se poist an li mire / ausi com an un mireor") may conceivably have been inspired by Ovid's lines, *cunctaque miratur quibus est mirabilis ipse*. Chrétien was the first, Colby says, to introduce the comparison of a maiden's beauty to a mirror into Old French verse. Likewise, the comparison of the eyes to two stars[22] does not occur anywhere else in the vernacular works before Chrétien's day. (Interestingly, this combination of traits—eyes like twin stars, *gemelli sideris*, and the flushed radiance of a lilylike complexion— does occur in a contemporary Latin text: in Alanus de Insulis's portrait of Natura, whom he addresses as "*speculum caducis*.")[23] The striking similarities that we find between Chrétien's and Ovid's texts strongly suggest that Chrétien is purposefully using the iconography of Narcissus to portray the hero's counterpart in beauty.

Chrétien continues to evoke the Narcissus theme in his emphatic insistence upon the visual nature of Erec's attraction to Enide, the visual mode of communication between them, and the visible equivalence of their beauty:

> De l'*esgarder* ne puet preu faire:
> quant plus l'*esgarde* et plus li
>   plest,
> ne puet müer qu'il ne la best;
> volantiers pres de li se tret;
> an li *esgarder se refet*
> molt *remire* son chief le blont,
> ses ialz rianz et son cler front,
> le nes et la face et la boche,
> don granz dolçors au cuer li
>   toche.
> Tot *remire* jusqu'a la hanche,

> le manton et la gorge blanche,
> flans et costez et braz et mains;
> mes ne *remire* mie mains
> la dameisele le vasal
> de boen voel et de cuer leal
> qu'il feisoit li *par contançon*
> N'an preïssent pas reançon
> *li uns de l'autre regarder*:
> molt estoient *igal et per*
> de corteisie et de biauté
> et de grant debonereté . . .
> Molt estoient d'*igal corage*
> et molt avenoient ansanble;
> li uns a l'autre son cuer anble;
> onques *deus si beles ymages*
> n'asanbla lois ne mariages.
>
> (*EE*, vv. 1466–96, my italics)

[He could not look at her enough: for the more he looks at her, the more she pleases him. He cannot help giving her a kiss. He is happy to ride by her side, and it does him good to look at her. Long he gazes at her fair hair, her laughing eyes, and her radiant forehead, her nose, her face, and mouth, for all of which gladness fills his heart. He gazes upon her down to the waist, at her chin and her snowy neck, her bosom and sides, her arms and hands. But no less the damsel looks at the vassal with a clear eye and loyal heart as if they were in competition. They would not have ceased to survey each other even for promise of reward! A perfect match they were in courtesy, beauty, and gentleness. And they were so alike in quality, manner, and customs, that no one wishing to tell the truth could choose the better of them, nor the fairer, nor the more discreet. Their sentiments, too were much like; so that they were well suited to each other. Thus each steals the other's heart away. Law or marriage never brought together two such sweet creatures (two such beautiful images).]

As Narcissus gazes in wonder at the loveliness of each feature he sees mirrored in the pool, so Erec fondles with his eyes the perfect anatomy of Enide whose beauty mirrors his own. The hypnotic repetition of "esgarder," "remirer," "regarder," registers the intensity of Erec's fixation upon Enide's radiant loveliness. Enide answers with silent assurances of her loyal heart and good nature—both expressions of her inward beauty—as if she were challenging him to reciprocate. The expression "par contançon," the counterpoising of competing gestures of two equal partners engaged in mutual contemplation, hints at mirror play. Their apparent resemblance in beauty, virtue, and desire is so striking that together they appear as replica images of each other: "onques deus si beles ymages / n'ansanbla lois ne mariages," the perfect specular couple.

Chrétien's description of the consummation of their love suggests further Ovidian motifs: the hunt, the fountain, the provocation of thirst, which becomes transformed into a passionate desire to satisfy a new inward thirst through carnal union (*situs altera crevit, dumque bibit*; "les cuers dedanz en aboivrent"),[24] the embrace (*cupit ipse teneri*; "einçois qui il s'antre tenissent"), the kiss (*poreximus osculo*; "des baisers qui amor atraient"), the inextricable union (*minimus est, quod amantibus obstat*; "si qu'a grant poinne se dessoivrent"):

Cers chaciez qui de soif alainne ne desirre tant la fontainne, n'espreviers ne vient a reclain si volantiers quant il a fain, que plus volantiers n'i venissent, einçois que il s'antre tenissent. Cele nuit ont tant restoré de ce qu'il ont tant demoré. Quant vuidiee lor fu la chanbre, lor droit randent a chascun manbre; li oel d'esgarder se refont, cil qui d'amor joie refont et le message au cuer anvoient, mes molt lor plest quanque il noient. Apres le message des ialz vient la dolçors, qui molt valt mialz, des beisiers qui amor atraient; andui cele dolçor essaient, que les cuers dedanz en aboivrent, si qu'a grant poinne se dessoivrent. (*EE*, vv. 2027-49)	Hic puer et studio *venandi* *lassus et aestu* procubuit faciemque loci *fontemque, secutus* *dumque situm sedare cupit,* *situs altera crevit* dumque bibit, visae correptus imagine formam spem sine corpore amat, corpus putat esse quod umbra est. . . . spectat inexpleto mendacem lumine formam perque oculos perit ipse suos . . . . . . *cupit ipse teneri:* nam quotiens *liquidis* *porreximus oscula lymphis* *hic totiens ad me resupino nititur* *ore* posse putes tangi: *minimum est,* *quod amantibus obstat.* (*Met.* 3. 413-17, 439-40, 450-53, my italics)

[The hunted stag which pants for thirst does not so long for the spring, nor does the sparrow-hawk return so quickly when he is called, as did these two come to hold each other in close embrace. That night they had full compensation for their long delay. After the chamber had been cleared, they allow each sense to be gratified: the eyes, which are the entranceway of love, and which carry messages to the heart, take satisfaction in the glance, for they rejoice in all they see; after the message of the eyes comes the far surpassing sweetness of the kisses inviting love; both of them make trial of this sweetness, and (inwardly) let their hearts quaff so freely that they can hardly leave off (sever their embrace.)]

[Here Narcissus,
Worn from the heat of hunting, came to rest,
Finding the place delightful, and the spring
Refreshing for the thirsty. As he tried
To quench his thirst, inside him, deep within him,
Another thirst was growing, for he saw
An image in the pool, and fell in love
With that unbodied hope and found substance
In what was only a shadow . . .
He watches, all unsatisfied, that image
Vain and illusive, and he almost drowns
In his own watching eyes . . .
He is eager for me to hold him.
When my lips go down
To kiss the pool, his rise, he reaches toward me
You would think that I could touch him—almost nothing
Keeps us apart.]

It is through these distinct echoes of the Narcissus myth that Chrétien invites us to contemplate the darker implications of the mirror symbolism. Enide's beauty ceases to function as a positive reflection of the hero's qualities, and, like the pool in the Narcissus myth, it begins to play the role of a fatal seductive mirror, the instrument of Erec's symbolic death in courtly society. Like Narcissus, or like Plato's deluded lover, Erec has become captivated by his own image, one that he himself has created in the person of Enide. For as he gazes into the mirror of her beauty, he perceives the image of himself as the perfected model—or "mirror"—of Arthurian knighthood, rather than the vision of the paragon he could yet become. He has made Enide reflect what he wants to see, to mirror his own sense of self-importance. He has chosen her as custodian of his public image, he has outfitted her from the queen's wardrobe so that she will appear a more fitting match for him, he has even given her her name, "Enide," a feminine echo of his own. And now that he has made his "bele ymage" the single "source" of his gratification, it is Enide, in her role as image, who is blamed for deceiving him and luring him to his downfall: "car si vos ai lacié et pris / que vos an perdez vostre pris" (vv. 2558–59; "For I have bound and imprisoned you so you have lost your worth").

Erec fails to realize that he has become the victim of a beautiful illusion, a prisoner of his own fiction, and that it is he himself who is responsible for his ruin. It is not his "ymage" that has deceived him, it is he who has deceived his "ymage," just as he has deceived the society to which he belongs. Through his narcissistic obsession with his counterpart in beauty, he has forgotten the vital role he is expected to play in society. For having abandoned his chivalric duties to lavish attention upon the consequence of his good fortune, he has relinquished his exemplary role in the Arthurian order. Erec resembles Enide in every respect except one: his own beauty has ceased to provide a mirror for others. Following Macrobius's chain of mirrors, he has become the soul the furthest removed from the summit of Being. Like Narcissus, he falls into a state of lifeless stupor ("adstupet ipse sibi vultuque *inmotus* eodem / haeret ut e Pario formatum marmore signum"), a frozen monument to courtly narcissism: a "chevalier recreant."

Yet even the most degraded of souls, when driven by love, can be moved to reverse their perspective, ascend the scale of Being, and correct their image.[25] The mirror metaphor, we recall, has been introduced by Chrétien to serve art as well as love. Like the reflecting surface of Narcissus's pool, it warns both hero and poet alike of the vanity and danger of becoming infatuated with the deceptive superficies of reflected forms and fleeting images, as it illuminates the way toward a more perfect conclusion. To rescue his romance from the brooding boundaries of Narcissus's gaze, Chrétien must awaken his hero to the recognition of his error and rechart his course. Having explored the resources of the static mirror imagery, he begins to exploit a more dynamic Ovidian device: the poetry of metamorphosis.

The main feature that gives unity to Ovid's collection of tales, according to Joseph Russo, is the creation of a situation of tragic conflict, the solution of which is reached by transposing the story onto a new plane of existence through metamorphosis. In Ovid's retelling of the myth, Narcissus's death does not bring his extinction; death is but a medium through which he becomes changed into a form that more truly represents his essential nature.²⁶ Similarly, in order to surmount the impasse in which he finds himself, Erec must accept defeat, forfeit his standing within the Arthurian context, and seek definition within a new frame of reference. Chrétien must forge a new beginning. This time, instead of opening with the "parole" of King Arthur as a solution to the problem (i.e., the re-enactment of the custom of the White Stag),²⁷ he will begin with the "parole" of Enide.

Envisioned in the first part of the romance as a silent *femme-image* and passive quest object, Enide is transformed into a *femme-langage* as she pronounces her "parole," the first syllables she utters in the romance, "Lasse, fet ele, con mar fui!," words that articulate the pathos and futility of her ill-fated love. Her utterance not only echoes and communicates to Erec the *planctus* heard at Arthur's court; it also distantly echoes the last cries of Ovid's Narcissus just before he dies: "Eheu: Eheu frustra dilecte puer!" ("Alas dear boy vainly beloved!"). This lament is repeated by Echo, the wood nymph who loved Narcissus in vain.

The introduction of the figure of Echo into the old Greek myth is one of Ovid's most spectacular innovations. By crossing the strands of their two destinies, the poet has created a hybrid tale of new and more poignant interest: a double drama of the self. A figure of self-effacing love, Echo's main function in the narrative is to provide a foil against Narcissus's self-centered indifference. Although she has been deprived of the power of initiating speech, she expresses her love for Narcissus by cleverly and playfully reversing the meaning of his words. Her echo behaves as a response, which Narcissus believes to be the voice of his image, and which unites the doubled self in dialogue.²⁸ The playful cleverness is of course Ovid's. In Echo's creative *imitatio*, Ovid has provided us, in fact, with an emblem of the adaptive process he is using to transform the old myth.

Chrétien's innovation is analogous to Ovid's. It is through his introduction of Enide into the original *Conte d'Erec* that Chrétien changes the old tale of the solitary knight errant into a double adventure, the *Roman d'Erec et Enyde*. Similarly, it is through Enide's speech act, the transformation from *femme-image* into *femme-langage* (compare Ovid's line, "Corpus ad hoc Echo non vox erat" ["Up to now Echo was body not voice"]), that she emerges as a central protagonist in the story, a creature with a will and a capacity for judgment. In Chrétien's story, however, Enide's fateful "Lasse, con mar fui!" is given a new twist; instead of bidding final adieu, it takes on the urgency of a magical exhortation.

What is the motivation behind Erec's departure, and why does he impose such a strict rule of silence upon his wife as he brutally exposes her to the dangers of the route? What is the purpose of this double adventure? Punishment? Penitence? Test? Quest? These are questions that have long confounded readers of this romance. But were they not meant to? Chrétien himself poses the riddle of Erec's motivation in an aside to the reader after the denouement of the adventure (when Erec himself steps into the role of narrator) as if he were testing our ability to interpret the true meaning of the tale:

> Erec ancomance son conte;
> ses avantures li reconte,
> que nule n'en i antroblie
> *Mes cuidiez vos que je vos die*
> *quex acoison le fist movoir?*
> Naie, que bien savez le voir
> et de ice, et d'autre chose
> si con ge la vos ai esclose.   (*EE*, vv. 6417–24, my emphasis)

[Erec begins his story, telling them of his adventures without forgetting any detail. Do you think now that I shall tell you what motive he had in starting out? Nay, for you know the whole truth about this and the rest, as I have revealed it to you.]

Such a challenge suggests that the author has control over each step in the development of the narrative as well as over the reader's level of understanding as the story advances. Norris Lacy once suggested that Chrétien may have so composed the poem as to intentionally restrict our vision, and that the very obscurity of Erec's motivation may be more important at that point in the romance than the motivation itself (359). Although Erec's behavior is deliberate, if blindly apprehensive, he moves mechanically, as if driven by some unknown force. With conventional heroic defiance, he places himself (and his wife) in the hands of uncertain fate, that unseen "transcendant authority" (the author's, of course), that decides the outcome of such adventure stories: "Erec s'an va, sa fame an moinne / ne set ou, mes en avanture" (2762–63; "Erec takes off with his wife. He knows not where except on an adventure"). Enide wonders what inner courage moves him ("Molt s'est Enyde merveilliee / que ses sires ot an corage" [2676–77]). Yet she is able to philosophically accept her sudden fall from Fortune's favor and her strange journey "en essil," and console herself in a manner reminiscent of Boethius's *alter ego*, Lady Philosophy, who reminds the "exiled" Boethius that knowledge of true happiness can be learned through the experience of misfortune: "Ne set qu'est bien qui mal n'essaie" (v. 2606).[29] Enide's love, like Philosophy's vision, provides her with a faith that enables her to participate in the larger scheme of things.

It is not until after the Limors adventure that we will learn that the couple has terminated a period of penitence, and their love has passed a double test of endurance ("Tant ont eü mal et enui / il por li et ele por lui, / c'or ont feite lor penitance" [vv. 5203-5]), and it is not until after Erec first hears the name of the "Joie de la Cort" adventure that he recognizes his true object of his quest: "Dex! an joie n'a se bien non fet Erec; / ce vois je querant" (vv. 5418-19); ("God, there can be nothing but good in *joie*; this is what I am going to seek").

The romance posits an ideal end point, the plenitude of a universal "joie pardurable," as the *summum bonum* that orients its movement. It is thus significant that Chrétien reserves his challenge to the reader until the end, when the hero, and presumably the enlightened reader, understand the full meaning of what was previously uncertain. The horizons of our perception are carefully controlled by his narrative strategy. If we read the narrative, not as a linear mimesis of a series of events, but rather, in the same way Macrobius read the *Aeneid*, as a self-referential verbal world, a literary microcosmos, whose implicit design reveals itself by increments both to the protagonist and to the reader, then we can begin to discern the comprehensive structure of meaning in the romance and solve such problems as character motivation and plot development. The mysteries of Erec's motivation, his harsh treatment of Enide, and Enide's heart-wrenching guilt, may be problems purposefully rooted in the mythical *matière* itself, a deliberate production of deceptive constructs designed to reveal the protagonist's (and the reader's) state of moral confusion. Just as Boethius's Philosophia exposes information concerning the nature and government of the cosmos to the dejected Boethius only in the measure that he can free his mind from the mutable world of Fortune, just as Alanus de Insulis's Prudentia is able to ascend to the firmament only after she has shed the inhibiting faculties of the senses and reason, and after Faith has supplied her with a mirror through which she can perceive divine truths, so the path of adventure initiates the hero (and the reader) into the mysteries of his fictional universe. In each case, the narration of the story coincides with the unfolding of consciousness and the completing of a preconceived plan.

To unriddle the problem of Erec's motivation, the reader must reflect backward from the ideal end point of the romance, its final locus of *sens*. It is only when we reach this point of illumination that we can recognize what the fated task of the hero is: to deliver the Arthurian world from its state of corruption (both moral and literary) and to restore its true meaning.

Erec's progress is paralleled, as Winthrop Wetherbee has observed, by a series of *integumenta* (239), the first of which is the mirror of Enide's beauty, a fictional reality that points to the supreme harmony of the cosmos. Her beauty is a mystery that Erec fails to penetrate and, as a result, he becomes bonded to the figural surface of his "bele ymage" and trapped in the "mendacious shades" of subjective contemplation. The critical turning point is reached when the wakeful Enide awakens the sleeping hero with her tears and her fateful *parole* lamenting her new husband's fall from grace in the Arthurian community. The tears that fall upon Erec's sleeping form recall the teardrops that ruffle the surface of Narcissus's pool obliterating the image momentarily and stirring the deluded boy to new consciousness. As Enide's voice wakens Erec fully to the recognition of his error ("de la parole s'eveilla / et de ce molt se merveilla" [2507–8]), reflection moves from the visual mode to the verbal, and passive contemplation yields to active introspection. The *parole* replaces the mirror as a mimetic instrument and as a more satisfactory mediating link between two inner worlds. Only the word has the power to dispel the illusory nature of the mirror and give expression to the mysterious boundaries between self and other; only the word has the capacity to evoke response and invite dialogue. Enide's speech act, like Echo's, discloses her otherness and dares to deconstruct the artificial symmetry of the specular bond that has become a travesty of true human love. Just as the disturbed surface of Narcissus's pool begins to separate the boy from the elusive object of his love, Enide's *parole* divides the couple against itself, and the "deus si beles ymages" become two separate beings both with a will of their own.

As the facets of the mirror's ambivalence first become translated into language, Enide's *parole*, the couple undergoes a crisis of interpretation. Erec feels betrayed by what he reads as a lack of trust. When he asks her why she is so distressed, Enide masks her grief and suggests he must have heard her speaking in a dream. Erec sees through her pretense and accuses her of lying. Just as Erec misreads Enide's mirror, he misinterprets her word. At the nadir of his existence, he is unable to see the true significance of things: he cannot look beyond the surface of the mirror, and he cannot read behind the *sensus litteratis* of Enide's *parole*. Yet he soon recognizes and acknowledges the sober truth beneath her deception. His apprehension of the underlying veracity of what at first appears to be false—be it *songe* or *mensonge*—marks the first step in the program of the hero's transformation, as the quest to reclaim lost honor gradually turns into the pursuit of a higher end. This dramatic moment of recognition also elucidates the deeper meaning of the rustic's proverb with which Chrétien begins his romance: "molt valt mialz que l'an ne cuide" ("much is worth more than what might at first be believed"), a remark that supposedly refers to Chrétien's literary project, a process by which the poet inscribes mendacious fictions with new meaning.

The logic of the mirror, however, prevails. When Enide's words cast reflections on Erec's inadequacy, his shame only kindles indignation, and he struggles to restore and test her function as idealizing mirror. Instead of correcting himself, he tries to correct his "ymage" by subordinating it to his will. As they set out together[30] upon a quest whose goal is uncertain, he orders his wife to beautify herself and resume her former silence as *femme-image*. What Erec unwittingly seeks is the *joie* of certainty itself, a lasting confirmation of his worth.

The narrative sequence that follows can be read as a new solution to the Ovidian story. Using the Narcissus figure as a prototype for his romance hero, Chrétien transcends the archetypal restrictions of the myth by grafting the mythic paradigm into the Neoplatonic program of ascent and return, a journey that will transform the "Narcissistic" soul into a "Ulyssian" (or "Aenean") soul. Chrétien uses Enide's *parole* (the expression of her sound judgment) as a unifying leitmotif by which he sets the narrative in motion, shapes the development of the plot, and determines the couple's ultimate fate. As they first set out, Erec continues to use Enide as a mirror—both as a visible sign of his value and as a lure to tempt adventure—in a vain effort to distinguish himself again in her eyes and to restore his lost *amour-propre*. But, at each encounter, it is instead Enide who proves her worth as she rescues Erec from certain peril by listening to the voice of reason; she must disobey him to save him. Each time, she must make the crucial choice between silence and speech, *teisir* and *parler*, a decision Chrétien requires himself to make in the prologue of his tale: "car qui son estuide antrelait, / tost i puet tel chose teisir / qui molt vandrait puis a pleisir" ("For he who neglects the concern of using his intelligence may likely omit to say something which will subsequently bring great pleasure"). Like Enide, Chrétien has chosen not to silence his wit.

The imperative to speak meets with great resistance within Enide, however, and at times the *parole* seems to have an independent life of its own as if it were some personified spirit struggling to free itself from the prison of her clenched teeth. Enide's choice between speech and silence is in effect a choice between remaining in the constricting role of *femme-image*, (i.e., the *imago* of the hero) or continuing in her liberating role as *femme-langage*, (i.e., the *imago vocis* of the poet).[31] For as Erec persists in manipulating the mirror for his purposes, Chrétien continues to use her *parole* in order to implement his own design: to "atorne a bien quel que il l'ait." The quickening magic of Enide's word enables him to reshape the couple's destiny by symbolically killing off the old hero and resurrecting the new. In the conflict between the obstinate and somnolent Erec, who would salvage his worth by reinvigorating the old beauty-prowess equation, and the vigilant and persevering Enide, who would obey the laws of reason and selfless love, the reader can follow the dynamics of a constructive dialectic between the old *matière* and the new *sens*.[32]

The romance can thus be read as an allegory of its own creation: Enide's inner person becomes the arena in which the *données* of the *conte* (i.e., the forces that drive Erec) and the dictates of Chrétien's *oeuvre* (those that compel Enide to use her better judgment) battle for supremacy.[33] As Erec, son of Lac, struggles to preserve his former dignity as Arthurian hero in obedience to the conventions of the preliterary *conte*, his physical strength and chivalric prowess diminish, and he becomes gradually more acquiescent to Enide's love-inspired ingenuity and strategies for survival. Her love, as if it were the embodiment of *Eros* itself, frees the Narcissistic paragon from the burdens of his inflated self-image. The adventure of the couple dramatizes a descent that is paradoxically an ascent: the demise of the hero (i.e., the dissolution of Erec's fictional self, his "faux moi") traces the deconstruction of the *conte* as it traces the reconstruction of Chrétien's *oeuvre* based on the recovery of Erec's "vrai moi" as the authentic hero of courtly romance.[34]

In the subsequent series of adventures, Chrétien uses the superior wisdom of Nature's "criature," a persona in whom he has allied the mediating roles of the courtly lady from the lyric tradition and of *Natura plagnens* (with whom Enide shares many attributes) from scholarly poetry. The fundamental purpose of Enide in the fiction is to mediate the psychomachia between the lower and higher impulses of the hero (like the curious emblematic stripe, "green as a grape leaf," that runs between the black and white colors of Enide's palfrey) and to restore him to his proper place in the cosmic order. It is through the *persona* and *parole* of Enide that Chrétien infuses the imperfect world of the *conte* with higher meaning and gives the crude *matière bretonne* a more sophisticated form.

It is finally in the kingdom of "Limors," whose very name associates the narcissistic terms of love and death, where *l'amor* triumphs over *la mort*. Believing Erec dead, Enide faults her *parole*, her "mortel parole antoschiee" [mortal empoisoned word], as the fatal instrument of the demise of the knight who once mirrored the ideal of Beauty itself ("qu'an toi s'estoit biauté miree" [4601]). Her cries once again awaken the sleeping hero and rescue him from death's threshold. (At the same time, it rescues Chrétien's story from the tragedy that ends the *Lai of Narcisus*: the double Pyramus-Thisbe like death of the two lovers.) Erec's experience with death becomes a final and necessary step in the metamorphosis of the hero and his discovery of the true bond of human love. It is only after he has fully recovered from his "plunge into the gloomy abyss" that Erec recognizes fully the constancy of Enide's love as expressed in her *parole*; it is only then that he becomes truly certain of his own worth and can return home to King Arthur's court with new integrity and purpose. From a false love bond, a Narcissistic union of "deus si beles ymages," Chrétien has fashioned a true bond, a "molt bele conjointure" between two generously loving hearts and minds.

As if to mark the importance of this pivotal juncture in the romance, Chrétien makes a curious allusion to the story of *Aeneid*, which, he tells us, has been carefully engraved on the richly ornate ivory saddle bows of Enide's new palfrey. It is interesting to note here that the summarized account of Aeneas's epic journey places particular emphasis on the chronological order, *ordo naturalis*, of the crucial events of his career. Chrétien, in fact, punctuates the order of this sequence with a succession of five anaphoras in his description of the ivory of the saddle bows:

s'i fu antaillee l'estoire
comant Eneas vint de Troye,
comant a Cartaige a grant joie
Dido an son leu le reçut,
comant Eneas la deçut,
comant ele pour lui s'ocist,
comant Eneas puis conquist
Laurente et tote Lonbardie,
dom il fu rois tote sa vie.   (vv. 5290–98, my emphasis)

[on which was carved the story of how Aeneas came from Troy, how at Carthage with great joy Dido received him to her bed, how Aeneas deceived her, and how for him she killed herself, how Aeneas conquered Laurentum and all Lombardy, of which he was king all his life.]

Scholars have traditionally dismissed this passage as thematically irrelevant. While Erec's transformation bears some resemblance to Aeneas's, the role of Enide cannot be sufficiently compared to that of either Dido or Lavinia. Joseph Wittig argues, however, that the arrangement of Virgil's epic, as it appears on the saddle, mirrors quite faithfully the narrative sequence of Chrétien's romance (240). The function of the *amplificatio*, he says, is to "broaden the context of the poem" by inviting the reader to observe the parallels between Erec's adventure and the epic of the *Aeneid* as it was read in the twelfth century (241). The Old French poet of the *Eneas* romance expanded the role of Lavinia (almost nonexistent in Virgil's story) and contrasted the mature love Aeneas shared with her at the end of his career to the earlier lustful relationship he had with Dido. The role of Lavinia is also very important in the tradition of Virgilian commentaries, as Wittig further points out (245). The legacy of this tradition, which originated with Macrobius's commentary on the *Aeneid* in his *Saturnalia* and which was continued in the twelfth century by Bernard Silvestris, viewed Virgil's epic the way Plotinus viewed Homer's *Odyssey*: as an adventure of the human spirit, its descent into corporeal matter, its coming to terms with its dual nature, and its freeing itself from the prison of the flesh. The figure of Dido, who obstructed Aeneas's destined path, was said to be symbolic of the "way of earthly pleasure"; Lavinia, who inspired him, represented the "way of the spirit." The purpose of the narrative, Bernard explains (citing Macrobius), is to guide us toward wisdom and self-knowledge (*se ipsum cognoverit*). He contends further that it is by following the *ordo naturalis*, the order of the story *ab ovo* from the fall of Troy (as opposed to the *ordo artificialis*, the poetical arrangement as recounted to Dido *in media res*,) that Virgil's epic traces *sub fabulosa narratione* the stages of the soul's journey. According to Bernard, Virgil observed both orders of narration: as a poet, the artificial, and as a philosopher, the natural or integumental.

The moral unity of Chrétien's romance depends, as Wittig sees it, on a comparison between Erec's progress in the tale and the pattern of psychological transformation experienced by Aeneas, who had been cast by the philosophical tradition as a type of "Everyman" (248). The development of Enide's character in the story represents a kind of progression from a Dido persona to a type of Lavinia. While Enide, like Dido, prevents the hero from fulfilling his more important duties, Wittig argues, she begins to inspire Erec after their moment of reconciliation as Lavinia had motivated Aeneas.

But does Enide not begin to serve as the motivational force behind Erec's transformation at an earlier stage in his carreer? As I have argued here, Enide begins to influence the restructuring of Erec's identity precisely at that dramatic moment in the story when, uttering her fateful *parole*, she provokes him to recognize the inadequacy of his role as Arthurian hero. It is at this point that Erec begins to undergo a metamorphosis from a persona modeled on the mythical Narcissus to a type of Aeneas. The "grant joie" that Aeneas knew in "Cartaige" corresponds to the false joie of Erec and Enide's first nuptial idyll as a specular couple. As in the *Aeneid*, a necessary crisis challenges the validity of the first "happy" ending and becomes the occasion for more trying adventures.

If Chrétien's romance follows the program of the "philosophical"

Aeneid, then the Dido-Lavinia dichotomy that divides Aeneas's career finds it equivalent in the ambivalent nature of Enide's mirror, her dual role as lover and wife. Enide is at once Dido and Lavinia depending on how Erec chooses to "read" the integument of her mirror. She is Dido in the measure that Erec misuses the mirror and allows himself to be distracted from fulfilling his destiny. Enide plays the Lavinia in Erec's career when, as Wetherbee puts it, "Erec's discovery of her true importance in his life involves coming to terms with himself" (237).

Erec undertakes the final adventure, ironically named "Joie de la Cort," as if he perceives through a glass darkly the promise of a true "joie." Erec is able to handle this adventure alone, because he has now internalized the courage, the vision, and the imperative of Enide's *parole* and integrated it into his own persona. Their newly defined love becomes operative in rescuing another couple, whose self-serving love-contract figuratively mirrors that of Erec and Enide before Limors. This couple represents what Erec and Enide might have become if Enide had not chosen to pronounce her "con mar fui!" Just as Narcissus took on the emblematic form of the passion that consumed him (the Narcissus flower), so this couple had become frozen into a mythical configuration that exposes them in the grip of their desire: imprisoned forever in a mythical *locus amoenus*, a colossal knight is condemned to defend the honor of his beguiling mistress (portrayed as a Celtic Lavinia), until the day he can be defeated in battle himself. As in Erec's story, true victory can only be had in defeat; each hero must be delivered from a prison of his own making. Erec's long battle with his mythical double—the symmetry of which is belabored by Chrétien to the point where, as Eugene Vance has noted, we begin to see a man dueling with his own image in a mirror (568)—can be seen as a struggle to gain a definitive victory over his own *desmesure*. As Erec defeats the oversized knight, the trappings of the Celtic Elysium vanish as does the spell of the false *joie*.

The epic combat in the enclosed garden, the *texte clos* of former storytelling, stands as a symbolic confrontation between *Erec recreant* and *Erec recreated* and as a kind of contest to determine the optimal "happy ending" of the love adventure. The metamorphosis of the mythic couple and their restoration to their true roles in life offers a metaphor for the creative process by which Chrétien "tret d'un conte d'avanture une molt bele conjointure." Erec's victory in the Edenic grove marks the triumph of the redeeming power of Enide's *parole* as well as the *verbum* of Chrétien's poetic art. As final celebration of Chrétien's literary achievement, his hero's destiny is "integumentally" realigned with the higher cosmic design, while his romance celebrates, still today, that legend, "qui toz jours mes an mimoire tant con durra crestïantez."

Notes

1. Frappier, *Chrétien de Troyes*, 61: "Perhaps Chrétien was in some measure the Ovid of Celtic mythology or of its [literary] reflections."
2. *Metamorphoses*, 1, 21. This is one of the first instances in Latin poetry of Nature personified as a creative power in the cosmos. See Curtius, and Economou, 72. In the concluding book of the *Metamorphoses*, where Pythagoras discourses on the subject of cosmic mutability, Nature is characterized as the "Great Renewer" (*novatrix rerum ex allis alias figuras reparat*), the innovating force that presides over the continual metamorphosis of the universe. The opening cosmogony thus provides a "natural" beginning and serves as a figural model for the evolutive design of Ovid's epic narrative.
3. Ghisalberti, "Arnolfo d'Orleans," 157–234. For additional comments on the significance of Arnulf of Orleans in the twelfth century and his acquaintance with the writings of the School of Chartres, see Marti, ed., *Glosule super Lucanum*, xxxiii.
4. Ghisalberti, "Arnolfo d'Orleans," 157–234; "Unde et anima Arnulfi qui has glosulas fecit Aurelianis defleri non debet. Et si eas bene fecit immo si quid habent veri vatum presagia, *vivam cum Ovidio*" (177).
5. Namely, "Les commandemanz Ovide," "L'Art d'amors," "le Mors de l'espaule," and "De la Hupe et de l'aronde et del rossignol la muance," which we assume to be Chrétien's adaptations of Ovid's *Remedia amoris, Ars amatoria, Pelops* (*Met.* 6.401ff.), and *Tereus, Procne, and Philomela* (*Met.* 6.412–674).
6. In his article, "The Influence of Ovid on Chrétien de Troyes," the only exhaustive treatment on the subject, Guyer states quite specifically, "Except for an incident modeled on the suicide motif of Pyramus and Thisbe story (4608ff.), there is no marked influence of Ovid on *Erec et Enide*." Guyer uses this observation to prove his conjecture that the list given in the *Cligès* prologue is chronological and that *Erec* was written before his interest in Ovidian love had been awakened through his translations of Ovid's works (241, 247). Without refuting his basic premise, Frappier (*Chrétien de Troyes*, 71) challenges his chronology on the grounds that Chrétien's *Philomela*, the only extant text of Chrétien's Ovidiana, is a mere "exercise d'école" in comparison to his *Erec*, a work that manifests a "maîtrise sûr de lui-même." (The only literary importance of the *Philomela*, he says, is to "jeter quelque lumière sûr les promesses d'un beau talent dans sa période d'apprentissage.") Scholars continue to accept Guyer's argument that the non-Ovidian *Erec* was Chrétien's first romance.
7. See Battaglia, "La Tradizione di Ovidio," 189. Whereas Virgil stood for disciplined conservative literary tradition, Ovid represented the new sense of adventure, revolt, crisis, and innovation in poetic expression. ("Virgilio rappresenta la tradizione, e Ovidio l'innovazione. Virgilio nel Medioevo e una idea, una costante, ma anche un'ancora conservatrice; Ovidio, invece, constituise la crisi, la rivolta, l'avventura. Vergilio e una disciplina, una scuola; Ovidio e una tentazione, significa l'imprevisto e il prohibito.")
8. Battaglia, 181: "Intencio est de mutacione dicere, ut non intelligamus de mutacione que fit *extrinsecus* tantum in rebus corporeris bonis vel malis sed

etiam de mutacione que fit *intrinsecus in anima*, ut reducat nos ab errore ad cogitione veri creatoris." The kind of correspondence Arnulf makes between cosmic mutability and inner spiritual transformation is typical of twelfth-century humanist thought. (See Wetherbee, 11–13.)

9. Battaglia, 181: "Quod Ovidius videns vult nobis ostendere per fabulosam narrationem motum anime qui fit intrinsecus, vel intendio sua est nos ab amore temporalium immoderato revocare et adhortari ad unicum cultu nostri creatoris." (The expression *narratio fabulosa* was coined by Macrobius to designate those fables he deemed appropriate in philosophical discourse.)

10. *Ovide moralisé* (1898). *Integumenta Ovidii* is the title of John of Garland's commentary on Ovid. Both works belong to the tradition initiated by Arnulf's *Allegoriae super Ovidii Metamophosin*. The expression *flos sine fructu* is found in John of Salisbury's *Policraticus* (5.247). Echoing Boethius's discussion of the "false goods" of Fortune, John says that he who strives after power, glory, wealth, and earthly beauty commits the same error as Narcissus, for he is striving after the visionary shadows of mere opinion.

11. For a study of the analogies between the theme of Narcissus and the quest of the twelfth-century courtly man, see Goldin. To illustrate his thesis, he examines the troubadour lyrics of Bernard de Ventadour and others, as well as the anonymous *Lai of Narcisus* and the *Romance of the Rose*; for a discussion of the Narcissus theme in the romances of antiquity in the love lyric and in Chrétien's romances see Frappier's article "Variations sur le thème du miroir," 134–58.

12. The kiss functions not simply as a prize (as does, for example, the decapitated head of the White Stag, which replaces the kiss in *Gereint et Enide*). Scheduled to coincide with the rites of spring, this ritualistic gesture of accord between the exemplary male and female can be understood as a sacramental reenactment of the original cosmogonic act, whose aim is to restore the integral wholeness of a community (see Eliade, *Myth of the Eternal Return*, 25). The kiss is appropriately conferred by Arthur, legendary heroic paragon, upon Enide, Nature's aesthetic paragon, and stands as official recognition of the concord that reigns between the worldly and celestial orders. Enide is described by Arthur as beauty to be seen only when heaven and earth meet ("où li ciax et la terre assamble" [1742]). (The kiss of the White Stag is also emblematic of Chrétien's *renovatio* in that it celebrates a preliminary *conjunctura* between Arthurian matter and clerkly inspiration.)

13. See Poirion, 26: "Narcissism characterized courtly aristocracy at every level, from the affectation of manners to the egocentrism of male desire" (my translation).

14. The allegorical tear in Natura's gown is a convention borrowed from Boethius's *Consolation of Philosophy*. Lady Philosophy explains to the dejected Boethius that pieces of her allegorical gown were ripped away by rivaling factions of philosophers after the death of Socrates in a violent struggle to appropriate her wisdom as if it were booty to be had. Chrétien may be making a similar statement about materialistic values. Enide's impoverished condition is the result of violent dispossession of her father's land and the material abuse of her

rich uncle. Erec's misgivings about her "tant povre robe et si vil" is shared by her uncle who offers her a dowry just to render her more marriageable: this gesture is contrasted to the loving concern of her father who refuses the uncle's gifts and chooses to save his cherished daughter for the one who would value her natural beauty as a sign of her inherent worth (vv. 428ff.) The verse "povre estoit la robe *dehors* / mes *desos* estoit biauz le cors" (vv. 409–10) underscores the author's focus on Enide's inward beauty as contrasted to her outward appearance, which is the object of Erec's obsessive concern.

15. Chrétien's presentation of Nature as a studious artisan capable of verbally judging and admiring her work is the earliest and most representative form of the Nature topos that occurs in the vernacular literature of his time (see Colby, 141). It is only in the Latin works of the twelfth century that Nature is personified through her speech. Chrétien has created more than just another stylized hyperbole; as a conscious literary artist working in the Ovidian and Macrobian tradition, he is focusing upon Nature's creative act, her perfect *imitatio*, as a model for his own poetic creation.

16. For a thorough discussion of the metaphorical exploitation of the multivalent properties of the mirror, see Grabes; also Bradley, 100–15.

17. As Goldin explains, "the mind of the knight must seek its certainty outside itself, regarding self-consciousness as worthless without its formal affirmation by others, for a knight can have no enduring sense of personal reality unless he is known by others. It is for others to ratify his existence, to formulate him. It is for this reason, Goldin adds, that "the loss of his sense of identity—the madness of Ivain, the indolence of Erec, the aimlessness of Parzival—always coincides with the loss of fame and reputation. The knight dies to himself when he ceases to be known."

18. *Enneads*, 1.6.8. A similar use of the Narcissus myth can be seen in the writings of a Christian Neoplatonist of the same school, Clement of Alexandria in his *Pedagogus* (2.2.2.3). Using Narcissus as a symbol for *vanitas*, he links the myth with a biblical passage (2 *Corinthians* 2:4.8), which contrasts the transience of things visible with the durability of things invisible and compares the "outward man," who destroys himself, with the "inward man," who continually renews himself. See Vinge, 36, 37.

19. The translations of Chrétien's *Erec et Enide* are taken from Comfort's *Arthurian Romances*.

20. The translations of Ovid's *Metamorphoses* are by Humphries.

21. Note Chrétien's choice of "crins," a direct translation of Ovid's *crinus* in preference to the more common Old French word for hair, "cheveu."

22. In the *Lai of Narcisus*, the eyes are described as "cler et luisant," and in the *Romance of the Rose*, the stars have been transmuted into crystals, an image that may have been inspired by the "cler plus que cristaux ne glace" of the *Lai*.

23. The fallen mirror of Nature, *speculum caducis*, refers here to both the text of Nature and the personification of Nature as perceived in the mirror of dream allegory. This apparent allusion to Ovid's portrait of Narcissus in Alanus's dream allegory may have been meant as a warning to the dreaming poet not to

put too much trust in the flawed state of mythological integuments. The perilous ambiguity of poetic images, as pointed out, is a major theme in the *De planctu*.

24. See Freeman, who suggests that the description in the *Rose* of Narcissus's drink at the fountain may well carry obvious Tristan connotations for medieval readers. Erec and Enide's thirst-quenching embrace may likewise have been intended to evoke the moment when Tristan and Isolde partook of their fatal lovedrink. (Chrétien's comparison between Enide and Isolde may not be fortuitous.) The lethal magic of the love potion becomes transposed into Enide's "mortel parole antoschiee" ("deadly poisoned word"), which brings the lovers to the brink of a shared death.

25. Erec's "recreantise," a military term used to acknowledge defeat, is derisively used here to refer to his uxorial sloth. With Chrétien's penchant for puns, it is conceivable that Chrétien also meant "recreant" as a play on the present participle of "recreer" (to re-create), in order to mark this moment as a pivotal point in his career. Erec's "defeat" is not definitive. The word "recreant" (meaning "re-creating") suggests a dormant stage in a regenerative process, or the potential capacity to re-create oneself. Erec's indolence can then be compared to Boethius's temporary *lethargus*, an affliction that Philosophy says is the "common illness of deceived minds."

26. Russo suggests further that, since Narcissus was the child of the river god Cephisus and the river nymph Liriope (meaning "lily"), his demise at the water's edge is in some sense a return to his true place in the world. His career has come full circle and has achieved a certain perfection.

27. See *Erec et Enide*, vv. 39–40: "Mon seignor Gauvain ne plot mie / quant il ot la *parole* oie," and vv. 61–62: "*Parole* que roi a dite / ne doit puis estre contredite."

28. See *Metamorphoses*, 5. 380: "Dixerat:—'Ecquis adest?' et 'adest responderat Echo' " (" 'Is anybody here?' and 'Here!' said Echo"), and vv. 391–92: " 'Emoriar, quam sit tibia copia nostri,' retullit illa nihil nisi 'Sit tibi copia nostri' " (" 'May I die before you have power over me.'—'I give you power over me', she says and nothing more").

29. Cf. *Consolatio Philosophiae*, 2, pr. 8: "Felix a vero bono devios blanditiis trahit, adversa plerumque ad vera bona reduces unco retrahit" ("Good fortune leads man astray by her flattery and makes them wander from the true good; bad fortune draws him back towards it as it were with a hook"). Echoing Boethius's words, Alexander Neckam, like John of Salisbury (see Wright, note 10), links the theme of deceptive good fortune with Narcissus's plight: "Arridet tibi, o homo, blandientis fortunae prosperitas, applaudet tibi favor popularis, fragilitas tuae memor sis. Venustate elegantis formae preditus est, vide ne cum Narcisso propria forma deluderis" (*De naturis rerum*, ed. Wright, 239).

30. It is customary for a knight to set out on a solitary adventure. Erec cannot leave alone, however, because he is inextricably "wed" to his "ymage." Cf. Ovid's lines: "Quod amas, avertere, perdes!" (3.433) ("What you love, you will lose when you turn away!") and "Tecum venitque, manetque, tecum discedet si tu discedere possis!" (3.435, 436; "With you it comes, with you it stays, and it

will go with you if you can go!'"). Erec's restriction of Enide's speech as punishment is also reminiscent of the way Juno denies Echo the control of her speech in retribution for having used it to deceive her: " 'Huius' ait 'linguae, qua sum delusa, potestas parva tibi dabitur vocisque brevissimus usus' " (vv. 366–67).

31. See Lacy, 361, for a discussion of Enide as the poet's "reflector." The expression *imago vocis* is used by Ovid himself to describe Echo's speech (*Met.*, 5. 385). Interestingly, Alanus de Insulis also uses the term *imago vocis* to describe Nature's speech (*PL* 210: 290).

32. Seinaert, 219, speaks of a similar antithetical play of meaning between narrative form and poetic content ("jeu antithétique significatif entre la forme et le fond") in the *Lais* of Marie de France: "Pour que l'oeuvre fût cohérente et que la forme épousât le fond, il faillait les opposer" ("For the work to be coherent, and in order to marry form with content, it is first necessary to place them in opposition to each other").

33. See Nightingale, "Chrétien de Troyes and the Mythographical Tradition," where I compare the theme of the couple's journey in *Erec et Enide* and Martianus Capella's *De nuptiis Philologiae et Mercurii*, both of which I show to be allegories of the mythographical process itself. The allegorical tale celebrates the "marriage" between the eloquence of mythological fable (personified by Mercury) and the persistent quest for knowledge (personified by Philology). Uitti (30–46) points out some obvious parallels between the personae of Erec and Mercury and between those of Enide and Philology, and suggests that Chrétien's romance may be a rewriting of Martianus's allegory in the idiom of the *matière bretonne*.

34. Seinaert, 220, points to a similar movement of ascent which transforms the original form of the *lais bretons* into her written *Lais*: "La véritable victoire . . . n'est pas celle de l'homme s'arrachant à l'étreinte dégradante d'une tarre irrémediable, sa véritable métamorphose est celle où, se dépouillant du vieil homme, l'homme nouveau se situe dans la perspective divine, transcendant ainsi sa condition tragique" ("The true victory is not that of a man tearing himself away from the degrading constraint of an irreparable flaw; his true metamorphosis is that of a man, taking off the persona of the old man, who transcends his tragic condition and situates himself, a new man, within the divine perspective").

Works Cited

Alanus de Insulis. *Liber de planctu Naturae*. *PL* 210: 488–574.
———. *The Complaint of Nature*. Translated by Douglas M. Moffat. Yale Studies in English, no. 36. 1908. Reprint. Hamden, CT: Shoestring Press, 1972.
Arnulf, of Orleans. *Glosule super Lucanus*. Edited by Berthe M. Marti. Rome: American Academy in Rome, 1958.
Battaglia, Salvatore. "La tradizione di Ovidio nel Medioevo." *Filologia Romanza* 6 (1959): 185–224.
Bradley, Ritamary. "Backgrounds of the Title *Speculum* in Mediaeval Literature." *Speculum* 29 (1954): 100–115.

Chrétien, de Troyes. *Erec et Enide, édité d'après la copie de Guiot (Bibl. nat., fr. 794) et publié par Mario Roques.* Paris: Champion, 1978.
Colby, Alice. *The Portrait in Twelfth-Century French Literature: An Example of the Stylistic Originality of Chrétien de Troyes.* Geneva: Droz, 1965.
Comfort, William Wistar, trans. *Arthurian Romances.* London: Dent; New York: Dutton, 1928.
Curtius, Ernst Robert. *European Literature and the Latin Middle Ages.* 1948. Translated by Willard Trask. 1953. Reprint. New York and Evanston: Harper and Row, 1963.
Dornbusch, Jean. "Ovid's *Pyramus and Thisbe* and Chrétien's *Chevalier de la Charrette.*" *Romance Philology* 36 (1982): 34-43.
Economou, George D. *The Goddess Natura in the Middle Ages.* Cambridge, MA: Harvard University Press, 1972.
Eliade, Mircea. *Myth of the Eternal Return.* New York: Pantheon, 1954.
Frappier, Jean. *Chrétien de Troyes: L'Homme et l'oeuvre.* Paris: Hatier-Bovin, 1957.
———. "Variations sur le thème du miroir de Bernard de Ventadour à Maurice Scève." *Cahiers de l'Association Internationale des Études Françaises* 11 (1959): 134-58.
Freeman, Michelle. "Problems in Romance Composition, Chrétien de Troyes, and *The Romance of the Rose.*" *Romance Philology* 30 (1976): 158-68.
Fulgentius. *Fulgentius the Mythographer.* Translated by Leslie George Whitbread. Columbus: Ohio State University Press, 1971.
Goldin, Frederick. *The Mirror of Narcissus in the Courtly Love Lyric.* Ithaca: Cornell University Press, 1967.
Grabes, Herbert. *The Mutable Glass: Mirror-Imagery in Titles and Texts of the Middle Ages and English Renaissance.* Translated by Gordon Collier. Cambridge and New York: Cambridge University Press, 1982.
Green, Richard Hamilton. "Alain de Lille's *De Planctu Naturae.*" *Speculum* 31 (1956): 649-74.
Guyer, Foster E. "The Influence of Ovid on Chrétien de Troyes." *Romanic Review* 12 (1921): 97-134, 216-47.
Hadot, Pierre. "Le Mythe de Narcisse et son interpretation par Plotin." In *Nouvelle Revue de Psychoanalyse,* vol. 13: *Narcisses.* Paris: Gallimard, 1976.
Husemoller, Jeanne A. *See* Nightingale, Jeanne A.
Lacy, Norris J. "Narrative Point of View and the Problem of Erec's Motivation." *Kentucky Romance Quarterly* 18 (1971): 355-62.
Macrobius. *Commentary on the Dream of Scipio.* Translated by William Harris Stahl. Records of Civilization: Sources and Studies, no. 48. 1952. Reprint. New York and London: Columbia University, 1966.
Musseter, Sally. "The Education of Enide." *Romanic Review* 73 (1982): 147-66.
Nightingale [Husemoller], Jeanne A. "Chrétien de Troyes and the Mythographical Tradition: The Couple's Journey." In *King Arthur Through the Ages,* 2 vols., edited by Valerie Lagorio. New York: Garland. Forthcoming.
———. "Court, Cosmos, and Conjointure: A Study of Chartrian Patterns of Thought in the Imagination of Chrétien de Troyes." Ph.D. diss., Bryn Mawr College, 1985.
Ovid. *Metamorphoses.* Edited and translated by Frank Justus Miller. 2 vols. Loeb Classical Library. 3d ed. Cambridge: Harvard University Press; London: W. Heinemann, 1977.
———. *Metamorphoses.* Translated by Rolfe Humphries. Bloomington and London: Indiana University Press, 1955. Reprint. 1972.
Plotinus. *Complete Works.* Translated by Kenneth S. Guthrie. 4 vols. in 1. Alpine, NJ: Platonist Press, 1918.

Poirion, Daniel. *Le Roman de La Rose*. Paris: Flammarion, 1974.

Rand, Edward Kennard. *Ovid and his Influence*. 1925. Reprint. New York: Longmans, Green and Co., 1928.

Russo, Joseph. "Narcissus/Narkissos: The Transfiguration of a Myth." Unpublished, 1977.

Seinaert, Edgar. *Les Lais de Marie de France: Du Conte merveilleux à la nouvelle psychologie*. Paris: Champion, 1978.

Stock, Brian. *Myth and Science in the Twelfth Century: A Study of Bernard Silvester*. Princeton: Princeton University Press, 1972.

Uitti, Karl. "A Propos de Philologie." *Litteratura* 41 (1982): 30–46.

Vance, Eugene. "Le Combat érotique chez Chrétien de Troyes: De la figure à la forme." *Poétique* 3 (1972): 544–71.

Vinge, Louise. *The Narcissus Theme in Western European Literature up to Early Nineteenth Century*. Lund: Gleerups, 1967

Wetherbee, Winthrop. *Platonism and Poetry in the Twelfth Century: The Literary Influence of the School of Chartres*. Princeton: Princeton University Press, 1972.

Wittig, Joseph S. "The Aeneas-Dido Allusion in Chrétien's *Erec et Enide*." *Comparative Literature* 22 (1970): 237–53.

Sources, Nature, and Influence of the *Ovidius Moralizatus* of Pierre Bersuire

William D. Reynolds

The *Ovidius moralizatus* of the fourteenth-century French Cardinal Pierre Bersuire (Petrus Berchorius)—sometimes confused with the better-known *Ovide moralisé* (see below, p. 85)—represents the culmination of a centuries-long series of attempts to invest the *Metamorphoses* with meanings beyond those directly conveyed by the text of Ovid's epic. Earlier scholars have done much to establish the history of commentaries on Ovid's *Metamorphoses*; to unravel the complexities surrounding the text of the *Ovidius moralizatus* (the fifteenth book of Bersuire's *Reductorium morale*); and to describe its pervasive influence upon artists, writers like Chaucer and Gower, and other mythographers.[1] But while these approaches have proved quite fruitful, important questions about the relationship of the *Ovidius moralizatus* to earlier Ovid commentaries and the exact character of Bersuire's allegorical method remain unanswered.

To suggest that attention be paid to defining the special place Bersuire created for himself in the mythographic tradition is not to question the validity of earlier scholarship. In fact, this essay will review such investigations both to pull together information from a variety of sources—many of them now quite difficult to obtain—and, more importantly, to demonstrate that Bersuire is a major figure deserving attention in his own right. For while it has been common practice to assume that anything true of the *Ovide moralisé* is also true of the *Ovidius moralizatus*, or to dismiss the *Ovidius moralizatus* as furnishing so many meanings as to become meaningless itself, my contention is that Bersuire occupies a unique place among mythographers. Though he was well aware of the various ways commentators had interpreted the *Metamorphoses* over the previous two hundred years, his selective use of this tradition indicates that he viewed his task not merely as removing the husk of fable until the kernel of truth appeared but as following the example of Scripture itself by actively using human fictions to confirm the mysteries of morals and faith.

Simply deciding what Bersuire wrote is in itself a complicated task because of the number of recensions that he himself created, the number of manuscripts and printed editions of his works, and the existence of texts that conflate the *Ovidius moralizatus* with the *Ovide moralisé*.

Further, many of his interpretations are derived from or at least shared with other mythographers and, at least as far as visual details are concerned, could have been passed along by visual, not verbal, sources, possibly even by ones now lost. But if one keeps these caveats in mind, broad patterns—if not always absolute proof of particular borrowings—are visible.

While Bersuire himself explains a great deal about the assumptions upon which his work rests, understanding the earlier history of medieval commentaries on the *Metamorphoses* helps to establish the nature of the tradition he inherited and reveal more clearly the significance of the changes he makes in it. As early as the sixth century, Fabius Planciades Fulgentius allegorized fifty of Ovid's stories, mostly in terms of ethics, relying on obscure, often bizarre etymologies of the names of the principal characters to reveal the true meanings beneath Ovid's fables.[2] And in the eighth century Bishop Theodulf of Orleans declared that beneath the false exterior of Ovid's tales lay hidden a core of truth (331).

The tradition of a consecutive but separate commentary on the *Metamorphoses* can probably be traced to the *Narrationes* of Lactantius or Luctatius Placidus; but scholars disagree on whether this work, whose earliest manuscript is dated 1462, was known to the Middle Ages.[3] Whatever the truth may be about the *Narrationes*, the Middle Ages began to develop its own commentary tradition as early as the eleventh century. And from the twelfth century on, it is possible to trace what Irving Lavin describes as "a nearly consecutive development" (262n.2), beginning with the *Allegoriae* of Arnulf of Orleans who also wrote commentaries on Ovid's *Fasti, Amores, Remedia Amoris*, and *Epistolae ex Ponto* and on Lucan's *Pharsalia*.[4]

Arnulf undertook a wide range of tasks in his commentary, glossing difficult or unfamiliar words, unraveling poetic conceits, and explaining genealogies. In addition, he placed prose allegorizations, which soon became independent entities, at the end of each book of commentary. Arnulf's method is to arrange the transformations in the order found in the *Metamorphoses* and then list a wide variety of possible explanations: moral, historical, or allegorical.[5]

The next work of this type is John of Garland's *Integumenta Ovidii* (ca. 1235), an allegorical narrative of two hundred and sixty distichs composed in classical Latin. Like Arnulf, whose interpretations he sometimes adopts, John furnishes a wide range of historical, physical, and moral explanations. Only rarely does John read a fable in more than one way, and, according to L. K. Born, seems to place particular emphasis on the moral message of Ovid's stories: "By far the greatest number (57) of the interpretations conclude with a distinct moral sermon. . . . Next come the fanciful interpretations (36), which may perhaps be regarded as a subdivision of the first class; and those (28) that seem only to have an etiological purpose. Finally there are some (44) that seem to be purely narrative and included merely for the sake of completeness" (182n.25).

During the first half of the fourteenth century, Giovanni di Antonio del Virgilio of Cesena, who borrows from both Arnulf of Orleans and John of Garland, produced his *Allegoriae librorum Ovidii* in 796 verses.[6] At first, del Virgilio announces that he intends to concentrate solely on furnishing moral interpretations.[7] In practice, however, del Virgilio includes euhemeristic and physical explanations, and his " 'moral' simply means an application to mores or manners" (Wicksteed and Gardner, 319). Thus, del Virgilio's morals are often tags, pieces of homey advice rather than spiritual instruction. For example, his commentary on the story of Jupiter and Danaë (*Metamorphoses* 6.113ff.) does not warn the reader about the weakness of women or the need to keep men of wealth away from one's wife. Instead, del Virgilio simply advises that any man who uses gold on women will be successful with them (Ghisalberti, "Giovanni," 59).

The most famous medieval allegorical interpretation of the *Metamorphoses* is the fourteenth-century *Ovide moralisé*, an Old French poem of more than thirty-five thousand octosyllabic couplets composed between 1316 and 1328 by an anonymous Franciscan and, like the *Metamorphoses*, divided into fifteen books.[8] In terms of the pre-Bersuire tradition of Ovid commentaries, the *Ovide moralisé* is significant principally for its single-minded presentation of specifically Christian interpretations of Ovid's tales. In identifying, for example, Perseus and Andromeda as Christ and the human soul, the *Ovide moralisé* demonstrates that, in the words of A. J. Minnis, by the early fourteenth century "pagan and Scriptural *auctores* had come together in terms of style" (Minnis, *Theory*, 141). As scholastic biblical exegesis followed the example of Albert the Great and Thomas Aquinas and concentrated on the literal sense, something "of the prestige, the new authority, which had been afforded to Scriptural poetry in particular, and to the poetic and rhetorical modes employed throughout Scripture in general, seems to have rubbed off on secular poetry" (Minnis, *Theory*, 142). Thus the author of the *Ovide moralisé* reads the *Metamorphoses* as other commentators did the Old Testament, using the familiar Pauline explanation that everything is written for our instruction as justification for his procedure of supplying every episode in the *Metamorphoses* with a Christian allegory.[9]

Another crucial part of the tradition leading up to Bersuire's *Ovidius moralizatus* is the *Fulgentius metaforalis* of the fourteenth-century Franciscan John Ridewall, who provided Christian interpretations for parts of the *Mythologiae* of Fulgentius. Ridewall identifies the gods with particular virtues: Saturn as Prudencia; Juno, Neptune, and Pluto as the three constituents of Prudencia—Memoria, Intelligencia, and Providencia; and Jupiter as Benevolencia. "To Pluto are subordinated Cerberus-Cupiditas and Proserpina-Beatitudo. Similarly, Apollo is Truth; Danaë, Modesty; Perseus, Courage, etc." (Seznec, 94). Ridewall is even more explicit than the author of the *Ovide moralisé* in maintaining that the spiritual meaning which he uncovers was intentionally placed there by the original author to lead his readers to live virtuously and detest vices.[10] It is particularly significant that in maintaining that theologians should concern themselves with secular poems that have spiritual meanings, Ridewall simply assumes that secular poems do in fact have such meanings.[11]

Ridewall uses Fulgentius as his starting point, but he draws heavily on encyclopedists, theologians, and particularly upon the twelfth-century *Liber imaginum deorum* of the third Vatican mythographer. He describes a picture of each god or goddess, then provides elaborate moralizations, making each "the text of a homily, with supporting quotations and *exempla* from Christian and pagan authors" (Smalley, *Friars*, 111). Finally, he readies the myths for preachers by a mnemonic device, rewriting Fulgentius in rhythmical lines.

At the end of this long tradition stands Pierre Bersuire. He was born in the thirteenth century and became a Franciscan when he was quite young; he transferred to the Benedictines sometime in the 1320s. Eventually, he left the cloister to go to Avignon where the papal court was established and, having found a patron in the influential Cardinal Pierre des Pres, obtained several advancements. During his stay at Avignon, Bersuire also became acquainted with the great Italian poet Francis Petrarch and conferred with him about classical studies during a visit to Vaucluse sometime between 1337 and 1341. From 1342 until his death in 1362, Bersuire was in or near Paris. In 1350 or 1351 he was placed in prison by the bishop of Paris, charged with heresy. He was freed by 1355 and around this time came under the protection of the king of France, John the Good, who first appointed him royal secretary and in 1354 raised him to be the prior of St. Eloi. In 1361 he met Petrarch, who was visiting Paris, for the last time. Bersuire died in Paris the next year.[12]

In addition to holding many ecclesiastical and political posts, Bersuire was also a scholar. His surviving works are: (1) the *Reductorium morale*, a moralized encyclopedia whose fifteenth book is the *Ovidius moralizatus*; (2) the *Repertorium morale*, a biblical dictionary; and (3) a translation into French of the Roman historian Livy. Two more works have been lost: the *Brevarium morale* and the *Cosmographia*. Although the *Repertorium morale* and the translation of Livy afford evidence of Bersuire's familiarity with both Christianity and the classics, the *Reductorium morale* is most important for the mythographic tradition.

The first thirteen books of the *Reductorium morale* follow the order of Bartholomaeus Anglicanus's *Liber de proprietatibus*, the most popular of the many encyclopedias produced during the thirteenth century. To these Bersuire added three more books. The fourteenth deals with the wonders of the world; the sixteenth is a brief moralization of the Bible; the fifteenth is the *Ovidius moralizatus*, a moralization of stories from the *Metamorphoses* and of a few myths from non-Ovidian sources.

The *Ovidius moralizatus*, which circulated independent of the rest of the *Reductorium morale*, survives in a number of versions, two of which were prepared at Avignon probably in the 1340s, the third after 1350 when Bersuire had moved to Paris. At Avignon, Bersuire read the standard mythographers: Fulgentius, Rabanus, the third Vatican mythographer, and others. But he was not satisfied with them, for none included a systematic account of how the gods should be described or painted. To remedy this deficiency, Bersuire consulted Petrarch's poem *Africa*; there, in Book 3, lines 138 to 264, he found the account he needed. These descriptions and Bersuire's allegorizations of them constitute the first chapter (the *De formis figurisque deorum*) of Book 15, while the allegorizations of the fifteen books of the *Metamorphoses* (the *Ovidius moralizatus* proper) make up the other chapters.[13]

Petrarch's *Africa* presented descriptions of fourteen pagan divinities: Jupiter, Saturn, Neptune, Apollo, Mercury, Mars, Vulcan, Pan, Juno, Minerva, Venus, Diana, Cybele, and Pluto. In the *De formis figurisque deorum* Bersuire rearranged the list to deal in their proper astrological order with the seven gods and goddesses identified with planets (Saturn, Jupiter, Mars, Apollo, Venus, Mercury, Diana), then with the remaining seven from Petrarch's list (with Bacchus interpolated), and finally with the punishments of Hades, the story of the Belides, the marriage of Peleus and Thetis, and an account of Alceste's love for Admetus.

After Bersuire moved from Avignon to Paris, Phillippe of Vitry introduced him to the *Ovide moralisé*. At this same time Bersuire read Ridewall's *Fulgentius metaforalis* and began to work on a revision of Book Fifteen, inserting into their proper places moralizations and allegorizations from the *Ovide moralisé* and the *Fulgentius metaforalis*, and reworking his text to accommodate these additions. Some critics have posited an intermediate version consisting of material from the second Avignon version and additional elements gleaned solely from the *Ovide moralisé*, but the most recent editor of the *De formis figurisque deorum* deems the existence of such a version neither proven nor necessary (Engels, Introduction, v).

Because it provided graphic descriptions of the pagan gods, something that no other mythological treatise did, the *De formis figurisque deorum* acquired an existence independent not only of the *Reductorium morale* but of the other chapters of the *Ovidius moralizatus*. According to Erwin Panofsky, "rivaled only by Boccaccio's *Genealogia Deorum* (and this exclusively in Italy), Bersuire's mythographic introduction and its derivatives constituted the most important source of information whenever classical divinities had to be depicted or described" (Panofsky, Preface, i). The later history of the *De formis figurisque deorum* is complex. Translated into French, it appears as an introduction to the *Ovide moralisé* in verse and in another version is combined with paraphrases of the *Ovide moralisé*. It also served as the basis for a more popular handbook in Latin, the *Libellus de imaginibus deorum*, where the moralizations were eliminated, additional visual details added, and the number of items doubled (Panofsky, *Renaissance*, 79n.2).

In the Prologue to Book Fifteen Bersuire explains his purpose and demonstrates clearly that he accepts the basic premise of works like the *Ovide moralisé* and the *Fulgentius metaforalis*, maintaining that through their fictions poets always wish to portray some other truth.[14] As an example of natural truth, he cites the story of Vulcan who is said to have been begotten by Juno, hurled from Paradise to earth, and made lame because he fell so far. According to the natural interpretation, Bersuire continues, Juno signifies the air that produces fire (Vulcan) and hurls it from on high by forcing it from the clouds as lightning; Vulcan is said to be lame because lightning always moves along a jagged course (Bersuire, *De formis*, 2). To illustrate a fable that conceals a historical truth, Bersuire mentions Perseus who is fabled to have killed the Gorgon and with her head to have turned Atlas into the mountain that bears his name when, in reality, a brave soldier named Perseus overcame Gorgon, the daughter of King Phorcus who ruled the southern islands, called Gorgons, and bore away her head—that is, her riches, authority, and power—and used them to gather an army with which he conquered King Atlas of Africa and forced him to flee into the mountains (Bersuire, *De formis*, 1–2).

But Bersuire pushes this line of reasoning even further than his predecessors, asserting that poets are simply following the explicit example of Scripture when they conceal other meanings beneath a story.[15] In support of his view, Bersuire cites Judges 9:8–15 where we are told that the trees wished to choose a king; Ezekiel 17:3, the story of the eagle that was said to carry the pith of the cedar; and 2 Kings 14:9 where the thistle of Lebanon wishes to find a wife for his son (Bersuire, *De formis*, 1).

Bersuire separates himself still further from his predecessors by announcing his intention to omit the natural and historical, and deal only with the moral. He gives three reasons: others, such as Fulgentius and Servius, have dealt with the literal meaning; in the first fourteen books of the *Reductorium morale* he had provided only a moral exegesis; and it would be very difficult, perhaps impossible, to give literal accounts of all the fables (Bersuire, *De formis*, 2).

But what is most distinctive about Bersuire is that his motivation for providing his readers Christianized allegorizations of the *Metamorphoses* is a specifically religious one. Because he had seen that Scripture uses fables to designate some truths, it seemed proper to him that after his moralization of the properties of things (Books 1 to 13 of the *Reductorium morale*) and of natural works (Book 14) he should set his hand to moralize the fables of poets so that through human fictions he might be able to confirm the mysteries of morals and faith.[16] Bersuire, then, chose an active role; his intention was not merely to produce a reference book but to contribute to his readers' moral improvement and to the moral improvement of persons influenced by his readers. For Bersuire pictured his audience as preachers looking for illustrations with which to move the hearts and minds of their listeners.

The view that Bersuire conceived of his audience as preachers explains many otherwise puzzling features of his style. Even someone familiar with the allegorizing tradition will probably be surprised by the sheer number of interpretations that Bersuire furnishes and by the variety of connectives that he uses to move from one explanation to another: sometimes phrases in first or third person (both singular and plural) such as "dicamus allegorice" or "Vel illud eciam exponitur"; more frequently ones in second person (again both singular and plural, often with the addition of "Karissimi") like "vel dic" or "Si vis . . . dic." But because Bersuire is writing for preachers, it is imperative that he provide a number of possible interpretations so his readers can locate Ovidean support for whatever points they wish to make. As for the alternation between singular and plural, and the intermingling of second-person phrases, Joseph Engels suggests that the imperative singular is addressed to the preacher composing his sermon while the second person plural is directed to the preachers' future audiences and that the passages introduced by *Karissimi* are ready-made *exempla* destined to be inserted into a future sermon.[17]

Similarly, in accord with the precepts of *Artes predicandi*, Bersuire reinforces or repeats the message of his exposition by furnishing one or more prooftexts. In addition to mythographers like Ridewall, Bersuire quotes a wide range of authorities (including St. Augustine, St. Bernard, Cicero, St. Gregory, St. Isidore, St. Jerome, Pliny, Rabanus Maurus, Seneca, and Solinus); but most frequently he chooses biblical passages, both Old Testament and New. Here, then, is the final stage of a process begun earlier in the fourteenth century by the friars of the "classicising group," as Beryl Smalley calls them. These scholars frequently used material from secular authors in their exegesis of Scripture (Smalley, *English Friars*, 1ff.), but Bersuire finds in Scripture affirmation—or rather restatement—of the spiritual truth he discovers beneath Ovid's fables; for what Bersuire identifies is one Truth, not several truths. As Judson Boyce Allen states:

> Spiritual sense meanings are simply stated, and the concordant authority or exemplum is added as a meaningful and verbal restatement of the same truth. Earlier, the literally allegorical senses were argued. Commentators included a good deal of analysis of etymology, of physical nature, and of the characteristics of virtue in order to justify their interpretations; the relation between a fictional story and its spiritual meanings, on the other hand, holds, not because there exists some arguable relation between the letter and the spirit—between vehicle and tenor—but rather because the meaning adduced is itself true. The proof is not an argument but a simple repetition. . . . (Allen, *Friar*, 76).

Bersuire's method is consistent throughout the *De formis figurisque deorum*, so an examination of his treatment of Diana (28–30) clearly illustrates his technique. Diana, Bersuire states, is depicted in the form of a lady holding a bow and arrow, and hunting horned stags. Around her dance bands of nymphs from the forest, mountains, fountains, and seas along with bands of horned satyrs who are said to be the gods of the fields. Despite his earlier disclaimer, Bersuire first furnishes a literal account (as usual, a very brief one) and then turns to the spiritual significance of what he has described. Identifying a series of separate details, he furnishes a series of explanations—*in bono* and *in malo*—incorporating all the individual points but not preferring one reading to another.[18]

As his first interpretation, Bersuire makes a typological comparison: through Diana can be perceived the Virgin Mary who is armed with the bow of easily-moved pity and with the arrow of prayer by means of which the proud devil (the horned stag) is overcome. Out of devotion, groups of holy souls should be near her: especially nymphs of the mountains, contemplative souls; nymphs of rivers and fountains, souls that stay in the river of the Scriptures; and nymphs of the seas, souls that live in the bitterness of contrition. Bands of satyrs—that is, sinners, "horned" because of their pride—should also dance and run about, seeking her kindness and mercy, and imploring her help. Or, Bersuire offers as an alternative reading, these satyrs may be prelates, especially mitred bishops, who should serve the Blessed Virgin Mary devoutly and frequent her altar through devotion, affection, and obedience.

Reading *in malo*, Bersuire identifies Diana as an evil woman (or an old Bawd or the sin of Luxury) who holds a bow and arrows because she pricks the foolish with booty and wounds them with temptation and desire. Such a woman draws after herself young women beguiled by her example and has with her wanton men raised up on the horns of rank. These young women who serve lust, Bersuire continues, are sometimes nymphs of the mountains because they are highborn, sometimes nymphs of the forests because they are rustics, sometimes nymphs of the seas because they are penitents and religious; for people from every level of society—noble or base, worldly or ecclesiastic—serve lust. Bersuire concludes his discussion of Diana with an alternate reading *in malo* according to which Diana is avarice or robbery, which never ceases wounding timid, poor people (the stags), and so around her dance proud "horned" princes and stubborn tyrants. All classes of persons are accustomed to obey her: the mountain nymphs, those who dwell on mountains and in towers and fortresses; forest nymphs, Cistercians and others who dwell in the woods; river nymphs, those who live on farms around which rivers flow; and sea nymphs, those who live in churches and monasteries.

In the *Ovidius moralizatus* proper, Bersuire summarizes the tales in question—attending of course to narrative details, each of which can later be invested with its own meanings—and explains the truth beneath the fiction. As in the *De formis figurisque deorum*, he continues to furnish brief historical and natural accounts (explaining Saturn as an early king of Crete and Juno as air, for example), but most of his interpretations are, as he claims, moral. Among his favorite techniques are seeing God, saints, and the devil behind such figures as Admetus, Hercules, Pluto, and Bacchus; he also frequently identifies the pagan divinities and their actions with general, abstract virtues or vices as when he uses Minerva as a figure of pride and Bacchus as the fervor of the Holy Spirit. But on occasion Bersuire singles out particular groups—most often worldly rulers, good or bad prelates, and good or bad women.

A typical example of Bersuire's technique is his treatment of Mercury's rescue of Io from the hundred-eyed watchman Argus.[19] Bersuire explains Jupiter's transformation of Io into a cow by making Jupiter a symbol of robbers who act in a similar way when, fearing that their secret deeds will become known, they wait for a dark, secret time and turn an innocent girl into a wanton woman. As one interpretation, Bersuire presents Jupiter as the devil who does not want the soul with which he fornicates by sin to be drawn back by the Church and so to keep her subject to his authority makes her into a carnal sinner alien to all spirituality. Explicating the rest of the allegory, Bersuire explains that Juno—that is, the Church—entrusts to Argus (that is, some circumspect prelate) custody of Io—that is, rule over subjects. But Mercury—that is, the flatterers who often surround such men—touches them with the rod of temporal power and makes them die the death of eternal damnation. As an alternative explanation, Bersuire suggests that Argus is the devil who kept Io (that is, sinful souls) in his power. But Mercury—that is, Christ—lulled the devil to sleep and conquered him by the wood of the cross. Thus, Bersuire continues, Christ freed human nature from the devil's power and in the end changed Io from a sinner into a just woman.

Not surprisingly, the least ambiguous influence of the *Ovidius moralizatus* is on another mythographic treatise, the early fifteenth-century *Archana deorum* of Thomas Walsingham—the last of the medieval moralizing commentaries on the *Metamorphoses*. Walsingham borrowed from Bersuire the plan of placing discussions of individuals gods and goddesses before his book-by-book commentary on the *Metamorphoses* and likewise drew on a number of Bersuires's paraphrases and natural/historical interpretations; but because he was writing for poets and for people interested in reading classical poetry, Walsingham omitted "every scriptural allusion and all . . . Bersuire's moral, allegorical, and spiritual comments" (van Kluyve, xiv).

Bersuire also influenced writers outside the mythographic tradition. Jacques Legrand (Jacobus Magni), a celebrated preacher of King Charles VI and himself the author of an *Introductorium sermocandi*, frequently included references—both direct and indirect—to the *Metamorphoses* in his sermons, taking many of his interpretations from the *Reductorium morale* (Engels, "L'Edition," 23). Moreover, Joseph Engels argues, the sixty surviving manuscripts of the *Ovidius moralizatus* and of the *Reductorium morale* suggest that Bersuire's work enjoyed a considerable vogue among other preachers as well ("L'Edition," 23–24). In a related field, Jean de Hesdin who lectured on theology at Paris during the third quarter of the fourteenth century names Bersuire—but no other contemporary writer—in his lecture on the Epistle to Titus and, according to Beryl Smalley, "quotes Berchorius' moralisations of the *Metamorphoses*, though not always verbally, sometimes expanding his original" ("Jean de Hesdin," 311).

Bersuire's influence on the visual arts is likewise unquestionable. Erwin Panofsky provides an account of the relationship between Bersuire's descriptions of the gods and goddesses and those illustrations found in manuscripts of the *Libellus de imaginibus deorum* and the *Ovide moralisé* in verse (*Renaissance*, 80-81n.2). Panofsky notes further that a "series of miniatures [which seems to have formed an independent picture book] inserted into a manuscript in the Bodleian Library at Oxford, MS. Rawlinson B.214 fols. 197v.-200 . . . corresponds exactly to the Berchorius sequence . . . except that one leaf, showing Neptune, Pan, Bacchus, and Pluto, is missing between fol. 199 and fol. 200" (*Renaissance*, 80n.2).

And, discussing a much later artist, Panofsky identifies Bersuire as the literary source of Dürer's engraving usually referred to as "The Judge" or "Justice": "[T]he subject of Dürer's engraving is the *Sol Iustitiae*, conceived, to be sure, as the Apocalyptic avenger rather than the merciful judge, and for this very reason strongly appealing to the spirit of the late fifteenth century. We can even name the literary source by which this interpretation was conveyed to Dürer: the *Repertorium morale* of Petrus Berchorius . . . [which] gives a description of the *Sol Iustitiae* which would appear as a literal paraphrase of the Dürer engraving were it not more than a century and a half earlier" (Panofsky, *Meaning*, 261).

A particularly amusing example of Bersuire's influence involves manuscript illustrations of Venus emerging from the sea. Erwin Panofsky cites one iconographic tradition, represented by Paris, Bibliothèque Nationale, MS fr. 373 (*Ovide moralisé* in verse, toward 1380), in which Venus is shown holding in her hand a large bird rather than a sea shell because the "concham marinam" of Bersuire's description ("Fingebatur igitur Venus puella pulcherrima nuda et in mari natans et in manu sua dextera concham marinam continens atque ges[ta]ns, que rosis erat ornata. . . ." [*De formis*, 12]) had been misread as *aucam marinam*, "sea goose" (*Renaissance*, 86). In Geneva, Bib. Publique et Universitaire, MS fr. 176 (*Ovide moralisé* in verse, end of the fourteenth century) an illustrator distinguishes a "sea goose" from an ordinary, garden variety goose by providing it with a fish tail and scales (*Renaissance*, 86-87). In another group of manuscripts, represented by Copenhagen, Royal Lib., MS Thott 399, 2, "concham marinam" has apparently been garbled into "canam laminam" and the comma before "que rosis" omitted, resulting "in the transformation of the sea shell into a slate (appropriately inscribed with a little love song); and it is this slate, and not the goddess, which appears 'adorned with roses and surrounded by doves' " (*Renaissance*, 87).

Determining the debt literary artists owe to Bersuire is a less certain pursuit. Scholars dealing with writers such as Chaucer, Gower, and Spenser frequently cite one or another of Bersuire's works to indicate that a particular idea or interpretation was in circulation during the fourteenth, fifteenth, or sixteenth century.[20] But the question of Bersuire's direct influence on any given writer or any given work gets caught up in the still larger question of whether and to what degree the "allegory of the theologians" and the allegory of the mythographers are to be found in secular literary works of the Middle Ages and Renaissance.

Nonetheless, the evidence is strong enough in some cases to support the claim that an author derived an idea or interpretation solely from Bersuire. Conrad Mainzer, for example, maintains that Gower "was using the *Ovidius moralizatus* in his section on the pantheon in the fifth book of the *Confessio*, in particular the preliminary section known as *De formis figurisque deorum*. It can be assumed [further] that he was also familiar with the rest of the work" (215).

Scholars have devoted still more attention to the possible influence of Bersuire on Geoffrey Chaucer. A. J. Minnis states that the "second recension of Bersuire's 'Moralized Ovid' (made around 1350) was the version used by Chaucer" (*Chaucer*, 11). Minnis concludes that Chaucer's interest in Bersuire was "literal and historical but rarely, if ever, spiritual or moral. That is to say, he inclined towards the astrological interpretation of the pagan deities . . . and he had a euhemeristic habit of mind . . . but moral allegory held no attraction for him, save as an object of humour or irony" (16).

As an example, Minnis—passing over the question of whether Chaucer knew the *Ovidius moralizatus* directly or through a work like the *Libellus*—examines the section of the *Knight's Tale* devoted to the statue of Mars, which dominates the temple devoted to him, and determines that Chaucer dropped all Bersuire's moral readings and concentrated solely on the visual details. In a late stage of his discussion, Minnis maintains that Chaucer's interpretation of Arcite, Emelye, Palamon, and Theseus is influenced in part by the qualities Bersuire assigns to the god or goddess with which each is associated (Mars, Diana, Venus, and Jupiter respectively) (111ff.).

In a series of related articles, E. H. Wilkins, J. M. Steadman, and Betty Nye Quinn examine the image of Venus in the *House of Fame* and the *Knight's Tale*.[22] Having examined Chaucer's two descriptions of Venus, Wilkins concludes that "at the only two points at which there is any difference between Bersuire and the *Libellus* [*de imaginibus deorum*]—the specification that Venus held the *conca* in her right hand, and the specification that the roses were both white and red—Chaucer agrees with the *Libellus* as against Bersuire. It follows that the *Libellus*, rather than the *Ovidius moralizatus*, was Chaucer's source" (521).

In his reply to Wilkins, J. M. Steadman presents the case for the *Ovidius moralizatus* as Chaucer's source. Steadman observes that Chaucer changed the traditional mythographic picture of Venus: "In neither of these poems does Venus bear a shell (*conca*). In the *House of Fame* she possesses, instead, a 'comb to kembe hir heed' (l. 136), and in the *Knight's Tale* she holds 'in hir right hand'—not a shell but a 'citole.' The latter detail links this description with Berchorius's *Ovidius moralizatus* rather than with the *Libellus*" (620). This last point (together with his conclusion that Chaucer had access to an unabridged version of Bersuire's work) Steadman justifies by tracing the citole to a prooftext Bersuire furnishes—Isaiah 23:10, 16—in which Venus and her *conca* are compared to a courtesan and her cithara (620-21).

Four years later, Betty Nye Quinn proposed that Wilkins's key reason for selecting the *Libellus* rather than the *Ovidius moralizatus* as Chaucer's source disappears when one recalls that Bersuire's work circulated in various forms. Both Wilkins and Steadman, Quinn observes, used editions of the *Ovidius moralizatus* printed by Badius in Paris in 1509 and 1511, editions that depend upon a version that Bersuire prepared before he had read John Ridewall's *Fulgentius metaforalis* and the *Ovide moralisé*. The version that incorporates what Bersuire found in these two works specifies that Venus carries the *conca* in her right hand; therefore, Chaucer could have used this version of the *Ovidius moralizatus* rather than the *Libellus* as Wilkins argued (479-80). Further, the presence of *comatur* in the Paris version suggests that Venus's comb in the *House of Fame* was based directly on Bersuire and not, as Steadman had suggested, on Claudian's *Epithalamium de nuptiis Honorii Augusti* or on a related tradition (480).

If Bersuire studies are to continue to progress, what is needed is easier access to what he actually wrote. While the ideal might be separate editions (or a parallel text edition) of each of the versions of the *Ovidius moralizatus* Bersuire prepared, first at Avignon and later at Paris, few scholars would feel disappointed with a complete critical edition following the pattern established by Joseph Engels and Marie S. Van Der Bijl. Once accurate texts have been established, a second priority should be determining more exactly the nature of Bersuire's moral interpretations and the relationship between his views and those of preachers and theologians contemporary with him. Finally, it seems likely that further investigation of Bersuire's influence on writers, authors, and preachers will prove profitable, particularly if attention is paid not simply to locating the source(s) of specific details but to identifying the principal thrust of both Bersuire's interpretation and that of the literary or artistic work being examined. For Bersuire's approach—as idiosyncratic or even wrongheaded as it may seem today—offers a sure and accurate guide to an important aspect of the medieval worldview.

Notes

1. The most significant earlier studies of Bersuire are Ghisalberti, "L'*Ovidius Moralizatus*" and Engels, *Etudes*. For information on works by and about Bersuire, see Engels, "Berchoriana," or Samaran and Monfrin. A generally accurate summary of the commentary tradition may be found in D. C. Allen. Engels summarizes the textual history of the *Ovidius moralizatus* in his Introduction. Four important works showing the later influence of Bersuire are Bolton, Kaske, Lavin, and Robertson. For additional studies of Bersuire's influence, see note 20.

2. The critical edition of Fulgentius's *Mythologiae* is found in his *Opera*. For an English translation, see Whitbread.

3. The text of *Narrationes* is included in Slater; also see Otis.

4. For an edition of the *Allegoriae*, see Ghisalberti, "Arnolfo."

5. "[M]odo moraliter, modo historice, aut allegorice" (Ghisalberti, "Arnolfo," 212).

6. The text of del Virgilio's *Allegoriae* may be found in Ghisalberti, "Giovanni."

7. "Quoniam uniuscuisque poete finis sit mentes hominum moribus informare in omnibus, unde in principio huius libri alibi dictum est quod ethice i. morali philosophie supponitur, ideo unaqueque transmutatio in hoc libro descripta merito ad mores est penitus reducenda" (43).

8. In addition to the verse form there exist two much abridged prose versions. The author of the *Ovide moralisé* was aware of the works of both John of Garland (whom he cites in 1.3126) and Arnulf of Orleans, quite possibly from a manuscript in which the texts of the two authors were conflated; Giovanni del Virgilio does not seem to have exerted an influence.

9. "Se l'escripture ne me ment, / Tout est pour nostre enseignement / Quanqu'il a es livres escript, / Soient bon ou mal li escript" (15:61).

10. "Institucio venerabilis viri Fulgencii in sua mithologia est sub tegmine fabularum a poetis fictarum describere diversa genera viciorum et virtutum eis oppositarum, ut cognita virtutum honestate et viciorum deformitate inducat auditores ad virtutum exercitacionem et viciorum detestacionem" (65).

11. "Nisi enim fabulae tales poetice ordinarentur ad mores theologi de eis se non deberent intromittere, sed eas pocius sicud vanas et frivolas devitare" (65).

12. For more details on the life of Bersuire, see Samaran and Monfrin.

13. For a critical edition of chapter 2 of the *Ovidius moralizatus* (Bersuire's commentary on Book 1 of the *Metamorphoses*), see Van Der Bijl.

14. "[F]ecerunt poete qui in principio fabulas finxerunt, quia s. per huius[modi] figmenta semper aliqua[m] veritatem intelligere voluerunt" (*De formis*, 1).

15. "Sic etenim Sacra Scriptura in pluribus passibus videtur fecisse, ubi ad alicuius veritatis ostensionem fabulas noscitur confecisse. . . . Sacra enim Scriptura . . . fabulis et fixionibus solet uti, ut exinde possit aliqua veritas extreahi vel concludi" (*De formis*, 1).

16. "Quia ergo video quod Scriptura utitur fabulis ad alicuius veritatis . . . congruum michi visum est, post moralizacionem proprietatum rerum postque iam [ad] mores reducta nature opera, eciam ad moralizandum fabulas poetarum manum ponere, ut sic per ipsas hominum ficciones possim morum et fidei misteria confirmare" (*De formis*, 2).

17. "La contradiction n'est qu'apparente, car l'impératif singulier s'adresse au prédicateur en train de composer son sermon, tandis que les Karissimi sont ses futurs auditeurs. Les exposés introduits par cette expression sont des fragments parachevés destinés à être insérés tels quels dans un sermon" ("L'Edition," 22–23).

18. Judson Boyce Allen observes that in each case "the interpretation as well as the letter has a certain narrative thread, but the dominant feature is the reduction of organized narrative to a series of essentially substantive bits, each the basis of a separate one-to-one equation. Interpretations are very precise, specific, and concrete. If the narrative under consideration is an especially popular or meaningful one, the interpretation is not therefore richer, more complex, or more general; there . . . [is] no real attempt at a concluding synthesis" (*Friar*, 73).

19. See Van Der Bijl, 40–45. Bersuire's account is based on *Metamorphoses* 1.588ff.

20. Allen and Moritz cite Bersuire's definition of "Iudicare" as a "helpfully comprehensive" (158) way to capture the medieval attitude toward judges; similarly, McCall demonstrates the link between the Greek goddess Pallas and prudence by citing Bersuire (165n.8). To see the same technique applied to other writers, consult Mainzer, esp. p. 222 where he parallels Gower's treatment of the non-Ovidian story of Admetus and Alcestis (7. 1917–43) with that found in the *Ovidius moralizatus*, Minnis, in particular p. 74 where he cites Bersuire to support the view that in old age the body cools and hence one's sexual urges diminish; Kaske, specifically notes 11, 19, and 20; and Nohrnberg, in particular p. 725 where Bersuire is cited as evidence of the existence of a tradition that makes the three theological virtues the Christian Graces.

21. Mainzer discusses this topic at greater length in *Study*.

22. Also see Twycross.

Works Cited

Allen, Don Cameron. *Mysteriously Meant*. Baltimore: Johns Hopkins University Press, 1970.

Allen, Judson Boyce. *The Friar as Critic*. Nashville, TN: Vanderbilt University Press, 1971.

Allen, Judson Boyce and Theresa Anne Moritz. *A Distinction of Stories: The Medieval*

Unity of Chaucer's Fair Chain of Narratives for Canterbury. Columbus: Ohio State University Press, 1981.

Bersuire, Pierre. *Reductorium morale, liber XV: Ovidius moralizatus, cap. i, De formis figurisque deorum.* Edited by Joseph Engels. Utrecht: Instituut voor Laat Latijn des Rijksuniversiteit, 1966.

———. *Reductorium morale, liber XV, cap. ii–xv, Ovidius moralizatus.* Edited by Joseph Engels. Utrecht: Instituut voor Laat Latijn des Rijksuniversiteit, 1962.

Bolton, W. F. "The Miller's Tale: An Interpretation." *Mediaeval Studies* 24 (1962): 83–94.

Born, L. K. "The Manuscripts of the *Integumenta* on the *Metamorphoses* of Ovid by John of Garland." *Transactions of the American Philological Association* 60 (1929): 179–99.

Engels, Joseph. "Berchoriana I: Notice Bibliographique sur Pierre Bersuire." *Vivarium* 2 (1964): 62–124.

———. *Etudes sur l'Ovide Moralisé, these de lettres*, chapter 2. Groningen, 1943. Rev. ed., 1945.

———. "L'Edition critique de l'*Ovidius moralizatus* de Bersuire." *Vivarium* 9 (1971): 19–24.

———. Introduction. *Reductorium morale, liber XV: Ovidius moralizatus, cap. i, De formis figurisque deorum.* By Pierre Bersuire.

Fulgentius, Fabius Planciades. *Opera.* Edited by R. Helm. 1898. Reprint. Stuttgart: B. G. Teubner, 1970.

———. *Fulgentius the Mythographer.* Translated by Leslie George Whitbread. Columbus: Ohio State University Press, 1971.

Ghisalberti, Fausto. "Arnolfo d'Orleans, un cultore di Ovidio nel sec. XII." *Memorie del Reale Instituto Lombardo di Scienze e Lettere* 24 (1932): 157–234.

———. "Giovanni del Virgilio espositore delle *Metamorfosi*." *Giornale Dantesca* 34, n. s. 4 (1933): 3–110.

———. "*L'Ovidius moralizatus* di Pierre Bersuire." *Studj Romanzi* 23 (1933): 5–136.

John, of Garland. *Integumenta Ovidii.* Edited by Fausto Ghisalberti. Milan: G. Principato, 1933.

Kaske, Carol V. "The Dragon's Spark and Sting and the Structure of Red Cross's Dragon Fight: *The Faerie Queene* I.xi–xii." *Studies in Philology* 66 (1969): 609–38.

Kaske, R. E. "The Summoner's Garleek, Oynons, and eeke Lekes." *MLN* 74 (1959): 481–84.

Lavin, Irving. "Cephalus and Procris: Underground Transformations." *Journal of the Warburg and Courtauld Institutes* 17 (1954): 260–87.

Mainzer, Conrad. "John Gower's Use of the 'Mediaeval Ovid' in the *Confessio Amantis*." *Medium Aevum* 41 (1972): 215–29.

———. "A Study of the Sources of the *Confessio Amantis* of John Gower." Ph.D. diss., Oxford University, 1967.

McCall, John P. *Chaucer among the Gods: The Poetics of Classical Myth.* University Park: The Pennsylvania State University Press, 1979.

Minnis, Alastair J. *Chaucer and Pagan Antiquity.* Woodbridge, Suffolk: D. S. Brewer, 1982.

———. *Medieval Theory of Authorship.* London: Scolar Press, 1984.

———. " 'Moral Gower' and Medieval Literary Theory." In *Gower's 'Confessio Amantis': Responses and Reassessments*, edited by Alastair J. Minnis, 50–78. Cambridge: D. S. Brewer, 1983.

Nohrnberg, James. *The Analogy of The Faerie Queene.* Princeton: Princeton University Press, 1976.

Otis, Brooke. "The *Argumenta* of the so-called Lactantius." *Harvard Studies in Classical Philology* 47 (1936): 131–63.

Ovide moralisé. Poème du commencement du quatorzième siècle. Verhandelingen der Koninklijke Akademie van Wetenschappen te Amsterdam. Afdeeling Letterkunde, n. r., 15, 21, 30, 37, 43 (1915, 1920, 1931, 1936, 1938). Reprint. 5 vols. Wiesbaden: Martin Sändig, 1966-68.

Panofsky, Erwin. *Meaning in the Visual Arts*. Garden City, NY: Doubleday, 1955.

———. Preface. *Reductorium morale, liber XV: Ovidius moralizatus, cap. i, De formis figurisque deorum*. By Pierre Bersuire.

———. *Renaissance and Renascences in Western Art*. Stockholm: Almqvist and Wiksell, 1960.

Quinn, Betty Nye. "Venus, Chaucer, and Peter Bersuire." *Speculum* 38 (1963): 479-80.

Ridewall, John. *Fulgentius Metaforalis*. Edited by Hans Liebeschütz. Leipzig: Teubner, 1926.

Robertson, D. W. "Why the Devil Wears Green." *MLN* 69 (1954): 470-72.

Samaran, C., and J. Monfrin. "Pierre Bersuire." *Histoire littéraire de la France* 39 (1962): 1-192.

Seznec, Jean. *The Survival of the Pagan Gods*. Translated by Barbara F. Sessions. 1953. Reprint. Princeton: Princeton University Press, 1972.

Slater, D. A. *Towards A Text of the Metamorphoses of Ovid*. Oxford: The Clarendon Press, 1927.

Smalley, Beryl. "Jean de Hesdin O. Hosp. S. Ioh." *Recherches de théologie ancienne et médiévale* 28 (1961): 283-330.

———. *English Friars and Antiquity in the Early Fourteenth Century*. New York: Barnes and Noble, 1960.

Steadman, John M. "Venus' *Citole* in Chaucer's *Knight's Tale* and Berchorius." *Speculum* 34 (1959): 620-24.

Theodulf of Orleans. "De libris quos legere solebam." *PL* 105: 331-33.

Twycross, Meg. *The Medieval Anadyomene, A Study in Chaucer's Mythography*. Medium Aevum Monographs, N. S. 1. Oxford: Society for the Study of Medieval Languages and Literature, 1972.

Van Der Bijl, Maria S. "Petrus Berchorius, *Reductorium morale, liber XV: Ovidius moralizatus, cap. ii*." *Vivarium* 9 (1971): 25-48.

van Kluyve, Robert A. Introduction to *Archana deorum*, by Thomas Walsingham.

Walsingham, Thomas. *Archana deorum*. Edited by Robert A. van Kluyve. Durham, NC: Duke University Press, 1968.

Whitbread, Leslie George. *Fulgentius the Mythographer*. Columbus: Ohio State University Press, 1971.

Wicksteed, P. H., and E. G. Gardner. *Dante and Giovanni del Virgilio*. Westminster: A. Constable, 1902.

Wilkins, E. H. "Descriptions of Pagan Divinities from Petrarch to Chaucer." *Speculum* 32 (1957): 511-22.

Christine de Pizan as Chivalric Mythographer
L'Epistre Othea

Judith L. Kellogg

Christine de Pizan, intellectually accomplished, spirited, and courageous as she was, would have been a remarkable woman in any age, and must be considered even more so having flourished so publicly and successfully in the late Middle Ages. Often called the first professional woman of letters, she arrived at such a career reluctantly. Born in Venice in 1364, she was educated by her father Thomas de Pizan, who was the most important formative influence on her life. He encouraged his eager and talented daughter to pursue diverse intellectual interests, this against the explicit wishes of her mother who thought it entirely unfitting for women to acquire too much education. When Christine was four, her father, who had been appointed court astrologer and physician to the French king, Charles V, brought his family to France. Throughout her life, Christine was able to profit from both the intellectual resources and the potential patrons she found at the French court. At fifteen she was happily married to a respected nobleman, Etienne de Castel, and at twenty-five tragically widowed, with three small children to support. When unscrupulous creditors provided added aggravation and humiliation, she turned to her study of philosophy and her writing, first for solace, then for survival.

Christine is best known for her earliest writing, her lyric poetry. Her first poems were devoted entirely to her husband and express her anguish over losing him. Her verses, which did become happier with time, remained strictly within the courtly tradition that appealed to her patrons' tastes, but eventually she came to consider this kind of poetry frivolous, and began to write longer and more learned works. In the course of her prolific career, she ranged over a wide intellectual territory, from social, political, moral, and religious comment, to scientific observation, and to philosophical meditations of various kinds. Her last work is a long poem in praise of Joan of Arc, the only extended work written about the French heroine during her lifetime. Christine died in 1430.[1]

Christine was generally conservative intellectually and socially, but she dramatically rebelled against accepted tradition in matters concerning women. She was passionately outspoken about the largely unquestioned misogynist attitudes of her day. And she turned vehemently against the idea of courtly love, "construing it as an ethic devised by men for men; courtly love, as Christine saw it, had no redeeming value for women. On the contrary, she saw it as a disruptive influence on their lives, destroying their greatest virtues, their chastity, their good name, and not least, their marital happiness" (Yenal, 8). Her most developed "defense" of women is her *Livre de la Cité des Dames*,[2] though we shall see that the *Epistre Othea* already shows Christine giving a prominent place to women as influential and enlightened shapers of civilization.

The *Epistre Othea* was probably written in 1400, just after she had rejected lyric poetry in her search for more meaningful material. Oddly, though it was the work most popular with her medieval audience, a medieval "best-seller,"[3] it is probably her work most maligned by modern critics. Yet when we here examine Christine's method in relation to other mythographers, we can put some of the charges against Christine that her interpretations are "bizarre" (Pinet, 280), or unpalatable (McCleod, 51), in perspective. It is true that this work does not conform to modern tastes (Bühler, xi), but her interpretations generally fall squarely and even conservatively within the range of accepted and expected mythographic norms. Furthermore, such a comparison with other mythographers will indicate that her work is hardly a stale or eccentric rehash of tired old ideas, as has been suggested.[4] A detailed trial examination of one section, that dealing with Ceres, will demonstrate that, while making informed and careful use of her inherited aesthetic possibilities, Christine brings considerable artistic innovation to her material. Though utilizing borrowed and traditional associations for her mythic figures, Christine streamlines and unifies her images with a consistency that deepens and strengthens their symbolic power.

Christine's innovation involves more than aesthetic freshness, for she brings to her work an original, imaginative, and effective layering of two established genres, those of the chivalric handbook and the mythographic text. Surprisingly, no one has yet attempted to explain in any detail why Christine chose to integrate the mythographic and chivalric traditions as she does. Mythography, of course, has always involved the moral allegorization of pagan fable and, later, specifically Christian spiritualization of these myths.[5] Christine adds a chivalric focus to this process by creating a framework that allows myth to bridge pagan and Christian time and makes knightly values the practical standard against which to measure ethical and spiritual perfection throughout history. Furthermore, throughout the layered chivalric and spiritual interpretations of myth, she interweaves a crucial feminist thread, for she suggests women's active place in making the historical synthesis possible. This essay then, seeks to establish that, although the *Othea* may be flawed, it demonstrates that Christine, even in her first major extended work, was already an original artist in control of her material and with a sophisticated vision of myth's power to represent the dominant forces defining and shaping universal history.

BEFORE examining her larger views, a general discussion of the construction of the *Othea* is in order. The full title of Christine's work, *L'Epistre Othea la deesse que elle envoya a Hector quand il estoit en l'aage de quinze ans*,[6] suggests her general frame. The work takes the form of a long letter written to the young Trojan hero by Othea, the goddess of prudence and wisdom, to aid him in his moral and spiritual preparation for virtuous knighthood. The name Othea seems to be Christine's invention, though in her attributes the goddess closely resembles Athena. It is unclear what contemporary young knight Christine means Hector to represent—probably a member of one of France's powerful families (Hindman, 33–51), but possibly her own son who would have been fifteen in 1400.

The *Othea* consists of one hundred fables, each representing a separate lesson. The structure of the one hundred individual fables is uniform, each consisting of three parts, what Christine labels the Texte, Glose, and Allegorie. The first part, the four-line poetic Texte,[7] briefly introduces a classical figure, situation, or motif. This "story-moment" (Tuve, 34) does not attempt any sustained narration, but suggests a significant symbolic direction. The Texte is followed by the Glose, in which Christine often elaborates on the basic plot of the tale in question, occasionally adding a euhemeristic interpretation, and then draws a moral lesson. Each Glose then concludes with a quote from an ancient thinker.[8]

Christine saves the specifically Christian application of the myth in question for her third part, the Allegorie. Here she develops ways the myth comes to symbolize the soul's quest for salvation, adds a quote from a Church father, and concludes with a passage from the *Vulgate*.[9] The qualitative difference between the moralization of the Glose and the symbolically deeper Allegorie is dramatic.[10] Where the Gloses teach one how to act before and among men, the Allegories suggest that one must continually examine the soul before God. The Allegorie, then, touches on the spirit in which the quest for worldly virtue must be undertaken. To attain the higher spiritual blessing of "goostli knyghthood," one must remember that since "alle erthli thinges be deceyuable, we shulde have in contynuel mynde the tyme for to come, which is withoute ende" ("comme toutes choses terrestres soient fallibles, devons avoir en continuelle memoire le temps futur, qui est sans fin"). That in essence is "the grete wisedome of parfit knyghthood" ("c'est la somme et parfaicte chevalerie"). The "esperit chevalereux" is not seeking the earthly recognition of a good name, but eternal glory. He becomes the pilgrim soul in seeking both to assist and to emulate the perfect spiritual knight, Jesus Christ.

The advice here concerns contemplation and understanding of Christian truths in their essence more than the active good works and the practical attention to moral improvement of the Gloses. The Allegories emphasize the notion that "the virtuous disposition of the soul is its adornment and beautiful raiment, not only its hard-won guerdon after conflict" (Tuve, 41). Because we are made in the image of God, it is necessary that the soul be "araid with vertues" ("aournez de vertus"), and ultimately with the final ornament when, if we are among the "victorious pepill" ("les victorieux"), we are "crouned in blis" ("couronnez en gloire").

There is no consistent narrative thread or chronology, but in the beginning at least there is some doctrinal relationship developed between clusters of these lessons. Fables 1–4 are intended to illustrate the four cardinal virtues, prudence, temperance, fortitude, and justice; 6–12, the seven planetary deities; 13–15, the three theological virtues, faith hope, and charity; 16–22, the seven deadly sins; 23–34, the twelve articles of the Apostle's Creed; and 35–44, the Ten Commandments. In fables 45–89, virtues and vices are more randomly presented, though certain loose thematic groupings are distinguishable.[11] With fable 90, the announcement of Hector's death, the tone changes and the last ten fables draw the rest of the *Othea* together by building up to the event that has informed the work from the beginning: the birth of Christ. It is in these last fables that the reasons why Christine has chosen a mythographic format with Hector at the center become clearest.

Though Christine's lessons generally have a universal ethical application, at the level of the Glose her direct audience is clearly noble.[12] The advice is appropriate for a medievalized Hector, an aristocratic boy of fifteen who has all the innate worthiness to promise a glorious future as a great warrior and statesman. As an example, in Texte 11, Othea introduces Mars as Hector's father whom "Thou shalte folowe . . . in euery mater; / For thin high and noble condicion / Drawith therto thine inclinacion" ("Tu ensuivras bien en tout pas; / Car ta noble condicion / Y trait ton inclinacion"). In the Glose she elaborates that "every knyght that loueth and suweth armes and deedis of knyghthode and hath a greet name of wurthynes may be callid sone of Mars" ("tout chevalier qui aime ou suive armes et fais de chevalerie et ait renommee de valeur peut estre appellé filz de Mars"). In the Gloses generally, the knight is encouraged to emulate admirable behavior, but is also cautioned to avoid the wicked example of, for instance, Leomedon ("Thin yvil mysdede foryete thou noughte," 61), the Trojan king who betrayed the Greeks who had previously helped him. The knight must keep in mind that "if he haue mysdon to any, that he kepe him weel, for he may be sekir it shal not be foryeten, but rather vengid, whan he may haue tyme and place" ("se il a a aucun meffait, qui il soit sus sa garde, car estre peut certain que cellui ne l'oublira mie, ains s'en vengera, quant il pourra, en temps et en lieu").

In the Glose, Christine sees each mythological figure as providing the knight the means to fight evil in this world by strengthening his moral character, combating society's injustices, and avoiding fleshly temptations. Certainly such virtue assists the Christian spirit gain salvation, but the immediate rewards are here on earth. And though Christine's direct audience may be the aristocratic, knightly world, her lessons are available to all who are willing to enter the moral battlefield of life, for "we may calle mankyndli lif verrai chyualrie" ("nous povons appeler la vie humaine droite chevalerie," 1). Hector becomes an Everyman, "Hector, the which in liche wise may be to all othir desiring bounte and wisedome" ("Hector, qui semblablement peut estre a tous autres desirans bonte et sagece"). To follow up the above examples, Mars, Hector's figurative father, becomes Jesus Christ, "father" of us all, who battled in this world for us and whom we must imitate by fighting vice within ourselves: "noon may ouercome the evilles outewarde that will not werre strongeli the synnes of theire soulis" ("ne pevent vaincre les maulx par dehors qui ne guerrie fort les pechez de son ame"). As for the treacherous and ungrateful Leomedon, the revenge taken upon him becomes a reminder that one will be damned if he does not amend his ways: "whan the good spirit feelith him in synne for defaute of resistence, he shulde thinke that he shal be ponyssched, as thei be that be dampned, if he amende him not" ("quant le bon esperit se sent en peché par faulte de resistance, il doit penser que punicion en sera faite, si comme il est des dampnez, se il ne s'amende").

The quality of the images of the Allegories is quite different from that in the Gloses, even though the images come from the same mythic figures. Christine's successful Allegories create a symbolic enrichment of the figures she uses, which depends on her being able to fuse the mythic image with the "maner of speche of goostli knyghthood" ("maniere de parler de l'esperit chevalereux") so that a classical figure can effectively come to represent the truth inherent in Christian doctrine and familiar Christian symbols. In other words, she invents no symbols (as for instance Spenser does), but attaches ancient images to Christian truths, thus strengthening their symbolic power and extending our understanding of the mystery these images have been asked to represent.

ONE of the best ways to understand the nature of Christine's method and intent and to illustrate the symbolic richness of her treatment of images is to focus on a single mythic figure. In this case, Ceres is a particularly apt subject for special attention because Tuve selects her as Christine's "best novel symbol for Christ's gift to men" (Tuve, 299). A comparison of several mythographers' use of Ceres will allow us to expand on Tuve's brief suggestion, and to situate Christine's work in the context of the mythographic tradition out of which the *Othea* grows.

Two of the most influential mythographic works that closely preceded Christine's work were the anonymous *Ovide moralisé*[13] and Pierre Bersuire's *Ovidius moralizatus*.[14] She certainly was familiar with the massive French work and borrowed heavily from it.[15] In fact, in the *Othea*, when she refers her audience to the original "fable" as her source, she is consistently referring, not to Ovid's *Metamorphoses*, as the stories might lead us to suspect, but to the *Ovide moralisé*. It seems, however, that she did not know Bersuire's commentary on the *Metamorphoses*, which comprised the fifteenth book of his encyclopedic *Reductorium morale*. In a revised version of the *Ovidius moralizatus*, Bersuire incorporated parts of the *Ovide moralisé*, no doubt in an attempt to provide a more comprehensive treatment of the myths in question, but in his initial version we see an approach to mythography quite distinct from that of the anonymous French work and the *Othea*.

The treatment of Ceres well illustrates the typical methods of each of these three writers. Bersuire, probably the most influential of all Ovid commentators, like other medieval mythographers, starts from the premise that "fables, enigmas, and poems must for the most part be read so that some moral sense may be drawn out from them and so that their falsity may be understood in terms of some familiar truth." He is not interested, he says, in natural or historical interpretations, but is only concerned with fictions by which he "may be able to confirm the mysteries of morals and faith" (Reynolds, 32–33).[16] The segments from Ovid that he uses for his allegorizations are succinctly and sketchily presented, more as points of departure for his moralizations than attempts at sustained narrative. He seems determined to gain as much allegorical mileage as possible from his mythic referents, varying his interpretations at different points in the story as he sees a possible new spiritual relationship emerging. In the course of narrating Ceres's ordeal over losing Proserpina (Reynolds, 238–46), the devoted mother goddess becomes alternately the pious prelate who tries to protect her subject (Proserpina)

through piety, Christ who rescues the human soul (Proserpina) from
the devil (Pluto), and finally, a beneficent God the Father who gives
seeds and fruits of grace to the world, these distributed by Christ (Triptolomous). Ceres remains an admirable figure throughout Bersuire's discussion, but such consistency is certainly not a necessity. Bersuire delights in testing different, even contradictory, interpretations of a single
figure, often using the same figure as an example both of good and
evil.[17] No attempt is made to harmonize these interpretations—they are
not presented as simultaneous, but as alternate readings. Thus the final
understanding of each figure is not fixed, except that it must ultimately
reveal or validate some Christian truth. To support his allegorizations,
Bersuire seeks to find scriptural parallels for each moral he has un-
earthed. It seems that the *process* of slowly and meticulously unraveling
the poetic veil that obscures God's truth fascinates him more than consistency. In fact, inconsistency, in a paradoxical way, even lends strength
to the validity of his method. In seeing how many wildly different interpretations he can make affirm Christian understanding, he is really asserting the power, unity, and plenitude of God's truth.[18] Of course, clear
threads run through the work, the most consistent no doubt being the
idea that the lessons should provide a kind of mirror for prelates.

The poet of the *Ovide moralisé* is more concerned with simple narrative coherence than Bersuire. He sees Ceres as grain, the sustenance of
the earth. In the more important spiritual sense, she is Holy Church,
who teaches us to "cultivate" (5. 2892) our service to God and who re-
plenishes our spiritual "fruit" (5. 2898). Holy Church increasingly works
to save the sinful soul (Proserpina) who has become a captive of
the devil (Pluto) until, like a loving mother, she provides the means for
repentence and thus the reunion of the soul with its Creator. Whereas
Bersuire swiftly glides over his source, lighting on those aspects that
serve his allegorical purpose, the *Ovide moralisé* recounts Ovid's stories
in detail. And while Bersuire tends to impose his larger ideas upon the
fables, the poet of the *Ovide moralisé* starts more exactly with the givens
of the stories and works out from these. After narrating the story
proper, he selects certain segments as focus, and within these he is compelled by his method to make doctrinal and allegorical sense of the
smallest details (5. 2782–3903). Even such minor props as the torches
that Ceres carries to light her way receive extended comment; these become the Scriptures. Digressions from the story take on an importance
equal to that of the central story. For instance, within the discussion of
Ceres's plight to rescue her daughter, Arethusa, a nymph transformed
into a fountain tells her own story, and the poet digresses for a separate
allegorical explanation. The danger in this approach, as Tuve points out,

is that "large numbers of unrelated separate significances are hustled in, but there appears to be no considered theoretical basis for this, such as choice of a deeper functioning of the image" (Tuve, 305).

In her own depiction of Ceres, Christine begins with a suggestion from the *Ovide moralisé*, but her images function more consistently. After Proserpina, the penitent soul, has been successfully returned to the company of Holy Church, the poet of the *Ovide moralisé* picks up a separate thread of Ceres's story, the gift of grain that Triptolomous is to spread throughout the world. Here Ceres becomes Christ and Triptolomous the Apostles of Christ. It is the Ceres-Christ parallel that Christine utilizes in her own work (24). But before she gets to her Allegorie, she manages to telescope Ceres's essential qualities in the brief sketch of the Texte:

La deesse Ceres ressemble,
Qui les blez donne et a nul n'emble;
Ainsi doit estre abandonnez
Bon chevalier bien ordonnez.

Be thou like to the goddes Ceres,
That took fro noon but yaf to corn encrees;
In such wise abandoned schulde be
The good knyghte, wel sette in his degre.

Ceres asks for nothing, but represents the purest spirit of generosity that should teach the knight the chivalric virtue of largess. In the Glose, the miracle of nature's abundance—the gifts of Ceres herself—remind the chivalric knight that part of his moral duty is to sustain others, to "be habundaunte to alle persones and to yeue his helpe and comforte aftir his powere" ("doit estre aussi bon chevalier a toute personne abandonnez et donner son ayde et reconfort selon son povoir"). Just as the spiritual knight is rewarded with salvation, the earthly knight is rewarded with that which makes his endeavor possible: "Be a liberal yeuere and thou shalte haue frendes" ("Soies liberal donneur et tu aras amis").[19] The knight has an identity and purpose only within a community of other men, whom he must inspire as well as provide with a mutual trust and loyalty.

In the Allegorie, Christine picks up the Ceres-Christ parallel suggested by the *Ovide moralisé* to illustrate the second article of the Apostle's Creed, belief in Jesus Christ, the one son of God. Christine builds spiritual resonance into the idea of generosity developed in the Texte and Glose by suggesting the most important way life can be sustained and grow fertile: through the largess of Christ. Ceres is emblematic of

Christ in that he "hath youen so largeli to us of high goodes" ("tant nous a largement donne de ses haulx biens") that make possible eternal rewards. Whereas the Glose, with its images of plowing and sowing the land, and the abundance of the harvest, inspires one to active good works, the Allegorie, by making the analogy between Ceres and Christ, asks simply for a refinement of one's understanding and a deepening of belief.

Christine's treatment of Ceres suggests how distinctively her method and intent differ from Bersuire's or the poet of the *Ovide moralisé*, for it demonstrates how economically she pares down, deepens, and sharpens the images she is using in the more effective of her sketches. In these she manages to capture the moral and spiritual essence that can be so easily lost in Bersuire's effort for variety and tendency to twist his material in contradictory directions, and in the *Ovide moralisé*'s floundering in overwrought attention to detail at the expense of a sustained larger picture. Christine's images are simple, but rarely simplistic. Because she carefully focuses upon one distinct figure, allied with one major statement in each Glose or Allegory, the force of each is unambiguous and stands out with a clarity that matches in the textual realm the kind of visual clarity that is possible in the illuminations of her works.[20] This concision, in combination with an often witty yoking together of chivalric and spiritual relationships, must have seemed a refreshing way for her audience to encounter some well-worn didactic clichés.

Christine's deviation from other mythographers' use of mythic detail clearly points to an original and calculated approach to her material, but certainly her most significant deviation from her tradition involves her overall plan to apply mythographic methods to the chivalric handbook so familiar to her audience. Thus she was able to combine two popular genres that risked individually becoming a little worn in Christine's day in a way that enriched and developed both. The far-reaching implications of her innovation can best be appreciated by examining the large structural frame set up in the opening and closing sections and her use of Hector as a pivotal figure. These suggest the ways she uses myth to develop a vision of universal history and to make some important statements about the place of chivalry within that scheme. Two separate, but related, issues are involved here. The first is the place of myth in bridging pagan and Christian time and history. The second involves the power of the chivalric model to represent what were considered to be absolute and eternal spiritual values.

The frame for the *Othea* sets up a complex, even paradoxical, time scheme. It opens (1), as we have said, with Othea introducing herself as goddess of prudence and wisdom to the young Trojan prince, "to the,

Hector, noble prince myghti, / That in armes is euer wurthi" ("A toy, Hector, noble prince poissant, / Qui en armes es adez flourissant"). She promises to tell him truly of those things that are necessary to virtue, honor, and one's good reputation, taking into account Hector's pagan existence when she adds that as a goddess who speaks "in the spirit of prophecee" ("en esperit de prophecie"), she knows of things that are to come, no doubt a veiled allusion to the circumstances of his premature death, but also an obvious reference to the coming of Christ—two events we shall see are related in the *Othea*. But she obscures the boundary between pagan and Christian time when she says that she hopes that by her teachings, Hector will be one of those to "clyme heuyn vnto" ("monter jusqu'a cieulx"), leaving the impression that she actually expects that he, a pagan, will attain salvation.[21] Such eternal rewards for a pagan are doctrinally impossible, yet Othea proceeds to teach Hector very explicit Christian lessons, encouraging him as she does to work toward Christian virtue, and inspiring him with the grandeur of Christ's example.

Significantly, the one other place where the line between pagan and Christian time is crossed is also the one other place where a female prophet enters. This echoing of the first section happens in the last section (100) when the Tiburtine Sibyl comes to tell Caesar Augustus of the coming of Christ—another prophetess come to inform a leading figure of the pagan world that the time has come for the unfolding and fulfillment of the true meaning of ancient culture, the same message Othea, in essence, has had for Hector.[22] The fact that the Sibyl lives within Christian time as well as ancient time gives her a validity and immediacy that she does not have when merely part of a pagan "fable." That is, she is not just a pagan "metaphor," an integumental figure, meant to represent some hidden, prefigured truth, but also a historical figure, instrumental in "true" (i.e., Christian) history.[23]

To understand more precisely what overriding statement Christine is making by the parallels she creates in the framing fables, we must look at the final segment of the *Othea*. The pivotal fable is 90, where the whole tone of the work changes as Hector's death is announced. The reminder that the spirit must continually think about death is an appropriate opening for the action, message, and tone of the next ten fables. In many ways, the general line of development followed in the body of the *Othea* has been rounded out in fable 89, which works as an effective hinge to sum up the preceding work and prepare for the end. This leaves the last eleven fables to make a statement vitally related to the rest, but separate in the power of their impact and the ultimate direction of their mythic references. Fable 89 recounts the fable of Nambroth, the giant who founded Babylon. The Texte warns that one should not trust Babylon's strength, then the Glose adds that the knight must not trust the strength of one's castle alone without worthy defenders inside, and, finally, the Allegorie cautions that the spirit should not trust the things of this world. This is certainly an appropriate spiritual summation for all that Othea, as emblem of wisdom and prudence, has to teach, resonating as it does at this point with the perils and temptations of the world that the goddess has illustrated, as well as with the gloriousness of the rewards of the next if such pitfalls are avoided. And it also appropriately puts the sequence of the last fables in perspective.

In these, where one might expect a final extolling of Hector for the worthy life he has led, we find just the opposite, criticism of his behavior along with that of a number of the great figures of the Trojan war. Fables 90–99, in fact, portray these deaths as degraded, stupid, and needless, resulting from ignorance, arrogance, and treachery. Hector first disgraces himself by his hubristic filial impiety (90), disobeying his father's request that he abstain from battle for one day. Hector then dies (91) because he does not keep his back covered, thus representing the spirit that allowed his senses to be open to the world, and so his conscience to fail him. His carelessness results from his coveting of worldly things (92)—the arms of the fallen Polibetes. Next Achilles (93) in becoming infatuated with Polyxena forgets that he should flee all that is foreign—that is, all this world—and love only those things from God. Ajax (94) is prideful in trusting only his own strength. Capping these deaths with the appearance of Antenor (95), who betrays his homeland and so represents all that is spiritually false and treacherous, intensifies the tone of degradation.

Christine then turns from the disastrous failures of ancient heroes to the danger involved in the place, Troy itself, and to the collective guilt of those who were destroyed. The Trojans, by having accepted the great horse into the Temple of Minerva (96), represent those who allow other than true prayers to be offered in the Church. Not only is the holy sanctuary abused, but also the secular stronghold as well, for Troy (97) contained those who grew lax trusting in the surety of their castle and indulging too much in the delights of this world. Worldly delights represent a false haven, the consequences of which are faced not only by the Trojans and Greeks who died at Troy but also by those who had yet to return home, for the survivors still had to face Circe (98), who turned men into swine. That is, self-indulgence turns men into hypocrites, people of two faces and natures, those of man and beast. So it seems that the Trojan war has only resulted in the moral degeneration of those involved.

Fable 99, which describes Ino, Athamas's wife who sows bad corn, seems like an odd and wrenching shift from the context of the Trojan war, yet the message both explains and sums up the intent of the previous devastating sections. For Ino represents the one who sows wisdom and understanding, which will not fructify because it has been wasted on the foolish. Othea here stresses that things that should be known are often not, and that there is no excuse for ignorance when proper perception is within reach. The fact that the explicit announcement of the birth of Christ is made immediately after this message puts the behavior and fate of the Trojans in perspective. They died disastrously and in sin, condemned to hell as all pagans must be. Yet their ignorance is understandable, and in fact, unavoidable. However, Christine stresses that our own ignorance is not excusable, for she emphatically reminds us at the end that Christ's message is available to us in a way denied the pagan world.

The humiliating end of the ancient heroes, set in the context of Christ's later appearance, also makes an important statement about chivalric ethics. The classical heroes were, after all, the best that the pagan world had to offer, and their behavior, as the medieval world saw it, and as Christine represents it in her Gloses, conformed to the strictest codes of chivalry. Such behavior was seen as necessary and good. But as we see from the ending of the *Othea*, it was not good *enough* in and of itself. Without Christian revelation, it was just a code of futile earthly behavior that led inevitably to the meaningless and debased deaths of even the most worthy.

The question for Christine then becomes how to salvage what was valuable and laudable from pagan culture and revitalize it for the Christian world. Christine's method and intent can be illuminated by looking at another related chivalric fiction, that of the Nine Worthies. It is no coincidence that the idea of the Nine Worthies emerges during roughly the same period in which Christine was maturing intellectually. It embodies attitudes toward myth and knighthood that certainly reflect back upon Christine's attempt to use mythography to develop the full significance of chivalric centeredness in human time and human history as the Middle Ages understood it. It also sheds light on Christine's particular choice of Hector to represent Othea's archetypal chivalric and spiritual disciple.[24] Significantly, though the line-up of figures included in the popular medieval configuration of Nine Worthies changes, Hector is always included among them.[25]

Maurice Keen describes particularly incisively the message the cult of the Nine Worthies had for the chivalric world from the time that Jean de Gonguyon introduced the three parallel triads of heroes in his fourteenth-century *Voeux du paon* (Keen, 121).[26] He explains how each of the first two layers represented by these heroes, those of the Old Law (Joshua, David, and Judas Maccabaeus) and those of pagan law (Hector, Alexander, and Julius Caesar), makes possible the triad of champions of new Christian Law (Arthur, Charlemagne, and Godfrey de Bouillon). The Christian heroes are

> thus the fruit of the marriage of the two older traditions, the pagan knighthood that God ordained to rule the world and to uphold peace in it, and the biblical knighthood that He ordained to guard the holy places and defend the religion of His chosen people. The three Christian heroes represent the armed force of His new chosen people, the Christian nation, whose mission derives from the earlier traditions; it being to uphold His Peace, to spread His Law, and to guard His Holy Places. They take their place as the three leading cult figures of Christian chivalry, the order whose terrestrial function mirrors more sharply and precisely than either of the earlier traditions the perennial and universal struggle of God and His angels against the forces of darkness, of turbulence and of sacrilege. (Keen, 122)

The place of the middle, pagan triad is especially important for the *Othea*, spanning as it does the essential history of the classical world, from the Trojan war to Julius Caesar, that is encompassed in Christine's work.

As Christine has structured her work, Hector represents both the beginning *and* the end of that period of human history. He exists literally in the beginning of the *Othea* as a Trojan prince, and, structurally within the *Othea*, he dies just before Christ's birth is announced to the pagan world. But his fate is not sealed with his death. Othea has, after all, promised him the opportunity to climb to heaven and has offered him the Christian revelation necessary to do it. The care Othea takes to instruct Hector in Christian virtue and its rewards only makes sense if Hector will be able to profit from his new wisdom. In many respects, then, he becomes like Caesar Augustus, a pagan to whom a prophetess offers enlightenment and transforms into a true believer. Hector, by his death and presumed salvation, has passed the threshold between the mythic and historical world in much the same way that the Sibyl manages to do. Remarkably, in changing spiritual contexts, he becomes his own fulfillment of the fable he represents. As he joins Caesar Augustus, son and moral heir to the great Worthy, Julius Caesar, in crossing from pagan into Christian time and from the mythic to historical world, he becomes far more than simply the virtuous pagan and worthy Trojan prince killed in battle. As a pagan, he must die along with his era, but he is also the embodiment of all that is best in the pagan world, reborn, revived, and sanctified by the added light of Christian revelation. The spirit of the redeemed Hector, joined by that of Christ, is transmitted by Caesar Augustus and ultimately fulfilled in the chivalric glory of the Christian Worthies, Arthur, Charlemagne, and Godfrey de Bouillon. So Hector provides a continuity from the beginning of pagan history into Christine's own medieval time frame.

It is really Hector who draws together the two levels of moral, chivalric Glose and Christian Allegorie and the separate kinds of lessons they involve. He provides a reminder similar to that of the last Worthy, Godfrey de Bouillon, who brings history up to the First Crusade and "more effectively than any of the others symbolized the fact that the story of chivalry's divine mission in the world was still in process, that that mission was an urgent and contemporary one, and that there was no reason why, with the nine, all the 'sieges' of the first circle of chivalrous honour should be regarded as occupied." Thus, "the Nine Worthies symbolized the significance of a story that was emphatically unconcluded, reminding men at once of the example of the past and that the history of chivalry was still a-making" (Keen, 123). Christine's work incorporates much the same message as that intended by the Nine Worthies. Like them, it is a reminder that every knight should strive to become the Tenth Worthy, and it offers the specific framework to teach both the literal knight as well as the figurative chivalric Everyman not just *how* he can achieve this distinction, but also *why* he must continue to do battle, for he can see the spiritual possibilities offered him more clearly in the context of human history. The final fulfillment of the mythic Hector then becomes the "New Hector," the boy of fifteen whom Christine addresses and who represents all the potential of the untried knight and spirit.

Christine is here doing something quite remarkable with mythography, which involves more than building layers of allegory upon pagan story. She also seems to be trying to revitalize the myths, making them a living part of the Christian world while still allowing them their symbolic value. As Christine brings her mythic layer into Christian time at the end, that moment of crossing gives additional resonance to the allegorical level she has described throughout. That moment becomes a reminder that the chivalric and Christian levels have never really been separate, though the lessons in each can certainly be contemplated separately and distinctly. Not only is Christine concerned to see the meaning of chivalry within God's eternal scheme, but she also feels compelled to remind the chivalric aspirant of the place of the eternal in the codes of chivalry. Christine is not using her mythological framework as an easy place to begin a mechanical equation (as Bersuire and the poet of the

Ovide moralisé so often do), but is developing her mythography with a consistent sense of universal history in mind and with chivalric virtues affording the continuity between pagan and Christian time.

THE *Epistre Othea*, addressed as it is to a young man about to take up the warrior calling of knighthood, has an overtly masculine orientation. And even if chivalric worthiness is at one level simply a metaphor for general moral and spiritual perfection, it remains a metaphor grounded in upper-class, male experience. Yet Christine has been called the "first feminist in the Western tradition" (Schulenburg, 34).[27] She is also the first woman mythographer. Thus it seems entirely appropriate that we ask whether her views on women figure in the *Othea* and affect her conception of mythography more generally.

We have seen that the framing sections, with the carefully structured parallels between Hector and Caesar Augustus, reflect the most obvious thematic intent and mythographic innovation in the *Othea*, yet a second clear parallel also exists in these two sections. Within each, the instigating and inspirational force is provided by a woman, Othea in the first and the Sibyl in the last, and in both, Christine comments explicitly on the importance of feminine counsel. In the first section, Christine relates that in ancient Troy "a full wise lady callid Othea" gave Hector "many grete and notable yiftis," including "this pistell." So Othea becomes more than an abstract representation of wisdom and prudence. On the literal level, she is also a type of all wise and virtuous living women, a reminder of their contribution to humanity generally, which is reinforced in the last section where, after relating in the Glose the story of Caesar Augustus's enlightenment and conversion, Christine moves to the moral in the Glose: "be-cause that Cesar Augustus, the which was prince of all the worlde, lerned to knowe God and the beleue of a womman, to the purpos may be seide the auctorite that Hermes seith: Be not ashamed to here trouthe & good teching of whom that euer seith it, for trouthe noblith him that pronounceth it" ("pour ce que Cesar Augustus, qui prince estoit de tout le monde, apprist a congnoistre Dieu et la creance d'une femme, peut estre dit a propos l'auctorite que dit Hermes: Ne te soit point honte de oyr verite et bon enseignement, qui que le die; car verite anoblist cellui qui le prononce"). In the Allegorie she further remarks: "There where Othea seith that she hath writen to him an hundrith auctorites and that Augustus lerned of a womman, is to vndirstand that good wordis & good techingis is to preise, of what persoone that seith it" ("La ou Othea dit que cent auctoritez lui a escriptes et de femme apprist Augustus, est a entendre que bonne parole et bon enseignement font a louer de quelconques personne que ilz soient dis").

After all the focus on the chivalric life, Christine's final statement suggesting the feminine source of enlightenment, prowess, and virtue on this earth may startle, but the figure of Othea has actually prepared for this idea from the beginning, and, in fact, it has been repeated and developed as a leitmotif throughout the work. Othea, as we have seen, represents wisdom, the "moost noble of all othir thinges" ("la plus noble de toutes autres choses," Glose 1), and prudence. Prudence and wisdom allied then become "moderis and conditoures of *all* vertues" ("mere et conduisarresse de toutes vertus," Allegorie 1, italics mine). So the formative power behind generating any further moral and spiritual progress is a feminine, maternal virtue. Othea's influence is reflected in the remarkable horse, Galanthe, which she presents to Hector. The image of the horse, besides its traditional associations with strength, virility, and beauty, carries for Christine when developed later through Pegasus, the special connotation of reputation. The gift of the horse is an emblem of Hector's potential—the outward manifestation of the innate worthiness that Othea must nurture to moral and spiritual perfection in the young prince.

Beyond the personal inspiration and counsel that women provide, they work on a broad cultural level. Remarkable female figures offer humankind some of its greatest practical gifts: Minerva (13), chivalric armor; Ceres (24), abundance of grain; Isis (25), the power of germination that gives plants "strengthe and growinge to multeplie" ("vigueur et croiscence de multiplier"). Especially significant is the association of Io (29) with letters which "yaf noryshschynge to vnderstandynge" ("trouva doulce nourriture a l'entendement"). Not only does she provide the foundation for all secular learning, but also the very means to salvation, for letters allow the recording and transmitting of Holy Writ and Scripture.[28] If Othea is the mother of all virtues, Io becomes Othea's necessary sister companion as disseminator of the wisdom and knowledge that make Christian virtue possible.

On a higher spiritual plane, two of these same civilizing figures, along with the goddess Diana, represent the most sacred of all eternal truths and the ultimate fructifying and generating power in the universe, the Trinity itself. Diana (23), because she is "withoute any spott of vnclene loue" ("sans tache aucune ameur de toute nettete"), represents "God of hevyn . . . the makere of hevyn and of erthe" ("Dieu de paradis . . . createur du ciel et de la terre"). As we have seen, Ceres (24), for her selfless generosity and the comfort she offers humankind, represents Christ. Isis (25), because she represents the mystery of life on earth, comes to signify the mystery of the conception of the Virgin and the breath of the Holy Spirit that makes spiritual life possible for humankind in allowing

Christ to be born on earth a man. Isis, then, is understood as "blessid concepcion of Jhesu Criste be the Holi Goost in the blissid Virgin Marie, moder of all grace, of whom the grete bounteis may not be ymagyned ne hoolly seide" ("la benoite concepcion de Jhesucrist par le Saint Esperit en la benoite Vierge Marie, mere de toute grace, de qui les grans bontez ne pourroient estre ymaginees ne dictes entierement"). Though individually these are not new associations, Christine's bringing this female triad together to represent the Trinity is a dramatic way to remind her audience that, although the Trinity consists of male figures, the qualities it reflects are equally shared by and available to women.

Not only do feminine figures represent great civilizing gifts and the source of spiritual life in the Trinity, but also valued human qualities. Cassandra (32) is a wise and pious woman who abhorred lying and served devoutly in the temple. Atalanta (72) is she who "hath grettir talent than thow" ("plus que toy grant talent a"). Penthesilea (15) becomes a particularly powerful figure. She completes a triptych of the three Theological Virtues begun by Minerva and Pallas, two separated aspects of the same goddess.[29] Minerva, who is named as figurative mother of Hector, is the inventor of armor, and thus the creator and patroness of knighthood. She is allegorically the virtue of Faith, the armor of God. Pallas, like Othea, represents wisdom, which is naturally joined with Hope. Penthesilea combines all the virtues embodied by Minerva and Pallas to represent Charity. On the chivalric level, she displays "merveillous wurthines in armes and in hardines" ("merveilleuse proece en armes et hardement"). Reflecting Pallas, she is "strong in vertu of witte and conscience" ("forte en vertu de sens et de constance"). In her aspect of Charity, she too becomes a kind of mother, generative spirit, for "charity is as the reyne the which fallith in the prime-temps, for it distillith the drops of vertues vnder the which greine good wil groweth and good hope fructifieth" ("charite est aussi comme la pluye qui chet en printemps, car elle distille les gouttes des vertus soubz la quelle germe la bonne voulente et la bonne opperacion fructifie").

In describing Penthesilea, Christine adds the notion of the framing sections that a good woman's strength, wisdom, and good example should not be ignored: "Bounte scholde be alowed where that it is perceyued" ("Bonte doit estre louee ou que elle soit apperceue"). The same idea is interspersed further throughout the *Othea*. Thomyris (57), the Amazon queen who conquered Cyrus, king of Persia, "schulde not be dispreisid though sche be a womman" ("ne doit estre desprisee pour tant se elle est femme"). One must "beleue the counceill" (79) of Alcione, the loving wife of King Ceys, who advised him not to undertake the perilous voyage that led to his violent drowning. Andromache, who tried to dissuade Hector from battle after having dreamt of his death (88), provides a reminder that one must "Dispite not the wijf, y counceil the, / Ne othir wommen that wise be" ("Ta femme du tout ne desprises, / Ne d'autres femmes bien apprises").

Aside from the good works and good examples that women offer humankind generally, women also make a special contribution to *mankind*. Though the good knight should avoid Venus (7)—that is, lecherie—he should look to Cupid (47)—that is, love—for a "wise wurschipfull lady" ("dame honoree et sage") for inspiration. Here Christine slips back to the courtly notions of woman as the ennobling force in men's lives, though she does stipulate that this love be chaste.

As insistently as Christine builds her positive portrait of women, she does not paint an overidealized or romanticized view of feminine nature. She realistically does not ask women to be better than men, but to come forward on an equal, fully rounded human footing. So women also represent flaws in human nature—for instance, Phoebe (10), unsteadiness and folly; Aglauros (18), envy; Arachne (64), boasting; and Cressida (84), false love and vainglory. But even here, a few female figures normally seen as reprehensible are dealt with in a surprisingly original and sympathetic manner. For instance, Medea (54), generally seen as treacherous, heartless, and lustful, is seen as victimized by Jason and serves to warn that one should not be ungrateful to one who helps him. Pasiphae (45) takes on a particularly strange twist. Though Christine, in accord with tradition, still sees the queen's actions as monstrous and bestial, she uses her to represent "a soule retournyd to God" ("l'ame retournee a Dieu").

It seems that Christine has taken the most offensive female exemplar she can find and has then asked her audience not to be too hasty to condemn her. Pasiphae was indeed a "fool," but even the most evil always retain the potential power to repent and return to the Creator. However, even if Pasiphae does not repent, and even if she remains a lost soul, Christine reminds her audience that one cannot make a judgment of all women on the basis of the behavior of one. Christine's plea in the Glose that the good knight "scholde neithir sey ne sustene that alle wommen schulde be like to hire" ("ne doit dire ne soustenir que toutes femmes soient semblables") seems a direct attack on the *process* by which misogynist beliefs and attitudes are generated. Remarkably, Christine has used a well-known example of female dissolution as defense against too hasty condemnation of women generally. She is fair and realistic about women's imperfections, but she also insists through her positive examples that the one-sided misogynist lens so often used to view women in her age be discarded. Women must be viewed not according to preset bias but according to experience, and thus be seen as contributing to the entire tapestry of human life, good and bad.

We have seen, then, that the *Othea* has employed two well-developed threads—attention to the chivalric and to particular qualities represented by notable feminine figures. What emerges is a satisfying dovetailing of these two interests in a way that expands the definitions of basic medieval attitudes toward history and chivalry. Christine has certainly used her mythographic text to develop a notion of human history that depends on the rightness and goodness of knightly values, but she has also universalized history by showing it as equally formed by and important for both men and women. She thus implies a reevaluation of the idea of the chivalric to include women more fundamentally and actively than as the traditional ennobling love object or helpless victim of circumstance in need of rescue. Women, as much as men, are responsible for the intellectual, cultural, religious, and even agricultural evolution of civilization. Though in the *Othea* this is still an undercurrent, already Christine makes clear her view that "women's achievements are so intimately woven into the fabric of civilization that any attempt to portray human history androcentrically is doomed at the onset" (Richards, 15). Although this statement was made about the *Livre de la Cité des Dames*, its applicability to the *Othea* shows Christine beginning to formulate a consistent philosophical framework regarding women's role in history early on in her career.[30]

The *Epistre Othea* turns out to be a complex and multifaceted work. Christine grounds her work in long-established mythographic format and method, but imaginatively builds something original upon that foundation, for she incorporates interlocking layers of elements from the chivalric handbook, spiritual treatise, and defense of women. In synthesizing these various elements, Christine attempts to describe large unifying forces within human history. Christine may still be experimenting with her ideas and techniques, yet her intent is ambitious, her artistic conception innovative, and her vision of human potential powerful.

Notes

1. The most recent, substantial biography of Christine de Pizan is that by Willard; see also useful biographies by Pinet, McCleod, and Pernoud.

2. The only modern edition available of Christine's Old French text is that of Curnow; the work has been recently translated by Richards, *The Book of the City of Ladies*.

3. The medieval popularity of the *Othea* is confirmed by its preservation in at

least forty-five manuscripts and its translation into English three times in the hundred years after it was first written.

4. Campbell, still considered the standard authority on Christine's use of sources in the *Othea*, sees much of Christine's borrowing as hackneyed and mechanical, and has set the tone for subsequent criticism of the *Othea*. This judgment extends to Christine's other works as well. Richards remarks in discussing the *Livre de la Cité des Dames*, "The traditional approach to Christine's thought is that she is a compiler of received notions" (*City of Ladies*, xxxi). See also, Mombello, "Quelques aspects." Clearly, certain criticisms of Christine's failure of artistry and imagination need reviewing and correcting.

Some of the most interesting recent comments on the originality of Christine's work have been made by feminist critics (see note 27). Few treat the *Othea* specifically, though Reno does provide a good starting place for the work. Reno discusses how Christine deals with various sources "so as to present certain female characters in a more favorable light." Ignatius makes important comments about Christine's originality by discussing the relationship between text and illuminations.

5. For a succinct overview of the mythographic tradition, see Chance, "Origins"; see also McCall. For a useful discussion of the relationship between mythography and the iconographic tradition into the Renaissance, see Seznec.

6. For the sake of accessibility, I will cite from Scrope's Middle English, generally quite literal, translation, ed. Bühler. The original French text is included for comparison, cited from the only modern edition presently available, edited by Loukopoulos. A modern English translation by Chance is forthcoming.

7. The quatrain form is uniform except in the first five Textes, which vary considerably in length.

8. Her source for quotations from ancient philosophers was primarily the collection *Dicta philosophorum*, according to Bühler.

9. Christine's primary sources for Christian authority were Thomas Hibernicus, *Manipulus florum*, for Church Fathers, and the *Flores bibliorum* for citations from the Bible, according to Campbell.

10. Tuve remarks, "whereas the first reading, in the Glose, has to do with building a character . . . the simultaneous additional second reading, the Allegorie, does not use literature or vicarious experience for that purpose—though advice on the good life is often near at hand as a by-product. The Good Spirit . . . reads in figures the reminder of its true condition as a creature, sometimes seeing its need for rescue, often seeing in the figures a repetition of the news of its way of deliverance or some definition of the nature of this deliverance" (39-40).

11. Examples of these groupings include 45-48, different kinds of love, most with disastrous consequences; 50-52, good and bad uses of counsel; 63-69, problems associated with idleness and self-indulgence, with repeated stress on hunting; 77-81, good and bad sources of counsel.

12. For a discussion of the internal evidence that the *Othea* was written clearly with an aristocratic audience in mind, see Bornstein, "Chivalry," 47-62.

Scrope's prologue to his Middle English translation (Appendix A of Bühler's edition) indicates the way a fifteenth-century noble audience viewed the *Othea*. In presenting his translation to his stepfather, Sir John Fastolf, Scrope implies that the work can be fully understood only by those who share chivalric experience.

13. This enormous work, composed of more than 72,000 octosyllabic verses, was known to exist by at least 1328. Though its primary base is Ovid's *Metamorphoses*, it incorporates some additional classical and medieval works. Edition used here is edited by de Boer.

14. When Bersuire wrote his first version of his *Reductorium morale* (1337–40), of which the *Ovidius moralizatus* is a part, he did not yet know the *Ovide moralisé*. However in 1342, when he completed his second version, he said he had used it.

15. For Christine's borrowings generally, see Campbell.

16. Compare Christine's statement that "poets hide truth under the cover of fable" (Glose, 29). She makes similar comments about the integumental nature of poetry in the Gloses of fables 1, 3, 4, 5, 8, 22, 60, and 82.

17. His treatment of Apollo is typical. In Bersuire's initial description (55ff.), Apollo becomes in succession the just judge or prelate, the evil prelate who exterminates the poor and innocent, Christ who through purity is ever young, truth, the just man who exterminates all evil in himself, and the evil tyrant who burdens and troubles his innocent subjects. Later, when Apollo appears in the tale of his pursuit of Daphne (136ff.), he comes to signify "those, either in the world or in the cloister, who glory in their virtues," or "those who desire worldly glory," or the devil "who entices the Christian soul [Daphne]," or "Christ the sun of justice."

18. Such a method, though it may seem eccentric to modern readers, conforms well enough to accepted medieval principles for allegorization, outlined, for example, by St. Augustine. Scientific logic was not the mark of successful allegory. As Robertson points out while introducing Augustine's *On Christian Doctrine*, "If the allegorical method fails to produce a single 'correct' interpretation for each passage but leads instead to the perception of a diversity of meanings, some of which may not have been intended by the author, this fact is regarded by St. Augustine not as a shortcoming but as a virtue, provided that all of these meanings are supported in other parts of the Scriptures" (xi).

19. Here Christine incorporates old, epic-feudal notions, where the terms *ami* and *amors* "extended to all members of one's warrior group" (Bloch, 141); see also Burgess, 142.

20. Throughout her career, Christine was personally interested in the illuminations that accompanied her texts. We know, for instance, that she personally supervised production of the illuminations for at least one of her *Othea* manuscripts, the magnificent MS fr. 606 of the Bibliothèque Nationale. On the relationship between text and illuminations in the *Othea*, see especially Hindman; also Ignatius, 127–42, and Meiss.

21. One cannot help but think here of Chaucer's *Troylus and Criseyde*, in which another (pagan) Trojan prince manages to climb to heaven, although

Chaucer intentionally makes more ambiguous what that ascent really signifies. Troylus is, of course, Hector's brother, and both are represented by their respective authors as superlative warriors. Both are also set up as examples of medieval virtue (though, again, in typical Chaucerian fashion, Troylus's virtue raises some larger ethical questions). Both heroes are instructed by women, though the instruction is of a very different nature. Other points of comparison are tantalizing, not the least of which concerns different ways a medieval author can use a pagan figure to make a Christian statement.

22. The story of Caesar Augustus's conversion is popularized in Jacobus de Voragine's *Golden Legend*; see Campbell, 78–79.

23. The Sibyls generally are powerful figures for Christine. In the *Livre de la Cité des Dames*, she remarks that "foremost among the ladies of the sovereign dignity are the wise sibyls, most filled with wisdom," and that the name "sibyl" means "knowing the thinking of God" (Christine, *Book*, 99–100). The Sibyls are the first women to be invited into her idealized city. In her dream vision, the *Chemin de long etude*, it is the Sibyl of Cumae who leads Christine on her quest for a more just and peaceful world.

24. One reason sometimes offered for the choice of Hector is the fact that French monarchy traced its legendary lineage back to the royal house of Troy, but Christine's reasons for selecting Hector go deeper than flattery of royal egos. Another approach to the appropriateness of using the young Hector is that of Loukopoulos, who provides an interesting discussion of the hero's mythic progress according to the paradigm set up by Mircea Eliade for an initiating ritual involving "the primordial social practice of leading the youth into the state of manhood . . . [whereby] the initiate is led away by a mystagogue to be instructed in the myths of his culture, undergo a mock death ritual, be invested with the trappings of manhood, and be shown the sacred symbols of his society's religion" (Loukopoulos, 109–10).

25. Hector's association as one of the Nine Worthies is represented in the illustrations of MS fr. 848 of the Bibliothèque Nationale, considered the earliest extant manuscript of the *Othea*. Here, Othea presents her epistle to Hector before eight crowned, sword-bearing lions. Mombello, *Tradizione*, 24, identifies these as the eight Worthies, Hector being the ninth.

26. See also Holgen; on Hector among the Nine Worthies, see Scherer, 63–65.

27. General discussions of Christine's place in feminist history include those of Davis and Altman. Other discussions of Christine's treatment of women include those of Rigaud, Bornstein, *Ideals*, and Finkel.

28. For a discussion of Christine's treatment of Io, see Reno, 273–74.

29. "Also where it is seide that Pallas scholde by ioyned with Minerve, the which is wele sitting, men schall vnderstande that Pallas and Minerve is all oo thing, but the names be dyuerse and be taken to ij vnderstandinges" (Glose, 14).

30. Christine's feminist attitudes make their most original, pointed, and entertaining appearance in the *Livre de la Cité des Dames*, which, briefly, recounts the construction of a remarkable allegorical edifice from the building blocks of exemplary female lives. This city is then populated with strong, virtuous, and

courageous women. In this work, Christine continues her mythographic innovation in a way particularly suited to her feminist stance.

Christine here takes further the revitalization of mythic figures that she experimented with in the *Othea*, particularly in the figure of Hector. We saw in her early work how she brought the full significance of Hector from the pagan world into her contemporary world by skillfully developing a balance between Hector the young Trojan prince, Hector the youthful medieval aspirant to knighthood, and then the layers of chivalric and spiritual values that he came to represent—this combined with a manipulation of the time frame so that the pagan hero was felt as a living presence within Christian time. In the *Livre de la Cité des Dames*, Christine continues to play off the symbolic associations of her mythic figures against her careful formulations of their biographies in order to make these legendary heroines just as immediately human and recognizable as Christine's contemporary patronesses who live beside them in her allegorical city. In this way, Christine attempts to sort through the layers of mythographic abstraction that have been imposed on these traditional female figures, often ignorantly and unjustly by men, and come to what is essential about them as women and as understood by other women, though always within fairly conservative medieval social, moral, and spiritual standards.

Not only does this city and its inhabitants thus provide an argument against the misogynist views of Christine's day, but it also provides a "compensatory history" (Schulenburg, 35), a figurative refuge for women from the artificial and hypocritical constraints and limitations placed upon them by men in society as a whole. If one of the aims of the *Othea* is to teach a young knight how he can become the Tenth Worthy, then the *Cité* matches the earlier work in teaching women how they can join the catalogue of "Female Worthies" (on Female Worthies, see Keen, 121, 171, and plate 29; also Warner, 205–7).

Works Cited

Altman, Leslie. "Christine de Pisan: First Professional Woman of Letters." In *Female Scholars: A Tradition of Learned Women Before 1800*, edited by J. R. Brink, 153–82. New York: New York University Press, 1980.

Augustine. *On Christian Doctrine*. Translated by D. W. Robertson, Jr. Indianapolis: Bobbs-Merrill, 1958.

Bloch, R. Howard. *Medieval French Literature and Law*. Berkeley: University of California Press, 1977.

Bornstein, Diane. "Chivalry as a Social Code." In *Mirrors of Courtesy*, 47–62. Hamden, CT: Archon Books, 1975.

———, ed. *Ideals for Women in the Works of Christine de Pizan*. Detroit, MI: Consortium for Medieval and Early Modern Studies, 1981.

Bühler, Curt, ed. *The Epistle of Othea*. See Christine de Pizan.

Burgess, Glyn S. *Contribution à l'étude du vocabulaire pré-courtois*. Geneva: Droz, 1970.

Campbell, P. G. C. *"L'Epître Othea": Etude sur les sources de Christine de Pisan*. Paris: Champion, 1924.

Chance, Jane. "The Origins and Development of Medieval Mythography: From Homer to

Dante." In *Mapping the Cosmos*, edited by Jane Chance and R. O. Wells, 35–64, 151–59. Houston, TX: Rice University Press, 1985.

Christine de Pizan. *The Book of the City of Ladies*. Translated by Earl J. Richards. New York: Persea, 1982.

———. *The Epistle of Othea*. Translated into Middle English by Stephen Scrope. Edited by Curt F. Bühler. Early English Text Society. London, New York, Toronto: Oxford University Press, 1970.

Curnow, Maureen Cheney. " 'Le Livre de la Cite des Dames' de Christine de Pisan: A Critical Edition." Ph.D. diss., Vanderbilt University, 1975.

Davis, Natalie Z. "Gender and Genre: Women as Historical Writers, 1400–1820." In *Beyond Their Sex: Learned Women of the European Past*, edited by Patricia H. Labalme, 153–82. New York: New York University Press, 1980.

de Boer, C. See *Ovide moralisé*.

Eliade, Mircea. *Birth and Rebirth*. Translated by W. Trask. New York: Harper, 1958.

Finkel, Helen R. "The Portrait of Woman in the Works of Christine de Pisan." *Les Bonne Feuilles* 3 (1974): 138–51.

Hindman, Sandra L. *Christine de Pizan's "Epistre Othéa": Painting and Politics at the Court of Charles VI*. Toronto: Pontifical Institute of Mediaeval Studies, 1986.

Hölgen, K. J. "Die 'Nine Worthies.' " *Anglia* 77 (1959): 279–309.

Ignatius, Mary Ann. "Christine de Pizan's *Epistre Othea*: An Experiment in Literary Form." *Medievalia et Humanistica* 9 (1979): 127–42.

Keen, Maurice. *Chivalry*. New Haven: Yale University Press, 1984.

Loukopoulos, Halina D. "Classical Mythology in the Work of Christine de Pisan, with an Edition of "L'Epistre Othea" from the Manuscript Harley 4431." Ph.D. diss., Wayne State University, 1977.

McCall, John. *Chaucer among the Gods: The Poetics of Classical Myth*. University Park: Pennsylvania State University Press, 1979.

McCleod, Enid. *The Order of the Rose: The Life and Ideas of Christine de Pizan*. Totowa, NJ: Rowman and Littlefield, 1976.

Meiss, Millard. *French Painting in the Time of Jean de Berry: The Limbourgs and Their Contemporaries*. New York: Braziller, 1974.

Mombello, Gianni. *La Tradizione manoscritta dell' "Epistre Othea" di Christine de Pizan*. Turin: Accademia delle Scienza, 1967.

———. "Quelques aspects de la pensée politique de Christine de Pizan d'après ses oeuvres publiées." In *Culture politique en France à l'époque de l'humanisme et de la Renaissance*, edited by Franco Simone, 43–153. Turin: Accademia delle Scienza, 1974.

Ovide moralisé. Poème du commencement du quatorzième siècle. Edited by C. de Boer et al. *Verhandelingen der Koninklijke Akademie van Wetenschappen te Amsterdam. Afdeeling Letterkunde*. Nieuwe Reeks 15 (1915): 1–374; 21 (1920):1–394; 30 (1931):1–303; 37 (1936):1–478; 43 (1938): 1–429. Reprint in 5 vols. Wiesbaden: Martin Sändig, 1966–68.

Pernoud, Régine. *Christine de Pisan*. Paris: Calmann-Levy, 1982.

Pinet, Marie-Josèphe. *Christine de Pisan: Etude biographique et littéraire*. Paris: Champion, 1927.

Reno, Christine. "Feminist Aspects of Christine de Pizan's 'Epistre d'Othea a Hector.' " *Studi francesi* 71 (1980): 271–76.

Reynolds, William D. "The *Ovidius Moralizatus* of Petrus Berchorius: An Introduction and Translation." Ph.D. diss., University of Illinois, 1971.

Richards, Earl J. "Christine de Pizan and the Question of Feminist Rhetoric." *Teaching Language Through Literature* 22 (1983): 15–24.

Rigaud, Rose. *Les Idées féministes de Christine de Pisan.* Neuchatel: Attinger, 1911.
Scherer, Margaret R. *The Legends of Troy in Art and Literature.* New York: Phaidon, 1964.
Schulenburg, Jane. "Clio's European Daughters: Myopic Modes of Perception." In *The Prism of Sex: Essays in the Sociology of Knowledge*, edited by J. Sherman and E. Beck, 33–53. Madison: University of Wisconsin Press.
Seznec, Jean. *The Survival of the Pagan Gods: The Mythological Tradition and Its Place in Renaissance Humanism and Art.* Translated by Barbara F. Sessions from the 1940 edition. New York: Harper and Row, 1953.
Tuve, Rosemond. *Allegorical Imagery: Some Medieval Books and Their Posterity.* Princeton: Princeton University Press, 1966.
Warner, Marina. *Joan of Arc: the Image of Female Heroism.* New York: Knopf, 1981.
Willard, Charity. *Christine de Pizan: Her Life and Works.* New York: Persea, 1984.
Yenal, Edith. *Christine de Pisan: A Bibliography of Writings by Her and about Her.* Metuchen, NJ: Scarecrow, 1982.

Christine de Pizan and the Judgment of Paris
A Court Poet's Use of Mythographic Tradition

Margaret J. Ehrhart

With her milieu the courtly culture of fifteenth-century France, Christine de Pizan was heir to a particularly rich body of mythographic lore. In the mid-fourteenth century, the anonymous *Ovide moralisé* and Pierre Bersuire's *Ovidius moralizatus*, outgrowths of the long medieval tradition of glossed Ovid manuscripts, had brought together allegorizing and moralizing interpretations of myth for the use of preachers. Drawing on such compilations, poets like Guillaume de Machaut had paved the way for courtly applications of classical myth. The long interpretive history that lay behind the medieval understanding of classical myths made them valuable repositories of meaning for use in the allegorical tradition stemming from the *Roman de la Rose*, a tradition that Machaut applied to his role as court poet. Indebted to both Machaut and the *Ovide moralisé*, Christine, like Machaut, applied her mythographic learning to the needs of a court whose leisure and wealth had developed its taste for classical culture.

This essay will deal with Christine's use of one particular Greek myth, the Judgment of Paris, which traces the Trojan war's origin to the Trojan prince Paris's decision that Venus was more beautiful than Pallas or Juno. The essay will demonstrate how Christine found in her mythographic sources the raw material for successive treatments of the Judgment that reflect her maturing sense of herself as a court poet during one of the most turbulent periods of French history.

Mastering much of the literature available to the later Middle Ages, Christine came to know the Judgment of Paris in a variety of sources.[1] She used the "historical" version of the Judgment, which proposed that Paris only *dreamed* his encounter with the goddesses, in the *Mutacion de Fortune* and in fable 68 of the *Epistre Othea*.[2] But it was the classical version of the story that captured her real interest. Here, the Judgment stems from the wedding of Peleus and Thetis, where a quarrel arose among the three goddesses when each claimed a golden apple destined for the most beautiful.[3] In the Christian Middle Ages, this version of the story was regarded not as history but purely as fable—fable with the potential for a moral or allegorical significance. Christine used this version of the Judgment in an early *balade*, in two chapters of the *Othea*, and in the *Livre du chemin de long estude*.

In the *balade*, an early work, Christine focuses only on the the Judgment's personal relevance. Rejecting Paris's choice of Venus and the life of pleasure that Venus represents, the speaker chooses Pallas and the life of wisdom, a choice very much in line with Christine's own decision early in life to devote herself to study and writing. In the *Othea*, which was written next, the choice represented by the Judgment is offered to Christine's noble audience. Implicit in the *Othea*—reflected even in the physical format of the presentation volumes whose production Christine oversaw—is the notion that Pallas is the worthiest choice. And a second source, not known to Christine when she wrote the *balade*, supplemented Pallas's wisdom with knightliness or *chevalerie*. Thus Christine could offer to Paris, and by extension to her audience, that union of *sapientia* and *fortitudo* most useful to a nobleman in discharging the duties of his station.

Finally, in the *Chemin de long estude*, she continued to probe the significance of the classical Judgment as she had come to understand it from her two sources. The *Chemin* exploits not only Pallas's link with wisdom and knightliness but also Juno's link with nobility and wealth. Flattering her audience, the princes of France, by assuming that they would not be swayed by Venus's gift of pleasure, Christine focuses on which of the four goods represented by these two goddesses is the best. As in the *Othea*, it is Christine's audience, given Paris's role, that must ultimately make the choice. Christine thus seized on the Judgment of Paris as a fable particularly suited to her purpose as court poet. Her successive retellings reflect not only variations in the details provided by her sources but also the role in which she cast herself as advisor to the court.

The *balade* represents Christine's earliest use of the Judgment, and it is based, I shall argue, on Guillaume de Machaut's *Dit de la fonteinne amoureuse*. Not only does the *Fonteinne amoureuse* account for all the details of the Judgment as it appears in the *balade*, but the *balade* is indebted to Machaut's poem for its overall conception. It is, in a sense, Christine's response to the *Fonteinne amoureuse*.

The second stanza and part of the third are devoted to a narrative of the Judgment:

Pallas, Juno, and Venus once wanted to argue their complicated
cause before Paris; each said that in her opinion she was more
beautiful and her great power more perfect in everything than that
of the others; they wanted to abide by [the decision of] Paris, who

judged then that Venus ought to be considered most beautiful and powerful. He said, "Lady, I want you because I have no comfort from Juno."

For the apple of gold, then, Venus came to help him gain Helen; on account of it he was afterwards dead and undone.

The first stanza, the remainder of the third, and the *envoi* place the speaker in Paris's position; like Paris, she chooses among the goddesses:

> If I could become acquainted with Pallas, I would never lack joy and all good because through her I would be on the path of comfort, bearing the load with which Fortune has overburdened me; but I am weak to sustain such a great burden, if she [Pallas] does not come to share part, to aid me through her powerful effort. Would God she might!—because I have no comfort from Juno.
>
> . . . .
>
> So my office is not with her [Venus], but my heart would be revived with joy if the worthy Pallas, by whom injuries are forsaken and every good regained, deigned to keep me for her servant: at last I would no longer have to desire to come to great good because I have no comfort from Juno.
>
> These three powerful goddesses make the world endure, their discord notwithstanding, but may God make me remember Pallas, because I have no comfort from Juno.[4]

An important dimension of the Judgment was the gifts traditionally offered Paris by the goddesses in exchange for the golden apple that was the prize of beauty. Interpretations of the story often focused on the choice among the goddesses as a choice among lives, each goddess representing a way of life associated with her proffered gift.[5] The *balade* clearly draws on this tradition, the choice of Pallas being seen as the choice of a life very different from the life chosen by Paris when he named Venus most beautiful. The *balade* seems to assume that readers would recognize the gifts or lives associated with Pallas and Juno; its point depends on this recognition though it does not name the gifts specifically. Since recognizing which tradition of gifts or lives Christine was drawing on will help identify her source, our first step will be to determine what identities for Pallas and Juno make the *balade* most coherent.

Pallas is most commonly linked with wisdom or military prowess, Juno with riches or royal power (Ehrhart, *Judgment*, s.v. Pallas, Juno). The thrust of the *balade* is that the speaker is in difficulties because she has no comfort from Juno. The early years of Christine's widowhood were shadowed by concerns about money (de Winter, 339–40; Yenal, 7; Hindman, 5–6). These were also the years of her early experiments with lyric forms.[6] Only later did she embark on the longer works that characterize her later output, thus attracting the patrons whose interest in her work would ease her financial difficulties. "I have no comfort from Juno" could easily mean that the speaker lacks money. Thus the *balade* is a complaint to the poet's purse, a complaint that sees no hope of remedy. It makes most sense, especially given its likely period of composition, if we link Juno with riches.

As far as Pallas is concerned, the *balade* regards that goddess as an antidote to the assaults of Fortune: lack of money, probably—and even Christine's loss of her husband. Christine had read the *Consolation of Philosophy* (McLeod, 79), and her view of Pallas in the *balade* recalls the role of Lady Philosophy in Boethius. As an antidote to Fortune, then, Pallas would most appropriately be associated with the gift of wisdom.

Thus, in looking for a source, we look for versions of the Judgment in which Pallas offers wisdom and Juno riches. The two redactions of the *Histoire ancienne*, which contain versions of the "historical" Judgment and are known to have been among Christine's sources for other works, are easily disqualified as sources for the *balade* for a number of reasons—most obviously because in neither redaction of the *Histoire* does Juno offer riches.[7] We are left, then, with the narratives of the classical Judgment in two sources that Christine is known to have used elsewhere: the *Ovide moralisé* (11.1242–2533) and Machaut's *Fonteinne amoureuse* (*Oeuvres* 3, vv. 1633–2144). Both have been acknowledged as sources for the Judgment in the *Othea*, Christine's first major work and thus near in time to the period of her lyric poetry (Campbell, 96–100).

The versions of the Judgment in these two works are quite similar because Machaut used the *Ovide moralisé* as his source for the Judgment in the *Fonteinne amoureuse* (Thomas, de Boer). In both works, the apple that provokes the goddesses' argument is gold, and each goddess claims to be not only most beautiful but also most powerful. These details are echoed in the *balade*. But the two versions of the Judgment differ in certain respects (Campbell, 99–100), and in each area of difference, Christine follows Machaut.

First there is the matter of the goddesses' gifts. In the *Ovide moralisé*, Pallas is linked with both strength and wisdom (11.1987–88), and Juno with both power and riches (11.1853–56). In Machaut's version of the Judgment, Pallas offers to make Paris the wisest of men ("plus sage" [v. 2061]); she points out that she holds in her sway all workers and also the seven liberal arts, as well as alchemy (vv. 2069–86). Juno offers him all the wealth that he could imagine; she is goddess of riches (vv. 2087-95). Thus, the *Ovide moralisé* includes wisdom and riches, but it includes other gifts as well, while Machaut's version of the Judgment includes wisdom and riches alone. Of course, Christine could have based her *balade* on two gifts even if she knew four, but the point of the *balade* depends so clearly on the recognition that Pallas is wisdom and Juno riches that it seems reasonable to assume she wrote it with Machaut's Judgment in mind. Moreover, other differences between the *Ovide moralisé* and Machaut point to Machaut rather than the *Ovide moralisé* as Christine's specific source.

The *Fonteinne amoureuse* differs from the *Ovide moralisé* in the order in which the goddesses speak. In the *Ovide moralisé*, sometimes Juno speaks first, sometimes Pallas. But for Machaut, the hierarchy is always Pallas, then Juno, then Venus. The *balade* follows the latter order. Moreover, the *Fonteinne amoureuse* differs from the *Ovide moralisé* in the point at which Paris learns of his royal ancestry. In the classical version of the story, he is living as a shepherd when the goddesses are brought to him because before his birth his mother dreamed he would cause the destruction of Troy. His father ordered the infant killed but his mother instead had him raised in obscurity. In the *Ovide moralisé*, he learns at the very conclusion of the goddesses' arguments that he is a prince (11.2082); in the *Fonteinne amoureuse*, on the other hand, his ancestry is revealed before the goddesses offer their gifts (vv. 1899-1910). He thus rejects the riches promised by Juno because he believes that henceforth his needs will always be taken care of (vv. 2127-29). This detail finds its echo in the *balade*, where Paris chooses Venus's gift on the grounds that he has no comfort from Juno; in other words, her gift of riches seems unnecessary to him.

The evidence suggests, then, that Christine used the *Fonteinne amoureuse* when she wrote this *balade*. I would like to argue further that not only did she take her version of the Judgment from the *Fonteinne amoureuse*, but that the entire conception of the *balade* owes to her reading of Machaut's narrative. The *balade* is her version of the *Fonteinne amoureuse*, a lyric rehandling of the Judgment theme. Just as Machaut's *Dit de la fonteinne amoureuse* defines—ironically—the métier of a prince, Christine's *balade* defines the métier of a poet-clerk, implicitly contrasting the pursuit of romantic love with the pursuit of wisdom.

In the *Fonteinne amoureuse*, Machaut uses the Judgment in the context of a fictionalized visit to the court of a lovelorn prince. Overhearing the prince's poetic complaint about his unrequited love, Machaut's narrator, a poet-clerk like himself, transcribes the complaint and presents it to his host. Then the two dream that Venus appears. She narrates the

Judgment of Paris and presents the prince with the woman for whom he is longing. The dream occurs beside a fountain whose water enamors those who drink it; the fountain is situated in a garden, and it is decorated with scenes from the story of Troy, including Paris's rape of Helen (vv. 1317-18). The *Fonteinne amoureuse* thus criticizes nobles who devote themselves to romantic love. The lovelorn nobleman resembles Paris. Each is a prince; each chooses a life of love and then receives his beloved from Venus. Because Paris won Helen, his kingdom was destroyed; similarly, the lovelorn prince's realm has fallen into decline, as a long, frequently overlooked passage makes clear (vv. 1161-1204; Ehrhart, "Machaut's *Dit*," 130-31).

The speaker in Christine's *balade* and the nobleman in the *Fonteinne amoureuse* are opposites with respect to sex, wealth, and power. One is a woman, poor and dependent; the other a man, rich and independent. Their positions are opposite as well. One is a poet: her estate is that of clerk; the other is a prince: his estate is that of knight. When the poet composes a complaint to her purse, the lyric's genre and its mode of composition signal her poverty, dependence, *clergie*. When the prince composes a complaint to his beloved, the lyric's genre and its mode of composition signal his wealth, independence, *chevalerie*. Machaut's nobleman is a patron of poets; his complaint is transcribed by Machaut's poet narrator. The prince's wealth and power enable him to conscript clerks to the service of love, the métier of the nobility in the scheme that the *Fonteinne amoureuse* ironically sets forth. Machaut's Paris declares that in choosing Venus's bribe of the beautiful Helen, he is choosing the estate of *chevalerie*, appropriate to his newfound identity as a prince (vv. 2132-34). Like Paris, Machaut's prince sees his time most fittingly devoted to love.[8]

For each figure, poet and prince, circumstance has narrowed Paris's threeway choice to two options. Like Paris, who declares that as a king's son he will always have enough, Machaut's nobleman is already rich: the court scene that leads up to the poem's central episode, the dream, makes that clear. Christine's speaker, on the other hand, is poor—hopelessly poor—and she sees no chance that Juno will favor her. Thus for each the remaining choices are wisdom or sexual pleasure. These are the métiers of *clergie* and *chevalerie*, and they are suited to poet and prince, respectively.

Though the compartmentalization implied by the three estates of knight, clerk, and laborer no longer reflected social reality, the estates lived on as an idea. Christine would later encourage the nobility to embrace wisdom; she would try to bridge the gulf between clerk's realm and knight's, *clergie* and *chevalerie*, radically annexing the clerk's wisdom to the power of the knight's estate. That was not to come yet, however. As a response to the *Fonteinne amoureuse*, the *balade* simply reflects what was—or at least what was thought to be. In the *Fonteinne amoureuse*, Machaut had depicted a nobleman who, like Paris, chose love; in the *balade* Christine depicts a clerk who chooses wisdom. That the clerk is a woman simply dramatizes the seemingly unbridgeable gulf between the two realms (and see Cerquiglini, "*Un engin*," 143–51).

The *balade*'s refrain, "Because I have no comfort from Juno," deepens in significance with each repetition, leaving the speaker content with her state and her choice. The first stanza posits a cause and effect relationship between the need for aid from Pallas and the lack of comfort from Juno. The second stanza places the refrain in the mouth of Paris; Juno's comfort does not satisfy him: he wants more, the pleasure that possessing the beautiful Helen will bring. The *balade*'s speaker, meanwhile, is moving in the opposite direction; she profits by the lesson of Paris. She knows that Paris chose Venus most beautiful and won Helen of Sparta, and that he died in the war which the Greeks waged in retaliation ("he was afterwards dead and undone" [vv. 22–23]). Thus she rejects the life of pleasure, recognizing that true joy lies with Pallas. In the third stanza, then, the meaning of the refrain differs subtly from its meaning in the first. At first, the speaker simply acknowledged her lack of comfort from Juno; now she recognizes that Juno *cannot* truly comfort. The fourth repetition of the refrain, in the *envoi*, exploits the ambiguity the words have acquired over the course of the poem. The speaker indeed lacks comfort from Juno, but she also recognizes that such comfort is not genuine or lasting.

Christine's reading of the Judgment in the *balade* is highly personal; she is interested in wisdom for her own benefit. Like Lady Philosophy in the *Consolation*, Pallas can help in regarding the reversals of fortune *sub specie aeternitatis*. Yet for Christine, wisdom was to have practical application too. Paradoxically, her learning was to attract the patronage of great nobles and the financial rewards that would bring her economic independence. In the *Fonteinne amoureuse*, Pallas had claimed to hold in her sway grammar, logic, geometry, arithmetic, music, rhetoric, and astronomy—the seven liberal arts (vv. 2073–81). The study of the seven liberal arts can lead to the wisdom that is an end in itself. But devotion to letters can also shape a career and secure a livelihood. When Christine's speaker in the *balade* requested Pallas's aid, Pallas answered her prayer with that learning on which Christine built her reputation as advisor to the court.

CHRISTINE used the Judgment again in her first long work, the *Epistre Othea* (ca. 1400). By the time she wrote the *Othea*, she had secured the interest of Louis of Orleans in her work, and she had come to see her writing as a means by which the wisdom of the past could aid the present. Thus, in devising the *Othea* as a handbook to shape the conduct of princes, and in dedicating it to Louis, the attractive and gifted brother of King Charles VI,[9] Christine embraced a mission that was to remain her guiding force. She would use the fruits of her reading to advise the powerful French princes and, later, their brother King Charles VI.

Christine lived in a turbulent era. By 1400 it had been clear for some years that Charles's spells of madness made him unfit to rule. The man to whom she dedicated the *Othea* was a leading contender for the power that Charles could not wield. Intrigues among Louis, the dukes of Berry and Burgundy, and the queen, Isabeau of Bavaria, were to culminate in Louis's murder by the duke of Burgundy in 1407. In the midst of hostilities with England, too, France could scarcely afford to have its sense of purpose weakened by internal dissension (Coville, 372–82; Hindman, 8–12). Christine's use of the Judgment in the *Othea* reflects first of all her perception that the Judgment echoes precisely the thrust of the *Othea* as a whole. As Paris was offered the chance to choose Pallas and the life she represented, Christine's noble audience is offered the chance to heed the words of the goddess Othea and to embrace the life laid out for them in Othea's lessons. Moreover, while her use of the Judgment continues to depend heavily on Machaut's *Fonteinne amoureuse*, Christine supplements the goddesses' promises with material derived from an additional source, the *Ovide moralisé*, where Pallas offers knightliness as well as wisdom, and Juno royal power as well as riches. Pallas's additional gift of knightliness, in particular, makes that goddess's offerings suited precisely to the role Christine sees for the French nobles, and for herself in the person of Othea, the voice of wisdom that can guide the ship of state through tumultuous seas.

The *Epistre Othea* is a "letter" from the goddess Othea to the young Trojan prince Hector. Othea is Christine's creation; the origin of the name remains a mystery, but the goddess is explicitly linked in fable 1 with prudence and wisdom (*Epistle*, ed. Bühler, 129, note to 6/18; Hindman, 23). Hector was regarded as a model of knightliness (Hindman, 34); moreover, the French nobles traced their heritage to dispersed Trojans who, like Rome's founder Aeneas, escaped Troy when the Greeks destroyed their city (Klippel; Heisig). Francio, the eponymous founder of France, was Hector's son, as Christine was to point out in the *Chemin de long estude* (vv. 3565–3622; Hindman, 35). Her dedication salutes Louis as coming of Trojan stock (Campbell, 34; Hindman, 37;

Meiss, 23). Thus her audience would appreciate her selecting Hector as the recipient of Othea's wisdom; in dedicating the *Othea* to Louis, she recognizes him as a modern-day Hector, even, like Hector, next in line to the throne (Hindman, 36–37). Implicitly, then, Christine is Louis's Othea, and the wisdom that Othea offers Hector will flow as well from her to her patron and the brilliant young nobles that surround him (Hindman, 34; de Winter, 371).

In form, the work is a collection of one hundred mythological stories. Some derive from the Trojan saga; others are Ovidian. The stories' arrangement, however, is based not on that of the cycles from which they are drawn but rather on their exemplary significance. Each story has its own chapter, and each chapter begins with a "texte"—a piece of advice for Hector, and thus, for Christine's audience. The overall arrangement of the hundred chapters, or fables, is determined by the relationships among the *textes*. Each of the first seven recommends one of the seven virtues; each of the next seven warns against one of the seven vices, and so on, through the twelve articles of the Creed, the ten commandments, and a miscellaneous assortment of virtues and vices. This organization of the chapters according to virtues, vices, and the rest is indebted to the tradition of the medieval *summa*, like Frère Lorens's *Somme le roi*.[10] As Rosemond Tuve puts it, the *Othea* is "an ingenious little classical *Somme le roi* with adornments" (286).

Within each chapter, the *texte* is glossed by a *glose*, which narrates the mythological story to which the *texte* alludes and then applies the chapter's lesson to action on the earthly plane. The *glose* is followed by an *allegorie*, which applies the same lesson to the spiritual plane. As Tuve has pointed out, the *Othea* shares with such works as the *Somme le roi* "an emphasis upon the 'two chivalries' " (Tuve, 39); in that it is aimed specifically at those who rule, it is in a sense also a courtesy book, a mirror for princes. Each chapter conduces to earthly chivalry, strengthening the reader in virtue, or more practically, I would add, fitting him for his role vis-à-vis the realm dependent on his political savoir faire. But each chapter also conduces to spiritual chivalry, forming the reader in the imitation of the *chevalier* Jesus Christ (Tuve, 44). The fiction implicit in the work is that in each chapter the *texte* represents Othea's words to Hector while the *glose* and *allegorie* represent commentary and interpretation added by others. When Christine created the *Othea*, then, she created a work whose text-cum-commentary format imitated the format that other books read in the Middle Ages had acquired only through the passage of time and through the contributions of many minds and hands.

Fable 60 introduces the Judgment of Paris by describing the origin of the goddesses' quarrel over their beauty and the selection of Paris as judge. The *texte* reads:

> Flee the goddess of discord;
> evil are her bonds and her cord.
> She disturbed the wedding of Peleus.
> Many people were gathered there then.[11]

The *glose* explains that when Discord was excluded from the wedding of Peleus and Thetis, she came without invitation. She brought a golden apple inscribed "Let it be given to the most beautiful," and cast it before Pallas, Juno, and Venus, who were seated together at a table. Each goddess claimed the apple, and Jupiter refused to settle the quarrel, sending them to Paris of Troy, who was living as a shepherd. The *glose* goes on to explain that Paris had been cast out of the royal household when his mother dreamed before his birth that he would cause the destruction of Troy. Mercury revealed to him his true identity when he brought the three goddesses to be judged.

The *glose* advises the good knight to avoid discord, and the *allegorie* picks up with advice based on the spiritual sense of the fable: the good spirit should flee all impediments of conscience and avoid contention and disputes.

Fable 73 continues the story of the Judgment with this *texte*:

> Do not judge as Paris judged
> because one receives many hard desserts;
> many have reaped evil
> by handing down a bad decision.[12]

The glose continues thus:

> The fable says that the three goddesses of great power—that is, Pallas, goddess of knowledge, Juno, goddess of wealth, and Venus, goddess of love, came before Paris holding a golden apple which said: Let it be given to the most beautiful and most powerful. There was great discord concerning that apple because each said that she ought to have it, and they were brought to Paris concerning this discord. Paris wanted to be diligent in determining each one's power for himself. Then Pallas said, "I am goddess of *chevalerie* [knightliness] and of wisdom and by me arms are distributed to knights and knowledge to clerks, and if you want to give me the apple, know that I will make you more knightly than all and [you will] surpass all others in all knowledge." Afterwards, Juno, goddess of wealth and of rule, said, "By me are distributed the great treasures of the world. And if you want to give me the apple, I will

make you more rich and powerful than any other." Afterwards, Venus spoke with extremely amorous words and said, "I am she who conducts the schools of love and of pleasure and who makes fools wise and makes the wise fools, who makes the rich beg, and makes exiles grow rich, nor is there power which compares to mine, and if you want to give me the apple, the love of the beautiful Helen of Greece will be given you through me—which will be worth more to you than any other possession." And then Paris gave his decision and renounced *chevalerie* and wisdom and wealth for Venus, to whom he gave the apple for which reason was Troy then destroyed. So it is to be understood [that] because Paris was not at all *chevalereux* and great knowledge did not matter to him, but all his thoughts were on love—it is understood that he gave the golden apple to Venus.[13]

The *glose* advises that "the good knight . . . ought not to do likewise," while the *allegorie* adds that the good spirit should entirely avoid judging others.

It is understandable that, in broadening her scope from the personal to the political, Christine continued to admire Machaut's work, as reflected in the close link between the Judgment in the *Othea* and in the *Fonteinne amoureuse* (Campbell, 100). Machaut had been associated with the court of Charles VI's father, Charles V, whom Christine regarded as the very exemplar of kingship. In her effort to encourage her own generation to emulate the wisdom and virtue of the past, she may have considered the literature of that previous generation a valuable model (Poirion, 195, 616). Determining to use the Judgment again in the *Othea*, she may have seen in Machaut's handling of the story a version still congenial to her tastes and aims, even though the *Ovide moralisé* provided her with the additional gifts for the goddesses, which, particularly in the case of Pallas, were useful in bringing the Judgment into line with the overall thrust of the *Othea*.

Though Machaut's version of the Judgment comes from the *Ovide moralisé*—at times he follows his source nearly word for word—he recasts the episode to reflect more accurately the milieu in which it is set— Jupiter's court on Mount Olympus—and to make it serve more readily as an exemplum for his noble audience. His alterations are significant in light of his own role as a court poet and in light of Christine's continued reliance on his version of the Judgment.

As we have seen, among the differences between Machaut's Judgment and that in the *Ovide moralisé* is the order in which the goddesses are mentioned. Though the *Ovide moralisé* mentions the goddesses now in one order, now in another, Machaut always follows the same order: Pallas, Juno, Venus. A longstanding tradition, stemming from Fulgentius, ranked the goddesses in an order based on the values of the lives they represent: contemplative (Pallas), active (Juno), voluptuous (Venus) (*Mythologies*, 2.1). Machaut, I would suggest, respects this hierarchy, as courtly protocol recognizes hierarchies based on rank. Moreover, Machaut's sense of courtly ceremony makes him alter the scene in which the golden apple is thrown among the Olympians. The *Ovide moralisé* envisions the wedding guests in a milling mass; all scramble for Discord's apple. Machaut, on the other hand, imagines the goddesses seated at a table of their own, where Discord finds them and casts the apple among them.[14]

We have seen too that a second difference between Machaut and his source is the point in the narrative at which Paris learns his true identity: near the end of his interview with the goddesses in the *Ovide moralisé*, but at the very beginning of the judgment scene in the *Fonteinne amoureuse*. Because the stories in the *Ovide moralisé* were aimed at preachers who would use them to enliven the sermons preached to popular audiences, the author of the *Ovide moralisé* might have wanted to keep Paris a shepherd for as long as possible. But if Paris is revealed as a prince at the beginning of the episode in which he must choose among the goddesses, he resembles much more the nobleman whose own choice of love Machaut makes Paris's story gloss, not to mention the members of Machaut's noble audience. Thus Paris's royal pedigree must be established before the episode begins.

Though Machaut's Judgment, then, offered a more courtly treatment of the story, one that appealed to Christine because of her analogous audience and her familiarity with a similar milieu, she preferred the *Ovide moralisé*'s expanded version of the goddesses' promises. Machaut, it will be recalled, had made Juno offer riches and Pallas wisdom. We saw that these two gifts inspired Christine to produce a *balade* in which the speaker lacked comfort from Juno and thus requested Pallas's aid. In the *Ovide moralisé*, however, Pallas tells Paris, "I will make you wise and strong [*sage et fort*], full of wisdom and power [*sapience et effort*]" (vv. 1987-88), and Juno, though she offers only riches (vv. 1901-3), identifies herself as powerful and noble, as well as rich (v. 1519). From the *Ovide moralisé*, Christine took, most importantly, Pallas's double identity, her link with strength—might in war—in addition to wisdom. She also took Juno's association with royal power as well as riches.

In the *Othea*, Pallas identifies herself as "goddess of *chevalerie* and wisdom"; she distributes arms to knights and knowledge to clerks. Her bribe to Paris is that he will become both more knightly and wiser than all others. Juno similarly identifies herself as goddess of wealth and of rule; she will make Paris richer and more powerful than all others. But Christine is more interested in Pallas's expanded identity than Juno's; this selective attention is demonstrated as the *glose* to fable 73 proceeds. In two subsequent references to the goddesses' bribes, Juno's two offerings are first abbreviated to one, and then omitted entirely, while Pallas's remain intact: "Paris . . . renounced *chevalerie* and wisdom and wealth for Venus. . . . So it is to be understood [that] because Paris was not at all *chevalereux*, and great knowledge did not matter to him . . . he gave the golden apple to Venus."

In the *Fonteinne amoureuse*, Machaut had demonstrated, with considerable irony, that some nobles regard the pursuit of love as their métier, equating the estate of *chevalerie* with the life of love. When Machaut's Paris declared himself for Venus, he explained that he had just learned he was a prince; thus he now saw his métier as love. Moreover, Machaut's Pallas offered only wisdom, traditionally the province of clerks. Paris shrugged off the possibility that Pallas's wisdom might be useful to a prince, explaining that if he needed advice he advised himself.

When Christine uses the word *chevalerie* to identify Pallas's additional gift, the gift that the *Ovide moralisé* had called *force*, she intends to redefine the goddess's gift. The *Ovide moralisé* had drawn on a long tradition when it made Pallas offer *force*. Victory or might in war was Pallas's earliest gift, going back to ancient Greek versions of the Judgment.[15] Louis of Orleans and the other nobles in the *Othea*'s audience are knights by virtue of their estate, and the knightly class is the warrior class, defenders of the realm. But the interests of one's realm are not always best served by military force. In France of the early fifteenth century, some threats came from within, in the power struggles among Louis and the dukes of Berry and Burgundy and in the king's own wavering sanity. Christine envisions a perfection of knightly qualities that will enable the French nobility to carry out most effectively the duties required by their station. Throughout the *Othea*, each chapter's lesson is aimed at forming the knight on both an earthly and spiritual plane. The *glose* offers lessons in noble conduct; fable 60, for instance, advises that the good knight avoid discord. The *allegorie* offers lessons in spiritual knightliness, the imitation of the *chevalier* Jesus Christ; in fable 60, again, the *allegorie* cautions against disruption of one's spiritual peace.[16]

Not only does Pallas offer a *chevalerie* that corresponds to Christine's ideal for the French nobles, but she continues to offer her traditional wisdom. In the *Fonteinne amoureuse*, Paris foolishly boasted that when he needed advice, he advised himself; thus he rejected Pallas's gift. By creating the figure of Othea, Christine made explicit her wish that Louis and the other nobles heed the voice of wisdom, the wisdom—derived from books—that could guide France's troubled government. Moreover, whereas the wisdom that Pallas offered in the *Fonteinne amoureuse* was, as we saw, a wisdom whose practical application was signalled by Pallas's patronage of the liberal arts, the wisdom with which she is associated in the *Ovide moralisé* is different. It is clearly wisdom as an end in itself, with a profound spiritual dimension. It is the wisdom that leads one to the recognition that the highest human goal on earth is to serve God. Pallas states in the *Ovide moralisé*, "I have placed my heart in the fear and service of God, because he is without doubt the source of all wisdom" (11.1934-36). To her come those who want to live blamelessly in the world (11.1979-80). With her offer of both *chevalerie* and wisdom in the *Othea*, then, Pallas offers Paris exactly the combination of qualities that Christine wishes for her own audience.[17] The spiritual dimension of the wisdom she envisions is implied by each chapter's *allegorie*, which applies the *texte* to the good knight seen in relation to his creator. Because uniting wisdom and *chevalerie* in her noble audience is Christine's aim for the *Othea* as a whole, she stresses particularly Paris's great loss in refusing these gifts.

Implicit within the *Othea* as Christine designed it, however, is the assumption that Louis and his nobles would have heeded Pallas's gift. The very format of the work offers what Patrick de Winter has called in a related context "discret hommage" (338); it assumes the union in the *Othea*'s audience of knightliness and wisdom, of *chevalerie* and *clergie*. Physically, the splendid book of the *Othea* reflects the noble splendor of Louis and the court. Christine was closely involved in producing the manuscripts in which she presented her works to her patrons (Ouy and Reno). They were sumptuous even by the standards of a sumptuous age. The one hundred and one miniatures—a frontispiece and one miniature to each chapter—that characterize most of the many surviving manuscripts of the *Othea* became a feature of the book very early. So remarkable were the illustrations Christine commissioned that artists she employed are identified by art historians in terms of works they illuminated for her: the Epistre Master, the Cité des Dames Master (Meiss, 9-10, 23-41). An early manuscript, B.N. fr. 848, copied by Christine herself (Ouy and Reno, 227), and possibly the manuscript in which the *Othea* was first offered to Louis, includes only four miniatures (containing six pictures in all), but its simplicity probably reflects only Christine's lack of capital at this stage in her career.[18] There is certainly no question that the *Othea*'s embodiment as a book reflects the splendid estate of Christine's noble audience.

But Christine also attributed to Louis and the other members of his court the clerkly dimension that the *Othea* was intended to foster. Read aloud or performed aloud, literature of all kinds had long required and won noble patronage, but books as objects were the province of clerks. The audience Christine envisions, however, is one that encounters a text privately and individually. Her view of her audience as an audience of readers is signalled by the golden apple episode as she retells it in the *Othea*. Her version contrasts distinctively with both her sources.

In the *Ovide moralisé*, Discord throws the apple among all the Olympians and all at first desire it. Only when Mercury, the god of eloquence, reads its message aloud do the Olympians realize that the apple is intended for the most beautiful (11.1473–1500). Like Mercury, the preachers for whom the *Ovide moralisé* was written interpreted the Word for those who could not read it for themselves. Partly because of his association with eloquence, Mercury himself was often depicted as a preacher (Ehrhart, *Judgment*, 106, 259n.97). In Machaut's *Fonteinne amoureuse*, even though the writing on the golden apple identifies it as a prize for the most beautiful, Discord shouts aloud as she throws it: "Let it be given to the most beautiful!" (vv. 1731–38) Many in Machaut's audience must have read for themselves. When his clerkly narrator in the *Fonteinne amoureuse* transcribes the nobleman's *complainte*, the nobleman reads it through as soon as he receives it (vv. 1519–24). Yet Machaut wrote his works to be read aloud, as his reference to the members of his audience as "ladies and he who reads" testifies (v. 19). Discord's procedure with the apple echoes Machaut's own procedure as a poet: a text is written to be read aloud. In the *Othea*, however, Discord silently casts the golden apple among the goddesses and each reads its message for herself.

Intended for an audience of readers, then, the *Othea* is not designed to be read aloud; its pages demand scrutiny. Christine's expectation that her readers will engage individually with her text is signaled most obviously by the close relationship between that text and the art that—perhaps literally—illuminates it. B.N. fr. 848, the earliest extant copy of the *Othea*, and the one possibly produced for Louis, has only six pictures, but the relationship between text and miniature is in certain ways more subtle and sophisticated than in the later cycles with a miniature for each fable. The pictures, according to Mary Ann Ignatius, "attempt to illustrate *simultaneously* the textual and allegorical significance" of the mythological material (135). In other words, the miniatures too offer an interpretation of the *texte*, parallel with *glose* and *allegorie*. Of course, the later manuscripts, with their much-expanded miniature cycle, likewise make the pages of the *Othea* visually engaging.

The arrangement of the text on the page in B.N. fr. 848 suggests too that Christine initially conceived the *Othea* as a text to be apprehended visually rather than aurally. In B.N. fr. 848, the *texte* appears in the middle of the page with *glose* and *allegorie* at either side (Ignatius, 133). Such a format, as Ignatius points out, "clearly guides us away from . . . a linear reading" (133). It invites individual study and contemplation even as it frustrates oral presentation. Read aloud, the effect that *glose* or *allegorie* can at any moment equally qualify the *texte* is lost. Here again the book of the *Othea* demands individual engagement.

The *texte, glose, allegorie* format of the *Othea*, however, implies more about the work's recipient than that he is simply a reader. It implies that his interests and skills are those of a clerk, that he has already annexed *sapientia* to his *fortitudo, clergie* to his *chevalerie*. When she designed the *Othea*'s format, Christine created a text that resembled the glossed texts through which the great works of the ancients were known in the Middle Ages, works usually in Latin and thus accessible to clerks alone.[19] The *Othea* is a vernacular imitation of such texts. Christine imitates the glossed texts of the ancients as she wishes the *chevaliers* of the French court to imitate the clerks who study those texts. Wisdom resides there, not only the wisdom that is an end in itself but the wisdom that can direct the ship of state.

Finally, there is another way too in which the *texte* and commentary format of the *Othea* represents a "discret hommage." Each chapter's *texte* simply alludes to a classical story. The omnipresent commentaries associated with the classics in the Middle Ages were necessitated partly by the allusive style of classical literature. Virgil wrote for an audience schooled in the Greek learning that forms a backdrop to the *Aeneid*. For a late-classical or medieval reader allusions needed to be explained—thus, for example, the popularity of Servius's commentary on the *Aeneid*.[20] But the learned reader eventually dispenses with commentaries, and recognizes with a rush of pleasure that he knows a story to which an allusion alludes. I would suggest that Christine designed the allusive *textes* of the *Othea* in imitation of classical style, and to allow her patron that same rush of pleasure that comes with recognizing, for example, who Paris is, and why one should not judge as he did, before glancing at the *glose* for the whole story.

Christine's desire to redefine *chevalerie* as a knightliness compatible with wisdom made her seize gladly on the *Ovide moralisé*'s Judgment, with Pallas offering not only wisdom but also strength, as a complement to the version of the story that she already knew from Machaut. Equally revealing of her relationship with her audience, however, is what Christine did not take from the *Ovide moralisé*—a further reflection of her relation with the court. In the *Ovide moralisé*, the narrative of the Judgment is followed by an allegorization and then a moral. The moral is applied directly to the lives of those who will hear the sermons into which the episode is incorporated. In the allegory, the three goddesses are taken to represent the three lives, active (Juno), contemplative (Pallas), and voluptuous (Venus)—an ethical interpretation that reached the Middle Ages through Fulgentius (*Mythologies*, 2.1). God gives humans free will to choose among the three lives, but humans make the wrong choice: "Man judged the contest badly: through empty pleasure, which delighted him, he took the bad, refused the good" (11.2504–6). Now, the *Ovide moralisé* goes on, in its moral application, all want to live "voluptuously." They think of nothing but gluttony and lust—and thus have come great harm and grief. Ribald scoundrels are everywhere; they betray chastity, pursuing the pleasure of lust even when Nature does not drive them on. Those most abandoned to lust and pleasure are most respected. This is what the world has come to! But the Last Judgment is at hand (11.2508–2533).

The author of the *Ovide moralisé* intended to draw from the fables of the ancients both truth and morality.[21] Christine likewise viewed myth as a beautiful covering for the truth. Both the *Ovide moralisé* and the *Othea* incorporate the Judgment into mythographical compendia whose declared purpose is to demonstrate the wisdom that lies beneath the surface of pagan stories. Yet the *Ovide moralisé* is directed at an audience of preachers who will employ the stories and their interpretations in sermons. As a poet, Christine has more in common with Guillaume de Machaut, whose *Fonteinne amoureuse*, like the *Othea*, is directed at a noble audience on whom its author depends for patronage. The *Othea* then shares its declared purpose with one of its sources for the Judgment, but it shares with the other its audience.

Louis of Orleans had a serious side to his character that led him to encourage Christine's writing; subsequent copies of the *Othea* retain the dedication to him that marks his close association with the work. But Louis, who would have been only twenty-seven or twenty-eight when Christine produced the *Othea*, had another dimension as well. His personality has been strikingly delineated by Daniel Poirion, who cites a document of 1398 in which Louis is charged with frequenting the company of harlots (35); in another he is accused of excessive devotion to his own pleasure (Poirion, 32). According to the fifteenth-century historian, Thomas Basin, Louis "whinneyed like a stallion after nearly every attractive woman" (1:13; cited in Poirion, 129), and his son, Charles of Orleans, said of him that he was "well known to the god of love" (Poirion, 275). His reputation as a gallant even extends to the claim that by 1405 he was engaged in an adulterous relationship with Isabeau of Bavaria, his brother's queen (Poirion, 35n.47; Mirot, part 1, 335-37; cf. Nordberg, 189-90) and it has been suggested that his assassination was motivated not by politics but by a liaison with the duke of Burgundy's wife (Basin, 1:13; cited in Poirion, 129). The atmosphere at the court of Charles VI has generally been cited for its moral laxity (Coville, 375, 378, 381).

When Machaut rehandled the *Ovide moralisé*'s Judgment, he not only reshaped the story from a courtly perspective, but he also suppressed the allegory and the moral interpretation. The *Ovide moralisé* sees Paris's choice of Venus as the choice of the voluptuous life, and it excoriates those who pursue such an existence, invoking the threat of the Last Judgment. But Machaut could scarcely seem to recognize and condemn lasciviousness in the lives of those among whom he found his patrons. As Kevin Brownlee sees it, in fact, the *Fonteinne amoureuse* "demoralizes" the Judgment (202). Not wishing to go this far, I have suggested that the Judgment's moral relevance lies implicit within the *Fonteinne amoureuse* (Ehrhart, "Machaut's *Dit*," 130-31). Unlike Machaut's scheme in the *Fonteinne amoureuse*, a dream-vision format that allows him to invite allegorical interpretation without providing an explicit moral, Christine's design for the *Othea* requires that she apply the Judgment explicitly to the lives of Louis and the other nobles who will read her work. But what moral can she draw from the episode?

As we have seen, Christine criticizes Paris primarily for what he renounces—*chevalerie* and wisdom—rather than for what he chooses—"love," as she calls it, in contrast to the *Ovide moralisé*'s "lust." Then Christine advises, "the good knight . . . ought not to do likewise." The *allegorie* applies the lesson to the spiritual plane: Augustine is brought forth to witness that one should avoid judging others because one does not know with what intentions they act and because one cannot know whether they will ultimately prove to be good or bad. Paris *judged*—he exalted one to the detriment of the others. Here we seem to be considering not *whom* Paris should have chosen but *whether* he should have chosen at all. On the earthly plane, the good knight must judge and he should be careful to do so well and responsibly, but on the spiritual plane he should mind the good of his soul and reserve judgment.

For all her emphasis on advice, what is most striking about Christine's use of the Judgment in the *Othea* is the extent to which she deflects the point of the story. Paris was a prince whose weakness for pleasure made him prefer the gift of a king's wife over other, more worthy, offerings. He thus brought ruin on himself, his family, and his realm. "He was afterwards dead and undone," Christine's *balade* recalled. The nobility should keep their minds off lust and avoid adultery:

this is the most obvious construction that one can put on the Judgment. The author of the *Ovide moralisé* made Paris's story a lesson not just for the nobility but for everyone, and he stated his point explicitly: all around us we see scoundrels betraying chastity as they pursue lust and pleasure even beyond the limits of natural desire. Paris would have been an even better exemplum for Christine's audience, princes like the Trojan prince himself, particularly since, using Machaut's version of the story, she had made Mercury reveal to Paris right at the outset that he was a prince. He could clearly serve then as a parallel to the princes that Christine envisioned as her audience for the work. Paris the Trojan was in some sense, like Hector, a brother to those French nobles sprung from Trojan stock, a brother whose reputation as a lover rather than a soldier had long made him suffer by comparison.[22]

But we must recognize in the *Ovide moralisé* a different relationship between text and audience. A cleric's estate raises him, both literally and figuratively, above a popular audience; the *Ovide moralisé*'s allegories and moralizations were destined for such an audience. Christine, on the other hand, looked up to her patrons, as attested, for example, by the dedication miniature in Harley 4431, fol. 95r, where she kneels before Louis while offering him her book.[23] In applying the Judgment to her patron's life, she might have taken as her starting point the *Ovide moralisé*'s "Man judged the contest badly," but she omitted "through empty pleasure." Paris did judge the contest badly, but Christine's moral becomes, blandly, "the good knight ought not to do likewise." She focuses more on what Paris did not do. He passed up the chance for wisdom and *chevalerie*, Pallas's gifts and the ones that correspond to Othea's vision of the knight that she hopes her "letter" will shape. Christine focuses less on what Paris did do. He allowed vain delight to lead him into a relationship with another man's wife.

Christine chose what stories to include in the *Othea*. The *Ovide moralisé* follows essentially Ovid's order in the *Metamorphoses*, with some extra stories—among them the Judgment—added. Christine's organization is based more on the meanings she wishes to draw from her stories than on the narrative relationship among the stories themselves. This ordering principle is particularly evident early in the collection when she is working with the series of virtues, vices, articles of the Creed, and commandments. The very fact that the wedding of Peleus and Thetis is fable 60 but the Judgment does not come along until fable 73 makes it clear that Christine's order is not based on narrative coherence. Thus she could have omitted the Judgment if she wished. Certainly, handled wrong, it could make a negative impression on Louis even if in 1400 he had not yet begun to contemplate a liaison with the queen. I would suggest that Christine included the Judgment, however, because the version of Pallas's promises in the *Ovide moralisé* harmonized so well with her overall scheme for the *Othea*: Paris was foolish when he passed up the chance to unite in his own person the highest attributes of the knight and the clerk, the union of wisdom and *chevalerie* that Christine hoped to urge on her audience.

WE TURN now to the third work in which Christine uses the classical Judgment, the *Chemin de long estude*, or "road of long study." Finished in 1403 (Solente, 361), the poem is a dream vision in which its narrator meets four queens, Wisdom, Nobility, Knightliness (*Chevalerie*), and Riches, entrusted by Reason with the task of choosing one man to rule the world. When each queen upholds as most crucial to this role the quality that she herself represents, Reflection (another personification) suggests that, like the goddesses who quarreled over their beauty, the four queens should enlist an arbitrator, and then tells the story of the Judgment. It is finally decided that the debate should be resolved by the French princes. Christine is to pose the question on her return to earth: Which quality should he have who governs the world? Wisdom, nobility, knightliness, or riches?

Christine dedicated the *Chemin de long estude* to King Charles VI (de Winter, 339); shortly after its completion she also gave copies to the dukes of Berry and Burgundy (de Winter, 351). A long tradition lay behind the concept of universal monarchy, and the theme was also current in the writings of Christine's contemporaries (Hindman, 169–70). Given her concern with the character of the princely class, as evidenced in the *Othea*, it is logical that she would be interested in the issue of what qualities would best suit a man to rule the entire world. We can see why she would dedicate the *Chemin de long estude* to the king; qualities suiting one to rule the world would be welcome in the ruler of France. Moreover, Christine might, as Sandra Hindman has suggested, have envisioned Charles himself as that universal monarch for whom the poem calls (Hindman, 170).

The version of the Judgment that Christine uses in the *Chemin* is very close to that in the *Othea*, and we know that by this time she was familiar with both the *Fonteinne amoureuse* and the *Ovide moralisé*.[24] The goddesses sit at a table. Discord throws the apple among them. They argue before Jupiter and his court, but are led by Mercury to "the excellent shepherd of Troy" for judgment. The Judgment itself is treated very sketchily. We are simply told that Paris gave the apple to Venus; the results of his decision are omitted (vv. 6149–92).

Christine altered the story slightly and simplified it greatly to make it serve her purpose in the *Chemin*. Usually the goddesses first submit their case to Jupiter, who sends them to Paris because he fears the bad feelings of the two goddesses who must inevitably lose. Here, however, Christine has the three goddesses submit their case to the entire court of Olympians, rather than simply Jupiter, just as the four queens submit their case to Reason's council. Most significantly, however, Christine omits the goddesses' promised gifts—even the promise from Venus that caused Paris to give her the apple. Clearly she wants to keep the focus on the goddesses' quarrel rather than on Paris's decision and what it led to.

The story of the Judgment is a good illustration of the point that an arbitrator can settle a debate. But the argument among Christine's queens finds in the goddesses' quarrel a more profound parallel as well, a parallel deriving from the cosmic dimension that Christine sees in the Judgment here. Reason's speech enlisting the queens' aid implies a relationship between the queens and the heavenly bodies. She addresses the four queens thus: "O you four, the Influences constrained to obedience to the high celestial directors, the moving officers of the skies—accompanied by Fortune and guided by the movement of the sky, you rule the entire world and drive human hearts with so many empty, erring desires. . . ." (vv. 2831–39). The queens rule the world and human hearts in the sense that human hearts are motivated by desires for what the queens represent: wisdom, nobility, knightliness, and riches. Yet the queens are subject to a higher force, "the moving officers of the skies." Thus they are seen as intermediaries between the ultimate forces of destiny in the cosmos and the humans subject to that destiny. As daughter of Charles V's court astrologer, Christine would have known the idea that human actions are ruled by the motions of the heavenly bodies (Willard, "Astrologer's Daughter," 101–3).

Christine knew too that the planets could be figured by the gods and goddesses who gave them their names and identities. The "children of the planets" iconography she designed for the opening chapters of the *Othea* depicts the planetary gods and goddesses showering their influences on crowds of humans below (Willard, "Astrologer's Daughter," 100–101; Meiss, 25–26). In the *Chemin*, the site of Peleus and Thetis's wedding feast, Mount Olympus, is referred to as "the places where the destinies have their seats." Implicitly, then, Christine is identifying the Olympians with the stars and planets that guide human destiny. Thus the quarreling goddesses, each championing her own power to sway human hearts, signify the conflicting forces the planets exert on humans. Each goddess traditionally claimed the apple on the basis of not only her beauty but also her power—that is, her influence on humans deriving from the quality or qualities she represented. This view of the goddesses illuminates as well the closing lines of the *balade*, in which the three goddesses are referred to as "these three powerful goddesses [who] make the world endure, their discord notwithstanding" (vv. 31–32).

Yet Paris chose among the goddesses. In a Christian world view, the planets may influence, but they cannot control. Each goddess claimed the apple, but Paris chose to give it to Venus. Seen in this cosmic light, the Judgment's significance is twofold: each goddess is powerful in that she influences human behavior, but Paris's opportunity to choose among them represents the freedom of one's will to choose one's own destiny. The planets may be the destiny that shapes our ends, but we choose the final design.

The debate among the four queens, the "Influences" who rule the world but submit to "the moving officers of the skies," repeats on a different plane the quarrel among the goddesses. Appropriately, as personifications of wisdom, nobility, knightliness, and riches, the queens personify gifts offered by the goddesses in the version of the Judgment that Christine knew from the *Ovide moralisé* and that she used in the *Othea*: wisdom and knightliness from Pallas, and riches and nobility, or royal power, from Juno. Paris always took into account the goddesses' gifts as he deliberated which goddess to declare most beautiful, but this contest which the princes of France are being asked to arbitrate is among the gifts themselves. Since the debate deals with what quality would best suit the ruler of the world, however, Venus and her gift have been omitted. Left with two goddesses, but knowing from the *Ovide moralisé* the tradition in which each offered two gifts, Christine created her four queens, representing those four qualities traditionally regarded as preferable to the sexual pleasure that Paris chose when he awarded the apple to Venus.

In the *Chemin*, Christine goes beyond her exploitation of the Judgment in the *balade* and the *Othea* to see in the goddesses' gifts a more complex choice than simply the choice between good and bad. In the *balade*, which used Machaut's version of the Judgment, the choices available to Paris and to the *balade*'s speaker were wisdom, riches, and sexual pleasure, and for her purposes there, Christine narrowed the choice to that between wisdom and sexual pleasure. It was easy to see which was superior. In the *Othea*, where the Judgment derived in part from that version which Christine found in the *Ovide moralisé*, Pallas's two gifts, wisdom and *chevalerie*, were precisely the qualities Christine wished to instill in her audience; thus, she particularly stressed Paris's rejection of those gifts and his folly in choosing Venus's gift. Christine alluded in the *Othea* to Juno's additional gift of royal power, but she did not really develop the implications of that gift, nor did she particularly stress the significance of Juno's gift of riches. In the *Chemin*, she removes sexual pleasure from the debate but she keeps the four gifts of Juno and Pallas. The choice which she offers her audience is thus more subtle than that in the *balade* or even the *Othea*. When Venus's gift was included among the alternatives, there was a simple polarity: sexual pleasure was bad and all the other gifts were better. Here, however, she is clearly questioning which of the better gifts is best—and which is worst.

The debate format allows her to examine the relative merits of qualities which, as far back as the Judgment's earliest appearances, were regarded as desirable in, or at least desired by, potential rulers. Her characterizing the four queens as "Influences" subordinate only to the planets and stars in shaping human destiny allows her to comment on the way the desire to possess these qualities shapes human action. Each queen's long speech in her own behalf makes a case for each quality as most important in the ruler of the world. Though the debate's ultimate resolution is left to the French princes, it is not difficult to see that the *Chemin* itself assigns the four queens a hierarchy. The order in which they are first introduced hints already at an evaluation, and there are other clues as well. Wisdom is named first and is clearly the optimum choice: the model of Charles V as a wise king is brought into the poem to uphold Wisdom's claim to rule. Nobility is second, and the power to rule that derives from Nobility is upheld, as is Knightliness, third, seen here more as military power than as that expanded *chevalerie* with which the *Othea* dealt. Riches is last, and lowest, with Reason explicitly chastising that queen for her role in human disorder (Hindman, 171–72).

By putting the resolution of the debate in the hands of the princes of France, however, Christine implicitly puts them in the position of Paris. When he judged the goddesses and chose Venus most beautiful, he demonstrated bad judgment but he exercised free will. The forces that the queens represent, which wage constant battle for human hearts, nevertheless cannot *control* unless humans choose to be controlled. That is why in a sense their debate is not resolved within the *Chemin*. The forces which they personify are always present, always tempting, and it is up to the individual to choose where to place allegiance. Just as the Judgment of Paris demonstrated not only the power of wisdom, sexual pleasure, and the rest to sway human hearts, it demonstrated too the freedom of the human will to determine its own destiny even in the face of the "moving officers of the skies." So too, the princes of France should choose the quality that makes the best case in the debate among the queens rather than that whose appeal is most seductive. Dedicating the work to the king and strongly hinting that wisdom is the quality that best suits a man to rule the world, Christine makes it quite clear that she is urging that quality upon Charles.

We have seen that Christine's three uses of the classical Judgment reflect not only the order in which she encountered two different versions of the story but also her own developing role as a court poet. In the *balade*, her application of the Judgment was personal. She knew from Machaut's *Fonteinne amoureuse* that Juno offered riches and Pallas offered a wisdom chiefly based on mastery of the seven liberal arts. The *balade* articulates its speaker's detachment from riches, her repudiation of a life devoted to sexual pleasure, and her commitment to wisdom both as an antidote to the reversals of Fortune and as an exercise in self-improvement. In that commitment, she contrasts with Machaut's prince, who emulates Paris in choosing a life devoted to love. Machaut had seen in Paris's threefold choice a scheme that enabled him to hint at a moral evaluation of his prince's actions without explicitly condemning them. Christine too recognized in the contrasting identities of the three goddesses a scheme within which she might contrast a prince's devotion to sexual pleasure with her speaker's commitment to the life of the mind.

When Christine came to write the *Othea*, she had a new agenda: rather than simply defining the poet-clerk as the antithesis of a figure like Machaut's lovelorn prince, she would speak directly to the prince instead. For a court in need of a steadying influence, she would provide a manual of advice that would use classical myth to urge the adoption of a new *chevalerie*. The prince who heeded the advice of the goddess Othea would be ready to fight the good fight on both the earthly and spiritual planes. Moreover, to his *fortitudo* would be annexed *sapientia*, or wisdom—a double wisdom. It would include not only that mastery of the liberal arts that would serve him in his earthly role, but a higher wisdom—its goal the worship of God—that would serve him in his spiritual role.

The application of the Judgment would accordingly have to be broadened. Christine found in her second source for the classical Judgment, the *Ovide moralisé*, a Pallas who offered a twofold gift: strength, as well as wisdom. Thus Paris's choice among the goddesses became more relevant to the noble estate. Machaut's Paris might have been forgiven for passing up wisdom alone, as if such a choice would negate his newly discovered princeliness, but to refuse wisdom annexed to *chevalerie* was clear folly. When Christine discovered the Judgment in the *Ovide moralisé*, she found a version of the story that echoed precisely the thrust of the *Othea* as a whole, and that allowed her to apply the story to the lives of her audience in keeping with her newfound public voice. Yet, like Machaut, she could not explicitly criticize her patrons. He used a dream-vision format to invite allegorical interpretation of the Judgment, an interpretation that would reveal its relevance to the life of the prince. Christine's form in the *Othea,* on the other hand, required that she provide explicit interpretation, but her relationship with her audience required that she deflect the Judgment's obvious moral.

Finally, having discovered in the *Ovide moralisé* an additional promise for each goddess, and having exploited in the *Othea* the usefulness of Pallas's twofold gift, Christine explored, in the *Chemin de long estude*, the political implications of Juno's gifts as well as Pallas's. The Judgment had been for two thousand years a parable of the way human hearts are swayed by the appeal of sensual pleasure, earthly power and gain, or the call of higher ideals—God and country. The goddesses themselves had nearly become personifications, each being so closely associated with the abstraction over which she offered mastery. Exploiting a tradition in which there were not merely three gifts, but five, Christine chose to invent her own fable, a fable that mirrors the Judgment but in which personifications of the goddesses' gifts take the place of the goddesses themselves. Yet she kept the goddesses in her narrative as well, as those stars or destinies that in a sense generate the forces that motivate human behavior. Dedicating the *Chemin de long estude* to the king himself, Christine aimed even higher in her quest to influence the powerful than she had in the *Othea*. The encouragement to pursue wisdom is reinforced here by citing Charles VI's father, who was, in Christine's eyes, a model ruler.[25]

Notes

1. On Christine's life, see Solente; McLeod; Yenal; Willard, *Life and Works*. For the spelling of her name, I am following Nicolini, and see Kelly, 770. On her learning, see McLeod, 77–85.

2. This version stems from the late-classical *De excidio Troiae* of "Dares the Phrygian." See Dares Phrygius, chap. 7; Frazer, trans., 138–39. Christine knew it from the *Histoire ancienne jusqu'à César*, whose first redaction contains a Judgment very close to that in Dares and whose second redaction contains a much expanded version of the episode. On the *Histoire ancienne*, see Meyer; on the Trojan material in the second redaction, see Williams. On Christine's acquaintance with the *Histoire ancienne*, see Campbell, 87–95; he suggests she may have known it in a MS that excerpted only the Troy section from the compilation (Campbell, 95). See also *Le Livre de la mutacion de Fortune*, ed. Solente, 1:lxiii-xcii. The Judgment appears in Book 6 of the *Mutacion*, vv. 15179–88 (3.63).

3. This version of the Judgment dates from the *Cypria*, roughly contemporary

150   Margaret J. Ehrhart

with the *Iliad*, but no longer extant. Its contents survive in two late-classical summaries. See *Hesiod*, trans. Evelyn-White, 489–91, and Apollodorus, trans. Frazer, 2:173. For a survey of the Judgment in ancient tradition, see Wüst.
   4.

   Se de Pallas me peüsse accointier
   Joye et tout bien ne me fauldroit jamais;
   Car par elle je seroie ou sentier
   De reconfort, et de porter le fais
   Que Fortune a pour moy trop chargier fais;
      Mais foible suis pour soustenir
   Si grant faissel, s'elle ne vient tenir
   De l'autre part, par son poissant effort
   Pour moy aidier, Dieu m'i doint avenir,
   Car de Juno n'ay je nul reconfort.

   Pallas, Juno, Venus vouldrent plaidier
   Devant Paris jadis de leurs tors fais,
   Dont chascune disoit qu'a son cuidier
   Plus belle estoit, et plus estoit parfais
   Ses grans pouoirs que de l'autre en tous fais;
      Sus Paris s'en vouldrent tenir,
   Qui lors jugia que l'en devoit tenir
   A plus belle Venus et a plus fort,
   Si dist: "Dame, vous vueil je detenir,
   Car de Juno n'ay je nul reconfort."

   Pour la pomme d'or lui vint puis aidier
   Vers Heleine Venus, mors et deffais
   En fu après; si n'ay d'elle mestier,
   Mais de joye seroit mon cuer reffais,
   Se la vaillant Pallas, par qui meffais
      Sont delaissié et retenir
   Fait tous les biens, me daignoit retenir
   Pour sa serve: plus ne devroie au fort
   Ja desirer pour a grant bien venir,
   Car de Juno n'ay je nul reconfort.

   Ces trois poissans deesses maintenir
   Font le monde, non obstant leur descort;
   Mais de Pallas me doint Dieux sovenir,
   Car de Juno n'ay je nul reconfort. (*Oeuvres poétiques*, 1:214–15)

   5. Notably, in Fulgentius's *Mythologies*, 2.1, a seminal passage for medieval understanding of the Judgment.
   6. McLeod, 39–44; Willard, 43–44; de Winter, 339. On her lyric poetry, see also Poirion, 237–54 and passim.
   7. The only discussion of specific sources for the *balade* that I know of is Dressler, 50–51. Citing Roy's view, in *Oeuvres poétiques*, 2:313, that Christine used the second redaction for some of the Troy material included in her lyrics, he concedes with some reserve that the Judgment in the *balade* may have come from that source too. But in the first redaction, Juno and Minerva promise wis-

dom and strength. British Library, Roy. 16.G.VII, fol. 71r. See Ehrhart, *Judgment*, 62 and 247n.126. In the second redaction, Juno promises to help Paris whenever he has need. British Library, Add. 25884, fols. 116v-117v. See Ehrhart, *Judgment*, 63 and 248-50n.132.

8. The implications of the *clergie-chevalerie* dichotomy that I stress in this paragraph were suggested to me by the interesting structural analysis of the poet-patron relationship in Cerquiglini, "*Un engin*," 107-38.

9. On the dedication of the *Othea* to Louis, see Mombello, "Per un'edizione," part 2, 1; de Winter, 367; Hindman, 12. Subsequent copies of the work, though prepared for other patrons, retain the dedication to Louis. See Campbell, 33-34; Mombello, "Per un'edizione," part 2, 1-3; Hindman, 34.

10. For the structure of the *Othea* as described here, see Tuve, 38-39; Ignatius, 130-33. For its relationship with another manual of virtues and vices, see Bühler, "The *Fleurs*."

11.

Fuys la deesse de discorde
Maulx sont ses liens et sa corde
Les nopces peleus troubla
Dont puis mainte gent assembla (n.p.)

Since there is no modern critical edition of the *Othea*, I have chosen to use the Paris 1522 edition of Philippe le Noir. Copies of the pages I needed were provided me through the kindness of Mr. Robert A. Tibbetts of the Ohio State University Libraries. This text represents the second redaction of the *Othea*. Though this redaction differs from the first in many passages, the fact that copies of the revised text made under Christine's supervision continued to carry the dedication to Louis of Orleans (e.g., B. N. fr. 606, Harley 4431) suggests that changes were not motivated by Christine's desire to alter the relevance of the text to her early patron. Gianni Mombello prints the contrasting passages in *La tradizione*, 292-301. On the two redactions, see Campbell, 18-23. Mombello recognizes the two redactions but sees additional complexities in the manuscript history. See "Per un'edizione," part 1, 410-11, and *La tradizione*, 289-328. For information on the early editions of the *Othea*, see Wisman, 148. Stephen Scrope's English translation is available in Bühler's edition. Loukopoulos's 1977 dissertation represents an edition of the *Othea* as it appears in Harley 4431. Translations in my text are mine.

12.

Comme Paris ne iuge pas
Car on recoipt maint dur repas
Par male sentence octroyer
Maintz en ont eu maulvais loyer (n.p.)

13. "Dit la fable que les trois deesses de grant puissance / cestassauoir Pallas deesse de scauoir. Juno deesse dauoir: et Venus deesse damours vindrent deuant Paris tenans vne pomme dor qui disoit Soit donnee a la plus belle et plus puissant / de celle pomme fut grant discord / car chascune disoit que auoir la debuoit et sur Paris sen furent mis de ce discord. Paris diligemment voulut en-

querre de la force de chascune a par soy. Lors dist Pallas / ie suis deesse de cheualerie et de saigesse: et par moy sont departies armes aux cheualiers et science aux clercz: et se la pomme tu me veulx donner: saches que sur tous te feray cheualereux et tous aultres passer en toutes sciences. Apres dit Juno deesse dauoir et de seigneurie / par moy sont departis les grans tresors au monde Et se la pomme me veult donner: riche et puissant te feray plus que nul autre. Apres parla Venus par moult amoureuses parolles et dist. Je suis celle qui tiens les escolles damours et de ioliuete et qui les folz fais estre saiges / et les saiges fais foloyer / les riches fais mendier / et les exillez enrichir / ne il nest puissance qui a la mienne se compare / et se la pomme tu me veulx donner: lamour a la belle Heleyne de grece te sera par moy donnee qui plus te pourra valoir que ne feroit nul aultre auoir. Et adonc Paris donna sa sentence et renoncea a cheualerie et a sagesse et a auoir. pour Venus a qui il donna la pomme pour laquelle achoison fut puis troye destruicte. Si est a entendre pource que paris ne fut point cheualereux et ne luy chalut de grant scauoir mais en amours furent toutes ses pensees: est entendu que a Venus donna la pomme dor" (n. p.; contractions have been silently expanded).

14. A banquet scene such as the one Machaut envisions here appears in an illustration to another of his works, the *Remède de fortune*, which describes a noble feast from his own milieu. Women and men even occupy separate tables. See Avril, pl. 25.

15. For example, in the *Cypria*, Euripides, Isocrates, Ovid, Apuleius, and Lucian. Hyginus made her offer both strength and wisdom; Fulgentius, wisdom alone. See Ehrhart, *Judgment*, 1-13, 23-27.

16. Hindman sees in the design of the miniature that accompanies this chapter in B. N. fr. 606 and Harley 4431 a specific topical reference: ". . . the conflict over the orb of rule that takes place at the upper table between the kings and emperor has a parallel in the conflict described in the text. . . . we can surmise that this chapter warns against [Louis of Orleans's] rivalry with his brother for the throne, with his cousin John of Burgundy for the regency, and with the emperor for the empire" (124-25).

17. See also fable 14 of the *Othea* on the union of Minerva and Pallas, or knighthood and wisdom—Christine takes the two names for two aspects of the same goddess. For the classical background of the theme, see Kaske, 424; on the importance of the theme in late medieval literature: Cerquiglini, "*Un engin*," 120-21, and "Tension"; on the importance of the theme in French historiography: Hindman, 171. Poirion: Christine "entend . . . consacrer tous ses éloges aux mêmes valeurs: celles qui s'inspirent d'un idéal fondé sur la tradition courtoise et chevaleresque, mais débouchant sur une monarchie philosophique" (246).

18. Hindman, xix, 14; Meiss, 9; Ignatius, 134-35. Mombello says it is the oldest extant, possibly the first (*La tradizione*, 28-29).

19. Ignatius also notes "a gloss is usually provided by a scholar for a text written by someone else" (132). Very near in time to the production of the *Othea*, possibly before, the first commentary written in the vernacular on a vernacular work appeared: the commentary on the *Echecs amoureux*. On it see most recently Guichard-Tesson. See also Badel, 290-315, and his bibliography,

n. 29, pp. 290–91. Its author has been associated with the court of Charles V, the milieu in which Christine was raised. See Badel, 291.

20. In the case of the Judgment of Paris, Virgil has simply "deep in her [Juno's] heart lie stored the judgment of Paris and her slighted beauty's wrong" (1.26–27). Servius's commentary spells out the whole story: 2.29–30.

21. On the *Ovide moralisé*, see Engels, Demats.

22. See Campbell, 93–94. Campbell cites Christine's *Le Livre de la mutacion de Fortune*: "Mais [Paris] n'ot la centiesme moitié / De son frere Hector la proece. . . ." (6.14936–37).

23. Reproduced as Hindman's frontispiece. Concerning the dedication miniature in B. N. fr. 848, Hindman stresses how the royal status of Louis is conveyed while "Christine wears a simpler garment suited to her bourgeois status" (43). Concerning her relationship with her audience, Poirion notes that "elle dépend de son public. . . . [But] la dépendance matérielle n'exclut pas toute liberté d'esprit; on peut montrer autant d'indépendance dans l'affirmation d'un idéal que dans la critique de la réalité" (246).

24. De Boer, 15:38–39n.1, said that Christine took the passage from Machaut's *Fonteinne amoureuse*, but for him the relationship was proven by Christine's seating the goddesses at a golden table, as in Machaut. As Campbell has noticed, 100–101, Christine's table is not gold.

25. Much of the material for this essay was gathered as part of a larger study, generously funded by the American Council of Learned Societies, which became my book, *The Judgment of the Trojan Prince Paris in Medieval Literature*. This essay, however, extends considerably the observations on Christine's use of the Judgment that appear in my book.

Works Cited

Apollodorus. *The Library*. Translated by James George Frazer. 2 vols. The Loeb Classical Library. Cambridge, MA: Harvard University Press, 1921.

Avril, François. *Manuscript Painting at the Court of France: The Fourteenth Century (1310–1380)*. New York: George Braziller, 1978.

Badel, Pierre-Yves. *Le Roman de la Rose au XIVe siècle: Etude de la réception de l'oeuvre*. Geneva: Droz, 1980.

Basin, Thomas. *Histoire de Charles VII*. Edited and translated by Charles Samaran. 2 vols. Les Classiques de l'Histoire de France au Moyen Âge, vols. 15, 21. Paris: Les Belles Lettres, 1933–44.

Brownlee, Kevin. *Poetic Identity in Guillaume de Machaut*. Madison: University of Wisconsin Press, 1984.

Bühler, Curt F. "The *Fleurs de Toutes Vertus* and Christine de Pisan's *L'Epître d'Othéa*." *PMLA* 62 (1947): 32–44.

Campbell, P.-G.-C. *L'Epître d'Othéa: Étude sur les sources de Christine de Pisan*. Paris: Champion, 1924.

Cerquiglini, Jacqueline. *"Un engin si soutil": Guillaume de Machaut et l'écriture au XIVe siècle*. Paris: Champion, 1985.

———. "Tension sociale et tension d'écriture au XIVème siècle: Les dits de Guillaume de

Machaut." In *Littérature et société au Moyen Âge. Actes du Colloque d'Amiens des 5 et 6 mai, 1978*, 111–29. Paris: Champion, 1978.

Christine de Pizan. *Les Cent hystoires de Troye [Epistre Othea]*. Paris: Philippe le Noir, 1522.

———. *The Epistle of Othea*. Translated by Stephen Scrope. Edited by Curt F. Bühler. London: Oxford University Press, 1970.

———. "*L'Epistre Othea*." Edited by Halina D. Loukopoulos. Ph.D. diss., Wayne State University, 1977.

———. *Le Livre du chemin de long estude*. Edited by Robert Püschel. 1881. Reprint. Geneva: Slatkine Reprints, 1974.

———. *Le Livre de la mutacion de Fortune*. Edited by Suzanne Solente. 4 vols. Paris: A. and J. Picard, 1959–66.

———. *Oeuvres poétiques*. Edited by Maurice Roy. 3 vols. Société des Anciens Textes Français. Paris, 1886–96.

Coville, A. "France: Armagnacs and Burgundians (1380–1422)." In *Cambridge Medieval History*, vol. 7, edited by J. R. Tanner et al., 368–92. Cambridge: Cambridge University Press, 1958.

Dares Phrygius. *De excidio Troiae historia*. Edited by Ferdinand Mesiter. Leipzig, 1873.

———, and Dictys Cretensis. *The Trojan War: The Chronicles of Dictys of Crete and Dares the Phrygian*. Translated by R. M. Frazer, Jr. Bloomington: Indiana University Press, 1966.

de Boer, Cornelis. "Guillaume de Machaut et l'*Ovide moralisé*." *Romania* 43 (1914): 335–52.

Demats, Paule. *Fabula: Trois études de mythographie antique et médiévale*. Geneva: Droz, 1973.

de Winter, Patrick M. "Christine de Pizan, ses enlumineurs et ses rapports avec le milieu bourguignon." *Actes du 104e congrès national des sociétés savantes (1979)*, 335–76. Paris: Bibliothèque Nationale, 1982.

Dressler, Alfred. *Der Einfluss des altfranzösischen Eneas-Romanes auf die altfranzösische Litteratur*. Borna-Leipzig: Robert Noske, 1907.

Ehrhart, Margaret J. *The Judgment of the Trojan Prince Paris in Medieval Literature*. Philadelphia: University of Pennsylvania Press, 1987.

———. "Machaut's *Dit de la fonteinne amoureuse*, the Choice of Paris, and the Duties of Rulers." *Philological Quarterly* 59 (1980): 119–39.

Engels, Joseph. *Études sur l'Ovide moralisé*. Groningen: J. B. Wolters, 1945.

Fulgentius. *Mythologies*, in *Opera*. Edited by Rudolf Helm. 1898. Reprint. Stuttgart: Teubner, 1970.

Guichard-Tesson, Françoise. "La *Glose des Echecs amoureux*: Un savoir à tendance laïque: Comment l'interpréter?" *Fifteenth Century Studies* 10 (1984): 229–59.

Heisig, Karl. "Zur fränkischen Trojanersage." *Zeitschrift für romanische Philologie* 90 (1974): 441–48.

Hesiod, the Homeric Hymns, and Homerica. Translated by Hugh G. Evelyn-White. The Loeb Classical Library. Cambridge, MA: Harvard University Press, 1936.

Hindman, Sandra L. *Christine de Pizan's "Epistre Othéa": Painting and Politics at the Court of Charles VI*. Studies and Texts, 77. Toronto: Pontifical Institute of Mediaeval Studies, 1986.

Ignatius, Mary Ann. "Christine de Pizan's *Epistre Othea*: An Experiment in Literary Form." *Medievalia et Humanistica* 9 (1979): 127–42.

Kaske, R. E. "*Sapientia et Fortitudo* as the Controlling Theme of *Beowulf*." *Studies in Philology* 55 (1958): 423–56.

Kelly, Douglas. Review of *Christine de Pizan: A Bibliographical Guide*, by Angus J. Kennedy. *Speculum* 62 (1987): 770–71.
Klippel, Maria. *Die Darstellung der fränkischen Trojanersage in Geschichtsschreibung und Dichtung vom Mittelalter bis zur Renaissance in Frankreich*. Marburg: Beyer und Hausknecht, 1936.
Machaut, Guillaume de. *Oeuvres*. Edited by Ernest Hoepffner. 3 vols. 1908–21. Reprint. New York: Johnson Reprint Co., 1965.
McLeod, Enid. *The Order of the Rose: The Life and Ideas of Christine de Pizan*. Totowa, NJ: Rowman and Littlefield, 1976.
Meiss, Millard. *French Painting in the Time of Jean de Berry: The Limbourgs and Their Contemporaries*. New York: George Braziller, 1974.
Meyer, Paul. "Les Premières compilations françaises d'histoire ancienne." *Romania* 14 (1885): 1–81.
Mirot, Léon. "L'Enlèvement du Dauphin et le premier conflit entre Jean Sans Peur et Louis d'Orléans." Parts 1, 2. *Revue des questions historiques*, n.s. 51 [=o.s.95] (1914): 329–55; n.s. 52 (1914): 369–94.
Mombello, Gianni. "Per un'edizione critica dell' 'Epistre Othea' di Christine de Pizan." Parts 1, 2. *Studi francesi* 8 (1964): 401–17; 9 (1965): 1–12.
———. *La Tradizione manoscritta dell' "Epistre Othea" di Christine de Pizan*. Memorie dell'Accademia delle Scienze di Torino: Classe di Scienze, Morali, Storiche e Filologiche, Serie 4^a, 15. Turin: Accademia delle Scienze, 1967.
Nicolini, Elena. "Christina da Pizzano: L'origine e il nome." *Cultura neolatina* 1 (1941): 143–50.
Nordberg, Michael. *Les Ducs et la royauté: Études sur la rivalité des ducs d'Orléans et de Bourgogne, 1392–1407*. Studia Historica Upsaliensia 12. Stockholm: Svenska Bokförlaget, 1964.
Ouy, Gilbert, and Christine M. Reno. "Identification des autographes de Christine de Pizan." *Scriptorium* 34 (1980): 221–38.
Ovide moralisé: Poème du commencement du quatorzième siècle. Edited by Cornelis de Boer, et al. *Verhandelingen der Koninklijke Akademie van Wetenschappen te Amsterdam, Afdeeling Letterkunde*. Nieuwe Reeks 15, 21, 30, 37, 43. 1915–38. Reprint. Wiesbaden: Martin Sändig, 1966–68.
Poirion, Daniel. *Le Poète et le prince: L'Évolution du lyrisme courtois de Guillaume de Machaut à Charles d'Orléans*. Paris: Presses Universitaires de France, 1965.
Servius. *Servianorum in Vergilii carmina commentariorum*. Edited by Edward K. Rand et al. 2 vols. Lancaster, PA: Lancaster Press, 1946.
Solente, Suzanne. *Christine de Pisan*. Paris: Klincksieck, 1961. Reprinted in *Histoire littéraire de la France*, 40: 335–422. Paris: Imprimerie Nationale, 1974.
Thomas, Antoine. "Guillaume de Machaut et l'*Ovide moralisé*." *Romania* 41 (1912): 382–400.
Tuve, Rosemond. *Allegorical Imagery: Some Mediaeval Books and Their Posterity*. Princeton: Princeton University Press, 1966.
Virgil. *Aeneid*. Translated by H. Rushton Fairclough. Rev. ed. 2 vols. Loeb Classical Library. Cambridge: Harvard University Press, 1978.
Willard, Charity Cannon. "Christine de Pizan: The Astrologer's Daughter." *Mélanges à la mémoire de Franco Simone: France et Italie dans la culture européenne, I, Moyen Age et Renaissance*, 95–111. Geneva: Slatkine, 1980.
———. *Christine de Pizan: Her Life and Works*. New York: Persea Books, 1984.
Williams, Clem C., Jr. "A Case of Mistaken Identity: Still Another Trojan Narrative in Old French Prose." *Medium Aevum* 53 (1984): 59–72.

Wisman, Josette A. "Manuscrits et éditions des oeuvres de Christine de Pisan." *Manuscripta* 21 (1977): 144–53.

Wüst, Ernst, "Paris." In *Real-Encyclopädie der classischen Altertumswissenschaft*, edited by A. Pauly and G. Wissowa, vol. 18, part 4, cols. 1494–1501. Waldsee: Alfred Druckenmüller, 1949.

Yenal, Edith. *Christine de Pisan: A Bibliography of Writings by Her and about Her*. Metuchen, NJ: Scarecrow Press, 1982.

Part II. Early England

Chaucer and the Mythographers

Pallas Athena and the Threefold Choice in Chaucer's *Troilus and Criseyde*

Patricia R. Orr

The problem of unity in Chaucer's *Troilus and Criseyde* has been to reconcile the pagan narrative that makes up most of the poem's length to the abrupt intrusion of foreign elements at its end, elements such as Troilus's sudden ascent from the field of battle, his perplexing laughter as he looked back to earth from heaven, and the apparently extraneous Christian sentiments at the poem's end.[1] To the modern reader, to whom no unifying threads are immediately apparent, the effect is at best awkward and at worst entirely perplexing. However, Chaucer's own warning that "th'ende is every tales strengthe" (2.260)[2] hints that unity exists in the poem; the question that remains is how best to discern its basis. One approach to finding the poem's unity is that of locating *topoi*, or commonplaces, unfamiliar to modern audiences but part of the intellectual climate of Chaucer's time, that Chaucer used to unify the poem and make of it an aesthetically satisfying whole.[3]

One such topos, which was noticed by D. W. Robertson two decades ago[4] but whose unifying thematic potential has not been fully realized, is that of the myth of the Judgment of Paris and the allegory the myth came to represent,[5] an allegory of choice among the lives of wealth, of lust, and of contemplation. Paris was allowed to choose only one life, but Chaucer's audience, alerted to the Judgment myth by Venus's conquest of Troilus in the very temple of wisdom, would be aware that Troilus, in loving and losing Criseyde, experienced each of the lives in turn. In tasting these lives Troilus, while making his celebrated movement upward on the wheel of fortune to the heights of his love for Criseyde and then downward to the depths of betrayal, made a simultaneous countermovement according to the values of the allegory, first downward into the life of lust and then upward into the realms of contemplation.[6] This contrapuntal movement downward and then upward underscores the poem's Boethian qualities and, in part because of the Christianization of the myth's allegory, helps to reconcile the pagan poem to its Christian conclusion.

The Judgment myth, already integral to the story of Troy by the time of Homer's *Iliad*, is told in the form in which it would be passed on to the Middle Ages by the late classical writer Hyginus:

Iouis cum Thetis Peleo nuberet ad epulum dicitur omnis deos convocasse excepta Eride, id est Discordia, quae cum postea superuenisset nec admitteretur ad epulum, ab ianua misit in medium malum, dicit quae esset formosissima attolleret. Iuno Venus Minerua formam sibi vindicare coeperunt, inter quas magna discordia orta, Iovis imperat Mercurio ut deducat eas in Ida monte ad Alexandrum Paridem eumque iubeat iudicare. Cui Iuno, si secundum se iudicasset, pollicita est in omnibus terris eum regnaturum, diuitum praeter ceteros praestaturum; Minerua, si inde victrix discederet, fortissimum inter mortales futurum et omni artificio scium; Venus autem Helenam Tyndarei filiam formosissimam omnium mulierum se in coniugium dare promisit. Paris donum posterius prioribus anteposuit, Veneremque pulcherrimam esse iudicavit; ob id Iuno et Minerva Troinis fuerunt infestae. Alexander Veneris impulsu Helenam a Lacedaemone ab hospite Menelao Troiam abduxit eamque in coniugo habuit. . . . (Myth 92, Rose, 68)

[Jove is said to have invited to the wedding of Peleus and Thetis all the gods except Eris, or Discord. When she came later and was not admitted to the banquet, she threw an apple through the door, saying that the fairest should take it. Juno, Venus, and Minerva claimed the beauty prize for themselves, and such quarreling arose among them that Jove ordered Mercury to take them to Alexander Paris on Mount Ida, and bid him judge. Juno promised him, if he should judge in her favor, that he would rule over all the lands and be pre-eminent in wealth. Minerva promised that if she should come out victorious, he would be bravest of mortals and skilled in every craft. Venus, however, promised to give him in marriage Helen, daughter of Tyndareus, most beautiful of all women. Paris preferred the last gift to the former ones, and judged Venus the most lovely. On account of this, Juno and Minerva were hostile to the Trojans.] (Grant, 82–83)

With Venus's help Paris later eloped with or abducted Helen, thus bringing about the Trojan war and the destruction of Troy. The goddesses' coarse bribery, an undignified prelude to the tragedy of Troy, was given a touch of earthy humor by other authors, who had Minerva and Juno parade around naked so that Paris might evaluate their charms, a privilege that he did not much care to prolong; Ovid had the nymph Oenone remark that Pallas would have done better not to have removed her impressive armaments.[7]

Within this rather disreputable tale the sixth-century mythographer Fulgentius, following the allegorical tradition that he was primarily responsible for passing on to medieval culture, found the wholesome nutmeat of an allegory of moral choice. Taking from Aristotle the notion that human beings have open to them three ways of life among which they must choose—the active, the contemplative, and the voluptuous[8]—the allegorists identified each of the goddesses with a corresponding way of life. Venus, goddess of love, whose gift to Paris was the beautiful Helen, became the exponent of the voluptuous life, lowest in moral value because of its absorption in the senses. Juno, who offered Paris riches and the rule of kingdoms, represented the active life of wealth and power, superior in moral value to that of Venus, but still inferior to the way of life represented by Pallas Athena. Pallas, who by Fulgentius's time was viewed primarily as a goddess of wisdom, personified the highest life of all, the life of contemplation and the search for truth (Helm, 36–40; Whitbread, 64–67).

The choice among the three lives was open to all human beings; a wrong choice was disastrous. Juno's life of temporal power was prey to greed, acquisitiveness, covetousness, and disregard of right action, and was dangerous because it was likely to lead to dishonor. The life of Venus was worse because it was without the possibility of honor; it was entirely given up to lust and sunk in corruption. Its affairs would end in shipwreck, and in choosing it Paris "denique brutum quiddam desipuit et ut ferarum ac pecudum mos est ad libidinem limaces uisus intorsit quam uirtutem aut diuitias inquisiuit," or as Whitbread translates, "did a dull and stupid thing and, as is the way of wild beasts and cattle, turned his snail's eyes toward lust rather than selected virtue or riches." The only worthwhile choice, the contemplative life identified with the goddess of wisdom, was free of the rage for profit, greed, and lust that beset the other ways of life; rather it was occupied with the search for truth and with meditation on what is right. It was arduous but offered the dazzling reward of immortality; immortal wisdom, according to Fulgentius, could not die (Helm, 38).

With the intellectual revival of the twelfth century came a renewal of interest in mythographic tradition and in the Judgment myth, which was not only recounted and valued in its Fulgentian form, but was also adapted to express notions of spiritual pilgrimage. The second Vatican mythographer recounted the myth and its meaning along Fulgentian lines, with some modification of Fulgentius's extremely severe condemnation of the active life, which this mythographer gave a more nearly Aristotelian stature midway between the voluptuous life, still viewed as catastrophic, and the contemplative life (*Mythographi Vaticani*, Kulcsár, Myth 50, 134–36).

It was Bernard Silvestris, writing in the same century, whose use of the allegory in his *Commentum super sex libros Eneidos Virgilii* transformed it to an active progression from the lowest life to the highest. Using the *topos* of the Pythagorean Y, the forked branch of which one limb represents evil and the other signifies good, to delineate the moral choice that confronted Aeneas, Bernard reinforced his allegory by a recounting of the Judgment myth and its representation of the three possible ways of life (Jones and Jones, 46; Schreiber and Maresca, 46–47). In the fifteenth century Cristoforo Landino was to take up Bernard's theme and allegorize Aeneas's journey as a progression through the three lives in turn; Aeneas began in the ruins of Venus's Troy, was diverted for a time to Juno's Carthage, but then made his way to Italy, seen to be the locus of wisdom and the *summum bonum* (Chance, "Medieval Sources," 146–50).

Fourteenth-century authors in their turn took up the Judgment myth and allegory; three authors known to and drawn upon by Chaucer recounted it, used it to underline comments on contemporary morality, and emphasized and elaborated upon the allegory's Christian implications. Petrarch, writing at the beginning of the century, was already treating the myth as a commonplace. In his *De viris illustribus* of 1338 Petrarch lamented that men of his time chose only between greed and pleasure, saying, "Sic non Venus tantum, sed Iuno etiam suorum iudicum prelata sentiis in precio est; Pallas sola negligitur"—that is, "not only Venus, but also Juno carried off the prize in the opinion of their judges, only Minerva is neglected." He needed only the names of the goddesses alone to call to his audience's mind the allegory of Paris's choice and add its weight to his complaint that lust and greed ruled his time (Martelloti, 218). Boccaccio included the myth and its allegory in his *Genealogie deorum gentilium*, attributing the allegory to Fulgentius and citing Aristotle as the source of the idea of the superiority of the contemplative life:

> Quas enucleare volentes, primo iudicium Paridis videamus, in quo sententia Fulgentii, meo judicio, sequenda est. Dicit enim tripartitam mortalium vitam esse, quarum prima theoretica dicitur, secunda practica, tertia phylargica, quas nos vulgatioribus vocabulis contemplativam, activam et voluptuosam nuncupamus. De quibus Aristotiles uti de ceteris potime facit, disseret in primo Ethicorum.
> (Romano, 1:303–4)

The foremost example of fourteenth-century interest in the allegory of the Judgment of Paris is no doubt found in the *Ovide moralisé*, the widely read work of an anonymous French author of that century. It is the most extensive exposition of the myth of the Judgment of Paris and its allegory extant; it runs to 1079 lines of verse, including 113 devoted to the allegory (De Boer, 4:11.1464–2543). The author united the familiar Fulgentian elements of the allegory with a full exploration of the Christian implications of the contemplative life of wisdom. He retained all the Fulgentian elements of the allegory; though less disapproving of the active life of Juno, he was censorious of the life of Venus: "c'est grant damage," it does great harm, the author says (4:11.2515). His treatment of the goddess of wisdom, whom he calls Pallas, was established on a firm Fulgentian foundation. Like Fulgentius, he gives a long list of vices from which the goddess and her gift of wisdom are free. He emphasizes the point that the gift of wisdom is not mutable:

Ma richesse ne peut perir
Ne ma gloire ne peut morir.   (4:11.1955–56 and passim)

[My wealth cannot perish, nor can my glory die.]

Unlike those conferred by Juno, the riches of Pallas are immortal. The author fully elaborates the notion that wisdom is derived from God; he posits that God is the object of the life of contemplation represented by the goddess of wisdom:

J'ai mis mon cuer in Dieu douter
Et servir, quar c'est sans doutance
La dois de toute sapience.   (4:11.1934–36)

[I (Pallas) have set my heart to fear and serve God, which is, without doubt, the duty of all wisdom.]

The author goes even further in a summation of the divine qualities of the contemplative life:

C'est la vie contemplative.
Cele est curieuse et pensive
D'une chose tant solement:
En Dieu cognoistre, en Dieu orer,
En Dieu servir, en Dieu loer.   (4:11. 2447–52)

[It is the contemplative life. It has care and thought for only one thing: to acknowledge God, to pray to God, to serve God, to praise God.]

The author ends the allegory with a remarkable addition of his own, a further development of the idea of judgment; he warns his readers, faced with their own choice of life, that the time is coming when God will destroy the world in which Venus and Juno hold sway and impose his judgment on humankind (4:11.2528–33).

Another fourteenth-century French author, Pierre Bersuire, or Petrus Berchorius, followed the anonymous author of the *Ovide moralisé* in using mythography to explicate the strongly moral inner meaning that medieval writers understood to exist behind Ovid's sometimes scandalous writings. In his *Ovidius moralizatus* he, too, subscribed to the notion that the wisdom associated with Minerva, as he called the goddess, was in truth not some abstract philosophical wisdom but was derived from the Christian God. He made this specifically religious connection by turning to a quotation from Ecclesiasticus 1:1, "All wisdom is of the Lord God" (ed. Ghisalberti, 5–136; Reynolds, 66–68, 78–82).

From these fourteenth-century authors, whom he knew well and borrowed from extensively, Chaucer, whether or not he was acquainted with Fulgentius, the second Vatican mythographer, and Bernard Silvestris, would have learned the Judgment myth and allegory. From Boccaccio's *Il Filostrato* Chaucer took and freely adapted the love story of Troilus himself, and Petrarch's Sonnet 88, paraphrased, became the first "Cantus Troili." The French *Ovide moralisé*, with its broad Fulgentian treatment of the allegory of the threefold choice and its identification of wisdom and of the life of contemplation with the service of God, was well known to Chaucer; he borrowed from it in a wholesale manner, taking words, lines, passages, and whole incidents for use in his own works.[9] Given his familiarity with these authors, it is unlikely that Chaucer would not have encountered the allegorized Judgment myth in the works of at least one of them, especially the *Ovide moralisé*, and perhaps in all.

The Judgment myth and the story of Troilus, the two love stories of the Trojan war, were, moreover, closely connected in fourteenth-century minds, and not just because both were part of the rather small, closely knit material that made up the "matter of Troy." In the *Roman de Troie* of Benoit de St. Maure and the *Historia Troiana* of Guido delle Colonne, it was Troilus who, after hearing his brother Paris's story of the judgment he had made in favor of Venus and the prize the goddess was to give him, impetuously overrode the objections of another and wiser brother Helenus and persuaded the people of Troy to undertake the expedition to bring Helen to Troy (Benoit, Constans, v. 1, 198–207; Guido de Columnis, Griffin, 63–64, trans. Meek, 62). Guillaume de Machaut's *Dit de la fonteinne amoreuse*, a work from which Chaucer drew for his *Book of the Duchess*, specifically links the two love stories. The fountain that is the poem's central image has engraved on it scenes concerning the abduction of Helen as well as a scene depicting the love of Troilus for Calcus's daughter; the subject of the narrative is the Judgment of Paris (Hoepffner, 3:190-91, 201-21). The love stories of Paris and Troilus, though the latter is the invention of the Middle Ages (Gordon, *Story of Troilus*, xii-xvii), had become sufficiently closely associated that one was likely to suggest the other.

Chaucer did not leave it to his audience to make the association between Troilus's story and Paris's choice by themselves; rather, he dramatically brought it to their attention by setting the scene in which Troilus is introduced to the poem's audience, gets his first devastating look at Criseyde, and begins his submission to Venus, the goddess of love, in the temple of the goddess of wisdom. This startling juxtaposition, the triumph of Venus in the temple of Pallas, constitutes another victory of Venus over Pallas analogous to the outcome of the Judgment of Paris, achieved once again by enticing a young man by means of the beauty of a woman, and serves as a striking reminder of that Judgment. Chaucer heightens the sense of Venus's achievement by repeatedly emphasizing the enormous importance of Pallas to Troy. Pallas, personified in her "relik, heet Palladion" (1.154), was "aldirmost in honour out of doute" (1.152), and the city's population had gathered at her temple to "herknen of Palladion the servyse" (1.164), to do honor to the cult statue, because it was "hire trust above everichon" (1.153), the deity to whom they looked for protection from the ravages of war with the Greeks.

If more was needed, there was even a subtle reminder of the allegory in the reiteration of the name of the statue. The medieval period derived most of its knowledge of classical deities from Latin sources and knew them by their Roman names. Chaucer's decision to retain from *Il Filostrato* the name "Palladion," derived from the Greek name Pallas, for the cult statue of the goddess, recalls the extended allegorization of the Judgment myth in the *Ovide moralisé*, Petrarch's complaint, and Boccaccio's account of the Judgment myth, all of which employ the Greek name "Pallas" for the goddess of wisdom.[10]

In the terms of the Judgment myth and allegory, thus suggested as a framework within which to view Troilus's actions, it becomes apparent that when Troilus enters the temple he is a servant of Juno. The hallmarks of his service are so much a part of his position that they could almost go unnoticed. He is, to begin with, a prince of the realm, "a worthy kynges sone" (1.226), and as such is involved in the rule over dominions associated with Juno. Along with his royal rank goes power sufficient that Criseyde would later be afraid of the consequences of bringing on his disfavor if she were to refuse his love (2.708-14). He is active in the defense of Troy, and when he enters the temple he is in charge of a group of knights younger and less experienced than himself. His service sits lightly on him and he enjoys twitting his charges with his very practical views of love, which strike him as requiring much labor and worry with little return. A lover, says Troilus, tosses and turns all night while his lady "slepeth softe," and the most likely outcome of lovers' efforts are "woo and penaunces" (1.195–96; 199–200).

Troilus soon left behind him both this extremely practical view of love and the life of Juno, and as he slipped into the service of Venus he signaled the change with this renunciation of the concerns of Juno: "myn estat roial I here resigne / into hire hond" (1.432–33)—that is, into the hand of Criseyde.[11] Criseyde, and through her Venus, was to gain his loyalty.

That Troilus, in falling in love with Criseyde, entered into subservience to Venus is not in dispute, but, just as the goddess of love wears two aspects in the poem, that of the patroness of lust from whom we get the word "venereal" and that of Cytherea, representative of divine love (3.1255),[12] so does Troilus's movement into love have a dual aspect in that it is both a rise and, simultaneously, a fall. Troilus's most readily apparent movement initially takes him upward. Chaucer himself describes Troilus's motion by saying that Troilus is "clomben on the staire, / And litel weneth that he moot descenden" (1.215–16), echoing the earliest lines of the poem in which we hear that Troilus's "aventures fellen / Fro woo to wele, and after out of joie" (1.2–3). This movement parallels the motion of the wheel of fortune that Pandarus will advise Troilus to catch on its upswing (1.850–54), but which inevitably casts down those whom it has carried up (*Boece* 2, Prose 1). Each movement encompasses a rise and subsequent fall.

According to the allegory of the threefold choice of life, however, this initial rise is actually a downward movement from the respectable if perilous life of Juno into the corruption of the voluptuous life of the senses; Chaucer's use of falling imagery indicates that he concurs. He uses the contradictory word "fellen" to describe Troilus's so-called rise from woe to weal, and goes on to underline the notion of falling by describing Troilus's supposed ascent into the heaven of love as a remarkable series of falls. Troilus's first act on emerging from the temple is to return home and sink down onto his bed, where he remains prostrate for some six hundred lines. In the scene in which Troilus gains Criseyde's love, he falls continually: onto his knees twice (3.953, 1080), and into a dead faint (3.1092); finally he has to be thrown into bed with Criseyde (3.1097). In the context of the climb on the stair and the rise on the wheel of fortune, Troilus's later descent into betrayal and misery reverses the direction; in the terms of the allegory of the choice of life, it is the logical culmination of the life embarked upon after the making of the wrong choice, the shipwreck of all its affairs that lust suffers and that Troilus seems to prefigure when he laments, "all sterelees withinne a boot am I" (1.416). The last fall that Troilus suffered, and the end of his life under Venus, was his fall on the battlefield on which he met his death.

Abruptly after Troilus's final fall came his seemingly inexplicable rise into heaven, his mysterious laughter at those who mourned for him, and the hymn of praise for Christ and Christian love that ends the work.[13] This bizarre sequence becomes reconcilable if Troilus's rise is understood to be an ascent into the locus of wisdom and contemplation, the realm of Pallas. Again Troilus signaled his passage from one realm to another by a statement of relinquishment, in this case the testament he made in anticipation of his death in battle; having left his arms to Mars, Troilus requests, "My sheld to Pallas yef, that shyneth clere" (5.308). No longer in need of offensive arms as he departs this life, he may safely leave them to the god of war, sometime consort of Venus. But, on entering a new life, he might well offer his shield, symbol of protection, to Pallas, former protectress of Troy, symbolically renewing the protective relationship she had had with the city for which he was named.

That Troilus, presumably received by Pallas, ascended into the realm of contemplation identified with her can be understood by a comparison with Dante's *Paradiso*. Chaucer tells us that, after Troilus's death, "His lighte goost ful blisfully is wente / Up to the holughnesse of the eighthe spere" (5.1808-09). Gerald Morgan has argued convincingly that Troilus's eighth heaven is established as corresponding with Dante's eighth sphere by Chaucer's placement of the planet Venus in the third heaven (*Troilus*, 3.1-4). Morgan notes that this correspondence is strengthened by the similarities between Dante's and Troilus's reactions to their view of the earth (Morgan, "Ending," 257-71). Dante, looking back from the eighth heaven, sees the earth and says:

> Col viso ritornai per tutte quante
>   le sette spere, e vidi questo globo
>   tal, ch'io sorrisi del suo vil sembiante;
> e quel consiglio per migliore aprobe
>   che l'ha per meno.   (12.133-37)

Or, as John D. Sinclair translates, "With my sight I returned through every one of the seven spheres, and I saw this globe such that I smiled at its paltry semblance. . . ."[14]

The remainder of the stanza is also worth quoting because it makes explicit the radical change in point of view achieved from the vantage point of the eighth sphere: "e chi ad altro pensa / chiamar si puote veramente probo" (12.137–38). Translated: "and that judgment which holds it for least I approve as best. . . ."

Thus Dante underlines the entirely new perspective and accompanying reversal of values that he saw as having been achieved in the eighth sphere. Troilus underwent a parallel spiritual reversal in the eighth heaven: Dante's smile was echoed in Troilus's laughter as he "fully gan despise / This wrecched world, and held al in vanite / To respect of the pleyn felicite / That is in hevene above" (5.1816–19). Furthermore, in a passage worthy of Fulgentius, Troilus "dampned al oure werk that foloweth so / The blynde lust, the which that may not laste" (5.1823–24). Thus he explained his startling laughter at those who mourned him: those who, not yet free of earthly values, regretted his passing from the world he now scorned.

Morgan identifies the eighth sphere of Paradise as the sphere of the Cherubim (Morgan, "Ending," 264), who are distinguished by their wisdom, the attribute of Pallas. As elaborated by the mythographers, especially the author of the *Ovide moralisé* from whom Chaucer borrowed extensively, wisdom was contemplation, and wisdom and contemplation alike had only one object, the love and service of God. Thus it is not surprising that, at the end of his renunciation of the follies of earthly life, Troilus reflected that we should "al oure herte on heven caste" (5.1825) and immediately went "ther as Mercurye sorted hym to dwelle" (5.1827). That is, he went to the place in heaven assigned to him by Mercury, an appropriate guide in that, according to the mythographers, Mercury's wings were the wings of contemplation because of his association with wisdom and science.

We are reminded of the Wife of Bath's statement that "Mercurie loveth wysdam and science" (whereas, as she said, "Venus loveth ryot and dispence," 3.699–700). Troilus had gained the immortality of wisdom, the gift that cannot die, and since that wisdom comes from and is directed toward God, Troilus's descent and subsequent rise can be seen to parallel, if at some considerable distance, that of Christ, "hym the which that right for love / Upon a crois . . . starf, and roos, and sit in hevene above" (5.1842–44), a correspondence that lessens the surprise of the poem's final references to Christ's love.

Another and very flattering parallel would be noticed by Chaucer's English audience; as Troilus fell and then ascended again into the place of wisdom, so Troy itself was to rise from destruction and come to glory in a place far removed from its defeat, reaching its finest culmination in their own native land. Chaucer's dedication to Virgil and Ovid (5.1792) would serve as a reminder, if any were needed, that Aeneas would escape from Troy and found Rome, the greatest empire the world had known. An English audience would have been aware that this would lead to another and, according to prophecy, even greater empire to be erected in Britain itself. According to a medieval English tradition a great-grandson of Aeneas by the name of Brutus founded Britain and was the ancestor of the British people. This tradition is found in sources as diverse as Laȝoman and the Gawain poet and even in the *Liber Albus*, London's book of city customs (Robertson, "Courtly Love," 10–12), but it is perhaps best to quote Geoffrey of Monmouth, whom Chaucer placed alongside Homer and Virgil upon an iron pillar in his *House of Fame*. In his *History of the Kings of Britain* Geoffrey has this prophecy for Brutus: "beyond the setting sun, past the realms of Gaul, there lies an island in the sea . . . and for your descendants it will be a second Troy." And Geoffrey expands on this: "A race of kings will be born there from your stock and the round circle of the whole earth will be subject to them" (Thorpe, 65).

This is not to say that Chaucer wholeheartedly subscribed to such nationalistic optimism; Robertson marshaled considerable support for his argument that Chaucer was warning Londoners that they, like Troilus, had chosen corruption and were in danger of destruction (Robertson, "Courtly Love," 10, 12, 13). The buoyancy of Troilus's rise, however, indicates that Chaucer was tempering the warning with a reminder that with the application of just a little wisdom they, like Troilus, could ascend to great heights.

The purpose of the Judgment myth and allegory in *Troilus*, however, is not to express Chaucer's concern with nations, but his concern with human beings: their absurdity, their frailty, their suffering, and their need of and capacity for redemption. The allegory does not operate in isolation; its value is in its contrapuntal function, its opposition to the dominant and more explicitly stated movements that Troilus makes. Under the worldly surface of this poem in which Troilus moves up and then down, climbing the ladder of love and then descending, and also riding the wheel of fortune first to its heights and then to its depths, can be discerned a countermotion in which Troilus passes from the life of temporal power downward into lust and then upward into wisdom and contemplation. This countermotion expresses otherworldly values and emphasizes the temporality, mutability, and impending tragedy of Troilus's ill-judged love by contrasting it with wisdom, which is heavenly, eternal, and leads to bliss.

This is not to suggest that Chaucer's use of the allegory is that of an earnest moral preacher; rather he fully exposes the absurdity of human experience. Troilus, who is ridiculous as a lover because he is passive to the point of helplessness, is equally so as a spiritual pilgrim; there is slapstick in his series of falls into lust and in the abrupt way in which he is whisked up to heaven. Nor does Chaucer use the allegory to advocate a complete renunciation of the world, despite his advice to young people that they "repeyreth hom fro worldly vanyte" (5.1837). Unlike Paris, who was allowed only one choice, Troilus experienced all three lives in turn, and this may have been part of the reason for his arrival at wisdom. According to a well-known etymological derivation of Isidore of Seville, *sapientia*, or wisdom, is derived from the verb *sapere*, to taste (*Etymologiarum*, Lindsay 1:10.240–41); perhaps Troilus could arrive at the life of wisdom only after he had tasted the other two.

Troilus's journey through the three choices of life reflects the course of the allegory from its birth in pagan antiquity to its fourteenth-century Christianization, and the allegory in turn helps to bind the pagan body of the poem to its Christian end. If, as Joseph E. Grennan argues, Chaucer knew of the life of contemplation from Aristotle's *Nicomachean Ethics*,[15] he would have known of the high moral purpose and divine object of that life; from Ovid he would have drawn the low comedy with which he invested Troilus's progress toward that object. It is not known that Chaucer ever read Fulgentius, though he would have known of him from Petrarch,[16] but there are oddly Fulgentian echoes in Troilus's rudderless boat that is in peril of shipwreck ("all stereless withinne a boot am I," 1.416), and in Pandarus's description of Troilus in terms that reminded one editor of the snail, a creature that Fulgentius used as a figure of lust.[17] Troilus's progression through the three lives adds a step to that of Bernardus's Aeneas, who went only from the lowest life to the highest, and prefigures Landino's identification of Aeneas's journey from Troy to Italy by way of Carthage as a journey from the life of lust to that of practical affairs and finally to the life of wisdom. The allegory's Christianization, in which Pallas's wisdom became identified with godly wisdom by Bersuire and with intimations of Christ's second coming and the day of judgment in the *Ovide moralisé*, is reflected in the expressions of Christian sentiment at the end of the *Troilus*, and helps to unify those sentiments with the poem's apparently pagan substance.

The allegory lends to the poem a Boethian sense of philosophical detachment, of a refusal to accept the perceived goods of the world, and an insistence instead on the search for the highest good. It also lends symmetry to the poem; the action that begins with Troilus entering the temple of Pallas ends with his entering her heavenly realms. More important, while the allegory incorporates the highest values of the pagan world, the Aristotelian search for wisdom and contemplation, in a specifically Trojan form that accords well with the pagan body of the poem, in its fourteenth-century Christianization it identifies wisdom with the love of the Christian God and contemplation with God's worship and service, thus lending credence to Troilus's rise into heaven and to the praise of Christ that conclude the poem. By calling our attention to Pallas and wisdom early in the poem, Chaucer gives us cause to believe that Troilus's rise into the heavens is the product of his experience throughout the poem, and that Chaucer's own remark, "Swich fyn his lust, swich fyn his noblesse" (5.1831), is not a lament, but a valedictory to two unsatisfactory lives as Troilus enters the best and highest life, that of wisdom, at last.

Notes

1. Steadman (6–12, 42–65) gives the most thorough and comprehensive treatment of the literary antecedents of Troilus's rise, concentrating on the literary sources available to Chaucer, arguing that these precedents demonstrate that the epilogue is less surprising than modern readers find it to be, and fully reviewing the scholarship that had preceded him. By far the most comprehensive bibliography of all aspects of Troilus's ascent is found in Vitto (163–65). Harmonizing the body of the poem with its end has inspired contradictory opinions; for example, Lewis (42–43) finds the palinode contradictory to the rest of the poem; but Donaldson (26–45) argues for the poem's consistency, saying that Chaucer manipulates the narrator's simplicity to point up the complex view of reality at the poem's end. Wheeler (105–23) argues that the palinode was the narrator's last, and only successful, attempt to achieve closure and express reality; and Pulsiano finds that Chaucer, aware of the dualities of language, employed corporal concerns to point to the eternal truths at the end of the poem. Reconciling the pagan and Christian elements has proved daunting; Covella (235–45) argues that there were in fact two palinodes for two audiences, one interested in the courtly love themes that appear in the body of the poem and another, the general audience, that would be reassured by the piety at the poem's end. Kamowski (405–18) believes that a rearrangement of some of the lines of the poem to provide a more logical transition is the best solution. Others look for thematic threads that bind the pagan and Christian elements. Vitto (141–42, 176–77) argues that Troilus is a parody of the Christian notion of the virtuous pagan and both his serio-comic arrival in heaven and Christian sermonizing could thus reasonably be expected; Hiscoe finds Christian elements of frailty and redemption that prefigure Troilus's acceptance into heaven and the praise of Christ that concludes the poem.
2. All quotations from Chaucer's work are taken from Benson.
3. See Vitto, 154–57, 160–61; Hiscoe, "Thorn."
4. Robertson, the only critic to have applied the allegorized Judgment myth to the *Troilus*, assumed general knowledge of mythographical themes, and, in a discussion that dealt with the allegory in very general terms and also with the na-

tionalistic assumption of the English that they were descended from the people of Troy, proposed the allegory as an alternative to interpretations, incorrect in his opinion, based on courtly love. Robertson, who treats several works in his article, explicates the judgment allegory, comments on the English belief in their nation's descent from Troy, and suggests that Chaucer uses the allegory to warn Londoners about the disorder and corruption of their time, 1–18.

5. Recent work by three critics has focused on the use of the allegorized myth of the Judgment of Paris in medieval and Renaissance literature. Erhart brings it closest to Chaucer's time in the work of Guillaume de Machaut and Christine de Pizan. Ehrhart shows how, with application of the allegory, Machaut's *Dit de la fonteinne amoureuse*, which critics have considered to be a facile and over-ornamented allegory, becomes a trenchant comment on a ruler who, overcome by love, neglects his responsibilities to the great detriment of his kingdom. Christine de Pizan, writing after the *Troilus* was completed, employed the myth in four different works. Ehrhart demonstrates that one of Christine's reasons for using the allegory was to give graceful lessons about public and private virtue to the class that were her patrons. See "Machaut's *Dit de la fonteinne amoureuse*," 119–37, and "Christine de Pizan and the Judgment of Paris: A Court Poet's use of Mythographic Tradition," infra. Ehrhart continues her examination of the French tradition of the Judgment of Paris, with some attention to the Latin tradition, in *The Judgment of the Trojan Prince Paris* (75–121 and passim). Chance examines the use of the allegory by Cristoforo Landino in the Italian Renaissance. Landino applied both the allegorized myth and the notion of the Pythagorean Y to Aeneas's journey as recorded in the first six books of the *Aeneid*. Chance explicates both the use of the allegory and its background in the medieval sources available to Landino, in "Medieval Sources," 45–60. Finally, Moss uses the treatment of the myth in the work of sixteenth-century French poets to show how the poetry of the period changed its focus from pointing the way to moral and spiritual truths beyond the literal sense to building its own world of pattern, allusion, and commonplace, a new world of aesthetic experience (6–16, 110–11, 116–17, 148–150, and passim).

6. The first mythographical approach to the *Troilus* was that of Kittredge (109–45), who gave consideration to the fall of Troy and its effect on the mood of the poem. The Root edition of the *Troilus* affords at least one mythographic reflection: the assertion that the festival of the Palladion is thought of as the pagan equivalent of Easter (413). For the debate on the eighth sphere of heaven, see Vitto, 144–46, 163–66. The discussion of Chaucer's treatment of Venus seems to center on the *Knight's Tale*, but Loomis, in discussing Venus as an aid to Natura and the beneficial and harmful effects of love, gives some attention to the Proem of Book III of the *Troilus* (182–95). Perhaps the broadest approach to mythography is found in two dissertations that undertake to identify all the references to the pagan gods and suggest possible reasons for their inclusion. See Costello and McCall, "Classical Myth." But often critics who discuss the mythographical and allegorical allusion in the *Troilus* either neglect or negate the wealth of mythographical and allegorical allusion that such material carried in the Middle Ages. Later, in his *Chaucer among the Gods*, McCall became much

more conservative about mythography and viewed Chaucer's use of it as straightforward and as utilized mainly to set a scene or to define character (17, 22–29, 156–58). Minnis, taking a similar position, is concerned with Chaucer's "historical approach to pagan antiquity" (7–30, 79–107). Miller denies a possible mythographical reading of one passage of the *Troilus* on the grounds of his own reading of Pandarus's character; because he views Pandarus as a kindly creature, he finds the allusions to Procne associated with Pandarus to be unsatisfactory and concludes that their purpose is mere ornamentation (65–68). The opposite point of view is found in the work of Fyler, who argues that fourteenth-century audiences had a sophisticated knowledge of mythology. Robertson (12–17) assumed a knowledge of both myth and allegory on the part of Chaucer's English audience.

7. "Illa dies . . . in qua Venus et Iuno sumptisque decentior armis / venit in arbitrium nuda Minerva tuum"; Ovid, *Heroides*, ed. and trans. Showerman, 60, 202. For the fullest description of the goddesses' parading unclothed, see *Lucian*, vol. 3, ed. and trans. Harmon, 385–409.

8. Aristotle, *Ethics*, 10.1178a; 6–14, 1179b; 11–15; ed. McKeon, 1105–06, 1108–09. Grennan argues that the *Nicomachean Ethics* is a more important source for Chaucer than has yet been acknowledged (125–38).

9. For Chaucer's use of *Ovide moralisé* see Witlieb, esp. 188–210, for the *Troilus*.

10. See, for example, *Ovide moralisé* 4:11.1907, 1999, 2163, 2426; Petrarch, 218; Boccaccio, 1:303–4.

11. Robertson, "Courtly Love," 14–16, cites these lines as evidence of an inversion of hierarchy signifying the decay of Chaucer's society, leaving implicit their function in marking the transition from the life of Juno to that of Venus.

12. Hollander gives a full treatment of the two aspects of Venus as found in Boccaccio; for Venus's duality in Chaucer, see for example, Steadman, 69, and Morgan, 221–35.

13. The debate concerning Troilus's rise and his ultimate destination, whether the seventh or eighth sphere and whether the count should be from the moon outward or from the Primum Mobile inward, has been summarized with extensive bibliography in Vitto, 144–46, 164–66, and more recently in North, 29–32.

14. Sinclair, trans., *Divine Comedy*, vol. 3: *Paradiso*, 322–23; all translations of Dante used here are from Sinclair.

15. Grennan identifies Troilus's rise as being to the ascent to the contemplation of truth, finding considerable irony in Troilus's lack of the leisure, full span of life, freedom from fatigue, and so forth, that Aristotle thought necessary for a philosopher who wishes to contemplate truth, as well as in Troilus's inability to achieve the detachment necessary for contemplation while "in the flesh" (132–34).

16. See above, p. 164.

17. Fisher, ed. *Poetry and Prose of Geoffrey Chaucer*, 408. Loomis thought that "Chaucer probably had access to many of the mythological treatises that were then current—Fulgentius, Hyginus, the earlier Albricus, either *in toto* or as they were excerpted in the encyclopedias" and goes on to point out that John

Ridevall, who was lecturing at Oxford in the 1330s, had written a work on Fulgentius; 190, 193.

Works Cited

Aristotle. *The Basic Works of Aristotle*. Translated by Richard McKeon. New York: Random House, 1941.
Benoit de Sainte-Maure. *La Roman de Troie*. Edited by Leopold Constans. Paris: Didot, 1904.
Bernard Silvestris. *Commentum super sex libros Eneidos Virgilii*. Edited by Julian Ward Jones and Elizabeth Francis Jones. Lincoln and London: University of Nebraska Press, 1977.
———. *Commentary on the First Six Books of Virgil's Aeneid*. Translated by Earl G. Schreiber and Thomas E. Maresca. Lincoln and London: University of Nebraska Press, 1979.
Bersuire, Pierre. "L'Ovidius Moralizatus de Pierre Bersuire." Edited by F. Ghisalberti. *Studj Romanzi* 23 (1933): 5–136.
———. "The *Ovidius Moralizatus* of Petrus Berchorius: An Introduction and Translation." Translated by William Donald Reynolds. Ph.D. diss. University of Illinois–Urbana, 1971.
Boccaccio, Giovanni. *Genealogie deorum gentilium libri*. Edited by Vincenzo Romano. 2 vols. *Opere*, vols. 10–11. Scrittori d'Italia, No. 200–1. Bari: Giuseppe Laterza, 1951.
Chance, Jane. "The Medieval Sources of Cristoforo Landino's Allegorization of the Judgment of Paris." *Studies in Philology* 81 (1984): 145–60.
Chaucer, Geoffrey. *The Book of Troilus and Criseyde*. Edited by Robert Kilburn Root. Princeton: Princeton University Press, 1926.
———. *The Complete Poetry and Prose of Geoffrey Chaucer*. Edited by John H. Fisher. New York: Holt Rinehart and Winston, 1977.
———. *The Riverside Chaucer*. Edited by Larry D. Benson. 3d ed. Boston: Houghton Mifflin, 1987.
Costello, Sister Mary Angelica. "The Goddes and God in the Troilus." Ph.D. diss., Fordham University, 1962.
Covella, Sister Frances Dolores. "Audience as Determinant of Meaning of the *Troilus*." *Chaucer Review* 2 (1967–68): 235–45.
Dante Alighieri. *The Divine Comedy*. Translated by John Sinclair. 1939. Reprint. New York: Oxford University Press, 1981.
Donaldson, E. Talbot. "The Ending of Chaucer's Troilus." In *Early English and Norse Studies, Presented to Hugh Smith in Honour of his Sixtieth Birthday*. Edited by Arthur Brown and Peter Foote. London: Methuen, 1963.
Ehrhart, Margaret J. *The Judgment of the Trojan Prince Paris in Medieval Literature*. Philadelphia: University of Pennsylvania Press, 1987.
———. "Machaut's *Dit de la fonteinne amoureuse*, the Choice of Paris, and the Duties of Rulers." *Philological Quarterly* 59 (1980): 119–37.
Fulgentius, Fabius Planciades. *Opera*. Edited by Rudolf Helm. 1898. Reprint. Stuttgart: Teubner, 1970.
———. *Fulgentius the Mythographer*. Translated by Leslie George Whitbread. Columbus: Ohio State University Press, 1971.
Fyler, John M. *Chaucer and Ovid*. New Haven and London: Yale University Press, 1979.

Geoffrey of Monmouth. *History of the Kings of Britain*. Translated by Lewis Thorpe. Harmondsworth, Middlesex, England: Penguin, 1966.

Gordon, R. K. *The Story of Troilus*. London: Dent, 1934. Reprint. Medieval Academy Reprints for Teaching 2. Toronto, Buffalo, London: University of Toronto Press, 1978.

Grennan, Joseph E. "Aristotelian Ideas in Chaucer's *Troilus*." *Medievalia et Humanistica: Studies in Medieval and Renaissance Culture* 14 (1986): 125–38.

Guido, delle Colonne. *Historia destructionis Troiae*. Edited by Nathaniel Edward Griffin. Cambridge, MA: Medieval Academy of America, 1936.

———. *Historia destructionis Troiae*. Translated by Mary Elizabeth Meek. Bloomington and London: Indiana University Press, 1974.

Hiscoe, David. "The Earthly, the Heavenly, Separations and St. Paul's 'Thorn' in Chaucer's *Troilus*." In *Traditions and Innovations: Essays on British Literature of the Middle Ages and Renaissance*, edited by David G. Allen and Robert A. White. Newark: University of Delaware Press, forthcoming.

Hollander, Robert. *Boccaccio's Two Venuses*. New York: Columbia University Press, 1977.

Hyginus. *Fabulae*. Edited by H. J. Rose. Leyden: A. W. Sijthoff, 1934.

———. *The Myths of Hyginus*. Translated by Mary Grant. Lawrence: University of Kansas Publications, 1960.

Isidore of Seville. *Etymologiarum sive Originum*. 2 vols. Edited by W. M. Lindsay. Oxford: Clarendon Press, 1911. Reprint, 1985.

Kamowski, William. "A Suggestion for Emending the Epilogue of *Troilus and Criseyde*." *Chaucer Review* 21 (1987): 405–18.

Kittredge, George Lymon. *Chaucer and his Poetry*. 1915. Reprint. Cambridge, MA: Harvard University Press, 1970.

Lewis, C. S. *The Allegory of Love*. London, Oxford, New York: Oxford University Press, 1936. Reprint, 1958.

Loomis, Dorothy Bethurum. "The Venus of Alanus de Insulis and the Venus of Chaucer." In *Philological Essays; Studies in Old and Middle English Language and Literature in Honour of Herbert Dean Merritt*, edited by James L. Rosier. The Hague: Mouton, 1979.

Lucian. *Lucian in Eight Volumes*. 8 vols. Edited and translated by A. M. Harmon. London: W. Heinemann; New York: G. P. Putnam's Sons, 1913–67.

McCall, John P. *Chaucer among the Gods: The Poetics of Classic Myth*. University Park and London: University of Pennsylvania Press, 1979.

———. "Classical Myth in Chaucer's Troilus and Criseyde: An Aspect of the Classical Tradition in the Middle Ages." Ph.D. diss., Princeton University, 1955.

Machaut, Guillaume de. *Oeuvres de Guillaume de Machaut*. Edited by Ernest Hoepffner. 3 vols. Paris: Didot, 1908–21.

Miller, R. N. "Pandarus and Procne." In *Studies in Medieval Culture*, edited by John R. Sommerfeldt. Kalamazoo: Western Michigan University Press, 1979.

Minnis, A. J. *Chaucer and Pagan Antiquity*. Cambridge: D. S. Brewer, 1982.

Morgan, Gerald. "The Ending of *Troilus and Criseyde*." *Modern Language Review* 77 (1982): 29–32.

———. "The Significance of the Aubades in *Troilus and Criseyde*." *Yearbook of English Studies* 9 (1979): 221–35.

Moss, Ann. *Poetry and Fable: Studies in Mythological Narrative in Sixteenth Century France*. Cambridge: Cambridge University Press, 1984.

Mythographi Vaticani I et II. Edited by Peter Kulcsár. Corpus Christianorum Series Latini 91c. Turnholt: Brepols, 1987.

North, J. D. *Chaucer's Universe*. Oxford: Clarendon Press, 1988.
Ovid. *Heroides and Amores*. Edited and translated by Grant Showerman. London and New York, 1914. Reprint. Cambridge, MA: Harvard University Press, 1947.
Ovide moralisé. Edited by C. de Boer et al. 5 vols. 1936. Reprint. Wiesbaden: Martin Sändig, 1966.
Petrarch, Francesco. *Prose*. Edited by G. Martelloti et al. La Letteratura italiana. Storia e testi, 7. Milan: R. Riccardi, 1955.
Pulsiano, Phillip. "Redeemed Language and the Ending of *Troilus and Criseyde*." In *Sign, Sentence, Discourse: Language in Medieval Thought and Literature*, edited by Julian N. Wasserman and Lois Roney, 153-74. New York: Syracuse University Press, 1989.
Robertson, D. W., Jr. "The Concept of Courtly Love as an Impediment to the Understanding of Medieval Texts." In *The Meaning of Courtly Love*, edited by F. X. Newman. Albany: State University of New York Press, 1968.
Steadman, John M. *Disembodied Laughter: Troilus and the Apotheosis Tradition; a 'Reexamination of Narrative and Thematic Contexts*. Berkeley: University of California Press, 1972.
Vitto, Cindy Lynn. "The Virtuous Pagan in Middle English Literature." Ph.D. diss., Rice University, 1985. American Philosophical Society: in press.
Wheeler, Bonnie. "Dante, Chaucer, and the Ending of *Troilus and Criseyde*." *Phililogical Quarterly* 61 (1982): 105-23.
Witlieb, Bernard L. "Chaucer and the *Ovide moralisé*." Ph.D. diss., New York University, 1969.

Chaucer's Zephirus

Dante's Zefiro, St. Dominic, and the Idea of the *General Prologue*

Jane Chance

Although Chaucer refers to many classical gods throughout the *Canterbury Tales*, he mentions only one mythological figure in the whole of the *General Prologue*—the West Wind, or Zephirus, in line 5. The passage begins with a dependent clause indicating the time when Zephirus most influences the natural world, that is:

> Whan Zephirus eek with his sweete breeth
> Inspired hath in every holt and heeth
> The tendre croppes, and the yonge sonne
> Hath in the Ram his half cours yronne,
> And smale foweles maken melodye,
> That slepen al the nyght with open ye
> (So priketh hem nature in hir corages). (5–11, Benson's ed.)

The passage ends with an independent clause indicating the consequence of Zephirus's influence on humankind:

> Thanne longen folk to goon on pilgrimages,
> And palmeres for to seken straunge strondes,
> To ferne halwes, kowthe in sondry londes;
> And specially from every shires ende
> Of Englelond to Caunterbury they wende,
> The hooly blisful martir for to seke,
> That hem hath holpen whan that they were seeke. (12-18)

In citing only one mythological figure, Chaucer's practice here contrasts with that in the *Book of the Duchess* and other early poems, *Troilus and Criseyde*, and the other *Canterbury Tales*. In his dream visions and poems (or tales) with pagan settings, he chooses mythological fables in accord with the theory of fabulous narrative as a "mask" or "cover" for underlying truths about the soul, or secrets of nature, enunciated by Macrobius in his commentary on the *Somnium Scipionis*, 1.2, and expanded by William of Conches in his commentary on Macrobius (Dronke, 25, 26, 70). His use of such mythological figures throughout

177

his poetry, including the *Canterbury Tales*, generally accords with the medieval mythographic practice, often used ironically, or with attention to his larger narrative purpose, as a variety of recent scholars have argued.[1] For this reason, given the context of the ironic English social comedy and ecclesiastical satire Chaucer develops in the *General Prologue*, his single reference to the pagan mythological figure Zephirus at its beginning seems highly incongruous. Why he uses Zephirus here at all, and for what purpose, are the questions this essay will seek to answer.

Chaucer's use of the Zephirus figure appears at first glance entirely conventional. Resembling other pagan figures and personifications, such as Aurora, Daybreak, frequently associated with spring openings in dream visions, Zephirus has generally been assumed to personify the West Wind and metonymize the advent of spring's fructifying breezes. Indeed, according to twelfth- and thirteenth-century dictionaries and encyclopedias by Papias and Giovanni Balbi, and commentaries like the fourteenth-century *Ovide moralisé*, the West Wind, also known as Favonius, makes the flowers and grasses bloom.[2]

Actually, Zephirus boasts a more complicated genealogy in the mythographic treatises, although a genealogy consonant with the conventional definitions of the figure. He is one of several winds, distinguishable from one another by their respective origins: according to the first Vatican mythographer (possibly the eighth-century Adanan the Scot), the Greek Zephirus is one of four winds, including the North Wind Boreus, the East Wind Eurus, and the South Wind Auster.[3] These winds, according to the second Vatican mythographer (possibly the tenth-century Remigius of Auxerre), were born as a result of the mythological coupling of Astraeus, one of the Titans who bore arms against the gods, and Aurora the dawn.[4] They are ruled by King Aeolus, also recognized as father of the winds by John of Garland in his thirteenth-century *Integumenta Ovidii*. In addition, the two directions of each wind bear different names; Zephirus seeks Circius in the Northwest, but Favonius (a frequently cited alternate name of Zephirus) in the West.[5]

Less meterologically and more mythologically, the power of Zephirus to engender flowers and plants through his anthropomorphized "breath" has been explained by Boccaccio in his fourteenth-century amalgamation of mythography known as the *Genealogie deorum gentilium*. Boccaccio primarily draws upon Ovid's *Fasti*, 5.183–371, Lactantius Firmianus's *Divinae institutiones*, 1.20.6, and Arnulf of Orleans's commentary on the *Fasti* to clarify the relationship of Zephirus and Flora, goddess of flowers. According to Ovid's *Fasti*, Zephirus the West Wind raped the nymph Chloris (a Greek name relating to "green," later changed to the

Roman Flora, a Latin name relating to *flos*) in the spring and later married her. Her name—and action—implicitly explain her function as goddess of the flowers, her enjoyment of perpetual spring, and her dowry, a fruitful garden nourished by a breeze and irrigated by flowing water. Her festival, the Floralia, which extended from April 28 to May 3, is described by Lactantius Firmianus as involving lascivious games and concupiscence of all sorts, perhaps, we might surmise, because of her identification in late antiquity with the Magna Mater (Bona Dea, Cybele, Ops, Juno, etc.).[6]

In line with these definitions, most of the acknowledged sources for the Chaucerian passage about Zephirus echo his literal role as revivifying wind.[7] Two important treatments come from Isidore in his *De natura rerum* (Huppé, 17) and from Pierre Bersuire in his *Reductorium morale* (Bowden, 20). Both passages mention zephyrs as synonyms for the balmy and fructifying westerly winds, as does Guido delle Colonne in his *Historia destructionis Troiae* (Huppé, 16), and of course Book 1, meter 5, of Boethius's *Consolatio Philosophiae* has been acknowledged as a source not only for the figure of Zephirus but also for the *reverdie* in Chaucer's *General Prologue* (Cummings, 86–90). Indeed, of all the possible sources for the *reverdie*, only the Boethius passage specifically mentions Zephirus. And in Boethius, as in other early passages, Zephirus, the wind of spring, the West Wind, functions exclusively as an agent for macrocosmic vitality and regeneration in contrast to Boreas, the North Wind associated with winter: Book 1, meter 5, of Chaucer's *Boece* addresses the "makere of the wheel that bereth the sterres" to note that "Thy myghte attempreth the variauntz sesouns of the yer, so that Zephirus, the debonere wynd, bryngeth ayen in the first somer sesoun the leeves that the wynd that hygte Boreas hath reft awey in autumpne."[8]

What continues to puzzle the student of Chaucer's *General Prologue* is the poet's more figurative use of Zephirus's role, structured as it is in the *reverdie* by means of the "when"/"then" conjunction (Huppé, 14–15; Chance, "Creation," 463). Such syntactical patterning invites an identification of the inspiration of the tops of leaves by Zephirus's "sweete breeth" with that of the pilgrims traveling to Canterbury, to echo the natural process of growth suggested by the mythic action with a more supernatural one—the "inspiration," or longing, of the pilgrims to visit Canterbury.

The analogy between the advent of spring and Easter, or natural and spiritual renewal, has been conventionally used throughout the Middle Ages in vernacular works, like the Middle English lyrics and French and English dream visions, and also Latin works, some of which Chaucer may have used as sources for his *reverdie* in the *General Prologue*. In some of these the figure of Zephirus also appears. For example, *Sir Gawain and the Green Knight* (Tolkien's edition) describes the passing of the seasons during the year Gawain must wait before setting out on his quest; in the season of summer, rather than that of spring, Zephirus manifests himself:

> . . . þe sesoun of somer wyth þe soft wyndez
> Quen Zeferus syflez hymself on sedez and erbez,
> Wela wynne is þe wort þat waxes þeroute,
> When þe donkande dewe dropez of þe leuez,
> To bide a blysful blusch of þe bryȝt sunne. (516–20)

The idea of a rebirth in the natural world brought on by Zephirus becomes ironic in this poem if the reader agrees with those critics who doubt that Gawain truly grows spiritually as a result of his three tests in Bertilak's castle. That is, still taking himself far too seriously when he breaks out into an angry, misogynistic diatribe in front of the Green Knight, Gawain also insists, rather pompously, on his many character flaws by wearing the green girdle as sign of failure upon his return to court. Or one might argue that Gawain grows into maturity, but that the court in its first age, which greets Gawain's story with laughter, does not.

Similar to the image of Zephirus in both *Sir Gawain and the Green Knight* and in the *General Prologue*, Zephirus functions in Chaucer's other poems as a revivifying agent generally adapted to signal a concomitant (often ironic) spiritual or psychological rebirth, sometimes with religious undertones, although this intention is clear to the reader only after analysis of the whole poem; given our limitations on space, we shall only suggest the way in which the reference functions in these poems. In the *Book of the Duchess*, Zephirus and Flora revivify the flowers together to suggest the richness and beauty of the idealized spring setting: after the whelp has joined the narrator in the dream portion of the poem, once Chaucer has emerged from the bedroom whose walls and windows depict literary figures, he leads the dreamer to a "floury grene," which the narrator imagines as the domain of Flora and Zephirus because of the many flowers abloom there:

> Doun by a floury grene wente
> Ful thikke of gras, ful softe and swete.
> With floures fele, faire under fete,
> And litel used; hyt semed thus,
> For both Flora and Zephirus,
> They two that make floures growe,
> Had mad her dwellynge ther, I trowe;

> For hit was, on to beholde,
> As thogh the erthe envye wolde
> To be gayer than the heven,
> To have moo floures, swiche seven,
> As in the welken sterres bee. (398–409)

The poet specifically antithetizes the rich plenitude of spring to the meager poverty of winter in order to enhance the role of Zephirus and Flora as vegetation forces and thus echo the appearance of Zephirus in conjunction with Boreas, the North Wind, in Boethius's *Consolatio*:

> Hyt had forgete the povertee
> That wynter, thorgh hys colde morwes,
> Had mad hyt suffre, and his sorwes;
> All was forgeten, and that was sene,
> For al the woode was waxen grene;
> Swetnesse of dewe had mad hyt waxe. (411–15)

The appearance of Zephirus and Flora in the idealized and verdant spring meadow setting acts by metonymy to suggest the psychological goal of both narrator and grieving Black Knight—the healing or renewal of self and soul. The narrator will catalyze this process by asking a series of simple, rather dense questions that prompt the Black Knight's mourning process—denial, anger, sadness, acceptance. By helping the mourner, the dreamer can himself "awaken" to a new dawn, after his long night of insomnia and numbness.

In *Troilus and Criseyde*, 5.10, Zephirus's yearly advent, marked by the arrival of tender green leaves, harkens back to the narrator's prefatory paean in the third book to the fair chain of love and the heavenly Venus and the harmonious music of Calliope; Troilus has ironically echoed this paean at the breaking of dawn close to the end of the third book after the lovers' first night of lovemaking, in his "Canticus Troili" addressed to "Love, that of erthe and se hath governaunce" (1744). That the love he shares with Criseyde remains physical, unlike the love he and the narrator celebrate in their twin apostrophes, reminds us that Zephirus's rejuvenation of the natural world, alas for Troilus, does not carry with it a rebirth of spiritual love. In 5.10, again for ironic contrast, Phoebus is said to melt the snows and Zephirus bring green leaves for three years of the relationship between Troilus and Criseyde—a happy rejuvenation that will end with her imminent departure to the Greeks, a sort of permanent winter:

> The gold-tressed Phebus heighte on-lofte
> Thries hadde alle with his bemes clene

> The snowes molte, and Zepherus as ofte
> Ibrought ayeyn the tendre leves grene,
> Syn that the sone of Ecuba the queene
> Bigan to love hire first for whom his sorwe
> Was al, that she departe sholde a-morwe. (8–14)

This cyclical repetition heightens the dramatic contrast between the ending of the relationship in this fifth book (and the literal as well as spiritual death of Troilus, plus the striking lack of fertility indicated by the "marriage") and the continuing new beginning of the natural world—and the advent of superior understanding after Troilus's death, a kind of rebirth as well as apotheosis, when he looks down from the eighth sphere on the wretched world beneath him and laughs aloud.

Zephirus and Flora rejuvenate flowers in the *Prologue* to the *Legend of Good Women* when they appear in May, a month of revivification in nature and in human love—indeed, their appearance together marks what might be termed the marriage of heaven (the West Wind Zephirus) and earth (Flora):

> And Zepherus and Flora gentilly
> Yaf to the floures, softe and tenderly,
> Hire swoote breth, and made hem for to sprede,
> As god and goddesse of the floury mede. (F171–4)

Such natural rejuvenation underscores the role of Alceste in choosing to die for her husband, descending into the underworld, and returning; she also appears in the form of a daisy with similar characteristics. Of course Alceste, the daisy, and even these references all work for the concept of fidelity within the context of love, Alceste allied with the God of Love as a queen of heaven analogous to the Virgin as the God of Love (in the conventional courtly manner) is analogous to the Christian God.

One other reference to Zephirus (at the end of the *Legend*, in the *Legend of Hypermnestra*, line 2681), depends upon the same conjunction of ideas, but for ironic purposes. The reaction of the central figure to her father Aegyptus's command to slit her husband's throat when he sleeps (he has been forewarned one of his nephews will kill him, and so commands all his daughters), or else die by her father's hand, is likened to the shaking of a branch by Zephirus, as if her father had the same power over her as the West Wind over nature. On the night her husband sleeps:

> She rist hire up, and dredfully she quaketh,
> As doth the braunche that Zepherus shaketh,
> And hust were alle in Argon that cite.

As cold as any frost now waxeth she;
For pite by the herte hire steyneth so. . . .   (F 2680-84)

The use of the normally positive and revivifying force of Zephirus to describe in a rough image the destructive and crazed—psychologically speaking, wintry, cold, barren—power of father over daughter is a brilliant turning *up-so-doun* of the normal associations of the classical figure, and of the revivifying power of spring (where else does a cold frost "waxeth," line 2683?). The image of Zephirus shaking the branch also invokes the genealogical cycle that normally renews the family by means of succeeding generations, in contradistinction to Aegyptus's frosty attempt to foreshorten that natural cycle in order to extend the duration of his own life.

In most of these works, but especially in the *General Prologue*, Chaucer's use of Zephirus depends upon the conception of the wind as a poetic correlative for spiritual renewal, as developed in the Latin mythographic tradition and in Dante. In many of the earliest medieval mythographic poems and tracts, Zephirus as a rejuvenating force is linked with the World Soul, in which the individual human soul was believed, in microcosm, to share. From this early association the figure of Zephirus gradually accumulates a potency suggestive of psychological renewal. But religious and even Christian associations for Zephirus derive from different sources.

The evolution culminates in the rich and complex treatment of Zefiro by Dante in the twelfth canto of the *Paradiso*, a text that I believe Chaucer was familiar with and that he used in part as a model for the roles of Zephirus in the *General Prologue*. The Greek concept of Zephirus as fructifying wind generally associates this West Wind with the breath of human life, in part because the World Soul, according to Stoic belief, was a macrocosmic equivalent of the human soul and responsible for its engendering. Indeed, according to Boccaccio's *Genealogie*, "life" or *vita* is the meaning of the Greek "Zephs" from which his name derives.[9] Other literary texts bear out this association. When the first Vatican mythographer discusses Zephirus in Myth 183.6, he cites a line from the *Aeneid* at the time of Dido's death noting that the winds (Zephirus is not singled out) bring and take away life. In this passage Iris the rainbow, Juno's messenger in the region of air ruled by the goddess, descends to Dido's head to free her from the flesh: "Dilapsus calor, atque in ventos vita recessit" ("With that she cut the wisp; at once all warmth / dispersed, and life retreated to the winds").[10]

The beginning as well as the ending of life for the soul is linked with Zephirus in several medieval texts. In the influential Fulgentian *Mitologiae* (3.6),[11] Zephirus seems to be associated with life, again in relation to the soul as represented by the character of Psyche. That is, Zephirus in the myth of Cupid and Psyche initially comes after her marriage to carry Psyche into the golden mansion of her new husband Cupid, a role denoting transportation and communication as well as beginnings—as in the beginning of a new relationship, particularly here one of marriage, which might herald creativity, fructification. In addition, this particular marriage, of Cupid—love, literally from *cupiditas*, cupidity, desire, concupiscence—and Psyche the human soul, argues for spiritual renewal as well, or for what could be interpreted as a change in consciousness as a result of falling in love. The second time Zephirus appears it is to carry Psyche to her worried sisters who fear she is dead because of her love for Cupid. Here the passage communicates reassurance of the continuance of life, or rather, the attempt to prevent worry and death. Zephirus serves in all cases as a messenger who announces the beginning of life, or at least a kind of beginning, symbolized in the wedding of Cupid and Psyche (to be understood on the literal and figurative levels), and also the ending of life (or its possibility), symbolized through the fear of Psyche's sisters that she is dead.

Such a connection between beginnings and endings also occurs in other, later works. Indeed, Zephirus, as Favonius, is declared by Boccaccio in the *Genealogie* to control beginnings and endings, particularly of germination beginning in spring and ending in summer, through the sweet and gentle nature of his influence and his complexion.[12] In Chaucer's *General Prologue*, too, the West Wind appropriately signals the return of life to the English countryside, awakening it from the "death" of winter and human mortality and suffering. Thematically the arrival of the West Wind in the *Prologue* also signals a "marriage"—of the body and the soul, Cupid and Psyche, or, within the eighteen lines of the *reverdie*, the natural urge of the birds to mate, in the first eleven lines, so to speak, coupled with the supernatural urge of the pilgrims to travel for penance, in the last seven.

Prior to Chaucer, the association of Zephirus with spiritual life in a specifically Christian context involving renewal of the soul occurs in a ninth-century passage from Rabanus Maurus's *De universo*. Rabanus uses as a base for his allegorical reading the more usual associations of Zephirus with the West Wind as fructifier of seed and flowers ("Occidentalis autem ventus, Zephyrus Graeco nomine appellatur eo quod flores et germina ejus flatu vivificentur") and the name Favonius because he warms (*foveat*: literally, "warms," figuratively "cherishes, embraces") that which is born ("Hic Latine favonius dicitur, propter quod foveat quae nascuntur," col. 282). In addition, Zephirus's appearance in spring, the time of year in which Christ died, carries with it the seeds of all virtue and good works which are born in the world ("Tunc autem hic ventus in bonam partem positus reperitur, cum mortis Christi et veri solis occubitum significat, unde omnium germina virtutum et bonorum operum in mundo nascuntur").

There is one link missing between the Zephirus of the Latin mythographic tradition and the Zephirus of Chaucer's *General Prologue*: Rabanus focuses only on the tropological interpretation of Zephirus as a rejuvenator of the human soul. Such an idea is used by Chaucer in the *Book of the Duchess* to suggest psychological renewal of the soul without any necessary and explicit Christian renewal, in contrast to the more explicit relationship celebrated in the *reverdie* of the *General Prologue*. Chaucer, however, if we understand his purpose correctly in the *General Prologue* and indeed at the end of *The Canterbury Tales*, wants also to use the anagogical significance of Zephirus as a rejuvenator of the Church.

The missing link can be found in Dante's treatment of Zefiro in canto twelve of the *Paradiso*, in an image that dominates this and surrounding cantos. Chaucer's interest in Dante and other writers of the Italian *trecento* may have been whetted by several trips to Italy, the most important of which (in terms of Dante's influence on his poetry) occurred in 1378,[13] some years after the writing of *The Book of the Duchess* in 1372.[14] Various studies have demonstrated his use of and familiarity with Dante, in particular, whose status as an *auctor* was made manifest before Boccaccio's death through a series of public lectures delivered by the scholar and poet on the early cantos of the *Inferno* and in the fourteenth century generally through scholarly commentaries.[15]

For Dante, Zefiro was in part responsible for the birth of a saint who revitalized the Church by battling ignorance and heresy. The chief champion of Christ's army is the "holy athlete" St. Dominic, founder of the order of the Dominicans (canto 11, who provide a counterpoint to the faithful Franciscans); the rigorous scholasticism and rationality of the former order is exemplified by St. Thomas Aquinas (canto 10), as the revelation, mysticism, joy, and love associated with the latter order is exemplified by St. Bonaventure. Both exemplars, and both orders, belong to the Sphere of the Sun, that of the theologians, and are harmonized and reconciled in Paradise, a perennially springlike other world symbolized by the Celestial Rose.

St. Dominic's birthplace is described in particular as touched by the sweet wind Zephirus in *Paradiso* 12.46–52:

> In quella parte ove surge ad aprire
> Zefiro dolce le novelle fronde

di che si vede Europa rivestire,
   non molto lungi al percuoter dell'onde
dietro a le quali, per la lunga foga,
lo sol talvolta ad ogne uom si nasconde,
   siede la fortunata Calaroga
sotto la protezion del grande scudo
in che soggiace il leone e soggioga:
   dentro vi nacque l'amoroso drudo
della fede cristiana, il santo atleta
benigno a'suoi ed a'nemici crudo;
   e come fu creata, fu repleta
sì la sua mente di viva vertute
che, ne la madre, lei fece profeta.   (ed. Grandgent, lines 46–60)[16]

[In that part where sweet Zephyr rises to open the new leaves in which Europe sees herself reclad, not far from the beating of the waves behind which the sun, after his long flight, sometimes hides himself from all men, lies favoured Calahorra under protection of the great shield in which the lion is subject and sovereign. In it was born the loving liegeman of the Christian faith, the holy athlete, gracious to his own and pitiless to enemies; and his mind, as soon as it was created, was so full of living power that in his mother's womb it made her prophetic. (Sinclair, 3:177)]

In this passage, Dante is making two crucial points by means of the figure of Zephirus. Literally, Zephirus the sweet West Wind "fructified" Castile to give birth to Dominic. More figuratively, St. Dominic himself acts as a type of Zephirus in tending Christ's garden, understood as the teaching that kept the vineyard of the Church vital:

   Domenico fu detto; e io ne parlo
sì come de l'agricola che Cristo
elesse a l'orto suo per aiutarlo.
   Ben parve messo e famigliar di Cristo; . . .
   Non per lo mondo, . . .
ma per amor de la verace manna
 in picciol tempo gran dottor si feo;
tal che si mise a circüir la vigna
che tosto imbianca, se'l vignaio è reo
   E alla sedia che fu già benigna
più a'poveri giusti, non per lei,
ma per colui che siede, che traligna, . . .
   contro al mondo errante

Chaucer's Zephirus

    licenza di combatter per lo seme
del qual ti fascian ventiquattro piante.
  Poi, con dottrina e con volere insieme,
con l'officio appostolico si mosse
quasi torrente ch'alta vena preme;
  e ne li sterpi eretici percosse
l'impeto suo, più vivamente quivi
dove le resistenze eran più grosse.
  Di lui si fecer poi diversi rivi
onde l'orto catolico si riga,
sì che i suoi arbuscelli stan più vivi.   (70–73, 82, 84–90, 94–105)

[He was called Dominic, and I speak of him as of the labourer whom Christ chose to help Him in His garden. He seemed indeed a messenger and of the household of Christ. . . . Not for the world . . . but for love of the true manna, he became in a short time so great a teacher that he began to go round the vineyard, which soon withers if the keeper is at fault; and to the seat which is now less kind to the upright poor than once it was—not in itself, but in him who sits there degenerate (Boniface VIII)—he appealed . . . for leave to fight with the erring world for the seed of which twenty-four plants encircle thee (i.e., the twenty-four saints that whirl around Dante in two circles, one representing the Franciscans and love, and the other representing the Dominicans and knowledge). . . . Then, with both learning and zeal and with the apostolic office, he went forth like a torrent driven from a high spring, and on the heretic thickets his force struck with most vigour where the resistance was stubbornest. From him there sprang then various streams by which the Catholic garden is watered, so that its saplings have new life.]

That is, figuratively, Dominic then restored the vineyard of the Church by planting new seeds of faith (the Dominican order) and creating future revivificators (streams feeding saplings).

    Closer attention to this seminal passage will enhance our understanding of the intertwined roles of Zefiro and Dominic. St. Dominic serves as the Christian analogue of the classical and even Stoic figure of Zephirus. To begin with the natural, literal, and macrocosmic level, it has been noted[17] that Spain is the country nearest the source of Zephyr, the West Wind, and that St. Dominic was born in Spain, all of which underscore the vitality of the region and the saint. But the reference transcends mere geographical proximity. St. Dominic planting seeds of faith in his vineyard resembles Zephirus producing seeds and flowers with his breath. Instead of the world reclad in flowery new garb, however, Dante images forth rebirth in the new leaves of the reclad and feminine Europe. The point (as we shall see later in the canto) is that from St. Dominic came the streams by which the gardens of the Church were watered, so that saplings had new life. In the *Legenda aurea,* "Dominicus" denotes the keeper of the vineyard of the Lord (from *domus* + *canes,* "watchdog of the house").[18] Thus the "new leaves" that regenerate the saplings come from the gardens we see emphasized in line 106: "From him there sprang then various streams by which the Catholic garden ["l'orto catolico," 104] is watered, so that its saplings have new life ["i suoi arbuscelli stan più vivi," 105]."[19] Earlier in this passage Dominic is described as the "labourer" ("l'agricola") whom Christ picked to help in his garden ("l'orto") (71). As teacher Dominic went around the "vineyard" ("la vigna," 86), "which withers if the keeper is at fault" ("che tosto imbianca, se'l vignaio è reo," 87). The point is that his scholastic work kept the garden alive, the garden being the Christian faith: he appealed in 1216 to Pope Honorius III for authorization for his order and thereafter preached against the Albigensian heresies. He appealed specifically "for leave to fight with the erring world for the seed of which twenty-four plants encircle thee" ("thee" is Dante, 96)—that is, for the faith that culminates eventually and perfectly in saints. Then follows the line, "From him there sprang then various streams by which the Catholic garden is watered, so that its saplings have new life."

Dante's reference to Zefiro thus sums up the wind's associations with macrocosmic and natural regeneration and microcosmic life, the latter understood spiritually and psychologically as well as naturally. Dante uses all the other classical associations of Zephirus with regeneration and vitality, both of the external world and of the little world man, but to these he adds the idea of Christian renewal ultimately typified in the figure of Christ and his Resurrection. St. Dominic thus is likened to the ultimate source of spiritual renewal in the Christian faith, Christ himself.

The earlier mythological contrast between winter and spring—Boreas and Zephirus, if we use the names of the North and West Winds—traced from late antique writers like Boethius thus becomes in Dante's hands an allegorical contrast between spiritual death and life—and between Fall and Redemption. The image of the garden reminds us of the Fall to indicate on the tropological level how human progress in the wilderness should lead to that earthly paradise at the top of Mount Purgatory, which Dominic's activities attempt through knowledge. For the macrocosm, then, the association of the Zephirus and garden images with the birth of Dominic marks an allegorical rebirth like that of spring in the natural world. For the microcosm man the association marks a tropological rebirth of human nature like that expressed through the resurrection of the second Adam, Christ, to which we may aspire in our search for purgation and redemption. Humankind has descended from Adam and like him is condemned to labor in the wilderness after the Fall. The gardening imagery used by Dante to describe Dominic's life reminds the reader that this saint is a model of human perfection in emulation of Christ.

How does the Dante passage relate to Chaucer's? Of course much of the opening passage in Chaucer focuses on what might be termed an unfolding of new life in a gardenlike setting thematically and imagistically reminiscent of Dante's passage—the emphasis on seeds, gardening, and the vineyard parallel Chaucer's heaths and holts, the burgeoning plant and animal life. Further and more significantly, the connection between St. Dominic and Zefiro also reminds us of St. Thomas à Becket and Zephirus. The "sweet wind" fructifying human nature for Dante brings Dominic; what was important for Spain initially and, later, Europe (that is, St. Dominic, says Dante), was equally important for England (that is, St. Thomas à Becket). In addition, the sweet wind (traditionally cause of revivification of life in the human soul) in England fructifies the human process of need for purgation so that pilgrims wish to journey toward Canterbury (more figuratively, the heavenly Jerusalem, as the Parson points out).

The reference to Zephirus in the *General Prologue* may also exemplify the underlying satiric theme of corruption in the Church and thus the need for renewal: just as Zephirus announces what might be seen as a pagan "marriage," in the first eleven lines, of a feminine and passive earth, or the roots, sap-vessels, and flowers of lines 2–5, to the masculine and active heavens, or the showers and wind of April of lines 1, 5–6,[20] so also Zephirus anticipates the analogous anagogical revivification of the Church, not by its ostensible leaders, the Prioress, Monk, or Friar, but by the truly Christian Parson and his brother the Plowman. Thus the previous association of Zephirus with female figures in all the sources—Dido in the *Aeneid*, Psyche in Apuleius, Europe in Dante ("dressing" herself, being reclad), the latter who, through the birth of St. Dominic and his work, will be reborn both politically and spiritually, given his many gifts to the Church—culminates in the figures of both Nature and the Church in the *General Prologue*.

In the works prior to the *General Prologue*, Zephirus is cast in the role of agent of macrocosmic and microcosmic life and generation understood on the physical and spiritual—even Christian—levels. This tension between pagan and Christian thus forms what might be termed the idea of the *General Prologue* as it functions on its two levels, literal (natural, physical, pagan) and figurative (supernatural, spiritual, Christian). Zephirus as the classical version of the West Wind has two significations: Latin mythographic sources reveal his association with the *Aeneid* and other works like that of Apuleius wherein he is a harbinger and messenger, a fructifier of the world in spring; and Dante, a vernacular and poetic source, reveals his association with the soul and good works within a more Christian context, the birth of St. Dominic. In this one classical allusion with its varied history of mythographic associations, then, Chaucer truly epitomizes what might be termed the idea of the *General Prologue*. To use a classical ("pagan") image ultimately within a Christian context serves to defuse artistically that dramatic tension between the desires of this world and those for the next from which we suffer and which is amply demonstrated in the pilgrims on the Canterbury journey.

Notes

1. Scholars have examined mythological figures in the dream visions—for example, the *Parlement* (Brown, "Priapus"; Loomis, "The Venus"), the *Legend of Good Women* (Clogan; Meech, "Chaucer"), the *House of Fame* (Fyler; Hall; Lord)—the *Troilus* (McCall, "Classical Myth," *Chaucer*; Miller; Minnis, *Chaucer*), the short poems (Storm), and several tales in the *Canterbury Tales* (the *Merchant's Tale*: Brown, "*Hortus*"; Donovan; Hoffman, "Ovid's Priapus"; Wentersdorf; the *Knight's Tale*: Green; Hoffman, "Ovid and Chaucer's Myth"; Loomis, "Saturn," "The Venus"; Quinn; Steadman; Wilkins; the *Wife of Bath's Tale*: Hoffman, "Ovid and the Wife of Bath's Tale," "Ovid's Argus," "The Wife of Bath"; Robertson, "Wife of Bath"; the *Physician's Tale*: Hoffman, "Pygmalion"; the *Pardoner's Tale*: Chance, " 'Disfigured' "). More generally, Hoffman, *Ovid and the Canterbury Tales*, and Robertson, *A Preface*, are full of suggestive glosses on the myths in Chaucer. I am now at work on a long study of the mythographic background of Chaucer's mythological figures, entitled The *Mythographic Chaucer*.

2. See the facsimile of Papias, *Vocabulista*, s.v.: "Zephyrus graece dictus qui flores et gramia eius flatu vivificentur: hic favonius dicitur latine," p. 380; and also the expanded but similar dictionary by Giovanni Balbi (Joannes Balbus), *Catholicon*, s.v. also under "Favonius." Of the commentaries, the *Ovide moralisé*, for example, mentions Zephirus in two places, once as one of the four winds, associated with the West and called Galerne (1.268, de Boer, 66) and once as the force that vivifies the flowers: "Unz vens plesans et delitables, / Zephirus, fesoit les floretes / Nestre: vers, indes, vermeilletes, / Jaunes, blaunches et d'autre guise, / Sans semence qui i fust mise" (1.508–512, de Boer, 72). For a brief discussion of the Zephirus tradition as it appears in Ovid's *Fasti* and the relationship between Flora-Chloris, see Wind, 116. No modern scholar has analyzed either Chaucer's use of Zephirus or the Zephirus tradition in the Middle Ages.

3. All references to the Vatican mythographers derive from Bode. In the first Vatican mythographer, Boreas is listed as Aquilones in Latin and Eurus as Africus; the mythographer mistakenly lists Auster as the corresponding Latin name for Zephirus rather than as the South Wind. For no. 183.6, pp. 55–56, Bode notes the sources of myth are the scholia on Statius's *Thebaid* 2.4 and Servius on *Aeneid* 1.132. A similar treatment of Zephirus and the other winds appears in Bede, *Didascalica genuina*, chap. 27, *PL* 90:248. The identification of Adanan the Scot as the first Vatican mythographer has been argued by Elliott and Elder, 198–99.

4. Put meteorologically, the mixing (mythologically, the mating) of air and water leads to the creation of winds: *nubes* (clouds) come from air, from *nubes* comes water, from the motion of water the winds were created. The comments in myth 51 are similar to those of the first Vatican mythographer, myth 183, and according to Bode derive from Hesiod's *Theogony* 378 and Servius on *Aeneid* 1.587. Here the mythographer provides a gloss on a line from the *Aeneid* in reference to Aeolus as king of winds. Aeolus's anger and his order to curb that anger are explained naturally (Bode, 92).

5. See John of Garland, *Integumenta*, lines 41–48 (ed. Ghisalberti):

Aeris in multas partes est fractio, ventus
  Frigoris et tonitrus vendicat esse pater.
Eurum sol oriens, Zephirumque cadens, mediusque
  Austrum cui Boreas obstrepit ore videt.
Dum Subsolano Vulturno cingitur Eurus,
  Hinc Austrum stipat Affricus, inde Nothus.
Circine, te Zephirus deposcit teque, Favoni.
  Hinc Aquilo Boream, Chorus et inde tenet.

See also the translation by Born. Favonius is regarded as especially fructifying in his effect on the double crops of India, as expressed in Martianus's *De nuptiis Philologiae et Mercurii (Marriage of Philology and Mercury)*, where Zephirus's Latin name, Favonius, is used: "nam in Eoum mare a meridiano porrecta, salubris Iauonii uegetabilibus flabris, secundo aestate annis singulis uegetatur bisque frugem metit; pro hieme etesias perfert" (Dick, 6, p. 345, or no. 694; "Stretching southward to the eastern Ocean, it [India] is a healthy land because of the invigorating breezes of Favonius; its soil is enlivened by a second summer each year, and it produces two crops," Stahl, 2:259).

6. Boccaccio, *Genealogie* 4.61 (1:217). Boccaccio cites Bede, Homer (*Iliad*), Lactantius in the *Divine institutes*, Ovid, and Pliny to uncover interesting details about the West Wind favoring the growth of flowers. His simplest gloss, probably taken from Ovid's *Fasti*, notes that a nymph named Cloris was loved and later married by Zephirus; her marriage dowry gave her rule over flowers and for this reason her name changed from Cloris to Flora: "De Zephyro talis recitatur fabula. Nynpham fuisse scilicet nomine Clorim, a Zephyro dilectam, et in coniugem assumptam, eique ab eo in munus amoris atque violate pudicitie omne ius [sic] in flores concessum, eamque ex Clora Floram vocavit."

The passage from Lactantius Firmianus euhemerizes the lascivious nature of the activities of the Floralia, which originated in a prostitute's donation to the Roman populace of a large sum of money intended for games on her birthday and dignified by the Senate through an identification of the prostitute with the goddess of flowers (who must be placated in order to ensure ample fruit and vines): "Dicit Lactantius in libro Istitutionum divinarum Floram feminam magnas ex meretricio quesisse opes, quarum moriens Romanum populum scripsit heredem, parte servata, que sub annuo fenore prestaretur, ex quo scilicet fenore voluit, ut suus natalis dies singulis annis editione ludorum celebraretur. Qui ludi Florales et sacra Floralia a Flora nuncupata sunt, quod quia senatui tractu temporis flagitiosum visum est, cum timore plebis rectractare non posset, ab ipso meretricis nomine argumentum summi placuit, ut rei pudende dignitas adderetur, et inde finxerunt Floram floribus preesse, eam oportere ludis placare, ut fruges cum arboribus aut vitibus bene prospereque florerent. Quem colorem secutus Ovidius [in the *Fasti* passage cited above], nynpham non ignobilem Zephyro nuptam et dotalitio munere, ut floribus presseet, accepisse a sponso. Qui ludi, ut dicit Lactantius, memorie meretricis conveniunt; nam omni lascivia et verborum licentia, quibus omnis obscenitas effunditur, positis flagitante populo a meretricibus vestimentis, que ludis in illis mymorum fungebantur officio, celebrantur."

Finally, Boccaccio draws upon Pliny's *Natural History*, 8.66.166, to indicate that near Lisbon, in Lusitania (Portugal), mares facing the west wind conceive the "breath of life" to produce a very fast colt; the mare from which this derived was known as "Thyella" and mentioned by Homer: "Quas dicit Plinius in concupiscentiam prolis suscipiende venientes hyulco gutture consuevisse flantes Zephyros suscipere, et ex eis concipere et parere velocissimos equos brevi tamen evo valentes. Sic forsan ex equa cui nomen erat Thyella, que impetus seu procella interpretatur, factum est, vel ut supra de equis Dardani ex Borea conceptis diximus."

Transmission of these little-used antique and late classical sources to Boccaccio and also to Chaucer, if he did not know the *Genealogie*, may have been fostered by the glosses of twelfth-century Arnulf of Orleans on the *Fasti*, which unfortunately exist today only in the crabbed script of about six different manuscripts, the best of which is Vat. Reg. 1548. Much of Arnulf's commentary reappeared in the more influential dictionary known as Huguccio of Pisa's *Magnae derivationes* (see Holzworth, "Hugutio's *Derivationes*," 259–76). Portions of the Arnulf commentary are excerpted and discussed in Holzworth, "An Unpublished Commentary."

7. For a discussion of other spring openings and this *reverdie*, see Tuve, "Spring," 9–16; Danby, 28–32; and Baldwin. There is a convenient summary of sources in Chance, "Creation," 459–64. As a literary device, the greening of the world during spring was initiated by Virgil's fourth eclogue; see also the concept of rebirth as linked with renaissance, in Ladner. Other sources Chaucer may possibly have used, in addition to those cited in the text, include Vincent of Beauvais's *Speculum naturale*, 15.66, "De vere," the *Secreta secretorum*, the *Pervigilium Veneris*, although most scholars accept Guido del Colonne's *Historia destructionis Troiae*, 4, as having primary importance.

8. Green's translation of Boethius, in a note to this reference, explains that the west wind was "said to produce fruits and flowers by his breath" (15), but does not indicate his source.

9. "Hyemem autem resolvit et germina floresque producit, et dicitur Zephyrus a Zephs grece, quod latine vita sonat," in *Genealogie*, 4.61, 1:217.

10. *Aeneid*, 4.705, in the Copley second edition. Although this phrase in Latin is not uncommon and may only suggest the effects of moving air, it may also relate to the ancient Italian animistic—and later Stoic philosophical—belief in the soul as breath analogous to the fiery World Soul, *anima mundi*.

11. As if underscoring this analogy between life, wind, and breath, Fulgentius describes Psyche as "gently wafted by the breath of Zephyr" ("Zephryi . . . anhelante vectura," Whitbread, 88; Helm, 68).

12. "Favonius autem eo quod faveat germinantia vel faveat germinibus; flat enim suaviter et placide a meridie usque in noctem, a principio veris usque ad estatis finem," in *Genealogie*, 4.61, 1:217.

13. For the Italian influence on Chaucer, specifically Boccaccio and Dante, see Howard Schless, "Chaucer and Dante," in Bethurum, *Critical Approaches*; and also his "Transformations." Schless notes that 1372 marks the first undoubted trip to Italy made by Chaucer; there may also have been trips to Spain and Italy in 1366 and 1368. Italian (Dantesque) influence on Chaucer's earliest dream vision, *The Book of the Duchess*, has been noted by Edwards, 189–204, although there may have been stronger influences on his poetry both by Boccaccio and Dante after the second and much more important visit to Italy, in 1378, to interview Bernabò Visconti and Sir John Hawkwood in Milan (about the king's wars), when Chaucer examined the Visconti libraries: see esp. Pratt, "Chaucer," 191–99. See also Schless's study, *Chaucer and Dante*, as well as the Boccaccio studies of Havely; Boitani ed., *Chaucer and the Italian Trecento*, esp. the essays by Boitani, "What Dante Meant to Chaucer," 115–39; Wendy Childs, "Anglo-Italian Contacts in the Fourteenth Century," 65–87, and J. A. W. Bennett, "Chaucer, Dante, and Boccaccio," pp. 89–113; Shoaf; Wetherbee, esp. chap. 5, "Dante and the *Troilus*."

14. Pratt believes that the *Book of the Duchess* was written in 1372 rather than 1369, the more commonly recognized date, as he will show in a forthcoming note in *The Chaucer Review*.

15. The Dante commentaries, which numbered at least twelve and which Chaucer may have seen, included those of the Ottimo Commento, the Anonymous Selmiano, Graziolo de Bambaglioli, Jacopo Alighieri, Jacopo della Lana, Boccaccio, Pietro Alighieri, Fra'Guido da Pisa, False Boccaccio, Benvenuto Rambaldi da Imola, Francesco Bartolo da Buti, and the Anonymous Florentine. (Robert Hollander's list, to appear in a forthcoming issue of *Dante Studies*, orders them differently: he begins with Jacopo Alighieri, continues with Graziolo de'Bambaglioli, the Anonymous Lombardus, Jacopo della Lana, Guido da Pisa, Ottimo, the Anonymous Selmiano, Pietro Alighieri, the Codex Cassinese, and then Boccaccio, followed by the "False Boccaccio" and the remainder of my list.) For additional information about the commentaries, see Sandkühler; for the

place of the commentaries within the whole of the mythographic tradition, see Chance, "Origins," 35–64. Hollander is compiling on computer many of these commentaries in what is known as "The Dartmouth Project."

16. The contemporary Dante commentaries have little of significance to add about Zefiro.

17. On *Paradiso*, 12.46–52, see Grandgent, *Companion*, 246. In support are cited these lines from Ovid's *Metamorphoses*, 1.63–4: "Vesper et occiduo quae litora sole tepescunt, / proxima sunt Zephyro" ("The Western shores which glow with the setting sun are the place of Zephyrus"). According to Gardner, Petrus Ferrandi compares St. Dominic to Hesperus, rising from the West (245).

18. See Grandgent, *Companion*, 246.

19. Lines 103–5, "Di lui si fecer poi diversi rivi / onde l'orto catolico si riga, / sì che i suoi arbuscelli stan più vivi."

20. See Huppé, 16, for the metaphor of impregnation and related rhetoric.

Works Cited

Arnulf, of Orleans. Commentary on Ovid's *Fasti*. Rome, Vatican Library. MS Reg. 1548.

Balbi, Giovanni (Joannes Balbus). *Catholicon*. 1460. Reprint facsimile. Westmead, Farnsborough, Hants, England: Gregg International Publishers, 1971.

Baldwin, Ralph. *The Unity of the Canterbury Tales*. Copenhagen: Rosenkilde and Bagger, 1955.

Bede. *Didascalica genuina*. PL 90: 123–614.

Bethurum, Dorothy. *See* Loomis, Dorothy Bethurum.

Boccaccio, Giovanni. *Genealogie deorum gentilium libri*. Edited by Vincenzo Romano. 2 vols. *Opere*, vols. 10–11. Scrittori d'Italia, no. 200–1. Bari: Giuseppe Laterza and Sons, 1951.

Bode, Georgius Henricus. *Scriptores rerum mythicarum latini tres Romae nuper reperti*. 2 vols. 1834. Reprint one vol. Hildesheim: Georg Olms, 1968.

Boethius. *The Consolation of Philosophy*. Translated by Richard H. Green. Indianapolis and New York: Bobbs-Merrill, 1962.

Boitani, Piero, ed. *Chaucer and the Italian Trecento*. Cambridge and London: Cambridge University Press, 1983.

Bowden, Muriel. *A Commentary on the General Prologue to the Canterbury Tales*. 2d ed. London: Macmillan; New York: Collier Macmillan, 1967.

Brown, Emerson, Jr. "*Hortus Inconclusus*: The Significance of Priapus and Pyramus and Thisbe in the *Merchant's Tale*." *Chaucer Review* 4 (1970): 31–40.

———. "Priapus and the *Parlement of Foulys*." *Studies in Philology* 72 (1975): 258–73.

Chance [Nitzsche], Jane. "Chaucer and Mythology." *The Chaucer Newsletter* 6:2 (Fall 1984): 1, 2.

———. "Creation in Genesis and Nature in Chaucer's *General Prologue*, 1–18." *Papers on Language and Literature* 14 (1978): 459–64. Reprinted in *Modern Critical Approaches to Chaucer's "General Prologue,"* edited by Harold Bloom, 67–71. New York: Chelsea Books, 1988.

———. " 'Disfigured is thy Face': Chaucer's Pardoner and the Protean Shape-Shifter Fals-Semblant (A Response to Britton Harwood)." *Philological Quarterly* 67 (1989): 422–33.

———. *The Mythographic Chaucer*. Forthcoming.

———. "The Origins and Development of Medieval Mythography: From Homer to

Dante." In *Mapping the Cosmos*, edited by Jane Chance and R.O. Wells, Jr., 35–64, 151–59. Houston: Rice University Press, 1985.

Chaucer, Geoffrey. *The Riverside Chaucer*. Edited by Larry D. Benson. 3d ed. rev. from Fred C. Robinson. Boston: Houghton Mifflin, 1987.

Clogan, Paul M. "Chaucer's Cybele and the *Liber Imaginum Deorum*." *Philological Quarterly* 43 (1964): 272–74.

Cummings, Hubertis M. "Chaucer's *Prologue*, 1–7." *Modern Language Notes* 37 (1922): 86–90.

Danby, John F. "Eighteen Lines of Chaucer's 'Prologue.'" *Critical Quarterly* 2 (1960): 28–32.

Dante Alighieri. *La Divina Commedia*. Edited by C. H. Grandgent. Revised by Charles S. Singleton. Cambridge, MA: Harvard University Press, 1972.

———. *The Divine Comedy*. Translated by John Sinclair. 3 vols. 1939. Reprint. New York: Oxford University Press, 1981.

Donovan, M. J. "The Image of Pluto and Proserpina in the *Merchant's Tale*." *Philological Quarterly* 36 (1957): 49–60.

Dronke, Peter. *Fabula: Explorations into the Uses of Myth in Medieval Platonism*. Mittellateinische Studien und Texte, vol. 9. Leiden and Cologne: E. J. Brill, 1974.

Edwards, Robert. "The *Book of the Duchess* and the Beginnings of Chaucer's Narrative." *New Literary History* 13 (1982): 189–204.

Elliott, Kathleen O., and J. P. Elder. "A Critical Edition of the Vatican Mythographers." *Transactions of the American Philological Association* 78 (1947): 189–207.

Fulgentius, Fabius Planciades. *Mitologiae*. In *Opera*. Edited by Rudolf Helm. 1898. Reprint. Stuttgart: B. G. Teubner, 1970.

———. *Fulgentius the Mythographer*. Translated by Leslie George Whitbread. Columbus: Ohio State University Press, 1971.

Fyler, John M. *Chaucer and Ovid*. New Haven and London: Yale University Press, 1979.

Gardner, Edmund Garratt. *Dante and the Mystics: A Study of the Mystical Aspect of the Divine Comedy and its Relations with Some of its Mediaeval Sources*. New York: Dutton, 1913.

Gawain Poet. *Sir Gawain and the Green Knight*. Ed. J. R. R. Tolkien and E. V. Gordon. 2d ed. rev. Norman Davis. Oxford: Clarendon Press, 1968.

Grandgent, Charles. *Companion to the Divine Comedy*. Edited by Charles S. Singleton. Cambridge, MA: Harvard University Press, 1975.

Green, Richard H. "Classical Fable and English Poetry in the Fourteenth Century." In *Critical Approaches to Medieval Literature: Selected Papers from the English Institute, 1958–59*. Edited by Dorothy Bethurum. New York: Columbia University Press, 1960.

Guido, delle Colonne [Guido de Columnis]. *Historia destructionis Troiae*. Edited and translated by Mary Elizabeth Meek. Bloomington and London: Indiana University Press, 1974.

Hall, Louis Brewer. "Chaucer and the Dido-and-Aeneas Story." *Medieval Studies* 25 (1963): 148–59.

Havely, N. R., ed. *Boccaccio—Sources of 'Troilus' and the Knight's and Franklin's Tales*. Chaucer Studies, vol. 5. Woodbridge, Suffolk: D. S. Brewer; Totowa, NJ: Rowman and Littlefield, 1980.

Hoffman, R. L. "Mercury, Argus, and Chaucer's Arcite: *Canterbury Tales* I (A) 1384–90." *Notes and Queries* 210 (1965): 128–29.

———. *Ovid and the Canterbury Tales*. Philadelphia: University of Pennsylvania Press, 1966.

———. "Ovid and Chaucer's Myth of Theseus and Pirithous." *English Language Notes* 2 (1965): 252–57.

———. "Ovid and the Wife of Bath's Tale of Midas." *Notes and Queries* 211 (1966): 48–50.
———. "Ovid's Argus and Chaucer." *Notes and Queries* 210 (1965): 213–16.
———. "Ovid's Priapus in the Merchant's Tale." *English Language Notes* 3 (1966): 169–72.
———. "Pygmalion in the *Physician's Tale*." *American Notes and Queries* 5 (1967): 83–84.
———. "The Wife of Bath as a Student of Ovid." *Notes and Queries* 209 (1964): 287–88.
Hollander, Robert. *The Dartmouth Project on Dante Commentaries: A Data Base*. Dartmouth: Dartmouth College, forthcoming.
Holzworth, Jean. "Hugutio's *Derivationes* and Arnulfus' Commentary on Ovid's *Fasti*." *Transactions of the American Philological Association* 73 (1942): 259–76.
———. "An Unpublished Commentary on Ovid's *Fasti* by Arnulfus of Orleans." Ph.D. diss., Bryn Mawr College, 1940.
Hugutio [Huguitio; Uguccione] da Pisa. *Liber derivationum* or *Magnae derivationes*. Oxford, Bodleian Library. MS 376.
———. Florence. Biblioteca Medicea Laurenziana. MS Pluteus XXVII Sinister, Codex 1. Fols. 1r–453v.
Huppé, Bernard F. *A Reading of the Canterbury Tales*. Rev. ed. Albany: State University of New York, 1967.
John, of Garland. *Integumenta Ovidii: Poemetto inedito del secolo XIII*. Edited by Fausto Ghisalberti. Testi e documenti inediti o rari, 2. Messina and Milan: Giuseppe Principato, 1933.
———. *Integumenta Ovidii*. Translated by Lester Kruger Born. In "The Integumenta on the Metamorphoses of Ovid by John of Garland—First cited with Introduction and Translation." Ph.D. diss., University of Chicago, 1929.
Lactantius, Firmianus. *The Divine Institutes, Books 1–7*. Translated by Sister Mary Francis McDonald. The Fathers of the Church, vol. 49. Washington, D.C.: The Catholic University of America Press, 1964.
Ladner, Gerhart B. "Vegetation Symbolism and the Concept of Renaissance." In *Essays in Honor of Erwin Panofsky*, edited by Millard Meiss, 2 vols. 1:303–22. De Artibus Opuscula, 40. New York: New York University Press, 1961.
Loomis, Dorothy Bethurum, ed. *Critical Approaches to Medieval Literature: Selected Papers from the English Institute 1958–59*. New York and London: Columbia University Press, 1960. Reprint. 1967.
———. "Saturn in Chaucer's *Knight's Tale*." In *Chaucer unde seine Zeit*, edited by Arno Esch, 149–61. Tübingen: Tübingen University Press, 1968.
———. "The Venus of Alanus de Insulis and the Venus of Chaucer." In *Philological Essays: Studies in Old and Middle English Language and Literature in Honour of Herbert Dean Meritt*, edited by James L. Rosier, 182–95. The Hague: Mouton, 1970.
Lord, Mary Louise. "Dido as an Example of Chastity: The Influence of Example Literature." *Harvard Library Bulletin* 17:1, 2 (1969): 22–44, 216–32.
Macrobius, Ambrosius Theodosius. *Commentarii in Somnium Scipionis*. Vol. 2 of *Macrobius*. Edited by James Willis. Leipzig: B. G. Teubner, 1963.
———. *Commentary on the Dream of Scipio*. Translated by William Harris Stahl. Records of Civilization: Sources and Studies, no. 48. 1952. Reprint. New York and London: Columbia University Press, 1966.
Martianus Capella. *Martianus Capella*. Edited by Adolf Dick. Corrected by Jean Préaux. Bibliotheca Scriptorum Graecorum et Romanorum Teubneriana. Stuttgart: B. G. Teubner, 1969.
———. *Martianus Capella and the Seven Liberal Arts*. Vol. 2: *The Marriage of Philology*

and Mercury. Translated by William Harris Stahl and Richard Johnson with E. L. Burge. New York: Columbia University Press, 1977.

McCall, John P. *Chaucer among the Gods: The Poetics of Classical Myth*. University Park and London: Pennsylvania State University Press, 1979.

———. "Classical Myth in Chaucer's *Troilus and Criseyde*: An Aspect of the Classical Tradition in the Middle Ages." Ph.D. diss., Princeton University, 1955.

Meech, Sanford B. "Chaucer and the *Ovide Moralisé*: A Further Study." *PMLA* 46 (1931): 182–204.

Miller, R. N. "Pandarus and Procne." In *Studies in Medieval Culture*, edited by John R. Sommerfeldt. Kalamazoo: Western Michigan University Press, 1979.

Minnis, Alastair J. *Chaucer and Pagan Antiquity*. Woodbridge, Suffolk: D. S. Brewer; Totowa, NJ: Rowman and Littlefield, 1982.

Ovid. *The Fasti*. Edited and translated by Sir James George Frazier. 5 vols. London: W. Heinemann; New York: G. P. Putnam's Sons, 1931.

———. *Metamorphoses*. Edited and translated by Frank Justus Miller. 2 vols. Loeb Classical Library. 3d ed. Cambridge, MA: Harvard University Press; London: W. Heinemann, 1977.

Ovide moralisé: Poème du commencement du quatorzième siècle. Edited by C. de Boer et al. *Verhandelingen der Koninklijke Akademie van Wetenschappen te Amsterdam. Afdeeling Letterkunde*. Nieuwe Reeks 15 (1915):1–374; 21 (1920):1–394; 30 (1931): 1–303; 37 (1936): 1–478; 43 (1938): 1–429. Reprinted in 5 vols. Wiesbaden: Martin Sändig, 1966–68.

Papias, the Lombard. *Vocabulista*. Turin: Bottega d'Erasmo, 1966.

Pratt, Robert A. "Chaucer and the Visconti Libraries." *ELH* 6 (1939): 191–99.

Quinn, Betty N. "Venus, Chaucer, and Pierre Bersuire." *Speculum* 38 (1963): 479–80.

Rabanus Maurus. *De diis gentium*. In *De universo libri XXII*, 15.6. In *Opera omnia. PL* 111: 426–36.

Robertson, D. W. *A Preface to Chaucer: Studies in Medieval Perspectives*. 1962. Reprint. Princeton: Princeton University Press, 1969.

———. "The Wife of Bath and Midas." *Studies in the Age of Chaucer* 6 (1984): 1–20.

Sandkühler, Bruno. *Die frühen Dantekommentare und ihr Verhältnis zur mittelalterlichen Kommentartradition*. Münchener romanistische Arbeiten, no. 19. Munich: Mac Hueber, 1967.

Schless, Howard. *Chaucer and Dante. A Revaluation*. Norman, OK: Pilgrim Books, 1984.

———. "Transformations: Chaucer's Use of Italian." In *Writers and their Background: Geoffrey Chaucer*, edited by Derek Brewer, 184–223. Athens: Ohio University Press, 1975.

Shoaf, R. A. *Dante, Chaucer and the Currency of the Word*. Norman, OK: Pilgrim Books, 1983.

Steadman, John M. "Venus' *citole* in Chaucer's *Knight's Tale* and Berchorius." *Speculum* 34 (1959): 620–24.

Storm, Melvin. "The Mythological Tradition in Chaucer's *Complaint of Mars*." *Philological Quarterly* 57 (1978): 323–35.

Tuve, Rosemond. "Spring in Chaucer and before Him." *Modern Language Notes* 52 (1937): 9–16.

Vatican Mythographers. *See* Bode.

Vergil (Virgil). *The Aeneid*. Translated by Frank O. Copley. 2d ed. Indianapolis: Bobbs-Merrill, 1975.

———. *Virgil*. Trans. H. Rushton Fairclough. 2 vols. Rev. ed. Cambridge, MA: Harvard University Press; London: W. Heinemann, 1978.

Vincent de Beauvais. *Speculum naturale*. Nuremberg, 1483.
Wentersdorf, Karl. P. "Theme and Structure in the Merchant's Tale: The Function of the Pluto Episode." *PMLA* 80 (1965): 522–27.
Wetherbee, Winthrop. *Chaucer and the Poets: An Essay on Troilus and Criseyde*. Ithaca and London: Cornell University Press, 1984.
Wilkins, Ernest Hatch. "Descriptions of Pagan Divinities from Petrarch to Chaucer." *Speculum* 32 (1957): 511–22.
Wind, Edgar. *Pagan Mysteries in the Renaissance*. 1958. Rev. ed. London: Faber and Faber, 1967.

Mercury in the Garden

Mythographical Methods in the *Merchant's Tale* and *Decameron* 7.9

Janet Levarie Smarr

Edmund Reiss, reviewing in 1974 the state of research on the question of Chaucer's knowledge of the *Decameron* and other writings by Boccaccio, declared in sum: ". . . no proof exists to show that Chaucer knew Boccaccio's great collection of stories or even Boccaccio's name" (Reiss, 16).[1] And he went on to conclude: "Although it used to be popular to consider Chaucer the English Boccaccio, such a view, as we may now see, is both misleading and wrong." Since then Donald McGrady (1–26) has pointed out the flaws in many of the arguments against Chaucer's knowledge of the *Decameron*, flaws either of logic or of outdated information.[2]

Whether scholars argue for or against Chaucer's knowledge of the *Decameron*, however, they have concentrated on story outlines and on surface details—who said or did what to whom—but not on what the authors make of the material they are treating. The plot of the *Merchant's Tale*, for example, is very close to that of a *Novellino* story and fairly unlike *Decameron* 7.9, to which it has sometimes been compared.[3] Yet the *Novellino* tale is a bare and simple narrative containing none of the symbolic and thematic developments that appear in both Boccaccio's and Chaucer's stories. My investigation of these two tales can in no way prove that Chaucer knew Boccaccio's story, but it does suggest—at least to me—that the two authors worked in very similar ways—in short, that in some sense Chaucer is the English Boccaccio after all.

A rapprochement between Chaucer's and Boccaccio's methods is encouraged by the last few decades of Boccaccio scholarship, which have revolutionized Boccaccio studies in a way that Chaucer studies had already been. Both authors, once considered chiefly the jolly tellers of popular and bawdy tales, have been seen anew as philosophical and ironic writers of great complexity and depth. Because the change in the scholarly view of Boccaccio has lagged slightly behind that pertaining to Chaucer, some Chaucerians still tend to think of Boccaccio as the relatively superficial good timer whose narratives Chaucer made into something more serious and complex. However, this perspective is becoming harder and harder to maintain as the complexities of Boccaccio's writing emerge. If anything, Boccaccio is more implicit, Chaucer more explicit in their working out of thematic developments.

David Wallace has suggested Chaucer's deep identification with Boccaccio as a writer seeking to combine Latin classics, Dante, French romance, and "adventurous use of iconography" with "more humble native resources" (159). It is especially the combination of native popular traditions with classical literature that allows both writers to develop the mythographical potentials of elements from popular comic tales: to connect the common themes of youth and age, spring and winter, with Mercury and Saturn, for example, and to be aware of the existing commentaries concerning these classical figures.

Both writers, envisioning the ancient poets as learned authorities, sought to raise the level of lively popular narrative by folding into it multiple layers of potential meaning. In one sense this might be to read folk tales as if they were classical myth, to be interpreted in multiple ways; or perhaps to recognize that the myths so interpreted had once been folktales. In another sense, it was to turn simple tales into something more complex by a conscious effort of reconstruction. It may well have been Dante who inspired both Boccaccio and Chaucer by his revision of the medieval poet's status as potentially akin to that of classical authors. But if Chaucer ever did see the *Decameron*, which was immensely popular among the Florentine merchants with whom Chaucer was engaged in business, he would have found a model even closer to his own interest in applying the learned poet's craft to shorter narratives and popular tales.

My investigation of the two tales will focus on certain aspects and not try to cover everything that might be said about these stories. It will also, inevitably, neglect the further meanings that arise from the interaction of each story with those surrounding it. Chaucer's tale really falls into two parts: the debate about whether January should marry and the consequences of his misguided decision. It is the latter part only that suggests some connection to Boccaccio's tale. Chaucer obviously drew (as did Boccaccio) from many sources of inspiration.

Decameron 7.9 is the tale about Lidia who falls in love with her husband's servant Pirro. To assure himself that she is not merely testing his loyalty, he sets her three difficult tasks. She outdoes the challenge by arranging to reap her reward before her husband's very eyes. They make love while her husband watches from a pear tree, and then blame the tree for enchanting his sight. The resemblance is slim but present to Chaucer's *Merchant's Tale*, in which young May makes love with her husband's servant in a pear tree, and when the blind spouse, regaining his sight, sees them at it, nimbly blames the faulty vision of his still dazzled eyes. Three thematic elements enhance the similarity of these tales: the erotic, anatomical identifications of the pear tree and garden; the importance of Mercury and his attributes as established by mythology and astrology; and the discussion of blindness in relation to the meaning of both tales. These three topics are discussed in turn in the three sections following. It is the combination of all three in both tales that is most striking.

JANUARY'S May is related by her very name to the little private garden in which her husband particularly likes to sport. His speech on behalf of marriage calls a wife man's "paradys terrestre" (1.1332); and he worries later because he has heard that man cannot have his paradise both on earth and in heaven (1637–52). After the wedding January embraces "his fresshe May, his paradys" (1822). The garden that January builds himself, all walled about with stone, is compared explicitly to the garden in the *Roman de la Rose* (2032), and Chaucer adds immediately after: "Ne Priapus ne myghte nat suffise, / Though he be god of gardyns, for to telle / The beautee of the gardyn and the welle" (2034–36). The garden is not simply May herself but rather, as the details and explicit associations make clear, a specific part of May's anatomy in which January takes such delight to "pleye, / That he wol no wight suffren bere the keye / Save he himself" (2043–45). "And whan he wolde paye his wyf hir dette / In somer seson, thider wolde he go" (2048–49). He alone, he thinks, has access to the garden through the narrow gate to which he has the key. But unknown to him, his servant Damian gets a second key; and while January thinks he is alone with May, Damian has already entered and "sat in the bush" (2155, 2208).

January's recitation from the *Song of Songs* reinforces the double meaning of the enclosed garden as two kinds of paradise both of which January hopes to have,[4] but his real interest is wholly in the Priapic aspect of the garden, as his proudly recounted life history of lechery makes clear.[5] Similarly the "fruyt" that May desires is obviously to be identified with the fruit of love, which in fact she obtains in the tree.

This kind of garden is common enough in literature. To start with some more abstruse but highly relevant examples, Alanus de Insulis in his *Distinctiones* (*PL* 210: 994c) glosses the phrase "ostia ventris" in Job 3:10 as a reference to the garden of Eden from which Adam and Eve were expelled as a child is expelled from the womb. Gregory the Great wrote similarly in his *Moralia* (4.12, *PL* 75: 649), "Paradise is the womb of the human race, whose gates the serpent opened" ("Paradisus humani generis uterus, cuius ostia serpens apersuit"). The *Roman de la Rose* was certainly a source known to both Boccaccio and Chaucer; nonetheless, it is worth noting that Boccaccio's tale, like Chaucer's, identifies the scene with an appropriate part of the human body. Just as May's name is the first link between her and the garden, so too the name of the servant in Boccaccio's tale identifies him with the pear tree; his name is Pirro, *pirum* being the Latin word for pear tree (or *pero* in Italian). If one reads with a sufficiently erotic mind, further evidence for the identification becomes apparent.

Pirro climbs the pear tree to satisfy his lady's desire for fruit; and looking down he claims to see his master and lady making love, exclaiming to his master, "vi dimenate ben sì, che se così si dimenasse questo pero, egli non ce ne rimarrebbe sù niuna" ("you are shaking yourself so hard that if this pear tree were similarly shaken, there wouldn't be one bit left in it"). At which the lady says, "io vi sarrei suso, per vedere che maraviglie sieno queste che costui dice che vede" ("I would like to climb up on it to see what these marvels are which he says he sees"). For her and Pirro the pear tree becomes not only an indirect means to their coupling, but also an indirect way for them to talk about what they are really after. The use of this signification continues through to the end of the tale, where Lidia blames the pear tree for causing dishonor to women and, in a displaced punishment, orders the tree cut down. Both pear tree and garden, then, are clearly anatomical signifiers within the context of the tales and both are identified by name with the character who is in each case the object of desire.[6]

THE ASSOCIATIONS in both stories with Mercury as a mythological and astrological figure are diverse but similar to each other. Let me start once again with Chaucer, for he explicitly sets the climactic scene of the tale with the sun in Gemini (2220–24). First of all, Gemini is linked with May, the month when it begins, in calendrical sequences and labors of the months in art throughout Europe (Fowler, 137–224; Tuve). Gemini is the house of Mercury; and the astrological influence of Mercury is agreed on by all astrologers and mythographers: it is based on the figure of Mercury in classical myth. As the messenger god, he betokens and produces eloquence; and his winged feet and cap represent the swiftness of winged words that travel, like Mercury, through the air.[7] He signifies, moreover, subtlety of wit, including the powers of deceit. Thus Boccaccio and Bersuire gloss his sleep-producing wand as the power of eloquence or persuasion. This in turn is linked to his piping, which caused Argus to close all hundred eyes, allowing Mercury to steal Io from his guard.

Mercury is thus the patron of thieves and deceivers. Isidore, for example, writes in his *Etymologies* (8.11.47), "They say he is also the master of thieves because speech deceives the minds of hearers." And Bersuire writes, "He is feigned to have the power of producing sleep because eloquence deceives even the wary (*oculatos*)" (Berchorius, *Reductorium*, fol. 8r–9r). D. W. Robertson (*Preface*, 257) has already noted the appropriateness of subtle wit and deceitful eloquence to May's prompt and false but persuasive explanation of what her husband saw her doing.[8] Chaucer underlines the theme by introducing the discussion between Pluto and Proserpine just before the climax. Pluto, sorry for January, declares he will restore the old man's sight and let him see his wife's true character. " 'Ye shal?' quod Proserpyne, 'wol ye so? / Now by my moodres sires soule I swere / that I shall yeven hire suffisant answere, / And all wommen after, for hir sake'" (2264–67). Her continuing, lengthy reply to Pluto is as triumphant as May's, for Pluto gives up and concedes his wife is right, just as does January.

Boccaccio's Lidia is similarly skillful at finding persuasive excuses for her behavior to her husband when she kills his hawk, plucks his beard, pulls one of his teeth, and finally makes love before his eyes. The sequence of more and more difficult tests functions as does the argument of Pluto and Proserpine to emphasize the theme of triumphant eloquence. Moreover, both Lidia and May launch into long complaints about their husbands' lack of faith in their fidelity, and both husbands hasten to conciliate the ladies, who have put on a very credible show of being offended.[9] Both ladies, in short, use eloquence as a means of blinding rather than enlightening, and the husband's eyesight is overcome by the mercurial rhetoric of the wife. This use of rhetoric is the opposite of the authors', who warn their readers against being blinded by folly or vanity, Chaucer by his comments on January, and Boccaccio by setting the story within a day of tales about the trickery of women.

Mercury is also considered the patron of medical doctors, as Boccaccio explains in his ever-helpful *Genealogie* (3.20); and in both tales the would-be lover falls sick or at least pretends to be ill. Lidia is feigning sickness when her husband visits her with Pirro, and they take her out into the garden to cheer her up. Damyan too is sick in bed when visited by May; her husband had declared that he would visit him with her, but then sends her alone with her maids, allowing the lovers to plot their garden escapade. Thus in both tales sickness becomes a means to the desired end, and the curing of these love-sicknesses can be considered a mercurial effect.

Mercury is relevant in another quite different way as well, for this is the merchant's tale, and Mercury is the patron of merchants and commerce, his name being derived in medieval fashion from *merces* and *mercatorum.*[10] Boccaccio not only calls him a god of commerce in his *Genealogie* but also uses his name in the *Comedia delle ninfe fiorentine* to represent wealth and banking (32.5). For as he explains in the *Genealogie* (4.35), Mercury born of Maia represents the treasures sprung from the earth. Like Chaucer's merchant narrator, January himself is a wealthy man, much given to worldly comforts and pleasures. He thinks of his wife as "the fruyt of his tresor" (1270), comparing her favorably to other gifts of Fortune "as londes, rentes, pasture, or commune, / Or moebles" (1313–14).

Lidia's husband is similarly "nobile uomo e ricco," and Lidia's servant tries to persuade Pirro to accept her lady's love in the following terms: "Quale altro troverrai tu che in arme, in cavalli, in robe e in denari possa star come tu starai, volendo il tuo amor concedere a costei? . . . ricordati che una volta senza più suole avvenire che la fortuna si fa altrui incontro col viso lieto e col grembo aperto; la quale chi allora non sa ricevere, poi trovandosi povero e mendico, di sé e non di lei s'ha a rammaricare" ("Who else will you find as well off as you in arms, horses, clothes, and money if you grant her your love? . . . remember that only once and no more does fortune approach one with happy face and open lap; and he who does not receive her then, later finding himself poor and beggared, has himself to complain of and not her"). Thus the benefits of possessing the lady in both cases are seen strictly in terms of economic value.

Proserpine not only exemplifies in Chaucer's tale mercurial powers of persuasion, but also was generally interpreted by mythographers, including Boccaccio (8.6), as signifying a person devoted to wealth because of her marriage to Pluto, whose name was too close to *plutus* or "wealthy" for medieval readers to avoid the connection.[11] This further explains Proserpine's connection to the mercurial theme of January's avarice and lust.

Of course, the Pluto and Proserpine pair suggests winter and summer, and their sympathies align with January and May respectively. Mercury is the son of Maia, for whom the month of May is named. As the importance of May is obvious in Chaucer's tale, it is worth attending to its less obvious relevance to Boccaccio's; for although Boccaccio's tale, like Chaucer's, is set in a season when one goes out into the garden to pick pears, Boccaccio never tells us a specific month for his narrative. There are, however, two iconographic models associated with May and Gemini that appear in Boccaccio's story. In calendars and carvings of the months throughout Europe, May is represented by a man on a horse very often with a hawk or falcon on his fist. This image, to name just some Italian examples, can be found in carved doorways at Modena,

Verona, Lucca, and Cremona; both in a doorway and on the baptistry at Parma; and in paintings at Padua. Written descriptions exist as well.

Bartholomaeus Anglicus in his discussion of the months in *De proprietatibus rerum* (9.13), describes May as a young man riding with a bird on his hand; and the Provençal *Breviari d'amour* identifies the bird as an *esparvier* (Tuve, 155–56, 152). Now the first thing Boccaccio tells us about Lidia's husband, Nicostrato, is that he likes to hunt and go hawking. When Lidia, to pass her lover's first test, kills her husband's favorite *sparviere*, she excuses her action by saying that the bird deprived her of her husband's attentions: "per ciò che, sì come l'aurora suole apparire, così Nicostrato s'è levato e salito a cavallo col suo sparviere in mano n'è andato alle pianure aperte a vederlo volare; e io, qual voi me vedete, sola e malcontenta nel letto mi son rimasa" ("for as soon as dawn appears, Nicostrato has gotten up and, mounted on horseback with his hawk on his hand, has gone off to the open fields to see it fly; and I, as you can see me, have been left alone and unhappy in bed").[12]

The image of her husband as the emblem of May is surely ironical, given that Lidia complains about her husband's old age and her consequent sexual dissatisfaction: "gli anni del mio marito son troppi, se co'miei si misurano, per la qual cosa di quello che le giovani donne prendono più piacere io vivo poco contenta" ("my husband is too old, if you measure his years against mine, wherefore I live discontented with regard to that in which young ladies take most pleasure"). As the hawk or falcon was a common symbol of male potency—hence too its association with springtime—the irony of the image is enhanced. Lidia is ironically implying that her husband's sexual infidelity rather than impotence is the cause of her sexual frustration, and is then symbolically destroying his sexual powers in order to replace them with her lover's. Chaucer would certainly have recognized this kind of calendrical image, for he used them himself in other tales.

Chaucer is playing not simply with May and Mercury but with the opposition between May and January, Mercury and Saturn.[13] If the hawk episode associates Nicostrato ironically with May, the following tests associate him more appropriately with Saturn, ruler of January and of old age. The husband's beard, object of the second test, relates him to the image of January or Janus, such as it appears also in Chaucer's *Franklin's Tale*. Lidia passes her third test, the extraction of a tooth from her husband's mouth, by pretending that his breath stinks and that one of his teeth must be rotten. Boccaccio in his *Genealogie*, 8.1, cites Albumasar's description of Saturn as an old man, "frigidum esse et siccum, melancolicum et fetidi oris" (that he is cold and dry, melancholic and of stinking breath). Boccaccio's own astrology teacher Andalo also described Saturn as producing men with stinking breath, "homines habentes anelitum fetidum ex ore" (Quaglio, 195). Thus all three of Lidia's tests refer in some way to her husband's age. The old husband and young wife, along with the saturnine qualities of frigidity and bad breath, and the May image of a hawker on horseback, suggest a pairing of Saturn and Mercury, January and May. The combination of both May and January images in association with Nicostrato may imply an incongruity in his own self-image akin to January's, as well as underlining the mismatching of his marriage.

The other iconographic model is the illustration of Gemini, which is often depicted as a naked couple with trees around them (Robertson, *Preface*, 256–57; Tuve). The baptistry at Parma shows a naked male and female with a tree between them, thus even more strongly suggesting Adam and Eve in paradise and the story of the fall. Didron (frontispiece, 5, and 177) discusses and illustrates a thirteenth-century candelabra from the Milan cathedral, whose four-sided base combines zodiac signs with virtues and scenes from the Bible. Gemini tops the side with Adam and Eve eating the apple and being expelled from the garden. That forbidden fruit-picking is, of course, very much to the point in both these tales, where the wives' explicit desire to eat fruit expresses obliquely their desire for illicit sexual union.

THE MOTIFS of the Fall merge with those both in Mercury's deception of Argus and in the tales at hand. The serpent was the original false persuader; Bersuire even writes that serpents "make others sleep by false coaxing" as does Mercury with the serpent-twined and sleep-inducing wand (fol. 2v; 1971, 39).[14] Mercury induced all hundred of Argus's eyes to close; but "in the day that ye eat thereof," says the serpent in Genesis 3:5, "then your eyes shall be opened." Then they ate, "and the eyes of them both were opened" (3:8). Hence come the discussions in both stories about blindness and seeing. January, who has become physically blind, opens his eyes and sees when his wife gathers the fruit of love in a tree. May claims that she is in the tree *in order to* restore her husband's vision. "Was no thyng bet, to make yow to see, / Than struggle with a man upon a tree" (2373–74).

Dempster has noted, disparaging the connection between these tales, that the husband in Boccaccio's story is not physically blind. Her objection is irrelevant because the importance of January's blindness is clearly figurative; he has become spiritually blinded by his prosperity.[15] "Allas! this noble Januarie free, / Amydde his lust and his prosperitee, / Is woxen blynd" (2069–71). Chaucer drives the point home by adding, "so been mo, / That wenen wisly that it be nat so" (2113–14). Boccaccio's

Nicostrato is similarly described by his wife—after a discussion of whether he is physically seeing straight—as having allowed "gli occhi dello'ntelletto" ("the eyes of the intellect") to be quickly blinded. Again the discussion of blinding or unblinding is occasioned by the wife's lovemaking, although this time the husband is in the tree and the couple below. The narrator of the story is Panfilo. Victoria Kirkham (1–23, esp. 5–7), in a persuasive demonstration of the associations between the three male narrators and the three parts of the soul, has identified Panfilo with reason. The identification reinforces his concern about the eyes of the mind and how clearly they can see, or how easily we rationalize what we do not want to witness.

Vincent de Beauvais remarks in the *Speculum naturale*, 30.32, that he who abuses his external vision in lust is justly punished by the blinding of his internal vision; a person dominated by concupiscence and devoted to *voluptas* "fenestrasque luminis ad tenebras cecitatis aperit" ("opens the windows of his eye to the darkness of blindness"). Here the eye *opens* into blindness, just as both husbands open their physical eyes only to be blinded mentally. Vincent cites Gregory's *Moralia*, which similarly relates blindness to concupiscence with special reference to the Fall. Through the phrase "ostia ventris" from Job, Gregory identifies the womb with the garden of Eden and the Fall with the opening of our eyes at birth to the world and to lust, which is paradoxically opening our eyes to darkness. Gregory concludes with the *sensus moralis* that our faith is blinded by both prosperity and adversity (*Moralia, PL* 75: 649–50).[16] Insofar as Chaucer's tale is told by a man who has discovered the woes of marriage, attributed to the wickedness of his wife, while Boccaccio's is part of a day devoted to tales about deceitful wives, the opening of one's eyes to darkness may apply also to the audience, to whom the tale is told partly as a revelation of the evil that lurks in what had seemed so good.

St. Augustine, glossing the lines from Genesis, "and the eyes of them both were opened," writes that we must not imagine Adam and Eve stumbling blindly about Eden and groping for the tree; the eye-opening refers to inner and not outer vision (*De Genesi ad litteram*, 11.31, *PL* 34: 445–46). January, of course, *is* groping for the tree, but the restoration of his physical sight merely emphasizes the extent of his mental blindness and willing self-delusion as he is immediately persuaded not to believe what he sees. "Ye maze, maze, good sire," says his wife. "So che voi falsamente avete veduto" ("I know that you have seen falsely"), says Pirro to Nicostrato. And Pirro adds, "la magagna di questo trasvedere dee procedere dal pero" ("the fault of this misseeing must come from the pear tree"). Augustine, however, argues at length that the forbidden fruit in Eden had no special powers or effects, and that the consequences of eating it were due entirely to the act of disobedience (8.6 and 13, *PL* 34: 337 and 383-84).

In sum, both Gregory and Augustine, through reference to Genesis 3:5, closely link the theme of the fruit tree and concupiscence with the theme of blindness and seeing.[17] Indeed, Gregory's commentary on the phrase "ostia ventris" accompanies his commentary on the verse, "expectet lucem et non videat," which he glosses by saying: "hi qui fidem sine operibus retinent, cum ea pro fide in extremo judicio salvari se posse confidunt, spes eorum frustrabitur" ("Let him expect the light and yet not see": "those who rely on faith without works, when they expect to be saved in the final judgment because of that faith, their hope will be frustrated") (*Moralia*, *PL* 75: 647-50, esp. 647). The application to January is self-evident.

The vision theme is further related, especially through the serpent's persuasion, to Mercury's blinding of Argus, as I noted. Argus, as the watchful guardian over a girl desired by Jupiter, easily becomes the jealous husband, blinded by his wife's deceit. Chaucer, often more explicit than Boccaccio, compares January to Argus:

> O Januarie, what myghte it thee availle,
> Thogh thou myghte se as fer as shippes saille?
> For as good is blynd deceyved be
> As to be deceyved whan a man may se.[18]
> Lo Argus, whiche that hadde an hondred yen,
> For al that evere he koude poure or pryen,
> Yet was he blent. . . .   (2107-13)

Boccaccio does not make this explicit comparison, but he does something subtler; he sets the tale "in Argo, antichissima città di Grecia" ("in Argo, a very ancient city of Greece"). Thus the name of Argo initiates the narrative.[19] It is directly preceded by the warning that one should not try to imitate the wife's escapade because "ne sono al mondo tutti gli uomini abbagliati igualmente" ("not all men in the world are equally blinded"). The word "abbagliar" returns at the end of the tale, as the wife accuses her husband of letting the eyes of his mind be blinded so quickly—an accusation understood in two ways. The husband understands it as a rebuke for his having so hastily believed in her infidelity, for allowing the supposedly magic vision in the pear tree to overcome his confidence in his wife's good character. But of course it is really a rebuke for allowing himself to be so easily hoodwinked by his wife's excuse.

Similarly ambiguous is the narrator Panfilo's final comment. Pirro and Lidia, he says, gave each other pleasure and delight; "Dio ce ne dea a noi." On the one hand, this sounds like a prayer that God grant us pleasure with our lovers. On the other hand, the outrageousness of such a prayer reminds us that the sort of joy God offers us is quite different from the joys of erotic love and is to be won through quite a different series of tests than the one that Lidia passed. Thus ultimately we are being nudged by Boccaccio to open our own eyes at this Edenic scene. January is subject to the confusion of earthly and heavenly paradise, and Chaucer's tale ends also with a prayer, though less ironically: "God bless us, and his mooder Seinte Marie!" The allusion to Mary counters the submerged allusion to Eve. The husbands' acceptance of their erring wives' persuasions repeats Adam's loving submission to the fallen Eve; it thereby suggests that their own fall is related to their inappropriate love not just for a young wife but also more generally for worldly comforts and pleasures. Both authors, while setting their tales in a frame of traditional misogyny about the dangers to men from the ever-treacherous daughters of Eve, use their stories to awaken the reader to the ease with which one rationalizes one's own mistakes and blinds oneself to their consequences. Thus the open criticism of women becomes turned against the foolishness of men.[20]

What about the other, acknowledged sources for Chaucer's tale? If we look at the three most likely sources—that is, the three most similar in plot—we do not find similar thematic developments, and certainly not the combination of them that occurs in the *Decameron* story. The *Comoedia Lydiae*, which was clearly Boccaccio's source, was possibly known to Chaucer too. The husband there, however, is not necessarily old at all; rather the author emphasizes the general deceitfulness and insatiability of women, exemplified by Lydia's passionate obsession. The theme of January and May or Saturn and Mercury is totally absent, and the husband is never referred to as blinded, either physically or mentally: he accepts at once the theory that the pear tree is causing him to see something untrue. Thus he never raises an outcry against his wife. Moreover, she has met with her lover before this pear tree episode. As blindness is not a theme, Argus is never mentioned, nor is the tale set in Argo. Rather, given the emphasis on female lust, the lovers are compared to Hippolytus and Phaedra. At least it does include the name punning of Pyrrhus with *pirum*, and goes on to comment on the other names as well.[21]

Other likely sources for Chaucer are "De caeco et ejus uxore" and a tale found in one manuscript of the fourteenth-century *Novellino* and put forth in Bryan and Dempster's *Sources and Analogues of Chaucer's Canterbury Tales*.[22] In these the characters are not named at all; the husband's physical blindness is not made to suggest a spiritual or mental blindness, but simply offers an occasion for demonstrating female lust and deceit. The garden is identified neither with the body nor with the garden of paradise. In sum, there is no exploitation of symbolic possibilities in these bare narratives.

Another of Boccaccio's works, the *Comedia delle ninfe fiorentine*, is commonly accepted as a source for Chaucer's description of a lusty but impotent old man's night in bed with his unhappy young wife. The young wife in this *Comedia* is named Agapes and represents charity among the seven virtues. Boccaccio here too introduces Mercury's name in connection with the devotion of Agapes' family to money-making. For mercenary ends they marry her to a wealthy and foolishly lusty old man who can be seen as the Adamic Old Man. Then she is introduced to Apiros, whose name, derived from the Greek *a-pyr*, means fireless or cold. This lover, though young, obviously bears some symbolic relation to Agapes' cold husband, whose frigidity she is urged to reject while warming Apiros with the fires of love. Apiros' name may possibly bear some relation to Pirro's as well; for Pirro is the hot young lover in contrast to Lidia's aged husband. Moreover, the word for pear was derived by medieval encyclopaedists from the Greek *pyr* because its color and shape were said to resemble that of a flame (Vincent de Beauvais, *Spec. nat.*, 14.36, "De piro"; Isidore of Seville, *Etymologiarum*, 17.7,15). However, the contrast in the *Comedia delle ninfe fiorentine* between Agapes' charity and the old man's concupiscence, within a context of the seven virtues and opposing vices, does not seem to be picked up in either of the tales we are considering.

Chaucer probably knew all these sources and may well have drawn from them for plot or episode. But the conjunction of thematic developments in his tale are much closer to those of the *Decameron* 7.9 than to any of these other sources. Possibly, reading the story elsewhere, Chaucer was reminded of Boccaccio's similar tale. The use of Gemini, of the mercurial qualities of persuasive eloquence, medicine, and commercial wealth, of the Argus story, and of the paired January and May or Mercury and Saturn, are combined with major themes in both stories: the pear tree in the garden where a love affair is consummated and by which certain relevant parts of the body are signified, and the discussion of blindness both physical and mental in an old, rich, unsatisfactory husband whose wife commits adultery before his eyes and gets away with it. If Chaucer is "the English Boccaccio," it is not because he may have borrowed a few stories from him but because he treated his materials in a similarly complex way and with similar interests.

Notes

1. So too Kirkpatrick (201): "There is no clear evidence that Chaucer ever used the *Decameron* as a source of material, and on examination his work reveals itself to be consistently different in character from Boccaccio's." He can emphasize the differences because he claims, astonishingly, to find an absence of irony in the *Decameron* and thus reads the work as "a vindication . . . of the natural impulses" (203, 226). A better sense of Boccaccio is conveyed in the same volume by Wallace, 141–59. I am using Branca's edition of the *Decameron* and *The Riverside Chaucer*, 3d edition, ed. Larry Benson.

2. See also his excellent bibliography on this subject.

3. Raith (69–70) suggested a connection to the *Decameron* tale. Bryan and Dempster (341–56) reject that connection, pointing to a much closer analogue contained in only one manuscript of the *Novellino* from about 1300, printed in Biagi (199–201). Beidler (266–84) reopens the discussion of a possible link. Other analogues, rather than sources, are offered by Benson and Andersson (206–73).

4. Robertson (*Preface*, 11, 256) discusses the two kinds of paradise, pointing out that January, like Janus, is trying to look in two directions at once; he refers also to the *Roman de la Rose* for a garden suggesting both erotic and religious paradise (242).

5. Cf. *Decameron*, 7.9, Lidia's desire to "trovar modo a'miei diletti e alla mia salute." She is, of course, not thinking about spiritual "salute."

6. Wentersdorf (50–53) lists examples from classical to medieval times associating the pear with sexuality.

7. Besides Boccaccio's *Genealogie*, 2.7 and 12.62, see also Rabanus, *De universo*, 15.6, "De diis gentium," *PL* 111: 429d–430b; Isidore of Seville, *Etymologiarum libri*, 8.11; Pierre Bersuire, *Reductorium morale*, Liber 15, cap. 1, *De formis figurisque deorum*.

8. North (275) comments about Damyan that "there is ample reason for thinking him mercurial. He was not only guileful, but he was capable of composing and writing a persuasive letter—a typical attribute of a subject of Mercury." Oddly, he neglects May's mercurial qualities, despite her name.

9. The accepted main sources for Chaucer's tale, "De caeco et ejus uxore" and the *Comoedia Lydiae*, do not include such a speech in the wife's general defense of her honor. Boccaccio in his *Genealogie*, 12.62, specifically interprets Mercury's cap as showing "quod adversus invidie fulmina eloquentia valido tegumento servetur" ("that against the blows of jealousy, eloquence serves as a powerful protection"). He states furthermore (3.20) that one of the Mercuries was the son of a certain Prosperina.

10. Bersuire, fol. 8r; Isidore, *Etymologiarum* 8.11.3 and 46; Boccaccio, *Genealogie* 7.36; et al. See also Gates (369–75).

11. Bersuire elaborates further: Proserpina represents a Christian soul busy gathering the flowers of the world—that is, the evanescent goods of fortune—who is carried off by the devil. Mercury has, for Bersuire, a significance close to

that of Proserpina, for *in malo* he represents the worldly-wise with a sleep-producing wand of deception and flattery, and a dog's head signifying avarice, as does the dog Cerberus in Proserpina's kingdom (*Reductorium morale*, fols. 15v–17r).

12. In the *Comoedia Lydiae*, Boccaccio's source, Lydia complains that her husband prefers the woods to her company, but does not describe her husband mounted on his horse with his hawk on his hand. The text, by Matthieu de Vendôme, is printed in *Poèsies inédites du Moyen Age*.

13. North (275) oddly describes January as "old, but not in the least saturnine," associating him rather with Venus, whose "knight" he is (II.1723–24), with Mars because of what I think is a misreading of lines 2065–66, which North interprets to mean that Scorpio (rather than Fortune) has been January's "freend." Surely the very name of January coupled with his old age is enough to make the Saturn associations outweigh these other two; January as Venus's knight is meant to be a ludicrous idea, akin to the presentation of Lydia's husband as a figure of May.

14. This is said within the interpretation of Saturn who, as an evil ruler, has false-speaking servants and officials, likened to snakes: "sicut aspis alios dormire faciunt false blandiendo."

15. Bartholomaeus Anglicus, *De proprietatibus rerum*, 7.20, ends his discussion of blindness with the comment: "Better is to a man to be blynde and have his iyen put out than have iyen and be deceyved and bigiled with fikelinge and flateringe thereof, as Gregory seith upon that word." On the figurative meaning of January's blindness, see Huppé (149 and 160); and Brown (231–43).

16. Robertson ("Doctrine," 44) comments that this scene in the Merchant's tale "reflects that of Adam and Eve in the garden of Eden." Bleeth (54) refers to the exegetical tradition of opening one's eyes to sin in Genesis, citing Ambrose and St. Augustine.

17. The use of a pear tree instead of an apple tree in these tales may have something to do with Augustine's use of the pear tree in his *Confessions* 2, where his theft of fruit, through his analysis of the incident, comes to represent evil action in general and man's mysterious motivation to do what he knows he should not. It is, in short, a version of the tree of good and evil.

18. Cf. note 15.

19. It is well known that Boccaccio makes significant use of names. For a review of this topic, see Sasso (129–74).

20. For a similar reading of Chaucer's tale as misogynistic on one level (e.g., the Merchant's and Harry Bailey's understanding) yet critical of men (both husbands and misogynist narrators) on a deeper level, see Arrathoon (241–328).

21. The Latin Lydia's name is linked with *ludere*, "to play." Curiously, her husband's name is not Nicostrato but Decius, allowing the narrator to explain that lustful Lydia would not be satisfied with ten men let alone one Decius. Boccaccio, who certainly took over the Pirro-pero pun and added the significant name of Argo for the setting, changed the husband's name; I do not know what the new name might signify or why the change was made.

22. "De caeco et ejus uxore" is tale 9 from the "Appendix to the Latin edi-

tions of Aesop's Fables printed in the Fifteenth Century," *Wright's Latin Stories*, 78. See also Furnivall, Brock, and Clouston, *Originals and Analogues*, 180.

Works Cited

Alanus, de Insulis. *Distinctiones*. *PL* 210: 687-1014.
Arrathoon, Leigh. "For craft is al, whoso do it kan," In *Chaucer and the Craft of Fiction*, 241-328. Rochester, MI: Solaris Press, 1986.
Augustine, St. *De Genesi ad litteram*. *PL* 34: 219-485.
Bartholomaeus Anglicus. *On the Properties of Things (De proprietatibus rerum)*. Translated by John Trevisa (1398). Oxford: Clarendon Press, 1975.
Beidler, Peter. "Chaucer's *Merchant's Tale* and the *Decameron*," *Italica* 50 (1973): 266-84.
Benson, Larry, and Theodore Andersson. *The Literary Context of Chaucer's Fabliaux*. Indianapolis: Bobbs-Merrill, 1971.
Bersuire, Pierre. *Reductorium morale*. Edited by J. Engels. Utrecht: Instituut voor Laat Latijn der Rijksuniversiteit, 1962, 1966.
———. *Ovidius Moralizatus*. Translated by William Donald Reynolds. Ph.D. diss., University of Illinois-Urbana, 1971.
Biagi, Guido. *Le novelle antiche dei codici Panciatichiano-Palatino 138 e Laurenziano-Gaddiano 193*. Florence, 1880.
Bleeth, Kenneth. "The Image of Paradise in the 'Merchant's Tale'." In *The Learned and the Lewed*, edited by Larry Benson, 45-60. Harvard English Studies, 5. Cambridge, MA: Harvard University Press, 1974.
Boccaccio, Giovanni. *Decameron*. Edited by Vittore Branca. Milan: Mondadori, 1976.
———. *Genealogie deorum gentilium libri*. Edited by Vincenzo Romano. 2 vols. *Opere*, vols. 10-11. Scrittori d'Italia, No. 200-1. Bari: Guiseppe Laterza, 1951.
Brown, Peter. "An Optical Theme in *The Merchant's Tale*." *Studies in the Age of Chaucer* 6 (1984): 231-43.
Bryan, William Frank, and Dempster, Germaine, eds. *Sources and Analogues of Chaucer's Canterbury Tales*. New York: Humanities Press, 1958.
Chaucer, Geoffrey. *The Riverside Chaucer*. Edited by Larry Benson. 3d ed. Boston: Houghton Mifflin, 1987.
"De cacco et ejus uxore." *See* Wright, Thomas.
Didron, Julien. "L'Arbre de la Vierge," *Annales archéologiques* 13 (1853): 5-15.
Fowler, James. "On Medieval Representations of the Months and Seasons." *Archaeologia* 44 (1873): 137-224.
Furnivall, F.J., E. Brock, and W.A. Clouston, eds. *Originals and Analogues of Some of Chaucer's Canterbury Tales*. London, 1888.
Gates, Barbara. " 'A Temple of False Goddis': Cupidity and Mercantile Values in Chaucer's Fruit-Tree Episode." *Neuphilologische Mitteilungen* 77 (1976): 369-75.
Gregory, the Great. *Moralia*. *PL* 75: 509-1162.
Huppé, Bernard. *A Reading of the Canterbury Tales*. Albany: State University of New York Press, 1967.
Isidore, of Seville. *Etymologiae*. Edited by W. M. Lindsay. Oxford: Clarendon Press, 1911.
Kirkham, Victoria. "An Allegorically Tempered *Decameron*," *Italica* 62 (1985): 1-23.
Kirkpatrick, Robin. "The Wake of the *Commedia*: Chaucer's *Canterbury Tales* and Boccaccio's *Decameron*." In *Chaucer and the Italian Trecento*, edited by Pietro Boitani, 201-30. Cambridge: Cambridge University Press, 1983.

McGrady, Donald. "Chaucer and the *Decameron* Reconsidered." *Chaucer Review* 12 (1977): 1–26.

North, J. D. " 'Kalenderes Enlumyned Ben They': Some Astronomical Themes in Chaucer." *Review of English Studies* n.s. 20 (1969): 129–54, 257–83, 418–44.

Quaglio, A. E. *Scienza e mito nel Boccaccio*. Padua: Liviano, 1967.

Rabanus. *De universo* 15–60. *PL* 11: 426–36.

Raith, Joseph. *Boccaccio in der englischen Literatur von Chaucer bis Painter's Palace of Pleasure*. Schrifftum und Sprache der Angelsachsen, 3. Leipzig: R. Noske, 1936.

Reiss, Edmund. "Boccaccio in English Culture of the Fourteenth and Fifteenth Centuries," In *Il Boccaccio nella cultura inglese e anglo-americana*, edited by Giuseppe Galigani, 15–26. Atti del Convegno di Studi, Certaldo, 14–19 settembre 1970. Florence: Olschki, 1974.

Robertson, D. W. "The Doctrine of Charity in Medieval Literary Gardens." *Speculum* 26 (1951): 24–49.

———. *A Preface to Chaucer*. Princeton: Princeton University Press, 1962.

Sasso, Luigi. "L' 'interpretatio nominis' in Boccaccio." *Studi sul Boccaccio* 12 (1980): 129–74.

Tuve, Rosemund. *Seasons and Months*. Paris: Librairie Universitaire s.a., 1933.

Vendôme, Matthieu de. *Comoedia Lydiae*. In *Poésies inédites du Moyen Age*, edited by M. Edelstand du Meril. Paris, 1854.

Vincent, de Beauvais. *Speculum naturale*. Nuremberg, 1483.

Wallace, David. "Chaucer and Boccaccio's Early Writings." In *Chaucer and the Italian Trecento*, edited by Pietro Boitani, 141–59. Cambridge: Cambridge University Press, 1983.

Wentersdorf, Karl. "Imagery, Structure, and Theme in Chaucer's Merchant's Tale." In *Chaucer and the Craft of Fiction*, edited by Leigh A. Arrathoon, 35–62. Rochester, MI: Solaris Press, 1986.

Wright, Thomas, ed. "Appendix to the Latin Editions of Aesop's Fables printed in the Fifteenth Century." In *A Selection of Latin Stories, from Manuscripts of the Thirteenth and Fourteenth Centuries: A Contribution to the History of Fiction during the Middle Ages*, vol. 9. London, 1872.

From Knossos to Knight's Tale
The Changing Face of Chaucer's Theseus

Melvin Storm

A century before Yorkist and Lancastrian chroniclers, diversely reviewing Richard II's reign, demonstrated how a single face can be made to show opposing aspects, Chaucer found his own double-visaged Richard, even his own Jekyll and Hyde, in Theseus, redoubtable doyen of the *Knight's Tale* and soothless betrayer of the *Legend of Ariadne* and the *House of Fame*. An examination of the changing face of Theseus can illuminate not only Chaucer's artistry and moral temperament but the flexibility of the uses of mythology in the Middle Ages as well. In Theseus the mythographic tradition provided Chaucer with a well-known figure possessed of a rich body of familiar lore. Working within that tradition—and occasionally testing its boundaries with some vigor—Chaucer demonstrates the ways in which the artist can, to suit his purposes, manipulate, reproportion, disguise, and sometimes distort a relatively fixed body of mythographic material. At the same time, I think it will be seen, a study of Chaucer's metamorphosing protagonist in the light of antecedent mythographic treatments suggests at least one of the *Legend of Good Women* narratives, the *Ariadne*, to possess a degree of subtlety not generally credited to that group of Chaucer's productions and offers yet another piece of evidence of the interrelationship among the diverse works of Chaucer's career. Finally, a reading of the *Legend of Ariadne* can illuminate our reading of that slightly later and much greater work, the *Knight's Tale*.

Theseus appears either as active figure or as referent in four of Chaucer's works—namely, in generally accepted chronological order, the *House of Fame*, the *Anelida and Arcite*, the *Legend of Good Women* (*Ariadne* and *Phyllis*), and the *Knight's Tale*. His role in the *House of Fame* is relatively slight, although it establishes the Mister Hyde characterization that is to be dominant in the *Legend of Ariadne*. In the *House of Fame* Theseus is a static figure, presented, so to speak, as first among recreant equals in the crime of betrayal of women. The narrator, describing the story of Aeneas as in his vision he saw it portrayed on the wall of Venus's temple of glass and concentrating particularly on the Dido episode, bursts out into a diatribe against men who, like Aeneas to Dido, have done "untrouthe" to women. He catalogues Demophon (388–96), Achilles (397–98), Paris (399), Jason (400–401), Hercules (402–404), and, finally, in the longest passage, Theseus (405–26), who, after Ariadne had saved his life:

> lefte hir slepynge in an ile
> Desert allone, ryght in the se,
> And stal away, and let hir be,
> And took hir suster Phedra thoo
> With him, and gan to shippe goo.   (*HF* 416–20)[1]

The central elements that will be important to the *Legend of Ariadne* are present here and are straightforwardly incorporated—the debt, the desertion, the supplanting sister—but we will note shortly the quite different way in which those elements are combined in that later work. One constant remains, however, and that is the vilification of Theseus, recurrent in the *House of Fame*, in the *Legend of Ariadne*, and, shortly thereafter, in the *Legend of Phyllis*, where he is the "false fader" who bequeathes to his son Demophon his nature as one "fals of love" (2464 and 2447).

But it is only in the *Ariadne* that we follow through the process whereby Theseus, beginning in innocence, earns the ill fame that he subsequently loses, so abruptly and so mysteriously, in the *Knight's Tale*. A look at what happens in the *Ariadne*, together with consideration of what the mythographical sources available in Chaucer's day offered by way of material, will repay our attention. The narrator of *Ariadne* begins his story with an account of Minos, who, on his way to besiege Athens in vengeance for his son Androgeus's death, conquered Alcathoe with the help of Scylla, its ruler's daughter. Setting the pattern that would subsequently be followed by Theseus, "wikkedly he quitte hire kyndenesse" (1918) once the victory was his and continued on to defeat Athens and establish the custom whereby Athenian youths were to be sent as sacrificial tribute to the Minotaur, "a monstre, a wiked best" (1928). When the lot eventually falls to Aegeus's own son, Theseus, to be sacrificed, the youth is sent to Crete and is imprisoned, fortuitously, where his laments can be heard by Ariadne and Phaedra. The narrative to this point holds few surprises, and most of the details can be attributed to one or another of the sources from which Chaucer evidently had bits and pieces of the story, a catalog generally agreed to include Ovid, Plutarch, Hyginus, Virgil, the *Ovide moralisé*, and Boccaccio.[2]

In the *Legend of Good Women* generally, Chaucer often is highly selective in the details he draws from his sources, for his narrative must always work toward the condemnation of false men and the corollary of implicit praise for the women whom they wrong. That approach is as true in the *Ariadne* as elsewhere, but because Chaucer is leading his audience into familiar mythological territory, we can assume, as he must have assumed, that whatever he omits will be readily supplied by the listener or reader. The narrator, for example, condemns Minos for abandoning Scylla after she helps him win Alcathoe and leaves it at that. Yet implicit in the story of Minos, which Chaucer presents as an instance of one man wronging one woman, are instances of two women wronging two men—that is, a daughter her father (Scylla's treachery to Nysus, ruler of Alcathoe) and a wife her husband (Pasiphae's bestial cuckolding of Minos from which union is born the Minotaur). Not only can the knowledge the audience brings to the legends sometimes serve to undercut the narrator's ostensible intentions, as would seem to be the case here, but critics have from time to time called into question the very tone of the narratives, suggesting that Chaucer is less than grave in recounting the travails of his heroines (see, e.g., Lounsbury, 3:338–39; Goddard; Garrett; Frank, 206–208; Fyler, 96–115).

The question of tone is surely raised in the present instance by the detail of Theseus's imprisonment adjoining a "foreyne" (1962), glossed in this context by *M.E.D.* as "privy," through which his lamentations rise to the ears of the two young women in the chamber above. In the Chaucerian context one may even be reminded of the *Merchant's Tale* and May's furtive disposal of Damian's letter. The unlikely detail is still more striking if we allow Lowes's suggestion that the particulars of Theseus's imprisonment derive from the same passage in the *Teseida* that Chaucer follows when he describes the imprisonment of Palamon and Arcite in the *Knight's Tale* (Lowes, 803–8). In the latter work Chaucer, more true to the spirit of the *Teseida*, assigns the youths' imprisonment to "a chambre an heigh" (*KnT* 1065) overlooking a garden.

But considerations of tone we may best hold in abeyance at this point and turn again to the movement of the story, for once Ariadne and Phaedra hear Theseus's "compleynynge," the narrative takes a surprising turn, a turn all the more remarkable in being so regularly ignored by critics.[3] The surprise lies in the prominent role of Phaedra in the salvation of Theseus, a role for which even the mythographical texts that include her—and many do not—offer no precedent. In giving Phaedra that role, and then in returning the focus of the story to the more traditionally appropriate Ariadne, Chaucer employs, as we shall see, extraordinary dexterity as a narrator, raising, at the same time, the question of why he made the exercise of that dexterity necessary in the first place. Hearing Theseus's lamentations, the sisters have compassion on him and Ariadne asserts that he should be helped. Thereupon Phaedra, affirming that "me is as wo / For hym as evere I was for any man" (1985–86), in a speech of thirty-nine lines (1985–2024), formulates the entire plan by which Theseus is to be saved.

Phaedra's speech is more than double the length of Ariadne's much noted lament, drawn from the *Heroides*, at the end of the poem. It is longer, in fact, than any of Ariadne's speeches, giving her considerable prominence in quantitative terms alone. It is Phaedra who plans to gain the "gayler's" collusion, who originates the idea of the balls of "wex and tow" to stop the Minotaur's mouth, and who devises the use of the "clewe of twyn" by which Theseus will find his way out of the labyrinth. Chaucer, in effect, catalogues every element of the escape that ever found its way into any of the sources and, having done so, transfers the exhaustive catalogue to the wrong woman.

Next, on the heels of such highly specific language and detail, the narrative suddenly becomes the epitome of vagueness:

What sholde I lenger sarmoun of it make?
This gayler cometh, and with hym Theseus.
Whan these thynges ben acorded thus,
Adoun sit Theseus upon his kne. . . .   (2025–28)

The passive voice in line 2027, as the passive is wont to do, makes quite uncertain who does the according and who presents the plan, but we cannot forget that the narrator has just attributed the plan to Phaedra and that it is she whom he has just quoted. In consequence of the ambiguity of the passage we are uncertain whom Theseus addresses in the lines that follow. Although knowledge of the myth would normally lead the audience to assume Ariadne to be the one addressed, that expectation must be weakened by the fact that Chaucer has already taken obvious liberties with the myth in depriving Ariadne of her traditional role as initiator of the escape plot. Logically, at least, the proximity of Phaedra's speech (albeit to Ariadne) and the fact that the plans were hers would make it not unlikely that it should be she whom Theseus addresses:

"The ryghte lady of my lyf," quod he,
"I, sorweful man, ydampned to the deth,
Fro yow, whil that me lasteth lyf or breth,
I wol nat twynne, after this aventure,
But in youre servise thus I wol endure." . . .   (2029–33)

The ambiguity is by no means resolved a few lines later when Theseus indicates that, despite the occasional references to the singular "lady" (i.e., 2029, 2054, and 2073), he is addressing all three, the "gayler" as well as both Phaedra and Ariadne:

> As wolde God, if that it myghte be
> Ye weren in my cuntre, alle thre,
> And I with yow to bere yow compaignye,
> Thanne shulde ye se if that I therof lye. (2056–59)

If the unlikely turn of narrative earlier and the ambiguity of transition have made it indeed possible that Theseus first addressed not Ariadne but Phaedra, these lines, which include all the trio of rescuers, serve the purpose of returning Ariadne pointedly to the narrative, effecting a gradual turn toward the lines immediately following Theseus's speech wherein she reclaims (if it be allowed that indeed she had lost it) the place mythology assigns her. Theseus's speech concluded, the narrator describes him and cites Ariadne's response:

> A semely knyght was Theseus to se,
> And yong, but of a twenty yer and thre.
> But whoso hadde seyn his contenaunce,
> He wolde have wept for routhe of his penaunce;
> For which this Adryane in this manere
> Answerde hym to his profre and to his chere:
> "A kynges sone, and ek a knyght," quod she,
> "To ben my servaunt in so low degre." . . . (2074–81)

Absent the established myth, the "*my* servaunt" might seem presumptuous in the context of what has just preceded, and there is perhaps a slight softening of the peremptory claim when Ariadne expresses the hope that she may find him "To me and to my syster here so kynde, / That I repente nat to yeve yow lyf!" (2087–88). But while we may see in Ariadne's inclusion of her sister evidence of Chaucer's making the transition less abrupt, there is no question but that the "lady myn" (2103) of Theseus's *next* speech is Ariadne, for she has by that point stated her intention, to which Theseus swears assent, that Phaedra be married to Theseus's son, Hippolytus, upon their return to Athens. (The question of how likely Theseus is to be of an age to have a marriageable son we may conveniently leave unexplored, just as Chaucer evidently did.)

It is noteworthy that the portion of the narrative just summarized comprises by far the greater part of Chaucer's *Legend of Ariadne*. After a speech by Ariadne to Phaedra in which she contemplates smugly—there is no other word for it—their life to come with the "regals of

Athenes" (2128),[4] the fight with the Minotaur and the escape are accomplished in a very few lines. The planning, as Chaucer proportions his narrative, is all, and the consequent prominence of Phaedra is difficult to forget even when Chaucer tells us that "by the techynge of this Adryane / He overcom this beste and was his bane . . ." (2146–47).

In giving Phaedra such prominence in the story, Chaucer has taken considerable liberties with the mythographical tradition. Ovid, for example, ignores Phaedra entirely when he deals with the Theseus-Ariadne myth in the *Fasti*, in the *Metamorphoses*, and in *Heroides* 10, Ariadne's lament. Ovid, in fact, never represents Theseus as deserting Ariadne for another woman; it is always a matter of simple desertion, with no rival involved. The closest Ovid comes to the Chaucerian account is in the *Fasti* when he deals with Ariadne's marriage to Bacchus, who indeed does leave her for another lover (*Fasti*, 3.8). Virgil, too, in his brief account in the sixth book of the *Aeneid*, omits mention of Phaedra, referring in the singular only to "the princess' great love" ("magnum reginae . . . amorem" [6.28]). Statius's *Thebaid*, so important an influence on the *Knight's Tale* in its account of Theseus's assault on Thebes, alludes merely to a single maiden (11.676) with no elaboration on the Cretan exploit. Plutarch summarizes several versions of Theseus's adventures in Crete and notes one account that has Theseus deserting Ariadne for another woman, but the woman he identifies not as Phaedra but as "Aigle child of Panopeus" (1:41 and 67). Phaedra does appear in Plutarch, but only in another context, Theseus marrying her after the death of Antiope (1:65). The account in Hyginus similarly draws no connection between the desertion of Ariadne and the marriage to Phaedra, noting merely that Theseus does the one and then later does the other (70).

Among the texts most likely to have influenced Chaucer, Phaedra is most prominently in evidence—as well she might be—in *Heroides* 4, her own letter to Hippolytus. There she accuses her husband, Theseus, of being as faithless to her as he had been to Ariadne. Yet, importantly, she credits herself with no role in the Cretan adventure. She attributes the labyrinthine aid solely to Ariadne (4.59–60) and says nothing of how she herself came to be Theseus's wife. The role of Phaedra as supplanter does appear in medieval texts. The *Genealogie deorum* thus depicts her (10.49), as does the *Ovide moralisé* (8.1329–39).[5]

Whatever the source, Gower, like Chaucer, picks up the detail in the *Confessio Amantis* (8.2556–58). But Gower also agrees with both the *Genealogie* and the *Ovide moralisé* in giving no credit to Phaedra for the plan itself. Here Chaucer stands conspicuously alone, even taking, it seems, Ariadne's *Ovide moralisé* soliloquy away from her and giving it to Phaedra to form the substance of her plan.[6] One may in fact suggest, if we grant the *Ovide moralisé* to be the source, that Chaucer's expansion of the original passage indicates his desire to emphasize it, to call attention to its anomalous presence. But however it comes about, representation of Phaedra as the instigator of the plan to free Theseus is evidently unique to Chaucer, and even her position as immediate supplanter of Ariadne is but dimly adumbrated in the sources and analogues, and the shift in Phaedra's position inevitably results in a change in Ariadne's.

The question of tone, which, as noted above, arises frequently in discussion of the *Legend of Good Women* narratives, can legitimately be raised regarding Ariadne's final soliloquy. The content of her soliloquy draws heavily on Ovid's *Heroides*, and because of that debt, perhaps, most critics are inclined to read the passage solemnly.[7] But while there are indeed lines of pathos (as in, notably, lines 2193–94, "The holwe rokkes answerde hire agayn. / No man she saw, and yit shyned the mone"), between Ovid and Chaucer some telling changes occur. While the colloquial curses the narrator levels at Theseus once he has sailed away with the fairer sister serve to set the lament into a less-than-solemn context ("a twenty devel-wey the wynd hym dryve!" [2177], "these false lovers, poysoun be here bane!" [2180], and "the devel quyte hym his while!" [2227]), perhaps the most intriguing choice of language lies in the remarkable verbal parallel between the discovery by Ariadne that Theseus has fled and the discovery by the miller's wife in the *Reeve's Tale* that she has almost—or so she thinks—entered the wrong bed. Thus Ariadne:

> Ryght in the dawenyng awaketh she,
> And gropeth in the bed, and fond ryght nought.
> "Allas," quod she, "that evere I was wrought!" (2185–87)

And thus the miller's wife:

> Soone after this the wyf hir rowtyng leet,
> And gan awake, and wente hire out to pisse,
> And cam agayn, and gan hir cradel mysse,
> And groped heer and ther, but she foond noon.
> "Allas!" quod she, "I hadde almoost mysgoon." . . . (*RvT* 4214–18)

Unless we assume language to be nuanceless and hence, even in larger syntactic units, limitlessly interchangeable, we cannot but think that an author's intended tone when he writes one passage is likely to be reflected when he uses essentially the same language to write another passage—unless, of course, the echo is used deliberately for purposes of irony, hardly the case here. From the beginning of the narrative to its end Chaucer weakens both in detail and in tone the stature of Ariadne as heroine, the specifics of the narrative calling into question even Ariadne's claim to Theseus's loyalty, and the framing of her lament calling into question the gravity with which her loss of that loyalty is treated. Her lament, finally, Chaucer breaks off abruptly, rather as he does Dorigen's tedious reflections on suicide in the *Franklin's Tale*, and suggests that his audience consult Ovid if they want it in its entirety:

> What shulde I more telle hire compleynyng?
> It is so long, it were an hevy thyng.
> In hire Epistel Naso telleth al. . . .   (2218-20)

I have dealt at length with Phaedra and Ariadne, although the center of the present study is Theseus himself. In mythology, the two sisters (or the one) serve primarily as appurtenances to his story, but our opinion of him in the *Legend of Ariadne*, after all, is shaped largely by what we know of the women with whom he is involved. Within the framework of the narrative itself in the *Legend of Good Women*, the liberties Chaucer has taken with mythological tradition may subtly serve the purpose, if not of vindicating the professedly vilified Theseus, at least of providing a degree of extenuation for Ariadne's fate. Theseus, if we attend closely to the narrator's actual telling of the story, may not be so fully the Mister Hyde the narrator insists him to be, or, at the very least, his victim may not be so deserving of the degree of sympathy the narrator insists we should reserve for her. It is possible that here, as many critics agree he had done in *Troilus and Criseyde*, Chaucer deliberately sets his narrator's stance at odds with the facts of the narrative, but even this possibility seems, finally, inadequate to balance satisfactorily the conflicting claims that the narrative, considered on all its levels, enforces on us.

Robert Worth Frank may be correct when he argues that Chaucer's artistry at this point, at least in the framework within which he was working, was unable to encompass the range of experience with which he found himself dealing (133). But if the *Legend of Ariadne* leaves us somewhat unsatisfied, a degree of resolution to what some may see as its uncertainties or inconsistencies can be found when we look upon it—and its presentation of Theseus—in relation to the *Knight's Tale*, where the villain of Crete becomes the paragon of Athens.

It is not unlikely that Chaucer had the *Legend of Ariadne* still in mind when he composed the *Knight's Tale*. Only a couple of years intervened between their respective compositions;[8] because of the tendency of readers to associate the quality of the legends themselves—though not of the *Prologue* to the legends—with Chaucer's poetic novitiate, it often comes as a surprise to realize that *The Legend of Good Women* falls chronologically between *Troilus and Criseyde* and *The Canterbury Tales*—that is, when Chaucer was nearing his fullest artistic maturity. Not only are the works chronologically contiguous, but, as Lowes long ago argued, there is a strong likelihood that the major source for the *Knight's Tale*, Boccaccio's *Teseida*, was exercising its influence on Chaucer even during his work on the *Ariadne*. In the account of Theseus's imprisonment, for example, which echoes strikingly the *Knight's Tale* account, based on the *Teseida*, of the incarceration of Palamon and Arcite, Chaucer describes the chambers of Phaedra and Ariadne as looking toward "the mayster-strete / Of Athenes" (1965–66). Although supported by the majority of manuscripts, it is a rather unlikely detail, considering that they are in Crete, but probably results from Chaucer's momentary inattention as he followed too closely the *Teseida* original (Lowes, 808n).

Parallels, whether *Teseida*-inspired or not, are numerous, transcending the mere fact of the poems' sharing a common protagonist, but they do not particularly occur where we would most expect them—that is, in the depictions of Theseus. In fact, specific reflection of the one Theseus by the other is largely limited to the shared tendency of each to swear by Mars (*Ariadne*, 2063 and 2109; *KnT*, 1708 and 1747). Such a detail, insofar as it indicates martial devotion, is of considerable significance as an index of character and is, as we shall see, thematically important; nevertheless, as in the example of imprisonment just cited, parallels most often are found joining the Theseus of the *Ariadne* not with the Theseus of the *Knight's Tale* but with Arcite. Theseus, for instance, in the lengthy speech discussed above wherein he addresses ambiguously either Phaedra or Ariadne or both, swears to "the ryghte lady of my lyf" (2029) that if he survives he will serve her and, like Arcite, "ben of youre court a page" (2037). Further, like the disguised Arcite, he will "me so wel disfigure and so lowe, / That in this world ther shal no man me knowe" (2046–47), and, also like Arcite, insists, not altogether credibly, that he has loved Ariadne from afar and has been her servant for "this sevene yer" (2120). Arcite, we recall, returns to Athens after a four-year absence and serves secretly under Theseus and Emelye for an additional three years before his identity is discovered and his love made known (see *KnT*, 1446 and 1452).

It is, we might observe, appropriate that in the *Knight's Tale* Arcite, rather than Theseus, should serve as echo of the *Ariadne*-Theseus, for Arcite, like the younger Theseus, exemplifies a martialism not yet matured, a martialism subject to the distractions of youth. Theseus in the *Knight's Tale* is, as we shall see, the exemplar of mature martialism, wholly dedicated to the discipline of the soldier, and hence at a considerable remove from his earlier counterpart.

Bearing in mind that there are definite links between *Ariadne* and the

Knight's Tale and that, because of their extensiveness and the relative proximity of Chaucer's writing of the two, the links are likely to be more than accidental, let us turn, finally, to the latter tale itself, particularly to the depiction of Theseus in that tale, where the villainous Mister Hyde, in an inversion of Stevenson's tragic sequence, emerges triumphantly as the benevolent Doctor Jekyll. Relatively few critics find the portrait of Theseus in the *Knight's Tale* to be other than highly positive,[9] and the positive nature of the portrait, among that majority of critics who accept it as such, is generally recognized as being accompanied by preeminence of narrative place, scholarship in recent decades commonly according Theseus the central position in the narrative. For example, according to Charles Muscatine's influential study, Theseus, not Palamon, Arcite, and Emelye, holds the center of interest in the poem, which, rather than being about love, is about "the noble life," of which love is only a part (78). According to Muscatine, the poem deals with the assertion of the order embodied in the noble life against the forces of disorder. While the love interest of Palamon and Arcite exemplifies only one of the concerns of nobility, Theseus stands at the center as "representative of the highest chivalric conceptions of nobility" (72).

In a similar vein John Halverson, taking as the poem's central theme order itself, exemplified in "three complementary aspects: the order of nature, the order of society, and the divine order of the cosmos," has suggested that, as regards social order, Theseus represents the knightly class fulfilling its traditional obligation to embody that order and preserve the society of which it is a part (606 and 612–13). Richard H. Green, carrying the theme of order associated with Theseus into the realm of mythology, has demonstrated that the mythological tradition supports Theseus's function as orderer, the triumph of Athens over Scithea representing the triumph of reason over appetite, and Theseus's marriage to Hippolyte the overcoming of "sensual indulgence" by "rational activity." So too, Theseus's victory over Creon is further triumph of virtue over vice in the restoration of order to what began in the rivalry of Eteocles and Polynices, and the Minotaur on Theseus's pennon serves to remind us of his "conquest of the monstrous product of Pasiphae's lust" (130–32). These studies all, we might note, quite ignore the forsaken Ariadne, but it will be seen that in the context of the *Knight's Tale*, where the Theseus-figure achieves its broadest significance, she too, albeit unnamed, has her thematic place.

In the *Knight's Tale*, Theseus is above all a martial figure, in the literal sense of being an avowed follower of Mars and as one whose warlike pursuits are indicated through actions, speech, and iconography. Our first view of Theseus is martial, for at his earliest appearance in the poem he is returning from war—the conquest of Femenye, the land of the Amazons—and, as it happens, he will almost immediately engage in still another one, the subduing of "the tiraunt Creon" (961). Theseus's banner, too, is witness to his martialism, carrying as emblem "the rede statue of Mars, with spere and targe" (975), a detail repeated from the parallel passage in *Anelida and Arcite* (29-31). His martial devotion is further emphasized by his habit of swearing by or invoking Mars, a habit that, as we noted above, he displays also in the *Ariadne* and which serves as one of the links between the two poems.

But the martial figure in Chaucer does not always thrive. In "The Mythological Tradition in Chaucer's *Complaint of Mars*" and "Troilus, Mars, and Late Medieval Chivalry," I argue that Mars in *The Complaint* and the Mars-devotee, Troilus, because they transfer their devotion to Venus, become courtly subservients and ultimately forfeit their accustomed strength. The pattern, debilitating to Mars himself, proves fatal to Troilus, as it does, in the *Knight's Tale*, to Arcite. Theseus in the *Knight's Tale*, however, represents a martialism different from that of his counterparts. His is a martialism untempered by venereal passion and hence not weakened, a chivalry that is concentrated on the military, not the courtly side of endeavor. Halverson, arguing Theseus to be the ideal representative of knighthood, notes that his admission to having once been a servant of love (1813-20) completes the ideal picture because "in medieval literature the ideal of love is added to that of chivalry to make up the perfect knight: these are the twin ideals of knighthood" (613; see also 614).

I would suggest, on the contrary, that we are able to look upon Theseus as the ideal, not because he *was* a servant, but because he no longer is. "In my tyme," he says, "a servant was I oon" (1814), clearly putting the experience in the past. His conquest of "al the regne of Femenye" (866), the land of the Amazons, and his wedding to Hippolyte, its queen, events accomplished before the poem opens and thereby giving to Theseus, at the outset, a character already established, not only suggests figuratively, as Richard Green points out, "the virile intellect subduing the feminine passions" (131; see also Robertson, 264-65); it is an unequivocal image of the subduing of woman by man, the correction of the inverted hierarchy implicit in the major interpretive tradition of the myth of Mars and Venus.[10] Theseus, by the conquest, demonstrates himself to be free from the subservience that, in the world of the romance, characterizes the courtly lover.

But while the *Knight's Tale* establishes internally the image of Theseus as the warrior freed from venereal bondage, the *Legend of Ariadne* provides an external, anticipatory exemplification of the theme. Theseus, that is, brings with him from the earlier poem an established character, specifically, a character imbued with precisely the nature appropriate to his *Knight's Tale* function as balancer of the conflicting claims of Mars and Venus that are embodied in Arcite and Palamon, their mortal devotees. The reader who comes to the *Knight's Tale* from the *Ariadne* brings with him a view of Theseus that more fully prepares him to comprehend the significance and function of the hero in the second work. In a sense, *Ariadne* dramatizes the process, the *Knight's Tale* the product. And that Theseus should be treated so positively in the one and receive such censure in the other may be a matter explicable on the basis of the differing personae the poet chooses to narrate the two works.

Theseus's career in the *Ariadne* is, if we incline to look at him as a warrior *gaining* freedom from the bondage of love, almost emblematic. He begins in literal imprisonment, swears not merely courtly subservience but literal, menial servitude to Ariadne and, after slaying the Minotaur in the labyrinth and escaping from Crete, leaves her. Stripped of its detail it is a spare narrative, but while one might counter that so bare an outline unfairly ignores the complexities and deeper emotions Chaucer infuses into the actual text, certain of those details themselves support an emblematic reading. Chaucer, for example, manages to insinuate through the words of Ariadne herself advocacy of the duty of the knight to avoid servitude. When Theseus offers to forego his heritage and serve in secret as Ariadne's page so that he can be near her, praying, ironically, that *Mars* give him a shameful death if he fail to do so (2060–69), Ariadne refuses the proffered vow, insisting that such a course would be unworthy of "a kynges sone, and ek a knyght," who ought rather to devote himself to the martial endeavor at hand:

> God shilde it, for the shame of wemen alle,
> And lene me nevere swich a cas befalle!
> But sende yow grace of herte and sleyghte also,
> Yow to defende and knyghtly slen youre fo. . . . (2082–85)

Thematically important also is the slaying of the Minotaur, portrayed on Theseus's pennon in the *Knight's Tale* and constituting Theseus's central action in the *Legend of Ariadne*. Even beyond its figurative application as the conquest of passion and the reassertion of reason, the exploit is significant to the present theme. The myth of the Minotaur, according to one mythographic tradition, is a corollary to the myth of Mars and Venus's adultery, in which the patron god of warriors, because he succumbs to his passion for Venus, ultimately finds himself entrapped and disgraced in the jealous Vulcan's net. The plight of Mars provided, in the medieval mythographical tradition, the emblem for the theme of masculine virtue weakened by love.

According to Fulgentius and the third Vatican mythographer, Venus took vengeance on the sun for having discovered the illicit liaison by inspiring the sun's daughters with various modes of shameful lust. One of those daughters was Pasiphae, from whose lust for the bull sprang the Minotaur (Fulgentius, 2.7; Mythographus Tertius, 11.6, Bode, 231). Thus Theseus vanquishes the offspring of a lust that derived, in turn, from the very lust that left his patron deity in captivity and disgrace. The conquest of the Minotaur is clearly pivotal in *Ariadne*, both in terms of plot structure—for thereafter Theseus contravenes his vow of servitude that preceded it—and in terms of the theme that is embodied in the exploit; considering the traditional signification accorded the figure of the Minotaur, it may not be too bold to suggest that in the act of killing the monster Theseus frees himself emblematically from love's fetters. But however one reads the tone of the *Legend of Ariadne*, and however much sympathy one brings to its heroine, it is clear that when we consider it in conjunction with the later narrative, Theseus moves from *Ariadne* to the *Knight's Tale* as the very image of unfettered martialism.

By the time Theseus emerges into the *Knight's Tale* from the long path over which Chaucer has led him, he has become a figure of far greater depth and complexity than his antecedents might have caused us to expect. There is little question but that the Theseus of the *House of Fame* is a one-dimensional figure: he is free from courtly subservience, to be sure, but free only in the simplest and least attractive sense of being wholly callous and self-serving. In the *Ariadne*, although the narrator insistently condemns him, the twists of narrative and the characterizations of the other figures make his actions—and, perhaps, his final position—somewhat more susceptible to sympathy or at least to understanding. By the *Knight's Tale*, he has come still further. Although he is free from courtly servitude, it has given place not to calculation and faithlessness but, instead, to the authority and steadfastness of the husband.

Theseus, in the *Knight's Tale*, is a figure of balance, his martialism matured and deepened in its humanity through the tempering and correction of time and experience. When he admits to having served Venus in the past, he says that he has "ben caught ofte in [love's] laas" (1817), echoing the bondage theme so important to the Mars myth, yet in the very act of admitting how easily one can become ensnared by love he sets his seal upon the activity of Arcite and Palamon as folly:

Now looketh, is nat that an heigh folye?
Who may been a fool but if he love?
Bihoold, for Goddes sake that sit above,
Se how they blede! be they noght wel arrayed?

>Thus hath hir lord, the god of love, ypayed
>Hir wages and hir fees for hir servyse!
>And yet they wenen for to been ful wyse
>That serven love, for aught that may bifalle.   (1798–1805)

Theseus's time of servitude—according to the *Ariadne*, perhaps, only an incipient servitude—is now behind him. It is no doubt significant that, having once served Venus, he is depicted in the *Knight's Tale* as serving both Mars and Diana (*KnT*, 1682). No slave to love's passion, in his marriage he represents the traditional medieval image of the appropriate hierarchy of the sexes as well as of reason and passion. With a character thus established on the basis of earlier mythological antecedents and on the basis of antecedents within the body of Chaucer's own work, Theseus stands in the *Knight's Tale* ready to bring to bear on the disorder around him the order that is, at last, embodied in his own person. It is no mere coincidence that the conflicting claims that the *Knight's Tale* challenges him to balance are those of Mars, Venus, and Diana.

We are left, finally, with the question of why, across Chaucer's writing, the face of Theseus undergoes so many metamorphoses, why he is here praised and there impugned. It would surely strain credulity to postulate that Chaucer deliberately began developing him, from the *House of Fame* through the *Ariadne*, so that he would come to the *Knight's Tale* properly accoutered, but it is not unreasonable to suggest that, when he composed the *Knight's Tale*, Chaucer had his earlier works in mind and was aware that many of his audience would have familiarity with those works as well and could draw upon them for illumination of the more recent.

I would propose, further, that we find in the changing faces of Theseus a clear record of the diverse ways in which the differing personae Chaucer employs for the respective poems can appropriately and diversely address a single theme and a single figure. The metamorphosing Theseus may, in fact, reflect Chaucer's changing point of view with regard to the conflicting claims of martial and courtly chivalry, but that is a matter of complexity beyond the scope of the present study.

We know that the author of the *Canterbury Tales* is one of the supreme masters of the art of speaking from behind a narrative mask and making his narrative accord with his persona. The works we have been examining offer no small evidence of that. When Theseus appears in the guise of simple villain in the *House of Fame*, unredeemable and unhesitatingly reviled, the presentation is indeed that which we would expect from the love-vision narrator that we come to know in Chaucer's early poems, especially the naive narrator of this particular vision, wandering credulously through Venus's temple. In the *Legend of Ariadne*, the narrator is not so credulous but has been constrained through the command of a deity to adhere to a particular line of narrative and a particular line of interpretation not necessarily congenial either to his own point of view or to his material. The narrator dutifully tells his story, replete with concomitant dutiful outbursts of vilification, yet adjusts, slants, and even distorts his material in such a way that his hero's crimes are seen in a different light. (The changes Chaucer makes with respect to the role of Phaedra are particularly striking in the light of the strong avowal, at the very beginning of the *Prologue*, that the authority of books is not to be questioned [1–29 and passim].)

Finally, in the *Knight's Tale*, Chaucer has moved a step beyond the personae of those earlier works in which he himself stood as narrator. No longer do we hear the voice of "Geffrey," but instead that of the Knight, a narrator mature, serious, and militarily dedicated. It is the Knight who shows us the final and most positive face of Theseus, a man like himself, a governor admired by all about him, an exemplar of morality, a sympathetic observer and corrector of the follies of others, a devotee of duty whose volition is directed toward setting right—as was the medieval knightly ideal—the disorder around him. It takes, one might suggest, Chaucer's Knight to see and to report the full significance of Theseus.

Notes

1. Quotations from Chaucer follow Benson, ed., *The Riverside Chaucer*.
2. *The Riverside Chaucer* (1071–72) provides a convenient and thorough list, the notes pointing out arguments that have been advanced for such additional candidates as Catullus, Machaut, and Filippo Ceffi's Italian translation of the *Heroides*.
3. Exceptions include Meech, 197–98; Baum, 380; and Fyler, 102–3.
4. I find it difficult to read these lines, as does Shannon, as merely evidence that Ariadne is "a romantic young princess" (249–50). Frank, I believe, accurately captures the tone of the passage in attributing to it "a curiously calculating quality" (119).
5. Meech suggests the possibility that the detail may have been provided to Chaucer by Filippo's prose translation of the *Heroides* (184).
6. Although Frank observes that the speech has been shifted, he finds no particular significance in the fact (120–21).
7. Even Frank, while finding considerable humor in the *Ariadne* as a whole, reads the soliloquy itself seriously (129–30).

8. According to Fisher's chronology in his edition of Chaucer, for example, the beginnings of the *Legend of Good Women* and of the *Canterbury Tales* fall within the same three-year period (960).

9. For a succinct summary of criticism unfavorable to Theseus, see Scheps, 19 and 31n.

10. Boccaccio (9.3) offers a thorough treatment of the myth of Mars and Venus and its implications for the relationship between man—particularly the warrior—and woman. In a similar vein are the treatments by Fulgentius (2.7); the second and third Vatican mythographers (Bode, 84–85 and 231–32); Arnulf of Orleans (210); Walter Map (4.3); and the *Ovide moralisé* (4.1488–1537).

Works Cited

Arnulf, of Orleans. *Arnolfo d'Orleans, un cultore di Ovidio nel secolo XII.* Edited by Fausto Ghisalberti. *Memorie del Reale Istituto Lombardo di Scienze e Lettere* 24 (1932): 157–234.

Baum, Paull F. "Chaucer's 'Glorious Legende.' " *Modern Language Notes* 60 (1945): 377–81.

Boccaccio, Giovanni. *Genealogie deorum gentilium libri.* Edited by Vincenzo Romano. 2 vols. Bari: Giuseppe Laterza, 1951.

Bode, Georgius Henricus, ed. *Scriptores rerum mythicarum latini tres Romae nuper reperti.* 2 vols. Reprinted in 1. Hildesheim: Georg Olms, 1968.

Chaucer, Geoffrey. *The Complete Poetry and Prose.* Edited by John Hurt Fisher. 2d ed. New York: Holt, Rinehart & Winston, 1989.

———. *The Riverside Chaucer.* Edited by Larry D. Benson. 3d ed. Cambridge, MA: Houghton Mifflin, 1987.

Frank, Robert Worth, Jr. *Chaucer and The Legend of Good Women.* Cambridge, MA.: Harvard University Press, 1972.

Fulgentius, Fabius Planciades. *Mitologiae.* In *Opera,* edited by Rudolf Helm, 3–80. 1898. Reprint. Stuttgart: B. G. Teubner, 1970.

Fyler, John M. *Chaucer and Ovid.* New Haven: Yale University Press, 1979.

Garrett, Robert Max. " 'Cleopatra the Martyr' and Her Sisters." *JEGP* 22 (1923): 64–74.

Goddard, H. C. "Chaucer's *Legend of Good Women.*" *JEGP* 7 (1908): 87–129; 8 (1909): 47–111.

Gower, John. *The English Works of John Gower.* Edited by G. C. Macaulay. 2 vols. EETS Extra Series 82. 1900. London: Oxford University Press, 1957.

Green, Richard H. "Classical Fable and English Poetry in the Fourteenth Century." In *Critical Approaches to Medieval Literature: Selected Papers from the English Institute, 1958–1959,* edited by Dorothy Bethurum, 110–33. New York: Columbia University Press, 1960.

Halverson, John. "Aspects of Order in the Knight's Tale." *Studies in Philology* 57 (1960): 606–21.

Hyginus. *Fabulae.* Edited by H. J. Rose. Leiden: A. W. Sijthoff, 1934.

Lounsbury, Thomas R. *Studies in Chaucer: His Life and Writings.* 3 vols. 1892. New York: Russell and Russell, 1962.

Lowes, John L. "The Prologue to the *Legend of Good Women* Considered in Its Chronological Relations." *PMLA* 20 (1905): 748–864.

Map, Walter. *De nugis curialium.* Edited by Montague Rhodes James. Oxford: Clarendon Press, 1914.

Meech, Sanford Brown. "Chaucer and the *Ovide Moralisé*—A Further Study." *PMLA* 46 (1931): 182–204.
Muscatine, Charles A. "Form, Texture, and Meaning in Chaucer's *Knight's Tale*." In *Chaucer: Modern Essays in Criticism*, edited by Edward Wagenknecht, 60–82. New York: Oxford University Press, 1959. Reprinted from *PMLA* 65 (1950): 911–29.
Ovid. *Fasti*. Translated by Sir James George Frazer. Loeb Classical Library. Cambridge, MA: Harvard University Press, 1931.
———. *Heroides and Amores*. Translated by Grant Showerman. Loeb Classical Library. 2d ed. Cambridge, MA: Harvard University Press, 1977.
———. *Metamorphoses*. Translated by Frank Justus Miller. 2 vols. Loeb Classical Library. 3d ed. London: W. Heinemann, 1977.
"Ovide moralisé": Poème du commencement du quatorzième siècle publié d'après tous les manuscrits connus. Edited by C. de Boer et al. *Verhandelingen der Koninklijke Akademie van Wetenschappen te Amsterdam*. 1915–38. Reprint 5 vols. Wiesbaden: Martin Sändig, 1966–68.
Plutarch. *Lives*. Translated by Bernadotte Perrin. 14 vols. Loeb Classical Library. Cambridge, MA: Harvard University Press, 1914–26.
Robertson, D. W., Jr. *A Preface to Chaucer: Studies in Medieval Perspectives*. 1962. Reprint. Princeton: Princeton University Press, 1969.
Shannon, Edgar Finlay. *Chaucer and the Roman Poets*. Harvard Studies in Comparative Literature 7. Cambridge, MA: Harvard University Press, 1929.
Sheps, Walter. "Chaucer's Theseus and the *Knight's Tale*." *Leeds Studies in English* 9 (1976–77): 19–34.
Statius. *Statius*. Translated by J. H. Mozley. 2 vols. Loeb Classical Library. 1928. Reprint. Cambridge, MA: Harvard University Press, 1969.
Storm, Melvin. "The Mythological Tradition in Chaucer's *Complaint of Mars*." *Philological Quarterly* 57 (1978): 323–35.
———. "Troilus, Mars, and Late Medieval Chivalry." *Journal of Medieval and Renaissance Studies* 12 (1982): 45–65.
Virgil. *Aeneid*. In *Virgil*, translated by H. Rushton Fairclough. Rev. ed. 2 vols. Loeb Classical Library. 1932–34. Reprint. Cambridge, MA: Harvard University Press, 1978.

Part III. Renaissance England

Shakespeare and the Mythographers

The Comedy of Love
The Medieval Venus and Shakespeare's *Venus and Adonis*

Theodore L. Steinberg

Until recently, Shakespeare's *Venus and Adonis* has been treated as Shakespeare's stepchild, or as a funny thing that happened to him on his way to *King Lear*. Most early critics, for instance, were concerned with the poem's moral stance, not recognizing either that they were examining a beautiful and delicate poem dealing with themes that occupied Shakespeare elsewhere in his works, or that the questions of whether it is a poem in favor of love or against love, whether Shakespeare approves of or disapproves of Venus, are largely beside the point. This is not to say that previous critics have not raised some of the more important questions about the poem, but only that their answers have often been unsatisfactory.

One of the most commonly raised problems, for example, concerns the changes that Shakespeare made in the original Ovidian story, and the resolution is often that Shakespeare simply forgot the original or, in order to make him seem somewhat less stupid, that he confused parts of the Venus and Adonis story with the story of Hermaphrodite and Salmacis. Neither of these alternatives is correct: Shakespeare did not simply change his source material, but rather manipulated it in order to create his own, quite different poem that deals humorously with vital questions about the role of Venus in human existence.

Shakespeare's use of Venus, however, illustrates some of the ways in which poetic mythography had changed since the Middle Ages, and it relies especially on the way in which Shakespeare developed the humorous potential that had always been inherent in medieval treatments of Venus. A large part of that humor results from the ambiguities associated with the goddess of love. For a critic like Fulgentius, of course, there are no ambiguities in the figure of Venus. If the Epicureans define her as "the good things of life," he is quite sure that the Stoics are correct in viewing her "as the empty things of life" (Whitbread, 66). This derision of Venus, associating her exclusively with lust, continued throughout the Middle Ages in most of the serious discussions of love.

Alanus de Insulis, however, offered a slightly more complex picture of the goddess in his *De planctu Naturae*, in which Nature explains that she was appointed by God as "a sort of deputy, a coiner for stamping the order of things." But, Nature continues, because she wanted to remain in the unchangeable, eternal regions, "in the outskirt world I stationed Venus, who is skilled in the knowledge of making, as underdeputy of my work, in order that she, under my judgment and guidance . . . might weave together the line of the human race in unwearied continuation" (44–45). Venus, as Nature explains later, soon grew tired of doing the same work over and over again and became "young and childish," turning to evil and degenerating into lust, which deserves only condemnation (54–55). Thus, although Alanus finally gave Venus a very orthodox significance, he also gave some indication of her complexity by recognizing the necessity of her role in the generative process. Furthermore, anyone reading Alanus who does not share that poet's moral stance could well find his narrative, with its descriptions of Venus subverting the works of Nature as a way of explaining human sexual behavior, fairly humorous.

It was Boccaccio, however, who brought the complexity and potential humor of Venus to the foreground in his *Genealogie deorum gentilium*, where instead of simply discussing Venus, he discussed two Venuses, whom he referred to as Venus Magna and Venus Secunda.[1] Boccaccio's first Venus is a divine Venus, from whom "comes the proclivity for love, friendship, delight, union, and society among animals, most particularly to urge those who are sluggish and reluctant in procreation." The second is a vulgar, wicked Venus, "the goddess of wantonness" (Schreiber, 523). While this dichotomy seems to be a direct reflection of the orthodox view described by Fulgentius, it becomes much more complex when Boccaccio "finds that both [Venuses] have the same iconographic attributes and that a clear differentiation between *Venus celestis* and *Venus scelestis* is impossible, in contrast with the earlier commentators such as Bernard Silvestris who sees a simple dichotomy" (522). The resultant ambiguity in Boccaccio's treatment of Venus takes on the greatest significance as Venus ceases to be a figure who must be almost automatically condemned. This does not mean, of course, that Venus suddenly became an allegorical representation of pure love or, heaven forfend, that carnal love suddenly became admirable. It simply means that Venus's complexity in human existence was acknowledged, that the kind of human love represented by Venus was recognized to be in itself neither good nor bad.[2] It also means that the figure of Venus can easily be used in a humorous way, for if an observer cannot tell whether a given manifestation of Venus is good or bad, the opportunities for comic confusion become limitless.

It was this kind of ambiguity that Chaucer exploited in his comical but very serious discussion of love and procreation in *The Parlement of Foules*. While Chaucer's bumbling narrator conceives of love as a single, pure element in both the human and cosmic spheres, the reader can see the ambiguities of Venus, of love, everywhere in the poem—in the relationship between the heavenly Cytherea and the carnal Venus in her temple; in the conflicting legends over the entrance to the garden, legends that promise opposite rewards for apparently similar behavior; and in the parliament of fowls itself, where the conflict between Nature and the royal birds is a conflict between loyalty to a good Venus, who rules over the natural demand for procreation, and an evil Venus, who controls the kind of love game that leads to sterility and, ultimately, to death.[3] Thus Chaucer takes the ambiguities inherent in the figure of Venus and gives them an ironic twist.

For Chaucer, the proper involvement in carnal sex becomes a sign of loyalty to the heavenly Venus, while refraining from sexual indulgence, as the royal birds do, becomes a sign of allegiance to the evil Venus. As he does everywhere in his works, Chaucer recognizes and accepts the ambiguities of human existence. He understands that human sexual love is fraught with peril, that it is easily abused; but his comic vision, his humanity, and his understanding of the humorous role of Venus in human life allow him to make that point without becoming excessively moralistic or doctrinaire. Dante consigns carnal lovers to the Inferno, where he weeps over them; but Chaucer acknowledges their failures by making us laugh at them.

Shakespeare, too, uses humor to discuss problems of sexuality and love in *Venus and Adonis*, though his use of Venus differs from Chaucer's in much the same way that the Renaissance mythographers' treatment of the goddess differed from that of their medieval predecessors. Whereas Boccaccio had said that there were two different Venuses who could easily be confused because of their similar names and iconographical representation, and whereas Chaucer attempted to clarify the distinction between the two by calling one Cytherea, Shakespeare emphasized the confusion between the two aspects of Venus inherent in the earlier writers by incorporating them in a single figure. In short, Shakespeare moves further along the path that Chaucer had laid out. In so doing, Shakespeare reflects the developments of Renaissance mythography.

For example, the sixteenth-century mythographer Natalis Comes wrote that by Venus we mean "the natural desire for procreation" (10), a sentiment echoed to some extent by Vincenzo Cartari, who underscored her complexity when he described her as "the goddess of libido and lust" and when he said that "she shows that hidden virtue by which the animals are all drawn to the desire for generations" (111). Venus, then, emerges as a complex and ambiguous figure who is, in the most basic terms, both good and bad, both necessary and to be shunned. She is the goddess of both carnal lust and "the natural desire for procreation"—that is, the sexual urge.

For these mythographers, Venus is no longer divided into two characters. Instead she is returned to her classical unity, but she now contains, in a single figure, all the attributes of Boccaccio's two Venuses. The dual potential of the medieval Venus that Schreiber described has become the focus, and the two potentials have become inseparable. Venus is no longer seen, as she was in much medieval mythography, as a necessary evil, a figure who embodies evidence of the Fall by having turned the need for procreation into recreational concupiscence. Instead, she reflects natural human sexuality, seen not as artificially bifurcated but as a problematical aspect of human life. Thus, keeping in mind Venus's significance as the sexual urge, a simple, brief statement can explain a great deal about *Venus and Adonis*, accounting for the changes that Shakespeare made in the original story and explaining why the poem is simultaneously tragic and humorous: puberty hits Adonis pretty hard. As I shall try to show, *Venus and Adonis* is an allegorical description and discussion of the onset of sexuality, represented by Venus, in a young man's life and his reaction to it.

Numerous commentators have noticed Adonis's youth, but A. C. Hamilton writes that Adonis "cannot be seen as the merely innocent boy too young to love, for Venus, who should know, says that he is old enough to be tasted" (12). In that same line (128), however, she says that he is "unripe," a description with which he evidently agrees:

"Fair Queen," quoth he, "if any love you owe me,
Measure my strangeness with my unripe years.
Before I know myself, seek not to know me.
No fisher but the ungrown fry forbears.
The mellow plum doth fall, the green sticks fast,
Or being early pluck'd is sour to taste."   (523-28)

Even the narrator mentions Adonis's "hairless face" (487). The point is that Adonis is just old enough to be "tasted," he has just reached the age when sexuality begins, metaphorically, to attack him. The metaphorical nature of the whole poem, in fact, is emphasized in the very first scene when Venus "plucks" him from his horse and carries him so effortlessly under her arm, illustrating her magnitude, the force with which she comes to him. This scene also offers the first example of the humor in the poem, the kind of good-natured humor which, under normal circumstances, we are likely to find in a young person's first attempts at coping with sexuality, as, for instance, when we see our children encountering the first problems of early puberty. Thackeray provides a good example in the thirty-fourth chapter of *Vanity Fair* when he describes James Crawley: "James Crawley, when his aunt had last beheld him, was a gawky lad, at that uncomfortable age when the voice varies between an unearthly treble and a preternatural bass; when the face not uncommonly blooms out with appearances for which Rowland's Kalydor is said to act as a cure; when boys are seen to shave furtively with their sister's scissors, and the sight of other young women produces intolerable sensations of terror in them."

This scene of Venus plucking Adonis from his horse also marks the beginning of the very important horse imagery in the poem, although most critics focus their attention on the later scene when Adonis's horse runs after the jennet. It is important to realize, however, that in spite of some shifts in emphasis in the two scenes, the horse retains its significance, originating in Plato's *Phaedrus* and in the prophet Jeremiah, as the bodily, fleshly aspect of man. This significance is emphasized later when Shakespeare concludes his description of the horse by saying, "Look, what a horse should have he did not lack, / Save a proud rider on so proud a back" (229–300).

Venus's appeal to Adonis, then, is not an appeal to his bodily, carnal appetites, as orthodox views of Venus would have it, but to his mental state, again reflecting the peculiar nature of puberty, when the body is ready for sexual activity but the mind is not. Consequently Adonis rejects all her arguments, though the readiness of the body is symbolized by his horse's attraction to the jennet.

Although Adonis's protection of his chastity, his rejection of Venus, has seemed admirable to numerous readers, his supposed virtue is undercut by many factors in the poem, especially by Venus's appeal, entirely in keeping with her significance according to Comes and Cartari, to the necessity of procreation. Thus the jennet is "a breeding jennet" (260) and Adonis's horse, in addition to enjoying himself, is obeying natural law by pursuing her. It is Adonis's desire for chastity that perverts natural law. He counters Venus's argument for procreation by saying, " 'You do it for increase; O strange excuse, / When reason is the bawd to lust's abuse!' " (791–92). But there is no denying that, in the end, Venus is correct: "By law of nature thou art bound to breed" (171). Adonis dies heirless. He wants to grow up more: "Before I know myself, seek not to know me" (525), he says; but his end shows the truth of Venus's " 'Fair flowers that are not gather'd in their prime / Rot and consume themselves in little time' " (131–32).

Part of the poem's complexity, however, a reflection of Venus's traditional complexity, lies in the fact that Adonis, while confusing the need for procreation with lust, is also potentially correct when he says that love " 'is life in death / That laughs and weeps, and all but with a breath' " (413–14).

Adonis's view is supported by the great quantity of bird imagery in the poem, as William Keach points out (65–66), in which Venus is referred to as "an empty eagle" (55) with "vulture thoughts" (551), while Adonis is like "a bird . . . tangled in a net" (67); and even Venus, after Adonis finally breaks away from her:

>   sings extemporally a woeful ditty;
> How love makes young men thrall and old men dote;
> How love is wise in folly, foolish-witty. . . .   (836–38)

Clearly sexual maturity, the psychological acceptance of the sexual urge as represented by Venus, does entail certain responsibilities and hardships, it does require leaving behind childhood's almost prelapsarian state of innocence. But it is also necessary, avoidable only if one chooses the kind of final death that comes when one dies without leaving an heir, as Shakespeare says over and over in the sonnets and plays. This concentration on the need for procreation, and on the psychological acceptance of that need, in order to achieve a species of immortality, of course, is of central importance in the sonnets, where it is not sexual activity but sexual abstinence that is considered immoral.

Nor is Shakespeare's use of this theme unique. One of the best examples of a contemporary who used the theme is Spenser, for whom chastity meant married life and the creation of children, and whose own wedding song, the *Epithalamion*, nears its conclusion with a prayer for many generations of progeny. Even more important are the numerous references in *The Faerie Queene* both to the complications that sexuality brings to life, the moral questions it raises, and the need for reproduction. We need think only of Belphoebe, of Britomart's story, of Arthur's quest for Gloriana, and of the events in Busirane's home to see many of the same problems that Shakespeare raises in *Venus and Adonis*. And Spenser uses the Venus and Adonis story with both a negative significance (as an illustration of lust) and a positive significance (as the basis for an explanation of generation) in cantos one and six of Book 3, thus exhibiting the same ambiguity, if not the same humor, as Shakespeare.

If, then, the problem in *Venus and Adonis* concerns the complex na-

The Comedy of Love

ture of Venus, of sexuality and psychology at puberty, what kind of conclusions does the poem reach? To answer this, it is necessary to consider the significance of the boar. The mythographers, almost without exception, saw the Venus and Adonis story in terms of a seasonal myth, making Adonis a symbol of the sun and Venus some aspect of the inhabited world.[4] Although Shakespeare's poem is clearly not based on the seasonal myth, his use of the boar is related to it, for the boar, according to the mythographers, is winter, the season that banishes the sun to Proserpina's realm and that consequently produces sterility and death on the earth.[5] In Shakespeare's poem, Adonis, by putting off Venus, the life-giving—or at least life-sustaining—force, chooses automatically the sterility of a death without heirs. As Shakespeare says in the seventh sonnet, "So thou, thyself outgoing in thy noon, / Unlooked on diest unless thou get a son."

Adonis, like the addressee of the sonnets, wants "to grow unto himself" (1180), but this desire destroys the immortality that can be achieved by mortals through progeny and is therefore sterile and self-defeating. This interpretation of the boar is dictated by the poem. When Adonis tells Venus that he must leave her to hunt the boar, she pulls him down on top of her, making, as Iago would say, "the beast with two backs." The sexual implications and the humor of this maneuver stand in contrast to the sterility of the boar, as does Venus's suggestion that Adonis hunt the rabbit, that ancient symbol of fertility and of the female genitalia. Furthermore, while Venus is still "in the very lists of love" (595), the goddess moralizes in terms that are strongly reminiscent of the sonnets, as she attempts to convince him to take advantage of the position into which she has put him:

"What is thy body but a swallowing grave,
Seeming to bury that posterity
Which by the rights of time thou needs must have,
If thou destroy them not in dark obscurity?
  If so, the world will hold thee in disdain,
  Sith in thy pride so fair a hope is slain.

So in thyself thyself art made away;
A mischief worse than civil homebred strife,
Or theirs whose desperate hands themselves do slay,
Or butcher-sire that reaves his son of life.
  Foul-cankering rust the hidden treasure frets,
  But gold that's put to use more gold begets." (757–68)

What Venus describes here is quite simply the inevitable result of preferring the boar hunt, sterility and death; and it is no accident that she compares this course of action to suicide.

At the end of the poem, then, it is not just Adonis's death that Venus bewails, because she, as an immortal goddess, would eventually have to mourn the individual mortal's death, nor is it the death of Platonic beauty. She is mourning Adonis's death without heir. In her celebrated apostrophe to Death, she says, " 'Thy mark is feeble age, but thy false dart / Mistakes that aim and cleaves an infant's heart' " (941–42). She must know that Adonis, even had he not hunted the boar, was fated to die. Her complaint is that " 'he is dead, and never did he bless / My youth with his . . .' " (1119–20).

Again, when she says in the apostrophe, " 'For he being dead, with him is beauty slain, / And beauty dead, black chaos comes again' " (1019–20), there is no need to call up notions of Platonic beauty. She is speaking hyperbolically of the beauty that, heeding her call, he would have passed on to his progeny. Because Adonis has died without passing his beauty on, it is dead, gone from the world. When Adonis's beauty is dead, Venus does not disappear—she just goes to Paphos to mourn. Shakespeare is still concentrating on his central theme, the advent of sexuality and the need to acquiesce to it, to be a sexual being, in spite of the problems it may bring, in spite, that is, of Venus's complex and ambiguous nature.

But here it is important to remember Venus's curse on finding the dead Adonis, a curse that begins:

"Since thou art dead, lo, here I prophesy:
Sorrow on love hereafter shall attend:
It shall be waited on with jealousy,
Find sweet beginning but unsavory end,
   Ne'er settled equally, but high or low,
   That all love's pleasure shall not match his woe.

It shall be fickle, false and full of fraud,
Bud, and be blasted in a breathing-while;
The bottom poison, and the top o'erstraw'd
With sweets that shall the truest sight beguile:
   The strongest body shall it make most weak,
   Strike the wise dumb and teach the fool to speak."   (1135–46)

As Hamilton notes, it seems as though Shakespeare has translated the action of the poem "into the prelapsarian state" (15), though this is complicated by two facts: Venus's curse echoes some of Adonis's earlier objections to love, and Adonis's horse and the jennet have already gone through a pantomime of the kind of courtly love that should result from Venus's curse. These complications are removed, however, by referring to the story of the Fall and the problem of prelapsarian sexuality.

In Genesis, the first consequence of the Fall is Adam and Eve's discovery of their nakedness, their sexuality, a fact that Milton emphasizes in *Paradise Lost*; and the question of prelapsarian procreation is one that challenged many of the Church Fathers, including St. Augustine, for example, who, in the fourteenth book of *The City of God* proposed a kind of passionless reproduction for the Garden of Eden's inhabitants. Furthermore, the curses that God proclaims against Adam and Eve do not really add anything totally new to their existence but rather affect the quality of what was already there. Shakespeare, dealing as he is with the ambiguities of Venus, her indispensability for the continuation of the world, and the problems that she poses for human existence, echoes the biblical Fall, making her curse not something new but simply a difference in quality: human love will henceforth reflect the system exemplified by the horses. Love will be really painful, the problems of sexuality will increase. And yet Venus, sexuality, "the natural desire for procreation," will be as necessary as ever, both for the continuation of the species and for the kind of personal immortality that she brings. The boar is the wrong thing to hunt; and Venus, even with all her ambiguities, must be succumbed to.

And yet, as the poem shows, there is something basically humorous about the whole situation. The poem does not present "a kind of subtle subversion of morality," as Frank Kermode says, "by playing up the comic and erotic elements for their own sake" (100). The morality of Venus's call is simply not a major issue in the poem except insofar as Adonis and a number of critics make it one by confusing sexual feeling and the necessity to procreate with lust. Rather the poem presents a humorous, frank examination of sexuality in contrast to the kind of moral stance that viewed any sexual feeling as immoral and therefore denied certain realities of the human situation. The poem's humorous, light tone and numerous funny scenes, with their sexual overtones—Venus plucking Adonis from his horse and lugging him under her arm, or Venus pulling him down on top of her as she pretends to swoon—serve as a corrective to the view that sexuality is inherently evil. Venus's call—the onset of sexuality—may put people in awkward and humorous situations, may even lead to the kind of excesses often represented by the rabbit; but recognized as a human necessity, as a call that must be answered, as Shakespeare says here and elsewhere, it sets one on the road to immortality, not immorality.

Shakespeare, then, relying on the mythographic tradition of Venus and reflecting the outlook of his age, has written a poem about the ambiguities inherent in human love and sexuality. He offers no simplistic or doctrinaire solutions. In fact it could be said that he offers no solutions at all, that the problems remain and that the poet simply offers a way in which human beings can accommodate themselves to those problems. Chaucer, relying on the tradition of the two Venuses who represent the extremes of acceptable and unacceptable love, indicated that in the mundane world neither extreme exists in pure form. People must aim for the ideal, but bear in mind their human inability to achieve that ideal. Love can lead to heaven or hell, and it is up to us to choose the kind of human love that will lead us to heaven; but the choice is difficult because the two kinds of love are often so similar.

Shakespeare takes this ambiguity even further by making his Venus, now more explicitly the natural sexual urge, simultaneously desirable and frightening but always necessary. We can resist her only at our peril, and yet she is no easier to live with than she ever was. She will "pluck us off our horse" whenever she likes, thereby complicating our lives; and if we refuse her, the result is tragedy, both for us as individuals and for society. Hence Shakespeare's Venus must be viewed comically: we must recognize her threat but accept her promise.

Notes

1. It is true that, as Earl Schreiber says, "From the time of the earliest mythographers she is invested with the dual potential of human love that can be either generous or selfish" (522), but Boccaccio was the first to make such a clear distinction while giving both aspects the name of Venus.

2. The best treatment of the two Venuses as Boccaccio conceived of them and used them in his writing is Robert Hollander's *Boccaccio's Two Venuses*, which is essential for understanding the subject.

3. For a detailed discussion of some of these points, see Economou, 125–50.

4. See, for example, Walsingham (156) as well as Boccaccio (102), Cartari (117), and Comes (118).

5. See, for example, Comes (287) and Cartari (118).

Works Cited

Alanus, de Insulis. *The Complaint of Nature*. Translated by Douglas M. Moffat. Yale Studies in English, no. 36. 1908. Reprint. Hamden, CT: Shoestring Press, 1972.

Boccaccio, Giovanni. *Genealogie deorum gentilium libri*. Edited by Vincenzo Romano. Bari: Giuseppe Laterza, 1951.

Cartari, Vincenzo. *Le imagini con la spositione de i dei de gli antichi*. Venice, 1556.

Comes, Natalis. *Mythologiae sive explicationum fabularum libri decem*. Venice, 1567. Reprint. New York: Garland, 1976.

Economou, George D. *The Goddess Natura in the Middle Ages.* Cambridge, MA: Harvard University Press, 1972.

Fulgentius. *Fulgentius the Mythographer.* Translated by Leslie George Whitbread. Columbus: Ohio State University Press, 1971.

Hamilton, A. C. "Venus and Adonis." *Studies in English Literature* 1 (1961): 1–15.

Hollander, Robert. *Boccaccio's Two Venuses.* New York: Columbia University Press, 1977.

Keach, William. *Elizabethan Erotic Narratives: Irony and Pathos in the Ovidian Poetry of Shakespeare, Marlowe, and Their Contemporaries.* New Brunswick, NJ: Rutgers University Press, 1977.

Kermode, Frank. *Shakespeare, Spenser, and Donne.* London: Routledge and Kegan Paul, 1971.

Schreiber, Earl G. "Venus in the Mythographic Tradition." *JEGP* 74 (1975): 519–35.

Shakespeare, William. *The Complete Works.* Edited by Hardin Craig. Glenview, IL: Scott, Foresman, and Co., 1961.

Walsingham, Thomas. *Archana deorum.* Edited by Robert A. van Kluyve. Durham, NC: Duke University Press, 1968.

Hercules in the Mind

Mythographic Tradition and the References in *Hamlet*

George D. Economou

In his essay on the labors of Hercules in the *Adagia* (3.1.1), Erasmus departs from his announced subject to remark on the hardships and disagreeable conditions of being a scholar, especially the kind of scholar devoted to restoring the literature of the ancients. Of such a dedicated individual Erasmus says, "I should like to know who would not be frightened off by these things from engaging in such work, unless he be a real Hercules in mind, able to do and suffer anything for the sake of serving others" (Phillips, 194).

Fortunately, the state of the profession has improved—or appeared to—since Erasmus's day, and, whatever the deterrents of our own time, we persist in responding to its manifold demands. Perhaps too specialized to repeat (without being charged with extravagance) Erasmus's claim for a mythological role-model, we still keep finding things to say about the texts, structures, ideas, language, and poetics of our literature. No matter how ambitious or limited the end, the burden of proof calls forth one of our primary labors, to share, possibly to convince, through written communication. It is only through these exercises, as well as through our teaching, that we may be said to have benefited others and thus to have humbly impersonated Erasmus's Herculean scholar.

By casting the humanist scholar in a heroic role figured by Hercules, Erasmus was simply making one more use of one of the most adaptable of all characters from classical myth and literature. For Hercules came to represent many things for many persons, though when we consider the legacy of his tradition to medieval and renaissance Europe we most often think of him as an *exemplar virtutis* or as a figure for Christ. Yet, because Hercules has done so many things and had so many things done to him, he has provided poets with an extraordinarily wide, and often contradictory, range of features to draw from (Galinsky). In the work of Geoffrey Chaucer, for example, besides numerous allusions and references, he is included among those great ones who trusted to Fortune and were laid low by that trust in *The Monk's Tale*, where he is portrayed in his familiar role as the flower of strength in his time, a virtuous hero victimized; while in the story of Hypsipyle in *The Legend of Good Women*, as the shipmate of the treacherous Jason, he plays the unflattering parts of conspirator and go-between. Original with Chaucer, this rather negative view of Hercules opposes the overwhelmingly dominant treatment of him in positive terms, centering usually on the labors, by Boethius, the second and third Vatican mythographers, and others.[1] But it also indicates that the heroic figure was susceptible to development by an individual poet and that the possibility of an ambivalent picture of him, however faint, persisted through the Middle Ages.

From the great diversity of physical exploits celebrated in the stories of the ancient world, along with the identification of the hero with local cult figures, to the elaborate system of allusions, comparisons, and references that flourished in the sixteenth century, there was always an opportunity to point at some deed or trait that was less than flattering or to expose an unworthy imitation. From the braggart soldier and sham Hercules of the New Comedy, to an admission by Macrobius in the *Saturnalia* (5.21) that the old hero had a weakness for strong wine, to the Lover's comparison in the *Roman de la Rose* of himself, laboring to break the maidenhead, to Hercules, repeatedly battering the gate to Cacus's cave,[2] the figure of Hercules, like that of Odysseus, provided negative instances of itself that served as comic and ironic foils to its predominant manifestations as the hero of the labors and the crossroads, as averter of evil and savior, and as exemplar of *virtus* and *fortitudo*.

Perhaps the best example of this tendency, especially as background to the unusual references to Hercules in *Hamlet*, is the sixteenth-century Gallic Hercules (Galinsky, 222–24; Jung, 73–93). Following the explanation in Lucian's *Heracles* that in Gaul it is Hercules not Hermes who stands for eloquence,[3] Renaissance humanists introduced a new theme to the standard symbolism of Hercules, one that had had very little importance in antiquity. The depiction of Hercules as an old man, dressed in his lion's skin and carrying his club and bow in each hand, leading a great crowd of joyous followers by delicate chains of gold that are attached to their ears and to the tip of his tongue, had great appeal for humanists like Erasmus and Budé, both of whom translated it from Greek into Latin, the latter retelling it in 1547 in his *Institution du prince*. This Hercules was to become not only the *typus eloquentiae* but also, through his Gallic identification, the patron of the culture and language of France. Consequentially, when the kings of France were portrayed through comparisons of them to the heroes of the ancient and early Christian worlds, Hercules was one of the most prominently used figures. Beginning with Francis I and culminating with Henry IV, the glory of their monarchy was celebrated by France's poets and artists by means of these flattering comparisons, but none was as elaborate or effective as the allegorical apotheosis of Henry IV presented by his identification with Hercules, particularly the Gallic version in an application "charged with complex political and religious significance" (Vivanti, 185; see Jung, 159–185).

Still, outside of France the Gallic Hercules could be viewed as spurious and ludicrous, a suitable figure for the satirization of humanist overconfidence in the powers of eloquence.[4] If the heroic Hercules of antiquity was not safe from negative representations and impersonations, neither was his Renaissance descendant, who could be contemporaneously cast on one side of the English channel in a medal as Hercules/Henry IV removing the crown from the head of a centaur/Charles Emmanuel and preparing to club him, while on the other side the Host of the Garter Inn addressed Sir John Falstaff as "My Bully Hercules" (*MWW* 1.3.6).[5]

In the work of William Shakespeare, the number of references to Hercules, his deeds and reputation, is not only varied but appropriately prodigious, although most readers primarily associate the mythic hero with the playwright's Antony, whose tutelary deity he is (Waith, 112–21). Yet the diversity of the Herculean reference in Shakespeare is no more apparent than when one remembers its best known comic instance, in which Nick Bottom proclaims, "My chief humor is for a tyrant. I could play Ercles rarely" (*MND* 1.2.24–25). Bottom's affinity for "Ercles' vein, a tyrant's vein" (1.2.35) recalls that earlier country bumpkin with a flair for the dramatic, the Herod-playing would-be lover, Absolon of Chaucer's *Miller's Tale*, in a fairly even trade across two centuries of the ranting king of the Mystery Cycles for *Hercules furens*.

That the impersonation of Hercules could be extended to a specific dramatic context for Shakespeare, even in the limited form of Bottom's declarations or Falstaff's pretension, provides a special lens through which the references to Hercules in *Hamlet* can be examined. For Shakespeare was certainly aware of the theme of the sham Hercules, even though he most likely had no direct knowledge of its origins and prosperity in the satyr plays and comedies of the Greeks (Galinsky, 81–100). Accordingly, a case can be made for a unitary interpretation of the four occasions in *Hamlet* in which reference or allusion is made to Hercules: 1.2.152–53; 1.4.81–83; 2.2.354; 5.1.278–79. The text of the play in general and the contexts of the references in particular strongly support such a consistent interpretation of them—once it is understood that Hercules to Hamlet means Claudius and that this is an utterly private identification of the usurper as a sham Hercules.

Perhaps it would be helpful to bear in mind two important qualities of Hamlet's characterization when considering these references, the first of which occurs in his first soliloquy. His culture and education, his literacy—as we might try to sum it up today—is both revealed and activated by the mythological references in this speech. Less obvious and of deeper consequence is his dramatic imagination, that dimension of his character that leads him to see things in "the mind's eye" (1.2.186), "to put an antic disposition on" (1.5.172), to put on Polonius (in one sense) as well as a play (in another). Thinking about his mother's hasty marriage with his uncle, he conceives a four-term comparison that shows the complexity of his sensibility and imagination: "My father's brother, but no more like my father / Than I to Hercules" (1.2.152–53).

That Claudius is to Hamlet's father as Hamlet is to Hercules, is what logicians call an analogy of proportionality. At once we register an explicit denial of any similarity between Hamlet and Hercules in equal proportion to the alleged absence of similarity between the brothers. As a unity and in its simplest form, the proposition works through two sets of counterparts, Claudius and Hamlet, Hamlet's father and Hercules. Though provocative and useful to Freudians and thus interesting to us all, this is not the only way to view the unity of the parts. As coefficients, they pair up dead father with son, Claudius with Hercules, a pattern that offers its own clues for dealing with the loyalties and conflicts in the play.

The suggested consistency of meaning in all four Hercules references makes this a plausible pattern to pursue, especially since Hamlet's limited knowledge at this point in the play yields only (and appropriately so) the possibility of an association between Claudius and Hercules. One basis for this association is the sham Hercules theme, which is hinted at by the combination of this reference with another a few lines earlier in this soliloquy, when Hamlet first compared the two kings, "So excellent a king, that was to this / Hyperion to a satyr" (1.2.139–140). Even if it is impossible to demonstrate with definiteness that the sequence of identifications, Claudius with a satyr followed by Claudius with Hercules, echoes and ultimately derives from the Old Comedy theme of satyric impersonation of Hercules, it should not be difficult to perceive the parallelism between such imposturing and that of a man who is described as a drinker, a lecher, and a beast, playing the noble king. Though still in an inchoate state, Hamlet's thoughts about the role of Claudius in everything that has happened are not only prophetically apt, they are mythographically consistent as well.

The second reference, an oblique one, is remarkable for its congruity with the emergent meaning of the first and for its advancement of the significance of the entire set of references. Still in the first act, just before

Hamlet speaks with the Ghost on Elsinore's fortifications, he prefaces his warning to Marcellus and Horatio to desist from preventing his following the apparition by exclaiming:

> My fate cries out
> And makes each petty artere in this body
> As hardy as the Nemean lion's nerve.   (1.4.81–83)

The initial impression of firm resolve, even of being dangerous, is shaken (at least for the reader, who has time to contemplate such things) by the recognition that the Nemean lion's greatest claim to fame is as one of Hercules' victims. By identifying Hamlet with the lion, this simile definitely agrees with the analogy in which Hamlet saw little, if any, similarity between himself and Hercules. It also has the disturbing effect of foreshadowing Hamlet's destruction. And equally disturbing is the immediate effect of the comparison as a bold, almost bombastic, statement of resolve that is confuted by some darker, hidden aspect of itself. Before he even knows what has been done and what he must do to set things right, Hamlet simultaneously announces his determination and courage, and betrays himself in some corner of his own mind as a victim.

Just as the first reference brought to mind the subject of the sham Hercules, this second one introduces further links with the figure of the counterfeit hero. A phony Hercules as "vanquisher" of the Nemean lion has historical and literary associations that support (though they need not prove) the integral meaning the text of the play gives the whole group of references. For instance, Suetonius reports that Hercules was one of the many theatrical roles Nero performed, and, more pertinent for its impertinence, that he planned to appear as Hercules in the amphitheater, naked before a carefully trained lion, which he would then either club to death or strangle. The currency of Suetonius in Shakespeare's time was such that knowledge of this notorious example of an imperial madman impersonating Hercules can hardly be stamped as esoteric.[6]

In the anonymous, slightly later, play *Nero*, for example, there are two references to the emperor's desire to be identified with the hero that could be effective only as commonplace information.[7] Still, the implied identification of Claudius with Hercules through Hamlet's self-identification with one of Hercules' opponents, raises the question unequivocally: How can a man like Claudius (who has committed such crimes) be thought of as Hercules? And the answer comes: In the troubled but sophisticated mind of Hamlet, who sees him initially as a usurper and a pretender to a station in life and country he does not deserve. Momentarily, he will learn worse things about him. If there is a meaningful connection between Shakespeare's evocation of the sham Hercules and the reputation of Nero in this characterization of Claudius, it is to convey a sense of corruption, of the peril involved for all, but one in particular, who are in his power, to hint, perhaps, at this ultimate downfall, and to reinforce our understanding of Hamlet's profound aversion for him. Could a possible Hercules-Nero connection with Claudius affect the expression of feelings in lines like these? "O heart, lose not thy nature; let not ever / The soul of Nero enter this firm bosom" (3.2.378-79).

If Nero could play Hercules, so could an ass—simply by wearing a lion skin, a trophy associated with Hercules' triumph over the Nemean lion. Using proverbial materials drawn from the *Adagia* and from Aesop (Baldwin, 1:625; 2:346-47), Shakespeare had already written these lines in *The Life and Death of King John* for Blanch and Philip the Bastard (fathered by Richard Cordelion on Lady Faulconbridge) in their taunting of Austria, who wears the lion skin that once belonged to the Bastard's father:

BLANCH: O well did he become that lion's robe,
That did disrobe the lion of that robe!
BASTARD: It lies as sightly on the back of him
As great Alcides' shows upon an ass.   (2.1.141-44)

The notion of an ass under the lion robe of Hercules (or under a royal mantle) might, in fact, be detected in Hamlet's lines to Horatio describing the king's "rouse" and "wassail" (touching upon one of the more embarrassing aspects of Hercules' career?):

And as he drains his draughts of Rhenish down
The kettledrum and trumpets thus bray out
The triumph of his pledge.   (1.4.10-12)

Although Claudius, like the devil, may be an ass, Hamlet's attitude toward him is dominated by the more general but relevant sense of an illegitimate and unseemly assumption of a role for which he is ill suited. In the first lines in which he refers to Claudius right after his meeting with the Ghost has ended, Hamlet emphasizes the role-playing as much as the moral hypocrisy of his uncle and king by noting, "That one may smile, and smile, and be a villain" (1.5.108).

This sense carries over to that part of the long second scene of the second act in which the players are announced, the locus of the third reference to Hercules in the play. Confirmation of Hamlet's feeling, qualified now by knowledge of how his uncle really got the throne, that Claudius's reign is more act than truly royal action, can be heard in his immediate response to Rosencrantz's report of the players' visit, "He that plays the king shall be welcome—" (2.2.314). But the full force of Hamlet's personal view of Claudius as a sham Hercules comes in his reaction to the only instance in the play in which another character refers to the mythological hero. Following his explanation of the boy actors' triumph in the War of the Theaters—in a probably coincidental but striking parallel to the story of the satyrs' theft of Hercules' bow, quiver, and club while he held the earth for Atlas (Galinsky, 82)—Rosencrantz answers Hamlet's question, "Do the boys carry it away?" with "Ay, that they do, my lord—Hercules and his load too" (2.2.353–54). The usurpation of the theaters by the boys makes very special sense to Hamlet (and hopefully to us, if not to his schoolmate), for he knows usurpation of another kind, and the acceptance and obeisance that result not only from the fickleness of the audience or subjects but from an effective impersonation as well:

> It is not very strange, for my uncle is King of
> Denmark, and those that would make mows at him while my
> father lived give twenty, forty, fifty, a hundred
> ducats apiece for his picture in little. 'Sblood,
> there is something in this more than natural, if
> philosophy could find it out.   (2.2.355–60)

Indeed, that the boys have carried away Hercules and his load cannot be very strange to one who knows of a king supplanted by a brother who himself carries off a strong performance of a heroic type. That the one explains the other in the mind of Hamlet is the "something in this that is more than natural"—if our philosophy has in truth found it out.[8]

The final reference to Hercules in the play stands far from the rest in the text and in time. Thus, it is all the more remarkable for its agreement with the others; for, when it surfaces again, Hamlet's reference to Claudius as Hercules (still in his own mind) comes with the same certitude with which he refers to himself publicly as "Hamlet the Dane" (5.1.244). After his fight with Laertes in Ophelia's grave, Hamlet delivers this exit speech:

>   Hear you, sir.
> What is the reason you use me thus?
> I loved you ever. But it is no matter.
> Let Hercules himself do what he may,
> The cat will mew, and dog will have his day.   (5.1.275–79)

Two recent distinguished studies of *Hamlet* indicate the degree of difference of opinion that can occur over a given Shakespearean passage. In what is possibly the most compelling Freudian reading of the play to date, Avi Erlich explains these lines in terms of Hamlet's weakness and relationship with an ambiguous father, whom he identifies with Hercules, that plagues him "but assists Claudius. Hamlet must 'mew' like a cat and plea that the father (Hercules act on his own behalf" (Erlich, 135). And Maurice Charney, in his gracefully written close analysis, pointing out that Hamlet has already strongly rejected any resemblance to Hercules, paraphrases the speech in a way that relates all the images to Laertes: "let this bombastic Hercules go through his *miles gloriosus* routines; we must allow cats and dogs to express their seriocomic, bellicose natures" (Charney, 278–79).[9]

But if by Hercules here Hamlet means Claudius, he is saying he is prepared now for *anything*. Surprised but not overdisturbed by Laertes's abuse, he is ready for whatever Claudius, his real antagonist, may do, for the one thing he has been sure of since returning to Denmark's shore is that he will succeed, though he does not know how. Trusting in the "divinity that shapes our ends" (5.2.10), Hamlet can now identify himself with small creatures, in contrast with his earlier identification with the mythical Nemean lion, with the cat and the proverbial dog—and the sparrow in whose fall "there is special providence" (5.2.208–9).

As in the other Hercules references, this one's meaning as Claudius depends partly on the effectiveness of their mutuality, but especially and primarily on its own good sense. Since "every dog has his day" was already proverbial in Shakespeare's time, and since its sense was invariably related to a desire and hope for vengeance and vindication (Tilley, D464), then the mewing cat, which seems to be original with Shakespeare, serves as a parallel that emphasizes the proverb's relevance. With Hercules as the code word for Claudius himself in the conditional clause, Hamlet declares his newfound confidence that he will be justly vindicated no matter what his enemy, with all the power and appearance of a great one, can do. The Herculean myth has been countered by a simple statement of belief just as Claudius's old power over Hamlet passes out of the now undivided world of his mind and action. Through its simplicity and directness of expression, this final reference, enriched by the cumulative effect of the entire series, suddenly and unexpectedly becomes another statement of that "ethical stance against overwhelming odds" that we recognize as inherent in Shakespearean tragedy (Levin, 50).[10]

Notes

1. See Kiser (114); on Book 4, m. 7 of *The Consolation of Philosophy*, see Courcelle (233–35); for the summaries of the Vatican mythographers, see Bode (126–27, 246–50); for an introduction to the question of the state and form of

mythological study in the late Middle Ages, see the admirable essay by Green, "Classical Fable and English Poetry in the Fourteenth Century"; the classic overview is the study by Seznec, and valuable for its background material is the work by Jung.

2. *The Romance of the Rose by Guillaume de Lorris and Jean de Meun*, trans. Dahlberg, 352; *Le Roman de la Rose*, ed. Lecoy, vol. 3, vv. 2159ff. See also Shoaf, esp. 147–48.

3. *Lucian*, trans. Harmon, 1:62–71. The learned Celt in Lucian's dialogue explains that Hercules, called Ogmios in their tongue, not Hermes, is eloquence: "We Celts do not agree with you Greeks in thinking that Hermes is Eloquence: we identify Heracles with it, because he is far more powerful than Hermes. . . . In general, we consider that the real Heracles was a wise man who achieved everything by eloquence and applied persuasion as his principal force" (4–6).

4. See Wind, " 'Hercules' and 'Orpheus'," 206–18. Panofsky disagrees with Wind in his *Life and Art of Albrecht Dürer*, 73–76.

5. See the figure of the *jeton* struck in 1602 facing p. 184 of Vivanti. All quotations and references to the works of Shakespeare are from *The Complete Works*, ed. Harbage. For parallels between Falstaff and figures from Greek myth, see Steadman, "Falstaff as Actaeon," 230–44, esp. 240–42, for the parallels with Hercules.

6. *The Lives of the Caesars*, 6.21 and 53 (2:19 and 183). See also the valuable study of Schilling, 31–57, esp. 49. For Suetonius in Elizabethan schools, see Baldwin, passim. Though there is no definite evidence Shakespeare encountered Suetonius in his own schooling, the work's place in school curricula and its general circulation is well attested.

7. *Nero and Other Plays*, ed. Horne. In *Nero* (1624, 1633) 1.2.14, 15, the emperor is twice identified by the Roman mob with Hercules—based most likely on Suetonius's life, 25, as Horne points out in his note. The second reference occurs in 4.5.68, when Nero says he will fetch Poppaea back from death—after having dealt her a mortal blow—in a parody of Hercules' rescue of Alcestis. See the description of this theme in Allen, 267.

8. Since the quoted speeches of Rosencrantz and Hamlet form the end-seam of one of the standard passages of dialogue added from the folio to the "good" quarto (see "Note on the Text," *The Complete Works*, 932), it is in order to raise the question of Shakespeare's intentions in making topical references to the boy actors and the Globe Theater, whose sign represented Hercules holding the world on his shoulders. In the context of this essay, what are the specific dramatic gains in having Hamlet react to the story of the boy actors' faddish success instead of to the general drop in popularity suffered by the players—i.e., to an effect without a cause? Or in having Hamlet associate his uncle's being king with an albeit metaphorical seizure of Hercules and the world instead of to the vicissitudes of a life upon the stage?

9. For the purposes of contrast with my own perspective, I would add here that Professor Charney connects his ranting Laertes with Bottom's "Ercles' vein is a tyrant's vein." For much earlier comment on the passage that is also provocative (but a little off the mark), see Furness, ed., *The Variorum Hamlet*, 411.

10. I would like to thank Professor Hope Phyllis Weissman of Wesleyan University for her valuable insights and advice when I needed a colleague in the field with whom to discuss this project. I would also like to thank my colleague Nicholas Howe for his late-hour advice on the final version of this essay.

Works Cited

Allen, Don Cameron. *Mysteriously Meant: The Rediscovery of Pagan Symbolism and Allegorical Interpretation in the Renaissance.* Baltimore: The Johns Hopkins University Press, 1970.
Baldwin, T. W. *William Shakespeare's Small Latine and Lesse Greeke.* 2 vols. Urbana: University of Illinois Press, 1944.
Bode, Georgius Henricus, ed. *Scriptores rerum mythicarum latini tres Romae nuper reperti.* Hildesheim: Olms, 1968.
Charney, Maurice. *Style in Hamlet.* Princeton: Princeton University Press, 1969.
Courcelle, Pierre. *La Consolation de Philosophie dans la tradition littéraire.* Paris: Études Augustiennes, 1967.
Erlich, Avi. *Hamlet's Absent Father.* Princeton: Princeton University Press, 1977.
Horne, Herbert P., et al., eds. *Nero and Other Plays.* The Mermaid Series, vol. 8. London, 1888.
Furness, Horace Howard, ed. *The Variorum Hamlet.* 14th ed., vol. 1. Philadelphia: Lippincott, 1905.
Galinsky, G. Karl. *The Herakles Theme: The Adaptations of the Hero in Literature from Homer to the Twentieth Century.* Totowa, NJ: Rowman and Littlefield, 1972.
Green, Richard Hamilton. "Classical Fable and English Poetry in the Fourteenth Century." In *Critical Approaches to Medieval Literature, Papers from the English Institute, 1958-59,* edited by Dorothy Bethurum, 110-33. New York: Columbia University Press, 1960.
Jung, Marc-René. *Hercule dans la littérature française de XVI siècle.* Geneva: Droz, 1966.
Kiser, Lisa J. *Telling Classical Tales: Chaucer and the Legend of Good Women.* Ithaca, NY: Cornell University Press, 1983.
Levin, Harry *Shakespeare and the Revolution of the Times, Perspectives and Commentaries.* New York: Oxford University Press, 1976.
Lorris, Guillaume de, and Jean de Meun. *Le Roman de la Rose.* Edited by Félix Lecoy. Les Classiques français de Moyen Age, 92, 95, 98. Paris: H. Champion, 1970.
———. *The Romance of the Rose.* Translated by Charles Dahlberg. Princeton: Princeton University Press, 1971.
Lucian. *Lucian.* Translated by A. M. Harmon, M. D. Macleod, et al. 8 vols., Loeb Classical Library. 1925. Reprint. Cambridge, MA: Harvard University Press, 1960-67.
Panofsky, Erwin. *The Life and Art of Albrecht Dürer.* 4th ed. Princeton: Princeton University Press, 1955.
Phillips, Margaret Mann. *The 'Adages' of Erasmus: A Study with Translations.* Cambridge: Cambridge University Press, 1964.
Schilling, R. "L'Hercule Romain en face de la reforme religieuse d'Auguste." *Revue de philologie,* 3d ser., 16 (1942): 31-57.
Seznec, Jean. *The Survival of the Pagan Gods: The Mythological Tradition and Its Place in Renaissance Humanism and Art.* Translated by Barbara Sessions. New York: Harper and Row, 1953.

Shakespeare, William. *The Complete Works*. Edited by Alfred Harbage et al. Baltimore: Penguin, 1969.

Shoaf, R. A. " 'Certius exemplar sapientis viri': Rhetorical Subversion and Subversive Rhetoric in *Pharsalia* 9." *Philological Quarterly* 57 (1978): 143–54.

Steadman, John M. "Falstaff as Actaeon: A Dramatic Emblem." *Shakespeare Quarterly* 14 (1963): 230–44.

Suetonius. Translated by J.C. Rolfe. 2 vols. Loeb Classical Library. London: W. Heinemann, 1920.

Tilley, Morris P. *A Dictionary of the Proverbs in England in the Sixteenth and Seventeenth Centuries: A Collection of the Proverbs Found in English Literature and Dictionaries of the Period*. Ann Arbor: University of Michigan Press, 1950.

Vivanti, Carrado. "Henry IV, The Gallic Hercules." *Journal of the Warburg and Courtauld Institutes* 30 (1967): 176–97.

Waith, Eugene M. *The Herculean Hero*. New York: Columbia University Press, 1962.

Wind, Edgar. " 'Hercules' and 'Orpheus': Two Mock-Heroic Designs by Dürer." *Journal of the Warburg Institute* 2 (1938–39): 206–18.

Sandys, Ovid, and Female Chastity
The Encyclopedic Mythographer as Moralist

Deborah D. Rubin

Misogyny in the literature of the European Middle Ages and Renaissance is a familiar topic, and to establish once again that it permeated many aspects of art and society during these periods is needless.[1] From time to time, however, one comes upon an instance of the workings of this social malady that seems particularly illuminating, hinting at the mechanisms and social sanctions that enabled it to flourish as it did. The medieval and Renaissance tradition of mythographical commentary offers an interesting example of how a method of literary criticism can be adapted to the presentation of certain social and individual biases. Mythographers, availing themselves of a particularly conservative yet contradictory tradition, are able to present highly subjective views behind the mask of erudition and respect for authority, thus institutionalizing certain attitudes toward myth and reality.

A case in point is George Sandys's commentary in *Ovids Metamorphosis Englished*. First published in 1632, this encyclopedic companion to an excellent English translation is a late representative of a long tradition of European allegorizing criticism of the Greek and Latin classics.[2] As such, it is riddled with truisms about female vice and virtue, praising the abstraction of chastity and little else about women, and casually revealing at times a phobia that transcends not only individual experience but even cultural stereotypes:

> . . . for Magicians were to abstaine from Venus (such an ape is the Divel) when they went about their infernal sacrifices. So none . . . at this day can see any thing in magical glasses, that have been polluted with women: in so much as ordinarily they set boyes to looke therein, and receive what is seen by relation. (256)

The problem is, of course, not unchaste or vicious women, but the sex itself. In the postclassical mythographic tradition, women are preeminently symbols of the body, the baser portion of human nature, and are of interest to male theorists for their unique—therefore sexually identified—human attributes. The resultant process of interpretation generates a false dichotomy, extrapolating from physiological to ethical differences. Rigidly patterned categorization and evaluation on the basis of gender is well established in medieval mythographies but proliferates in late Renaissance encylopedic works. Through Sandys's commentary, this mythographic trend finds expression in the England of James I and Charles I, a place and period notably hostile to women in its culture, and increasingly secular and political in its values.

This feature of Renaissance mythography deserves more attention than it has received. Recent accounts of the tradition focus their analysis on the genre's role as mediator between pagan and Christian values or between traditional belief and early modern empiricism. Jane Chance, for example, concludes her essay "The Origins and Development of Medieval Mythography: From Homer to Dante" thus: "If classical mythography of the Greek and Roman poets explains literature to the philosophers, then medieval mythography explains the gods and heroes to the theologians—and to medieval poets like Dante" (64). Jean Seznec makes a similar distinction: "In spite of the immense revolution created by Christianity, medieval thought found points of agreement and formulas for reconciliation with the pagan spirit. The Renaissance, on the other hand, perceived this historical distance, and had to make a conscious effort to establish harmony between two worlds separated by a lapse of centuries" (322).

In this essay I have addressed a different function of the genre—the literary construction of gender—and have attempted to show how distinctive features of late encyclopedic mythography are exploited not only to preserve a connection with classical poetry and pagan wisdom but also to maintain an ideology of gender identity and social relations. How Sandys employs the very structure of his commentary to enforce such a viewpoint may be seen by examining his treatment of related Ovidian tales: Actaeon and Callisto; and Hercules, Perseus, Paris, and Atalanta.

IN THE first pair, Actaeon and Callisto,[3] the thematic similarities are striking. Both figures innocently offend against the chastity of Diana and both are cruelly punished by transformation into a beast. Actaeon, in the form of a stag, is torn apart by his own hounds, and Callisto, in the form of a bear, is nearly killed by her son. Actaeon and Callisto differ, however, in their sex, and those aspects of the myths that correspond less perfectly may be attributed to this difference. Actaeon's offense is an act—that of violating Diana's body with his eyes—while Callisto's is her polluted nature after having been raped. Actaeon's punishment is designed to deny him the power of further action through speech, while Callisto's punishment is designed to deprive her of the beauty that makes her sexually desirable. While Actaeon's punishment is more absolute, culminating in his dismemberment and death, Callisto is the passive victim of four gods' whims—raped by Jupiter; expelled by Diana; transformed by Juno; metamorphosed again by Jupiter; and subject at last to the will of Tethys, goddess of the sea.

In responding to such riches, Sandys relies on a vast tradition of classical, medieval, and Renaissance commentaries that he knew directly or through secondary sources.[4] Borrowing from these, he accepts as well a didactic tripartite view of the meaning of myth, employing alternately the euhemeristic ("historical"), "physical," and "ethical" modes of interpretation. According to the first, myths describe mortal men and women whose remarkable personalities and actions had earned them a reputation as gods or supernatural heroes. The second reads myths as allegories for events in the material world, the mythographical figures representing elements of climate, yearly growth and decay, and other aspects of the natural environment. The third interprets myths as allegories of vice and virtue. Such a structure for critical thought discourages individual reassessment of its values, categories, and epistemology, but it does allow for differences in emphasis and comprehensiveness of treatment.

A first reading of Sandys's commentary on Callisto yields the impression of wide learning, casual but balanced organization, and a lively curiosity to explore many viewpoints:

> *Jove* like a common father, is solicitous in repairing
> the ruines of these disorders [the results of Phaeton's
> fall]; but cannot order his owne affections. He burnes
> in love with *Calisto*, the daughter of *Lycaon* whom be-
> fore he had turned into a Wolfe: and now turnes him-   5
> sclfe into the figure of chastitie; *Diana Calisto's*
> Goddesse. Vice is ashamed of vice: and so ugly, that
> it cannot deceave but under the pretext of Virtue; as
> the Divell in the shape of an Angell of light. The
> virgin is devirginated, and cast by *Diana* out of her   10
> chast assembly: whom *Cupid* in *Lucian* complaines that he
> never could wound, in that ever exercised in hunting.
> But Juno (said to be the wife of *Jupiter* in that the
> ayre is subjacent to Heaven; and his sister, because
> both, according to *Macrobius*, were ingendred of the   15
> same substance) will not be so pleased. Jealousie is
> unplacable; as rash as fire, & more cruell then the
> grave. Shee dragges her by the haire, beats her with

> her fist, and lastly converts her into a Beare. So
> loose they their faire figures, and resemble deformed
> beasts, who abandon their chastities; the excuse of
> ravishment being convinc't by conception. *Calisto*
> signifies beauty: the more beautifull the more perspic-
> uous their blemishes. *Palaephatus* reports how, hunting
> in the mountaines, shee entred a Cave, and there was
> torne in peeces by a Beare: when her companions raised
> this rumor of her change; the Beare comming forth
> alone, and shee never seene after. Others, how having
> vowed virginitie, and guilefully deflowred by the *Cre-
> tan Jupiter*, shee was expulsed by her subjects: who
> fled into the woods, and there was delivered of *Arcas*:
> where they lived obscurely; till impatient of so sal-
> vage a life, he attempted to kill his mother. Shee
> fled to *Jupiter*, who reconciled, & restored them to
> their kingdome of *Arcadia*. From whence grew the fable,
> how, when ready to have beene slaine by *Arcas*, they were
> both assumed into heaven by compassionate *Jupiter*; and
> converted into neighbouring constellations within the
> Artick circle. Those foure starres which make a quad-
> rangle on the side of the greater Beare, are called the
> Waine. . . .   (70–71)[5]

In the complete passage, Sandys offers two physical readings (lines 13–16 and 39 on, beyond the passage here cited), two euhemeristic readings (24–28, 28–39), and four ethical readings (on Jove: 7–9; on Juno: 16–18; on Callisto: 20–24). He intersperses his commentary with running narrative and with factual "asides" (4–5, 11–12), and alternates modes to maintain a light, informative tone.

While the ethical mode with its condemnatory pronouncements catches our attention, Sandys maintains a certain balance by examining Jupiter and Juno as well as Callisto. In allegorical fashion, he assigns a symbolism to each of the figures (Diana's does not require further development) and draws a lesson about human lust, jealousy, and unchastity. Even here the reader might observe that, given the narrative context, the moral drawn from Callisto is strained. While Jupiter and Juno are defined by their actions within the myth, Callisto is defined as intrinsically deformed. Her fate in the myth is the external sign of a preexisting flaw: "the more beautifull the more perspicuous their blemishes."

The reductive literalness of interpretation in the ethical commentary is especially problematic: lust is vice, "devirgination" is defilement, sexual jealousy is consuming, the abandonment of chastity is bestial. This quality is particularly striking in Sandys's conflation of the direct and indirect consequences of Callisto's rape, her pregnancy, and her transformation into a bear: "So loose they their faire figures, and resemble deformed beasts, who abandon their chastities; the excuse of ravishment being convinc't by conception." The implication that pregnancy is a deformation or a punishment suggests a view of female sexuality and procreation that is itself distorted. To describe it in terms of the loss of human form, and to relate a pregnant woman to a beast is still more strange. If women in their role as mothers are monstrous, then only men and asexual women are truly human.[6]

Taken as a whole, such a passage reveals a preoccupation with female sexuality and the accompanying prescription of chastity or dire punishment, but it does not suggest an abuse of the technique of mythographical commentary to any particular end. However, a comparison of the Callisto passage with Sandys's commentary on Actaeon places the matter in a different light. Overall, the second passage is as balanced and diverse, but its central ethical statements are utterly unlike those in the Callisto passage:

> But this fable was invented to shew us how dangerous a curiosity it is to search into the secrets of Princes, or by chance to discover their nakednesse: who thereby incurring their hatred, ever after live the life of a Hart, full of feare and suspicion: not seldome accused by their servants, to gratulate the Prince, unto their utter destruction. For when the displeasure of a Prince is apparent, there commonly are no fewer Traitors then servants, who inflict on their masters the fate of *Actaeon*. Some such unhappy discovery procured the banishment of our *Ovid*: who complaining of his misfortunes, introduceth this example.
>
> > Why had I sight to make mine eye my foe?
> > Or why did I unsought-for secrets know?
> > *Actaeon* naked *Dian* unaware
> > So saw; and so his hounds their master tare.
> > The Gods sure punish fortune for offence:
> > Nor, when displeased, will with chance dispence.
>
> Guard we therefore our eyes; nor desire to see, or knowe more then concernes us: or at least dissemble the discovery. *Iulius Montanus* meeting with *Nero* in the darke, by his unseasonable respects upbraiding, as it were, his ruffianly licentiousnesse, was put to death:

The act was understood (saith *Tacitus*) by *Mutianus*; but the disguising of his knowledge was a point of obedience. (100)

The ethical portions of Sandys's Callisto commentary concern individual vice and virtue, but those in the Actaeon commentary concern public qualities. While Callisto personifies the unchaste woman, Actaeon personifies the impolitic courtier. His failure is not a moral one, but one of simplicity or ineptitude. In fact, in several ways the courtier described by Sandys gains in stature by failing to secure his prince's favor. His crime is to see and to reflect accurately what he has seen. To avoid knowledge of certain truths is wisest, argues Sandys, and to preserve silence of what we know is next best. In a society where expedience takes precedence over morality, where disguise is "a point of obedience," we feel sympathy for the innocent whose unschooled instincts lead him to destruction. Sandys's commentary on Actaeon raises fundamental philosophical issues: What is the relation between knowledge, intent, and action? Is virtue absolute or relative? What constitutes innocence, guilt, or justice? Each of these issues, in turn, suggests the ambiguity of human acts and moral codes, the wisdom of examining a narrative from many sides.

Actaeon's status is further enhanced and complicated by Sandys's quotation from the *Tristia*.[7] In it, Ovid, by comparing himself with Actaeon, reaffirms his own blamelessness regarding the mysterious event that led to his exile: each had unsought knowledge thrust upon him and each was punished for the vagaries of fortune. Sandys, in turn, dignifies Actaeon by a comparison with Ovid, who has special status as the author of the work under discussion and the (re)creator of Actaeon. Subsuming Actaeon under the identity of the poet, Sandys displaces him from a position of perilous centrality in the allegory. As Ovid recounts the myth, the central event occurs deep in the forest, in a clearing by a stream, where both Diana and Actaeon have taken refuge from the heat of the day and the violence of the hunt.[8] Their awful, primal confrontation surely lends itself to the same kind of obsessively one-dimensional reading as does that of Callisto and Diana in the same setting. But Sandys's comparison of Ovid and Actaeon releases the latter from this impasse, casting upon him—an antidote to Diana's avenging drops of water—a mist of moral ambiguity, aesthetic distance, and historical perspective.

Finally, the more effectively to promote Actaeon, Sandys demotes Diana:

Juno in *Lucian* upbraides *Latona* that her daughter *Diana* converted *Actaeon*, having seene her naked, into a Hart; for feare he should divulge her deformity: and not out of modesty; being so farre from a Virgin, as continually conversant at the labours of women, like a publicke midwife. (100)

In keeping with the political reading of the myth, Sandys here sweeps away the last shred of the ethical absolutism by means of which he had wrought the downfall of Callisto in his commentary. If obedience and disguise replace virtue as the highest good, then Diana may be as secretly corrupt as the most illegitimate of princes. By such reasoning, Callisto might have seen an earlier end to her sorrows if only her attempt to conceal her pregnancy had been more successful. Perhaps it was the revelation and not the fact of her unvirginal state that threatened to pollute the waters of Diana's pool.

A reader of the *Metamorphoses* must be struck by the elaborate parallels between the stories of Callisto and Actaeon, and also by the crucial differences in their symbolic roles. Diana's outrage at her aggrieved virginity lies at the heart of both myths, but in the first, the protagonist is a tragic double of the threatened goddess, and in the second, the protagonist is the threatening male. Innocence of intent and defenselessness before a deity cannot save the protagonists from punishment for their participation in a guilty act, although Callisto is ultimately the more fortunate.[9]

Given the centrality of these myths to Ovid's theme in the *Metamorphoses*, and given the similarity of their preoccupations, it is significant that Sandys presents them to the reader so differently. Most striking in his treatment of Actaeon is the degree to which his critical interpretation has been detached from the sexual content of the myth. In Sandys's ethical commentary on Callisto, there is a relentless focus on sexual transgression—Jupiter's lack of control, Juno's jealousy, Diana's outraged prudery, Callisto's corruption. Each figure is fixed in a single role, a single emotion hard as an amber tear. In his treatment of Actaeon, the subject does not arise, and Actaeon is permitted more than one role. The contrast is all too familiar. While Callisto is defined entirely in sexual terms—first as a devotee of chastity, then as a fallen woman, and finally as a mistress—Actaeon is defined as an individual with a public, social identity. Disregarding the primal scene of exposure and confrontation, the commentator is able to free Actaeon from the contamination of sexuality and place him in a masculine world of status, intrigue, and individual action. The political has supplanted the ethical as the framing critical mode,[10] and our interest is focused not on Actaeon's essential nature but on relativistic codes for behavior and survival. Characteristically, in his reference to Montanus and Nero, Sandys argues along with Tacitus that obedience and concealment, not virtue, are the issue.

One of Sandys's euhemeristic interpretations of Actaeon—in a striking instance of interpretive flexibility—actually presents him as the prince, rather than the imprudent courtier:

> And some imagine how he was said to be devoured by his hounds, in that he impoverished his estate in sustaining them. But what was that expence to a Prince? I rather agree with those, who thinke it to bee meant by his maintaining of ravenous and riotous sycophants: who have often exhausted the Exchequors of opulent Princes, and reduced them to extreame necessity. (100)

While piecemeal allegorical interpretations lend themselves to such inconsistencies, the ease with which Actaeon may be presented as both courtier destroyed by his prince and prince destroyed by his subjects demonstrates the flexible standard by which he is judged. In Sandys's treatment of Actaeon, one senses a greater freedom to explore the Ovidian material. "But why may not this fable receave a double construction? Those being the best that admit of most senses" (100), exclaims Sandys as he moves from the ethical to euhemeristic views of Actaeon. The plot yields a symmetrical reversal from Actaeon, an unwilling aggressor against Diana and her band, to Actaeon, victim of his own unwitting hounds, and Sandys feels at liberty to explore such symmetries on the allegorical level as well. If this involves presenting the prince first as corrupt yet commanding obedience, and then as innocent and destroyed by generosity, there is no obstacle. If this involves reversing Diana's very nature, the commentator is equally free to select from among his sources a supporting reference. The multiple constructions that Sandys seeks are typical of the genre: each component episode is segmented, and the figure of the protagonist is reduplicated in a series of shifting configurations. Typically, the reader of such a commentary loses a sense of the plot as a whole, or of a clear train of causality from one event to the next. Actaeon surprised in the presence of Diana yields one set of readings, and Actaeon destroyed by his hounds yields another. In place of the plot, we have a series of disconnected tableaux of approximately equal importance.[11]

Given the commentator's latitude for symbolic redefinition and inversion, one must ask why the myth of Callisto did not receive a comparable treatment. Diana could equally well be viewed as a prince here, and the entire drama translated into political terms. Callisto's eventful career—considerably more complex than Actaeon's—could be segmented and its episodes explored from different points of view. Her story is actually better suited to a political reading than is Actaeon's, turning as it does upon a power struggle among the gods that resembles nothing more than the internal intrigues of a royal court. Beyond this, the possibilities for an ingenious allegorizer are endless. The answer seems to be that for Sandys female sexuality is too compelling—indeed obsessive—a topic to be viewed as representing anything else, and it elicits, consequently, the most reductive and censorious of critical responses.

At the heart of both the myths and their interpretations lies the issue of concealment, and Sandys's commentarial strategy also involves this issue. Just as Callisto cannot conceal her disgrace and downfall, so the mythographer seems unable to cloak her story in the cool, intellectual terms of politics or the natural sciences. One might conclude that he feels she should not be spared. Conversely, the message seems to be that men can and should conceal their indiscretions. Sandys's reading of the Actaeon myth and in particular his reference to Nero and Montanus make this clear. The discretion urged by Sandys in this reading is particularly interesting since it protects through concealment both subject (Actaeon / Montanus / the courtier) and object (Diana / Nero / the prince). The commentator holds forth the possibility of both saving one's skin and fulfilling one's social obligations, an exquisitely utilitarian way out of the dilemma. And this is finally the way out taken by the commentator, who casts a veil over Actaeon's sexual confrontation and shifts the frame of reference for his entire sex.

THE GOLDEN apples of the garden of the Hesperides—ambivalent emblems of divine favor and discord—provide another example of Sandys's manipulative mythographic practice. These apples, a wedding gift to Hera from Mother Earth, appear in the myths of Heracles, Perseus, Paris, and Atalanta but have their origin in pre-Hellenic and Celtic mythology. The three Hesperides, whose western garden is associated with sunset and death, guard the apples, the biblical fruit of the tree of life and "passports to . . . paradise" (Graves, sec. 12.5). With the coming of the Achaeans and the institution of "a new form of sacred kingship" (sec. 53.3), these apples become "the gift by which her [Aphrodite's] priestess decoyed the King, the Sun's representative, to his death and eternal life" (sec. 33.7).

While the medieval and Renaissance mythographers lost sight of the origins and earlier significance of the myth, some traditions continued to view the golden fruit as precious, the worthy goal of a hero's quest. In his commentary on Hercules' exploits in Book 9 of the *Metamorphoses*, Sandys offers an etymological account for a seeming fantasy: "the Golden Apples; which was [sic] *Atlas* sheepe with yellow fleeces; the name equivocall to either: sheep being so honoured by the ancient for enriching their owners, that riches in mony or cattle was of them so named.".[12] Sandys's unmentioned authority bases his essentially euhemeristic interpretation on the fact that in many Indo-European languages, terms for wealth and money had their origin in terms for cattle. The Latin *pecunia* and *peculare*, the English *pecuniary* and *peculate*, can be traced from the Latin *pecu* (flock, herd); the modern English *fee* (Old English *feoh*) unites the meanings of cattle, wealth, and money in early usage. The golden apples are thus golden sheep, whose golden fleece recur throughout Western myth and folklore as desirable quest-objects. Sandys continues, in a moralizing vein, "But allegorically, *Hercules*, or Virtue, cannot reape the fruit of his indeavours, those golden Apples, untill he have killed the Dragon, Malice and Envy, which continually watch to frustrate his reward."[13]

Sandys reiterates and extends the euhemeristic interpretation in his discussion of Perseus, who Themis prophesied would rob the tree of the Hesperides (*Metamorphoses*, 4:642–45). In addition, he offers two physical interpretations for the apples: they are "the store of gold wherewith *Mauritania*[14] aboundeth, digg'd up at the foot of that mountaine" (167) or "astronomically those apples are taken for starres, shining like gold, and in figure orbicular; said to grow in the West, in that they appear not before Sun-set; the Zodiack, or our Hemispheare, being the Serpent: all of them supported, in regard of his excellency in Astronomy, by *Atlas*" (167). He touches here also on the more common medieval view of gold as a false value, a temptation to avarice, but balances that judgment with an appeal to moderation:

> The wakefull Dragon [is fained of] those restlesse cares which afflict the covetous in the tuition of their riches: a blessing to the liberall, but to the miser a punishment. (167)

Gold, then, is not incompatible with the heroic quest and heroic virtue; it is indeed the means to princely generosity.

If we turn now to two female figures associated with gold or the apples, we see again the devious uses to which mythic polysemy may be put. Commenting on Atalanta's pursuit of the golden apples, through which she loses the race with Hippomenes (Ovid, 10.560–680), Sandys writes, "This fable deciphers . . . the unconstant minde of a woman; diverted by gold, or pleasure, from her intended course, and obedience to the heavenly Oracle, to her fore-knowne and assured destruction" (365). Sandys offers as well an allegorical interpretation straight from Bacon's *De sapientia veterum* ("Atalanta," 743–44):

This fable is said to signifie the contention between Art and Nature. Art expressed by *Atalanta*; which in her owne virtue, if not interrupted, is swifter by far than Nature, or *Hippomenes*; and sooner arrives at the proposed end, as almost is evident in all things. . . . Yet these Golden Apples give impediment to this prerogative and vigor of Art, to the infinite detriment of humane affaires. Neither is there any of the Arts and Sciences which constantly proceed in a true and legitimate course to the end prefixed; but interrupt their undertakings, and desert the Palme, like *Atalanta* diverted by inticing lucre. And therefore no marvell though Art overcome not Nature, and destroy not the vanquished, according to the compact of their contention: when contrarily it falls out, that Art is under her command, and obeyes her as a wife doth her husband. (365)

Atalanta's predicament in the mythographical tradition is as desperate and inevitable as it is in the myth itself. Perseus, diverted by the sight of Andromeda as he wings his way back to Seriphos bearing the head of Medusa and further diverted by the apples of the Hesperides when he lands on Mount Atlas to rest, returns with his trophies a hero. But the mythographers find Atalanta's diversion by the apples to be ignoble. Her situation is different in that she falls victim to a plot contrived against her by Aphrodite and Hippomenes, and she fails in the larger task (the race) as a result. Perseus is able to be diverted and yet, in the accretive fashion that characterizes so much of Western myth, tale, and folk song, to return to his starting place crowned with prizes and honors undreamt of when he departed. This is perhaps to say that Perseus is a hero and Atalanta is not, as the myth came to be shaped and viewed in the Hellenic age and after. A token of this reality is Sandys's characterization of Hercules, the other heroic male questor after the apples, as "Virtue" and Atalanta as a possessor of "the unconstant minde of a woman." Just as Actaeon represents the courtier but Callisto the unchaste woman, so Hercules represents virtue, a human trait, and Atalanta the failings of her sex. The contagion of her nature spreads to the apples, which are no longer appropriate quest-objects but instead sexually tinged ("gold, or pleasure") lures "from her intended course, and obedience to the heavenly Oracle." Bacon (and, following his reading, Sandys), in characterizing Atalanta as Art and Hippomenes as Nature, more or less reverses the traditional medieval view of woman as body and man as soul,[15] but does not fail to draw the conclusion that the former must be subjugated to the will of the latter.

It is characteristic of Atalanta's story as it has been passed down to us that the protagonist is continually in conflict.[16] When she consults the oracle of Apollo about marriage, she is told, according to Ovid, "You have no need of a husband, Atalanta. You should avoid any experience of one. But assuredly, you will not escape marriage and then, though still alive, yet you will lose your own self."[17] Her strategy of racing with and destroying her suitors is, on a psychological level, an expression of her ambivalence, resistance overcoming obedience. Her choice to pursue the apples and forfeit the race is another expression of that ambivalence, a reluctant capitulation to her destiny made easier by an attractive and clever suitor. Historically, however, Atalanta's dilemma is the product of two conflicting mythologies: the earlier, pre-Hellenic one according to which her race is the love chase, where "the moon-goddess as Nymph . . . pursued the sacred king . . . and finally devoured him,"[18] and the later one in which marriages of the goddess and her priestesses rationalize the transfer of power to a male hierarchy. The race, as conceived by Atalanta, endlessly replays the earlier plot, for she is swifter than any man and can destroy all comers. The race, as sanctioned by her father, manipulated by Aphrodite, and engaged in by Hippomenes/Melanion, is of another kind—a contest to discover the most suitable husband—and thus open to another outcome. Apollo's oracle seems to acknowledge both interpretations, and prophesies the catastrophic losses that result from their conflict.

Since Atalanta emerges from classical times already a captive in the contradictions between two incompatible mythologies—condemned to "win" a husband only by losing, and then to lose herself and her dubious prize because of her "victory"—it is not surprising that later mythographers should have found her an emblem of instability. The irony of her name—"unswaying" (Graves, index)—cannot have escaped scholars of Greek, and a central medieval tradition interpreting the judgment of Paris—wth its reiteration of the theme of the golden apple—as the choice between three modes of life—the philosophical (Athena), active (Juno), and sensual (Aphrodite)—colored later readings of Atalanta's seemingly impulsive and avaricious pursuit of the apples. While in the hands of Juno or Athena, Paris's award would have signified the virtues of heroic action or philosophic wisdom, in the hands of Aphrodite it was irrevocably identified with the vicious perversion of natural gifts and of choice, and with an act that led to the corruption and downfall of a great city.

Danae shares with Atalanta the displeasure of a father and an unfortunate prophecy brought to pass by the potency of gold. She shares with Callisto a mysterious rape against which she cannot arm herself or flee.

While she is imprisoned in a tower by her father Acrisius to forestall the birth of a murderous grandson, Zeus comes to her as a shower of gold, and she gives birth to Perseus, who must later rescue her from the violent overtures of King Polydectes. Despite her chaste isolation, however, Sandys follows Lactantius in blaming Danae as well as Jupiter for her fall: "Jupiter, saith *Lactantius*, endeavoring to violate Danae, with store of gold corrupted her chastity" (166).

In Sandys's preferred mythographic tradition, women who are raped are considered vicious, while those who flee or are saved are considered virtuous.[19] The corruption here is literal in two senses: Danae is corrupted by her sexual experience, and doubly so because the agency of seduction is gold. The earlier association of the golden shower with the rays of the sun in a myth that, according to Graves, "must refer to the ritual marriage of the Sun and the Moon" (sec. 73.4) had been lost even by late classical times. Sandys is able to quote as well Horace's ode on contented poverty, in which Danae's story is cited as an example of cynical trickery and bribery:

Inclusam Danaen turris aenea
robustaeque fores et vigilum canum
tristes excubiae munierant satis
    nocturnis ab adulteris,

si non Acrisium virginis abditae
custodem pavidum Iuppiter et Venus
risissent: fore enim tutum iter et patens
    converso in pretium deo.

aurum per medios ire satellites
et parrumpere amat saxa, potentius
ictu fulmineo. . . .[20]

Given a choice between a unifying general truth and a divergent interpretation highlighting details of a myth, Sandys generally pursues the latter, producing a fragmented and contradictory opus that classifies rather than synthesizes. In this context, we can see how potent a stimulus for doctrinaire interpretation must be the mythical juxtaposition of women and gold. While gold in itself or as an object of male desire may be interpreted severally, as Sandys does in his passages on Perseus and Hercules, sexuality has no part in these interpretations. The quest may be equated with heroic virtues or with the vice of avarice. Either way the issues do not involve gender. But when a woman is involved, however reluctantly, the moral terms are altered. Horace's ironic phrasing in Ode

16 makes this clear, for there are no sentinels to be bribed or pathways to be revealed, and "Acrisiu[s] virginis abditae custo[s] pavidu[s]"[21] is not even on the scene. While on the literal level Jupiter encounters no obstacle at all—because his form eludes the barriers erected by the anxious father and cannot be perceived by his passive object—figuratively, Horace implies, the coopted and cooperating party is Danae herself. A woman who takes gold from a man, as Danae does from Zeus and as Atalanta does from Hippomenes, is ultimately a whore.

Because Diana, the emblem of chastity, is female, mythographical allegories regarding chastity and sexual corruption are further complicated. As we observed above, in his interpretation of the Actaeon myth, Sandys cites Lucian's "Dialogues of the Gods," in which Hera and Leto abuse each other's offspring in a malicious and slangy manner. Of Diana, Hera says that she is cannibalistic and wild, and furthermore:

> your pretty maid is so pretty that, when she found out that Actaeon had seen her, she was afraid the young fellow would tell everyone how hideous she was, and set her hounds on him. I won't bother pointing out she could never have been a midwife, if she were a virgin herself. (*Lucian*, vol. 7, 325–27)

In the context of Sandys's commentary, his paraphrase of Lucian illustrates a displacement of guilt and responsibility from Actaeon to Diana. Actaeon's illicit action—eavesdropping on sacred mysteries—is reinterpreted by Lucian as commendable, the public exposure of a fraud. Furthermore, Actaeon's metamorphic decline from man to beast is supplanted in the narrative by Diana's revelation as "hideous" and unchaste. Sandys's paraphrase is strongly worded in its reference to Diana's "deformity," a term implying not mere lack of beauty but an unnatural and shameful quality intimately related to sexual experience. That she is "*conversant* at the labours of women," "a *publicke* midwife," [emphasis mine] strengthens this impression.[22]

When one considers the context of Lucian's words, Sandys's selection of this passage seems more bizarre, since the piece is satirical, deliberately undermining received interpretations of the myths, and a dialogue as well. Neither Hera nor Latona is reliable by any standard; to the contrary, their motives for slander are obvious. Lucian would have laughed to see his frivolous trifles so solemnly inserted into Sandys's mythographical edifice. The issue is not what Lucian has Hera say to Latona, but the uses to which Sandys puts the passage, inserting it blandly into a collection of serious comments on Ovid's text and the matter described therein.

IN DEALING with a genre as thoroughly conservative—which is to say plagiarizing—as Renaissance mythographical commentary, it is difficult to determine responsibility for thematic materials. An author such as Sandys, working late in the tradition, is largely affirming by repetition the opinions, citations, and principles of organization of others. To the degree that this is so, it would be inappropriate to attribute to Sandys in particular either the views on men, women, and sexuality that can be deduced from his commentaries or an intention to manipulate the genre for his own purposes. These particular passages, free from the lively personal allusions that form part of his most original commentaries, are in their elements entirely derivative from earlier works.

An essential feature of such commentaries is their inclusivity. Often repetitive, contradictory, more concerned with being complete than with arriving at the truth, the late mythographies represent a potpourri of Christian and enlightened pagan wisdom. Certain views, of course, are simply unknown and certain authors excluded from consideration, but within the pale of acceptable fact and opinion the mythographer is undiscriminating. Sandys, however, by exercising greater restraint in selecting among his sources, incurs a greater responsibility for what he includes and what he omits. Perhaps under the influence of late sixteenth-century and early seventeenth-century essayists, he has chosen to write with greater concision, a stronger critical voice, and a higher level of rhetorical organization than was common during the Renaissance. He has declined to give the endless philological variants of Giraldi, the moral summations and resummations of Comes, the line-by-line explications of Latin prosody of his contemporary, Jacobus Pontanus. In their place, he offers a fast-paced, smoothly seamed, pleasantly argumentative running commentary that Don Cameron Allen has called "the most readable discussions ever written on Ovid" (192).

A consequence of this heightened style is a more unified focus within episodes, a more distinct thesis on the part of the commentator. Thus we see Sandys emphasizing sexual ethics in Callisto's tale and political ethics in Actaeon's. He does not create these interpretations, but he selects them from among many, and he intensifies their impact on the reader by judicious pruning and shaping of the surrounding material. By this means, Sandys unobtrusively cultivates a bias of the age. In a genre where wide selection among authorities is approved, a commentator may conceal a considerable amount of highly directed argument under a surface appearance of casual shifts of subject and critical mode. The consequence in Sandys's work is a style of humanistic speculation and detached, broad-ranging scholarship superimposed on certain arbitrary, narrow, and highly emotional responses. These formalized critical modes, assisting indirectly the expression of an ideology of gender, permit a scholar such as Sandys to voice in a traditional, authoritative, and genial manner subjects of fear and loathing.

Notes

1. Recent work on women, gender, patriarchy, and misogyny in the Renaissance is extensive. For historical introductions, see Kelly; Ferguson, Quilligan, and Vickers; and Delaney. For discussions of the social and literary limitations imposed on Renaissance women and their responses to them, see Kelso, Hannay, Rose, Jones, and Hull. Two books on the English Renaissance "controversy about women" are by Henderson and McManus, and Woodbridge. The extensive bibliographies of these works point to other important sources, including a growing literature on Renaissance women writers.

2. The first five books of Sandys's translation were published separately in 1621, and the entire translation without commentary for the first time in 1626. I have used the Garland facsimile. Also available is the Hulley and Vandersall edition. For more bibliographical and biographical information on Sandys, see Davis; for a longer study of Sandys's commentary, see Rubin. Beyond these two books and brief discussions in major surveys of Renaissance mythography, little has been written on Sandys's *Ovid* in this century.

3. *Metamorphoses*, ed. Miller, 3:138-252, 2:409-531. All citations of the *Metamorphoses* are from this edition and are identified by book and line numbers.

4. For general background on late classical, medieval, and Renaissance traditions of mythographical commentary, see D. C. Allen, Bush, Chance (35-64), and Seznec. For discussions on the more rationalistic approaches to myth and fiction that emerged in the Renaissance, see Nelson, Shapiro, Knoespel, and Baker.

Sandys's "principall Authors" among the modern writers, as he himself declares with unusual forthrightness, were the Italian mythographers Giraldus and Comes, the Ovidian commentators Sabinus and (Jacobus) Pontanus, as well as Ficino, Vives, Scaliger, Bacon, and Valeriano (Bolzani).

5. In citing Sandys, I have changed *i* to *j* in conformance with modern English spelling (*Juno* instead of *Iuno*, *subjacent* instead of *subiacent*). I have retained his italicization of proper names, where it occurs, but have not attempted to reproduce other distracting uses of italicization (for instance, to signal quotations).

6. Stallybrass discusses views of woman's body as "naturally 'grotesque' " (126). See also Kelly on the "loathing for women and the female body" (73) characteristic of medieval clerical writing and persisting into the seventeenth century in "Early Feminist Theory." For a discussion of the Renaissance modification of "the literature and values of courtly love . . . in the direction of asexuality," see Joan Kelly Gadol, "Did Women Have a Renaissance?" 137-64.

7. The lines Sandys has translated are *Tristia* 2:103–8.

8. A compelling discussion of this *topos* is Parry's essay, which considers interconnections and reversals between the hunt and the erotic chase. Parry examines the myths of Actaeon, Callisto, and Atalanta, among others. He concludes that these myths share the theme of "rape and violence . . . at the ultimate place of refuge: in the dark recesses of the woods, where the heat of the sun is excluded, in a virginal setting, in those very woods where Diana maintains her realm as the defender of virginity" (277). Perella traces the same *topos* from Dante through the twentieth century, demonstrating the persistent centrality of the Actaeon myth.

Moss emphasizes the sexually charged setting of the pool, also, citing several sixteenth-century French illustrated versions of the myth of Salmacis that describe "the emasculating properties of the pool and [equate] it with the female sexual organ" (98).

9. Claimed for mercy by the domain of love—"imperium," "regnum," "vires Amores," as Venus refers to the portions of the universe under her sway (5:371–72, 374, 378)—and for punishment by the domain of virginity, her survival and translation to the heavens suggest that the primal forces of creation are stronger than any concept of personal integrity, identity, or justice. Even Diana recognizes this, casting her out of the band but sparing her life and that of her unborn child. Actaeon, aloof as yet from the domain of love and lacking a champion of this kind, is destroyed.

10. As is frequently the case, Sandys's source for typically Renaissance political readings of myth is Bacon's *De sapientia veterum*. (See "Actaeon or Pentheus," 719–20.) Such readings, strongly influenced by Machiavelli, represent a major departure from medieval ethical interpretations. While Bersuire refers constantly to good and bad princes, prelates, preachers, etc., his types are ideal, and appropriate behavior is determined by virtue, not expedience. Gower, in *Confessio Amantis*, also defines Actaeon's sin as one of wrong seeing—"Ensample touchende of mislok"—but with the medieval insistence on individual responsibility rather than political reality (2:45). For other Renaissance political readings of Actaeon, see Barkan and Vickers.

11. This aspect of Renaissance mythography may be traced back to the medieval tradition of *in bono* and *in malo*, which encourages the commentator to segment the text in order to extract many morals, and to view each element both as an emblem of virtue and as an emblem of vice. An extraordinarily elaborated example of this technique is Bersuire's *Ovidius moralizatus*. The Renaissance vogue for hieroglyphics and emblems gave a new impetus to such fragmented readings. See, for instance, Alciati, Bolzani, and Quarles. Vickers's discussion of the fragmentation and dispersal of the female form in the Petrarchan tradition and Mathieu-Castellani's deconstructive reading of the Actaeon myth place this phenomenon in a broader critical context.

12. Page 324. This page is wrongly numbered 334 in the 1632 edition reproduced by Garland, and should not be confused with the proper page 334.

13. Pp. 324–25. These pages are wrongly numbered 334–35, and should not be confused with the proper pages 334–35.

14. Where the garden of the Hesperides was said to be located, on Mount Atlas.

15. A frequently used example is Orpheus and Eurydice, whose passages to the underworld were quite differently interpreted by medieval mythographers: Eurydice's represented the "vicious descent" (the temptations of the flesh) while Orpheus' represented the "virtuous descent" (the philosophical study of worldly things in order to guard against their influence). See Nitzsche, 50–55.

16. In Apollodorus's account, she was "exposed by her father, because he desired male children," suckled by a she-bear, and raised by hunters, 1:399 (3.9.2). Atalanta's status as virgin huntress suggests service to Diana, to whom also the she-bear is sacred (Graves, sec. 80.4). Perhaps for this reason she is able to land the first blow against the Calydonian boar, also Diana's sacred animal and a scourge sent to avenge a slight against the goddess. Atalanta, however, is fated to obey the will of the father who cast her off, abandon the service of the goddess who preserved her, and incur the wrath of Aphrodite for a sacrifice of virginity made too reluctantly and too late (Graves, sec. 80 passim).

17. *Metamorphoses*, 10.564–66. I have quoted from Innes's translation, 240.

18. Graves, sec. 62.1. See also Graves, sec. 80.4, and Cornford, passim.

19. Although Sandys says of Semele that "to be embraced by a God was held no impeachment to chastity but contrarily a high honor" (101), his general interpretive practice does not follow this dictum. Women such as Coronis, Daphne, and Syrinx, who suffered metamorphoses into non-human forms to escape a lustful god, are treated favorably or lightly passed over, while women such as Callisto and Danae are condemned.

20. *Carminum*, Liber 3, Ode 16, pp. 232–33. Bennett's translation is as follows: "Tower of bronze, doors of oak, and the strict guard of watch-dogs had quite protected imprisoned Danae from nocturnal lovers, had not Jupiter and Venus laughed at Acrisius, anxious keeper of the hidden maiden. For they knew that the way would be safe and open, when the god had turned to gold. Gold loves to make its way through the midst of sentinels and to break through rocks, for 'tis mightier than the thunderbolt" (233).

21. "Acrisius, anxious keeper of the hidden maiden," 233.

22. A similar displacement of shame onto Diana can be seen in Sandys's treatment of the myth of Hippolytus, which in the *Metamorphoses* includes the protagonist's rescue, cure, and renaming by his patron Diana. After a relatively neutral summary of Ovid's plot, Sandys writes:

> But what saith *Lactantius*? *Diana* when she had allmost lost her lover, much bruised and torne by his unruly horses, called *Aesculapius* . . . to his timely helpe, whom she as soone as he was recovered, conveyed to those sequestred aboads. What showed this diligence in his concealed cure? these private retreates? his long conversation with a woman.[sic] and that in a place unfrequented? the change of his name? and lastly her detestation of horses? but the guilt of her incontinency, and of such a love as agreed not with a virgin. (523–24)

It is hard to believe that such blatant and extraneous distortion of divine worship and service could arise were the deity male. Just as the mediation of golden tokens in Atalanta's marriage and Danae's rape lessens the credibility of the women in the tales for Sandys, so the just intercession of a deity—in anger or in love—is discredited because the deity is female.

Works Cited

Alciati, Andrea. *Emblematum*. 1621. Reprint. New York: Garland, 1977.

Allen, Don Cameron. *Mysteriously Meant: The Rediscovery of Pagan Symbolism and Allegorical Interpretation in the Renaissance*. Baltimore: Johns Hopkins University Press, 1970.

Apollodorus. *The Library*. Translated by Sir James George Frazer. 2 vols. Loeb Classical Library. 1921. Reprint. Cambridge: Harvard University Press, 1946.

Bacon, Francis. *De sapientia veterum*. In *Works*, edited by James Spedding, Robert Leslie Ellis, and Douglas Denon Heath. Vol. 6 of 14 vols. 1870. Reprint. New York: Garrett, 1968.

Baker, Herschel. *The Race of Time: Three Lectures on Renaissance Historiography*. Toronto: University Toronto Press, 1967.

Barkan, Leonard. "Diana and Actaeon: The Myth as Synthesis." *English Literary Renaissance* 10 (1980): 317–59.

Bersuire, Pierre. "*The Ovidius Moralizatus* of Petrus Berchorius: An Introduction and Translation." Translated by William Donald Reynolds. Ph.D. diss., University of Illinois, 1971.

Bolzani, Giovanni Pierio Valeriano. *Hieroglyphica*. 1602. Reprint. New York: Garland, 1976.

Bush, Douglas. *Mythology and the Renaissance Tradition in English Poetry*. 2d ed. New York: Norton, 1963.

Chance, Jane. "The Origins and Development of Medieval Mythography: From Homer to Dante." In *Mapping the Cosmos*, edited by Jane Chance and R. O. Wells, Jr., 35–64, 151–59. Houston: Rice University Press, 1985.

Cornford, F. M. "The Origin of the Olympic Games." Chapter 7 in *Themis: A Study of the Social Origins of Greek Religion*, by Jane E. Harrison, 212–59. 2d ed. 1927. Reprint. Cleveland: Meridian-World, 1962.

Davis, Richard Beale. *George Sandys, Poet Adventurer: A Study in Anglo-American Culture in the Seventeenth Century*. London: Bodley Head; New York: Columbia University Press, 1955.

Delaney, Sheila. *Writing Woman: Women Writers and Women in Literature, Medieval to Modern*. New York: Schocken, 1983.

Ferguson, Margaret W., Maureen Quilligan, and Nancy J. Vickers, eds. *Rewriting the Renaissance: The Discourses of Sexual Difference in Early Modern Europe*. Chicago: University of Chicago Press, 1986.

Gadol, Joan Kelly. "Did Women Have a Renaissance?" In *Becoming Visible: Women in European History*, edited by Renate Bridenthal and Claudia Koonz, 137–64. Boston: Houghton-Mifflin, 1977.

Gower, John. *Confessio Amantis*. Vol. 2 of *The Complete Works*, edited by G. C. Macaulay. 1901. Reprint. Grosse Pointe, MI: Scholarly, 1968.

Graves, Robert. *The Greek Myths*. 2 vols. Harmondsworth, Middlesex, England: Penguin, 1960.

Hannay, Margaret Patterson, ed. *Silent But for the Word: Tudor Women as Patrons, Translators, and Writers of Religious Works*. Kent, OH: Kent State University Press, 1985.

Henderson, Katherine Usher, and Barbara F. McManus, eds. *Half Humankind: Contexts and Texts of the Controversy about Women in England, 1540–1640*. Urbana: University of Illinois Press, 1985.

Horace. *The Odes and Epodes*. Translated by C. E. Bennett. Cambridge, MA: Harvard University Press, 1914.

Hull, Suzanne W. *Chaste, Silent and Obedient: English Books for Women, 1475–1640*. San Marino, CA: Huntington Library, 1982.

Jones, Ann Rosalind. "Surprising Fame: Renaissance Gender Ideologies and Women's Lyric." In *The Poetics of Gender*, edited by Nancy K. Miller, 74–95. New York: Columbia University Press, 1986.

Kelly, Joan. *Women, History, and Theory*. Chicago: University of Chicago Press, 1984.

Kelso, Ruth. *Doctrine for the Lady of the Renaissance*. Urbana: University of Illinois Press, 1956. Reprint. 1978.

Knoespel, Kenneth. "From Poetry to Historiography: Ovid's *Metamorphoses* and Seventeenth-Century Historiography." Special Session on Ovid and Renaissance Poetry, MLA Convention, New York, December 28, 1983.

Lucian. *Lucian*. Translated by M. D. Macleod. Vol. 7 of 8 vols. 1925. Reprint. Cambridge: Harvard University Press, 1961.

Mathieu-Castellani, Gisele. "Acteon ou la rhétorique du mythe dans la poésie baroque." In *La Mythologie au XVIIe Siècle*. Eleventh Conference of the Centre Meridional de Rencontres sur le XVIIe Siècle (C.M.R. 17) January 1981. Org. Claude Faisant. Nice: C.M.R. 17—Centre National des Lettres et de l' U.E.R., University of Nice, n.d.

Moss, Ann. *Poetry and Fable: Studies in Mythological Narrative in Sixteenth-Century France*. Cambridge: Cambridge University Press, 1984.

Nelson, William. *Fact or Fiction: The Dilemma of the Renaissance Storyteller*. Cambridge, MA: Harvard University Press, 1973.

Nitzsche, Jane Chance. *The Genius Figure in Antiquity and the Middle Ages*. New York: Columbia University Press, 1975.

Ovid. *Metamorphoses*. Edited and translated by Frank Justus Miller. 2 vols. Loeb Classical Library, 3d ed. Cambridge, MA: Harvard University Press; London: W. Heinemann, 1977.

———. *The Metamorphoses of Ovid*. Translated by Mary M. Innes. Harmondsworth, Middlesex, England: Penguin, 1955.

———. *Tristia and Ex Ponto*. Edited by Arthur Leslie Wheeler. Cambridge, MA: Harvard University Press, 1924.

Parry, Hugh. "Ovid's *Metamorphoses*: Violence in a Pastoral Landscape." *Transactions and Proceedings of the American Philological Association* 95 (1964): 268–82.

Perella, Nicholas J. *Midday in Italian Literature: Variations on an Archetypal Theme*. Princeton: Princeton University Press, 1979.

Pontanus, Jacobus. *Ex P. Ovidii Nasonis Metamorphoseon Libris XV*. 1618. Reprint. New York: Garland, 1976.

Quarles, Francis. *Emblems*. In *Complete Works*, 3 vols., edited by Alexander B. Grosart, 3:41–184. Edinburgh, 1880–81.

Rose, Mary Beth, ed. *Women in the Middle Ages and the Renaissance: Literary and Historical Perspectives*. Syracuse: Syracuse University Press, 1986.

Rubin, Deborah. *Ovid's Metamorphoses Englished: George Sandys as Translator and Mythographer*. New York: Garland, 1985.

Sabinus, Georgius. *Metamorphoses seu Fabulae Poeticae*. 1589. Reprint. New York: Garland, 1976.

Sandys, George. *Ovids Metamorphosis Englished, Mythologiz'd and Represented in Figures*. 1632. Reprint. New York: Garland, 1976.

———. *Ovid's Metamorphosis Englished, Mythologiz'd, and Represented in Figures*. Edited by Karl K. Hulley and Stanley T. Vandersall. Lincoln: University of Nebraska Press, 1970.

Seznec, Jean. *The Survival of the Pagan Gods: The Mythological Tradition and its Place in Renaissance Humanism and Art*. Translated by Barbara F. Sessions. Bollingen Series, 38. Princeton: Princeton University Press, 1953.

Shapiro, Barbara J. *Probability and Certainty in Seventeeth-Century England: A Study of the Relationships Between Natural Science, Religion, History, Law, and Literature*. Princeton: Princeton University Press, 1983.

Stallybrass, Peter. "Patriarchal Territories: The Body Enclosed." In Ferguson, Quilligan, and Vickers, 123-42.

Vickers, Nancy J. "Diana Described: Scattered Woman and Scattered Rhyme." *Critical Inquiry* 8 (1981): 265-79.

Woodbridge, Linda, ed. *Women and the English Renaissance: Literature and the Nature of Womankind, 1540-1620*. Urbana: University of Illinois Press, 1984.

Part IV. Bibliographic Epilogue

Eleven Unpublished Commentaries on Ovid's *Metamorphoses* and Two Other Texts of Mythographic Interest

Some Comments on a Bibliography

Judson Boyce Allen

To speak of a commentary as a textually definite entity is to impose modern precision on a portion of the medieval culture of manuscripts in which it does not belong. Though certain glosses, such as the *Glosa ordinaria*, might indeed attain a measure of uniformity, and though even literary glosses might tend roughly to occur in groups, or with a consistent *accessus*, there is still a good deal of the kind of variation that makes it imprudent to claim that a certain author used a certain commentary without identifying the particular manuscript involved. Ovid's *Metamorphoses*, after the Bible the most popular medieval storybook, are no exception to this rule. I have, in the course of working on problems of literary theory, had occasion to look at a great many manuscripts of Ovid's *Metamorphoses*, in most of the major European libraries. Classifying manuscripts as copies of this or that particular commentary was not my project; on the contrary, I was interested in recording in as much detail as possible particular glosses and *accessus* variants in an array that could document and define medieval attitudes toward literary theory. The notes that resulted from this research necessarily contain facts of bibliographic interest.

The miscellany that follows is my attempt to share these facts, such as they are, with people who might have some need of them. Their context can be defined by four preliminary generalizations. First, the texts that have been published and are well known: pseudo-Lactantius Placidus, John of Garland, Arnulf of Orleans, Pierre Bersuire, and Giovanni del Virgilio, fairly represent what can be called the ideology of medieval *Metamorphoses* commentary. At the early end of the tradition, the manuscripts deriving from Manegold von Lautenbach have a poetic-mystical attitude toward language and nature which much resembles Bernard Silvestris,[1] and at the later end a fragment of commentary by Peter Lavinius is more explicitly Christian than are any of the well-known commentaries.[2] Bibliographically, each of these texts deserves separate entry. Ideologically, however, they confirm more than they revise.

The tradition that all these commentaries define has two major characteristics. The story summaries, chiefly found in the early *narratio* of the pseudo-Lactantius and in the late retelling of Giovanni, but also repeated and amplified in the *Ovide moralisé* and in the works of such storytellers as Beryl Smalley's classicizing friars and Bromyard's *Summa predicantium*, tend to be more realistic and more circumstantial with the passage of time. Ghisalberti, Giovanni's editor, thus characterizes his *narrationes* as *novelle*.[3] In addition, the interpretations tend to become more and more explicitly Christian, and to depend with less and less reservation on the techniques of reading defined by biblical exegesis. The reason for this tendency, I think, is that Ovid's poem, which commentators first approached as a text to be justified and explained, became by virtue of their very work a corpus of accepted exemplary stories which, like all accepted stories, were liable to typological applications.

Fourth, finally, and in contradiction of these large modern views based on having seen large numbers of manuscripts, I must emphasize that any given medieval reader's sense of *Metamorphoses* commentary was of a quite static body of received information. Most readers would have had only one manuscript, or at most a very few—seen probably at various times in widely separated places. Even Pierre Bersuire, who himself wrote one of the major medieval commentaries and whom Petrarch aided with bibliography, dealt with the various sources that he so assiduously searched out more by compiling them additively than by sorting them into kinds or traditions.[4] And Robert Holkot, who knew the *Metamorphoses* quite well but seems to have had access to no known commentary, interpreted the stories from Ovid, which he repeated in his own works in a fashion perfectly consistent with all the various practices of the commentators—sometimes euhemeristically, sometimes in terms of science or cosmology, sometimes tropologically.[5]

Thus, medieval readers may have known both the names of various commentators and that they from time to time wrote differing glosses on the same passage. But these readers nevertheless seem to have been prepared to receive glosses from different and even inconsistent commentary traditions as all part of the same great body of apparatus. Bersuire's work is full of alternate and essentially unrelated interpretations.

But even these generalizations are modern. The medieval reader does not read the Zeitgeist; he reads a codex, a particular copy. The important modern scholarly task is not to blur differences between copies under labels like "Arnulf" and "Giovanni," but to make differences and distinctions as clear as possible. The task is made more difficult by the nature and condition of surviving manuscripts. Glosses and *accessus* tend to be added—for literary texts, the *Glosa ordinaria* format is both late and rare. The page most easily lost from a manuscript is the flyleaf or pastedown; the page most likely to be rubbed is the first; the part of the page most likely to be damaged is the margin. Not all glossed Ovids therefore have intelligible incipits or *accessus*. Further, especially in the case of manuscripts involving or depending on Arnulf, *accessus* tend to be transmitted more reliably than the attendant glosses, which will naturally include everything a given compiler found of value. Arnulf's *accessus* sometimes introduces gloss collections that, though like his in character, are very far from being faithful copies of what Ghisalberti prints; the modern decision as to whether a given manuscript contains contaminated Arnulf or something that can be called a commentary with its own integrity is often quite arbitrary. The manuscripts I discuss in this paper contain, in my judgment, enough material specifically different from that in print to justify separate description.

They can be divided into three classes. First, there are collections like those of Arnulf of Orleans in general character, but sufficiently different in specific content to warrant separate consideration. Second, there are commentaries and compilations of glosses that are substantially different from those in print—upon occasion, one might call such material more invented than compiled. Finally, there is one grammatical commentary.

This last is the *Liber Titan* of Ralph of Beauvais, whose professional life extended from perhaps 1140 to 1185. It has been identified in two manuscripts by R. W. Hunt, who says that "it contains long grammatical notes on select lines in the *Metamorphoses*."[6] There are other glosses on quotations from Lucan's *Pharsalia*. The British Library exemplar, which I have seen, is formidably illegible.

Depending on how one counts, Ghisalberti treats over two dozen manuscripts that either contain Arnulf's commentary or report it extensively;[7] my own survey confirms that Arnulf's glosses are the dominating core of this tradition. Nevertheless, there are three manuscripts, two mentioned by Ghisalberti, that seem to me to deserve separate mention: British Library Additional manuscript 15733 and Vatican Ottoboni manuscript 1294, both fourteenth-century Italian books, and Vatican fondo Vat. lat. manuscript 1949, from fourteenth-century France. The first quire of the Ottoboni manuscript is missing, and identification is therefore made difficult, but it seems to relate to Additional 15733. Their allegories are methodologically like Arnulf's, but they are sometimes fuller, and there are interpretations of more stories than those for which Ghisalberti prints a gloss.[8] Manuscript Vat. lat. 1479 is developed and amplified from both Arnulf and Giovanni, and contains some explanations more explicitly Christian than either of them.[9] It is further worthy of mention because it contains, in addition to the *Metamorphoses* and its commentary, the *Ars major* of Donatus with other grammatical material, the *Distichs* of Cato, the *Eclogues* of Theodulus, the *Remedia amoris* of Ovid, the versified *Tobias* of Matthew of Vendome, and the *Alexandreis* of Walter of Châtillon. All but the first two of these texts are elaborately surrounded by commentary, written in the full *Glosa ordinaria* format. The book is a large folio, obviously made for a rich patron as a library in one volume, written large for old eyes.

In addition to these, there is one further manuscript mentioned by Ghisalberti as dependent on Arnulf, Paris B.N. lat. 8253 (fourteenth century), which has a distinctive *accessus*. In this *accessus*, the established *schemata*—material, intention, usefulness, and the like, are treated, but there is also treatment of the four Aristotelian causes. Further, formal cause is not here defined in terms of the late medieval convention of a duplex form, *forma tractatus* and *forma tractandi*, but in terms of "quod est in esse rei."[10] Otherwise, predictable material occurs in a language that is a compromise of original insight and garbling.

Next I should mention two summaries. Both of them are literal. One, in verse with prose glosses, very brief, is preserved in a fifteenth-century Italian manuscript now in Vienna, Vindob. 3379 in the Imperial Library. It is fundamentally only a mnemonic, by means of which one can call to mind all the major stories of the *Metamorphoses* in sixteen Latin lines. The effect is rather like that of the one in English listing British sovereigns, which begins: "Willy, Willy, Harry, Ste / Harry, Dick, John, Harry three. . . ." The other summary is long and circumstantial, with indirect discourse and dialogue. It is preserved in Oxford, Merton College MS 299, bound with a copy of Bersuire attributed to Nicholas Trivet. According to Merton's catalog, it is by John Segward.

Finally I mention three more commentaries, even more distinctive because they have a date and author or provenance, or because the glosses are more personal than traditional. The first of these, preserved in Paris manuscript BN. lat. 16238, is the *Constructio Ovidii Magni* of Johannes Bolent, dated in the winter of 1348, and noting that "in illo anno moriebantur per totum mundum" (fol. 166v). Its *lemmata* account thoroughly for Ovid's text; there is substantial paraphrase, and some use of the French language. The second, now MS Vat. lat. 5222, is endorsed by Damianus de Polo as the book he lectured on at Padua in 1415. Other courses are recorded for 1430 and 1442, in Venice and Padua; yet another two "readings" are probably student work, because the names of the supervising masters are recorded.[11] Damian illustrates his opinions with personal experience (fol. 31va), refers to folio forty-five of his book of genealogies (fol. 85v) and folio four of his copy of the *Aeneid* (fol. 169v), and emends his text on the basis of Priscian's quotation of the line in question (fol. 182r). For the most part, his explanations consist of paraphrase and literal annotation. The last of this group of three manuscripts is an "Allegorie Hovidii," preserved in MS Vat. lat. 2877, a fourteenth-century Italian codex. The author develops his material freely from Giovanni and Arnulf, and includes a good deal of his own opinion and a number of apparently phonetic spellings of Latin. He is quite self-conscious about poetry and its relation to philosophy.[12]

These specifications are both tentative and diffident. Another scholar might read the manuscripts, or indeed my notes on the manuscripts, and distinguish a different list. Other manuscripts may turn up—at least one has, for which I am happy to thank Margaret Gibson of Liverpool University, who has told me that Copenhagen Royal Library MS Fabricius 29.2 (twelfth century), of which there is no printed catalog notice, is solid with glosses, and includes the *Thebaid* as well as the *Metamorphoses* and a number of other texts. It may, of course, turn out to be another copy of Arnulf, but its existence justifies adding a delightful city to an *iter codicum*.

I began this brief list by framing the commentary tradition. At the one end, the three Munich manuscripts related to Manegold von Lautenbach, safely before Arnulf. At the other end, the biblically figural fragment of commentary written just before 1700 by Peter Lavinius. The trend they define is from a text that must be explained to a body of stories that can, as *exempla*, be used. I close the list with two mythographic texts that, perhaps better even than in Lavinius, illustrate the late medieval use of this material.

The first text is the *Fulgentius metaforalis* of John Ridewall, long familiar in the edition of Hans Liebeschütz. I include it only in order to point out that Liebeschütz edited from a single manuscript, which unfortunately contained only about half the text. All but one of the complete manuscripts can be identified from Liebeschütz's notes; I have located one more, Oxford University MS Bodl. 571. In its full version, the character of Ridewall's "Fulgentius metaphored" is even clearer. It is a commentary on a commentary, which makes metaphors of virtue and vice out of the gods constructible from Fulgentius's mythographic explanations.[13]

My final text is the *Concordatia* of poetry, philosophy, and theology of John Calderia, a fifteenth-century Venetian physician.[14] In this work, theology is represented by an allegorical flight into the heavens, philosophy by conversations with philosophers whose island one reaches by means of a bridge allegorical of mental process, and poetry by an allegorized collection of mythological and pseudo-mythological figures from sources as diverse as Ovid's *Metamorphoses* and Holkot's *Moralitates*. The interpretations are various; many are specifically Christian. Leda, for instance, represents Holy Mother Church. In another context, Saturn equals God, Jupiter Christ, Juno Mary, and Terra Peter. In yet another, there is a description of the pope, which is literally a borrowed description of Cybele. From the point of view of literary theory, the text is important, because it defines poetry as that discourse on which, in Rosemond Tuve's words, allegory may be "imposed." In the mythographic tradition, it is the ultimate extreme case of that medieval assimilation that Seznec illustrated by discussing Ridewall's *Fulgentius metaforalis*.

Our modern interest in all this material has been, for the most part, an interest in a developing tradition, viewed as a whole. What remains to be done, and what is I think more important, is to describe various specific medieval views: Chaucer's mythography, or Dante's, or even John Calderia's. We must seek, not to establish texts, but to understand surviving codices—what gets bound with what, what a particular manuscript's array of glosses means. For this enterprise, the variety of manuscripts, the cross-contamination of glosses, the circulation of set descriptions under various names—all that which makes the work of modern bibliography so difficult—is needed and useful evidence.

Notes

1. Manegold's own commentary apparently does not survive. Munich MSS clm. 4610, 14482, and 14809, all preserving texts of the twelfth century or earlier, seem to be interrelated with each other, and to reflect Manegold's views. *Accessus* from these commentaries are printed by Young (1–13). Manegold is quoted by MS clm. 4610 at *Metamorphoses* VII.121 (fol. 70r), VIII.183 (fol 71r), XI.214 (fol. 77v). For discussion, see Manitius 3:178.

2. Peter's commentary, which is very full, breaks off at the Flood; a note is printed at the end of Book 1 (fol. 27r) explaining that the printer was in such a hurry that he published without allowing Peter to finish, or check, his work. Peter explains that he had been able to work at the commentary during Lent, but not during Easter, and hopes that if he can get back his copy of the *Metamorphoses* he will continue. Apparently he never did.

3. "Maestro Giovanni . . . transforma l'antico e serio evemerismo della tradizione patristica in un realismo che sa di novella" (Ghisalberti, "Giovanni del Virgilio," 29–30).

4. For the fullest studies of Bersuire's versions, and the sources on which they were based, see Engels, "Berchoriana I," 62–134; "Berchoriana: Les Pseudo-

Bersuires," 128–48; "Note sur quelques manuscrits mythologiques," 102–7; "La Letter-dédicace de Bersuire," 62–72; "Note complémentaire," 73–78; and "L'Edition critique de l'*Ovidius moralizatus* de Bersuire," 19–24.

5. For proof of this generalization, see my article "The Library of a Classicizer," 721–29. I compiled and annotated all the mythographic materials in Holkot's works in my dissertation, "Mythography in the Bible Commentaries."

6. The manuscripts are B.L. Add. 16380, fols. 111r–119v, s. XIII early; and Bern Stadtbibliothek 519, fols. 116r–135v, s. XIII. See Hunt, "Studies on Priscian in the Twelfth Century II," 11–14, and Alton and Wormell, 28.

7. Ghisalberti, "Arnolfo d'Orléans," 157–234.

8. The following interpretation of Ganymede, for instance, is not in Arnulf: "Per ganimedem pulcerrimum puerum possumus accipere vitam contemplativam que impeditur multotiens ab activa, pincerna efficitur quia contemplatio in lacrimas mutatur ut patet in magdalena que vitam contemplativam gerens pedes lavit lacrimis domini salvatoris. inde auctor: arripit yliadem etc." (British Library MS Add. 15733, fol. 114v).

9. On Europa: "Moralitas talis est: iupiter iuvans pater idest deus misit mercurium idest facundiam angelum suum erurope idest bone rippe marie que rippa et finis fuit veteri testamenti. Mutavit [se] iupiter in speciem tauri quia deus assumpsit formam humanam assumens quod non erat non reliquens quod erat. niveus erat per nivem intelligimus virginitatem. europa ascendit super eum quia maria totam mentem in deum posuit unde mare idest mondum transivit quia mundi viciis caruit et deus ex illa natus fuit sic dicitur iupiter rem con [sic] illa habuit non corrumpendo sed consternando illam" (Vatican, MS Vat. lat. 1479, fol. 71r).

10. The *accessus* begins: "Quatuor sunt cause principales in cuiuslibet operis compositione scilicet causa efficiens, causa materialis, causa formalis, causa finalis. Causa efficiens est illud a quo res agitur. sicut est ipse deus quia est causa efficiens cuiuslibet rei. Causa materialis est illud a quo res agitur. sicuti sunt ligna et lapides que sunt causa materialis domus. Causa formalis est illud quod est in esse rei sicuti divinitas in deo, humanitas in homine. Causa finalis est illud propter quod res agitur. sicuti est bonitas. quia propter bonitatem et ut ad bonum finem deveniant omnia procreantur. Unde patet in versibus. efficiens causa deus est formalis ydea, finalis bonitas. materialis yle" (Paris, MS B.N. lat. 8253, fol. lv).

11. "Hunc ovidium emendavi ego damianus de pola anno domini 1415 sex tamen primos libros antea correxeram et legi eum a principio usque ad finem padue et publice et complevi die 6 octobris 1415 ad laudem dei omnipotentis et omnium sanctorum suorum. Amen. et meus est liber iste. [In another hand]: nunc est francisci dime quem a nostre emit ducis et padue paulo [three words illeg.] obirem diem meum.

"Rursus complevi lecturam huius ovidii venetiis in schola mea de sancto leone die lune 25 septembris 1430 hora 23. tercio legi hunc ovidium publice padue in schola mea et complevi lecturam die veneris 12 Ianuarii 1442 hora quasi 24. Prius autem legeram ipsum bis / primus otonello de mediis er[e]mitibus deinde francisco de perusio olim fratri magistri Gentilis et sic quinques legi" (fol. 247v).

12. "Vulcanus philosophys primus fuit, qui traderet dissiplinam de coniunti-

one martis et veneris, et sic eos cepit et propalavit, quia tales coniuntionem docuit. Sed quia talem coniutionem scivit et collegit per motum et cursum solis, idcirco dictus est hoc fecisse, ex inditio philosophi, set per catenas et retia ita suctilia intendit, ita suctiles rationes ex quibus hoc habuit quod oculi videre non possunt, et sicut retia intueantur, ita ille rationes" (fol. 6r). ". . . Per euridicem nos inteligimus pohesim seu philosophiam que inventa ab apolline per pratum scientie currens morsa ab uno philosopho sofista mortua est idest perdita. Orfeus autem diu speculatus est super ipsa et pulcro textu eam descripxit sed cum retro vertitur se ad infernum idest ad errores perdidit eam" (fol. 15r).

13. I deal with the textual problems of the *Fulgentius metaforalis*, with certain texts derived from it, and with the implications for literary theory of this material, in "Commentary as Criticism," 25–47.

14. Calderia's *Concordatia* was apparently published once (1547); a manuscript exists: Vatican Palat. lat. 985. Calderia also wrote an exposition of the *Distichs* of Cato (British Library MS Add. 15406, dated 1450). In it, he lists his works: "Speculum divinale, Speculum sapientiale, Speculum historiale, Gemmam medicinalem, Lucidatorium, Omnes partes philosophiae descripsimum, Librum de causis et causatis, Expositio psalmorum, Expositio comedie dantis aldigeri, Concordantia philosophorum, etc., Expositio Catonis, Familiares epistolas ad omnis mundi principes" (fols. 100r–100v). For further discussion, see my "The Allegorized Mythography of Johannes Calderia," forthcoming in the *Acta* of the Fourth International Congress on Neo-Latin Studies, held at Bologna, Italy, in August 1979.

Works Cited

Allegorie Hovidii. Rome. Vatican Library. MS lat. 2877.

Allen, Judson Boyce. "The Allegorized Mythography of Johannes Calderia.' In *Acta*, 4th International Congress on Neo-Latin Studies at Bologna, Italy, August 1979. Forthcoming.

———. "Commentary as Criticism. The Text, Influence, and Literary Theory of the Fulgentius Metaphored of John Ridewall." In *Acta Conventus Neo-Latini Amstelodamensis*, edited by P. Tuynman, G. C. Kuiper, and E. Kessler, 25–47. Munich: Wilhelm Fink Verlag, 1979.

———. "The Library of a Classicizer: The Sources of Robert Holkot's Mythographic Learning." In *Arts libéraux et philosophie au Moyen Âge*, 721–29. Montreal: Institut d'Études Médiévales, 1969.

———. "Mythology in the Bible Commentaries and *Moralitates* of Robert Holkot." Ph.D. diss., Johns Hopkins University, 1963.

Alton, D. E. H., and D. E. W. Wormell. "Ovid in the Mediaeval Schoolroom." *Hermathena* 94 (1960): 21–38, 95 (1961): 67–82.

Bolent, Johannes. *Constructio Ovidii Magni*. Paris, Bibliothèque Nationale. MS lat. 16238.

Calderia, John. *Concordatia*. Rome, Vatican Library. MS Palat. lat. 985.

———. *Concordatia*. Venice, 1547.

———. Exposition on Cato's *Distichs*. London, British Library. MS Add. 15406.

De Polo, Damianus. Commentary on Ovid. Rome, Vatican Library. MS Vat. lat. 5222.

Engels, Joseph. "Berchoriana I: Notice bibliographique sur Pierre Bersuire, Supplement au Repertorium Biblicum medii aevi." *Vivarium* 2 (1964): 62–124.

———. "Berchoriana: Les Pseudo-Bersuires." *Vivarium* 3 (1965): 128–48.

———. "L'Edition critique de l'*Ovidius moralizatus* de Bersuire." *Vivarium* 9 (1971): 19–24.

———. "La Letter-dédicace de Bersuire à Pierre de Prés." *Vivarium* 7 (1969): 62–72.

———. "Note complémentaire sur les manuscrits Berchoriens de Worchester." *Vivarium* 7 (1969): 73–78.

———. "Note sur quelques manuscrits mythologiques." *Vivarium* 6 (1968): 102–7.

Ghisalberti, Fausto. "Arnolfo d'Orleans, un cultore di Ovidio nel sec. XII." *Memorie del Reale Istituto Lombardo si Scienze e Lettere* 24 (1932): 157–234.

———. "Giovanni del Virgilio espositore delle 'Metamorfosi.' " *Il giornale dantesca* 34, n.s. 4 (1933): 3–110.

Hunt, R. W. "Studies on Priscian in the Twelfth Century: The School of Ralph of Beauvais." *Mediaeval and Renaissance Studies* 2 (1950): 1–56.

Lavinius, Peter. *P. Ovidii Nasonis poete ingeniosissimi Metamorphoseos libri xv. In eosdem libros Raphaelis Regii luculentissime enarrationes. Neque non Lactantii et Petri Lavinii commentarii non ante impressi.* Venice, 1527.

Manitius, Max. *Geschichte der lateinischen Literatur des Mittelalters. Erster Teil. Von Justinian bis zur Mitte des zehnten Jahrhunderts.* 3 vols. In *Handbuch der klassischen Altertums-Wissenschaft*, vol. 9, part 2. Munich: C. H. Beck'sche, 1911–31.

Manegold, von Lautenbach [Lutterbach]. "Explicationes Metamorphoseon Ovidii." Munich. Staatsbibliothek. MSS Monacensis Latinus 4610, 144872, 14809.

Ovid. *Metamorphoses*. Anonymous Commentary, Copenhagen, Royal Library. MS Fabricius 29.2

———. *Metamorphoses*. Anonymous Commentary. London, British Library. MS Add. 15733.

———. *Metamorphoses*. Anonymous Commentary. Oxford, Merton College. MS 299.

———. *Metamorphoses*. Anonymous Commentary. Paris, Bibliothèque Nationale, MS lat. 8253.

———. *Metamorphoses*. Anonymous Commentary. Rome, Vatican Library. MS Vat. lat. 1479.

———. *Metamorphoses*. Anonymous Commentary. Rome Vatican Library. MS Ottoboni 1294.

———, *Metamorphoses*. Anonymous Summary. Vienna, Imperial Library. MS Vindob. 3379.

Ralph, of Beauvais. *Liber Titan*. London, British Library. MS Add. 16380. Fols. 111r–19v.

———. *Liber Titan*. Bern, Stadtbibliothek. MS 519. Fols. 116r–35v.

Ridewall [Ridevall], John. *Fulgentius metaforalis*. Ed. Hans Liebeschütz. In *Fulgentius metaforalis, ein Beitrag zur Geschichte der antiken Mythologie im Mittelalter*. Studien der Bibliothek Warburg, no. 4. Leipzig and Berlin: B. G. Teubner, 1926.

———. *Fulgentius metaforalis*. Oxford, Bodleian Library. MS 571.

Smalley, Beryl. *English Friars and Antiquity in the Early Fourteenth Century*. Oxford: Basil Blackwell; New York: Barnes and Noble, 1960.

Young, Karl. "Chaucer's Appeal to the Platonic Deity." *Speculum* 19 (1944): 1–13.

Bibliography

Primary Works

Alanus de Insulis. *Liber de planctu Naturae. PL* 210: 488–574.

———. *The Complaint of Nature.* Translated by Douglas M. Moffat. Yale Studies in English, no. 36. 1908. Reprint. Hamden, CT: Shoestring Press, 1972.

———. *Liber in distinctionibus dictionum theologicalum. PL* 210: 687–1014.

Albericus, of London (third Vatican mythographer). *See* Bode.

Alciati, Andrea. *Emblematum.* 1621. Reprint. New York: Garland, 1977.

Alfred, King. *King Alfred's Old English Version of Boethius: De consolatione Philosophiae.* Edited by Walter John Sedgefield. Oxford, 1899.

———. *King Alfred's Version of the Consolation of Boethius.* Translated by Walter John Sedgefield. Oxford: Clarendon Press, 1900.

Alighieri, Jacopo. *Chiose alla cantica dell'Inferno di Dante Allighieri atribuite a Iacopo suo figlio.* Florence, 1848.

———. *Chiose di Dante le quali fece el figiuolo co le sue mani: messe in luce da F. D. Luiso.* Vol. 2: *Purgatorio.* Florence: G. Carnesecchi and Sons, 1904.

Alighieri, Pietro. *Petri Allegherii super Dantis ipsius genitoris Comoediam commentarium nunc primum in lucem editum.* Edited by Vincentio Nannucci. Florence, 1845.

Allegorie Hovidii. Rome, Vatican Library. MS lat. 2877.

Anonymous Barberinus. In "Barberini Manuscripts 57–66 and 121–30," edited by Ann Rose Raia. Ph.D. diss., Fordham University, 1965.

Anonymous Florentine. *Commento alla Divina Commedia d'Anonimo Fiorentino del secolo XVI.* Edited by Pietro Fanfani. 3 vols. Bologna, 1866–74.

Anonymous of St. Gall. Commentary on Boethius. The shorter. Naples. MS IV G 68. Fols. 1r–92r. The longer. St. Gall. MS 845. Fols. 3–240.

Anonymous Selmiano. *Chiose anonime alla prima cantica della Divina Commedia di un contemporaneo del poeta pubblicate per la prima volta a celebrare il sesto anno secolare della nascita di Dante da Francesco Selmi con riscontri di altri antichi commenti editi ed inediti e note filologiche.* Edited by Francesco Selmi. Turin, 1865.

Anonymous Teutonicus. *Commentum in Theoduli eclogam e codice Utrecht, U.B. 292 editum (1).* Edited by Árpád P. Orbán. *Vivarium,* 11 (1973): 1–42; 12 (1974): 133–45; 13 (1975): 77–88; 14 (1976): 50–61; 15 (1977): 143–58.

Apollodorus. *The Library.* Translated by Sir James George Frazer. 2 vols. Loeb Classical Library. 1921. Reprint. Cambridge, MA: Harvard University Press, 1946.

Aristotle. *The Nicomachean Ethics.* In *The Basic Works of Aristotle,* edited by Richard McKeon. New York: Random House, 1941.

Arnulf, of Orleans. *Allegoriae super Ovidii Metamorphoses.* In "Arnolfo d'Orléans, un cultore di Ovidio nel seculo XII," edited by Fausto Ghisalberti. *Memorie del Reale Istituto Lombardo di Scienze e Lettere,* 24 (1932): 157–234.

———. Commentary on Ovid's *Fasti.* Rome, Vatican Library. MS Reg. 1548.

———. *Glosule super Lucanus.* Edited by Berthe M. Marti. Rome: American Academy in Rome, 1958.

Asser. Commentary on Boethius. Edited by Fabio Troncarelli. In the Appendix to *Tradizioni perdute: L'antica "Fortuna" della "Consolatio Philosophiae,"* 141–201. Padua: Editrice Antenore, 1980.

Augustine, St. *De civitate Dei contra paganos libri.* Edited and translated by William M. Green. 7 vols. Loeb Classical Library. London and Cambridge, MA: Harvard University Press, 1963.
———. *De civitate Dei libri XXII.* Revised by Bernhard Dombart and Alfonsus Kalb. Bibliotheca Scriptorum Graecorum et Romanorum Teubneriana. 5th ed. Stuttgart: B. G. Teubner, 1981.
———. *De Genesi ad litteram. PL* 34:219–485.
———. *On Christian Doctrine.* Translated by D. W. Robertson, Jr. Indianapolis: Bobbs-Merrill, 1958.
Bacon, Francis. *De sapientia veterum.* In *Works,* edited by James Spedding, Robert Leslie Ellis, and Douglas Denon Heath. Vol. 6 of 14 vols. 1870. Reprint. New York: Garrett, 1968.
Balbi, Giovanni (Joannes Balbus). *Catholicon.* 1460. Reprint facsimile. Westmead, Farnsborough, Hants, England: Gregg International Publishers, 1971.
Bambaglioli, Graziolo. *Il commento Dantesco di Graziolo de'Bambaglioli dal "Colombino" di Siviglia con altri codici raffrontato.* Edited by Antonio Fiammazzo. Savona: D. Bertolotto, 1915.
Bargigi, Guiniforto delli. *Lo Inferno della Commedia di Dante Alighieri col comento di Guiniforto delli Bargigi.* Edited by G. Zacheroni. Marseilles and Florence, 1838.
Bartholomaeus Anglicus. *On the Properties of Things (De proprietatibus rerum).* Translated by John Trevisa (1398). Oxford: Clarendon Press, 1975.
Baudri, de Bourgueil. Poem no. 216, "Fragment of a Moralized Mythology." In *Les oeuvres poétiques de Baudri de Bourgueil (1046–1139),* edited by Phyllis Abrahams, 273–316. Paris: Librairie Ancienne Honoré Champion, 1926.
Bede. *Didascalica genuina. PL* 90:123–614.
Benoit, de Sainte-Maure. *Le Roman de Troie.* Vol. 1. Edited by Leopold Constans. Paris: Librairie de Firmin Didot et Cie, 1904.
Bernard Silvestris. *The Commentary on the First Six Books of the Aeneid Commonly Attributed to Bernardus Silvestris.* Edited by Julian Ward Jones and Elizabeth Frances Jones. Lincoln and London: University of Nebraska Press, 1977.
———. *Commentary on the First Six Books of Virgil's Aeneid.* Translated by Earl G. Schreiber and Thomas E. Maresca. Lincoln and London: University of Nebraska Press, 1979.
———. *The Commentary on Martianus Capella's De Nuptiis Philologiae et Mercurii Attributed to Bernardus Silvestris.* Edited by Haijo Jan Westra. Studies and Texts, 80. Toronto: Pontifical Institute of Mediaeval Studies, 1986.
———. *Cosmographia.* Edited by Peter Dronke. Leiden: E. J. Brill, 1978.
Bernard d'Utrecht. "Bernard's *Commentum in Theodulum: Editio Princeps.*" Edited by Morton Yale Jacobs. Ph.D. diss., University of North Carolina–Chapel Hill, 1963.
———. *Commentum in Theodulum.* Edited by R. B. C. Huygens. Biblioteca degli "Studi medievali." Spoleto: Centro italiano di studi sull'alto Medioevo, 1977.
Berne Scholia. *Scholia Bernensia ad Vergilii Bucolica atque Georgica.* Edited by Hermann Hagen. Jahrbücher für classische Philol. Suppl. Vol. 4, pt. 5. Leipzig, 1867.
Bersuire, Pierre. *De formis figurisque deorum.* Cap. 1 of *Reductorium morale,* liber XV: *Ovidius moralizatus.* Edited by Joseph Engels. Utrecht: Instituut voor Laat Latijn der Rijksuniversiteit, 1966.
———. *Reductorium morale, liber XV, cap. ii–xv: Ovidius moralizatus.* Edited by Joseph Engels. Utrecht: Instituut voor Laat Latijn der Rijksuniversiteit, 1962.
———. "The *Ovidius Moralizatus* of Petrus Berchorius: An Introduction and Translation." Translated by William Reynolds. Ph.D. diss., University of Illinois–Urbana, 1971.

Boccaccio, Giovanni. *Decameron*. Edited by Vittore Branca. Milan: Mondadori, 1976.

———. *Genealogie deorum gentilium libri*. Edited by Vincenzo Romano. 2 vols. *Opere*, vols. 10–11. Scrittori d'Italia, No. 200–1. Bari: Giuseppe Laterza, 1951.

———. *On Poetry*. Translated by Charles G. Osgood. 1930. Reprint. Indianapolis: Bobbs-Merrill, 1956.

Boccaccio (False), of Roveta. *Chiose sopra Dante testo inedito ora per la prima volta pubblicato*. Edited by William Warren Vernon. Florence, 1846.

Bode, Georgius Henricus. *Scriptores rerum mythicarum latini tres Romae nuper reperti*. 2 vols. 1834. Reprint in one vol. Hildesheim: Georg Olms, 1968

Boethius, Anicius Manlius Severinus. *De consolatione Philosophiae*. Edited by L. Biehler. Corpus Christianorum, vol. 164. Turnhout: Brepols, 1957.

———. *The Consolation of Philosophy*. Translated by Richard H. Green. Indianapolis and New York: Bobbs-Merrill, 1962.

Bolent, Johannes. *Constructio Ovidii Magni*. Paris. Bibliothèque Nationale. MS lat. 16238.

Bolanzi, Giovanni Pierio Valeriano. *Hieroglyphica*. 1602. Reprint. New York: Garland, 1976.

Bryan, William Frank, and Germaine Dempster, eds. *Sources and Analogues of Chaucer's Canterbury Tales*. 1941. Reprint. Atlantic Highlands, NJ: Humanities Press, 1958.

Buti, Francesco di Bartolo da. *Commento di Francesco da Buti sopra de Divina Comedia di Dante Allighieri*. Edited by Crescentino. 3 vols. Pisa, 1858–62.

Calderia, John. *Concordatia*. Rome, Vatican Library. MS Palat. lat. 985.

———. *Concordatia*. Venice, 1547.

———. Exposition on Cato's *Distichs*. London, British Library. MS Add. 15406.

Cartari, Vicenzo. *Le imagini con la spositione de i dei de gli antichi*. Venice, 1556.

Chaucer, Geoffrey. *The Complete Poetry and Prose*. Edited by John Hurt Fisher. 2d ed. New York: Holt, Rinehart & Winston, 1989.

———. *The Riverside Chaucer*. Edited by Larry D. Benson. 3d ed. rev. from Fred C. Robinson. Boston: Houghton Mifflin, 1987.

Chrétien, de Troyes. *Erec et Enide, édité d'après la copie de Guiot (Bibl. nat., fr. 794) et publié par Mario Roques*. Paris: Champion, 1978.

Christine de Pizan. *Les Cent hystoires de Troye [Epistre Othea]*. Paris: Philippe le Noir, 1522.

———. *L'Epistre Othea*. In "Classical Mythology in the Works of Christine de Pisan, with an Edition of 'L'Epistre Othea' from the Manuscript Harley 4431," by Halina D. Loukopoulos. Ph.D. diss., Wayne State University, 1977.

———. *The Epistle of Othea*. Translated into Middle English by Stephen Scrope. Edited by Curt F. Bühler. Early English Text Society. London, New York, Toronto: Oxford University Press, 1970.

———. *The Letter of Othea to Hector, Translated, with Introduction and Interpretive Essay*. Translated by Jane Chance. Cambridge, MA: Focus Information Group, 1990.

———. *Le Livre du chemin de long estude*. Edited by Robert Püschel. 1881. Reprint. Geneva: Slatkine Reprints, 1974.

———. " 'Le Livre de la Cité des Dames' de Christine de Pisan: A Critical Edition." Edited by Maureen Cheney Curnow. Ph.D. diss., Vanderbilt University, 1975.

———. *The Book of the City of Ladies*. Translated by Earl J. Richards. New York: Persea, 1982.

———. *Le Livre de la mutacion de Fortune*. Edited by Suzanne Solente. 4 vols. Paris: A. and J. Picard, 1959–66.

———. *Oeuvres poétiques*. Edited by Maurice Roy. 3 vols. Société des Anciens Textes Français. Paris, 1886–96.

Comes, Natalis. *Mythologiae sive explicationum fabularum libri decem*. Venice, 1567. Reprint. New York: Garland, 1976.
Comfort, William Wistar, trans. *Arthurian Romances*. London: Dent; New York: Dutton, 1928.
Dante Alighieri. *La Divina Commedia*. Edited by C. H. Grandgent. Revised by Charles S. Singleton. Cambridge, MA: Harvard University Press, 1972.
―――. *The Divine Comedy*. Translated by John Sinclair. 3 vols. 1939. Reprint. New York: Oxford University Press, 1981.
Dares Phrygius. *De excidio Troiae historia*. Edited by Ferdinand Meister. Leipzig, 1873.
Dares Phrygius, and Dictys Cretensis. *The Trojan War: The Chronicles of Dictys of Crete and Dares the Phrygian*. Translated by R. M. Frazer, Jr. Bloomington: Indiana University Press, 1966.
de Boer, C. *See Ovide moralisé*
"De caeco et ejus uxore." *See* Wright, Thomas.
De Foxton, John. *Liber Cosmographiae: An Edition and Codicological Study*. Edited by John Block Friedman. Brill's Studies in Intellectual History, vol. 5. Leiden and New York: E. J. Brill, 1988.
De Polo, Damianus. Commentary on Ovid. Rome, Vatican Library. MS Vat. lat. 5222.
Digby Mythographer. "An Edition of an Anonymous Twelfth-Century *Liber de natura deorum*." Edited by Virginia Brown. *Mediaeval Studies* 34 (1972): 1–70.
Duemmler, Ernest, ed. *Poetae Latini Aevi Carolini. Poetarum Latinorum Medii Aevii*. Vol. 1, *Monumenta Germaniae Historica*. Berlin, 1881.
Ecloga Theoduli. Edited by John Gottlob Samuel Schwabe. Altenburg, 1773.
―――. *Theoduli eclogam recensuit et prolegomenis instruxit Joannes Osternacher*. In *Fünfter Jahres bericht des bischöflichen Privat-Gymnasiums am Kollegium Petrinum in Urfahr für das Schuljahr 1901/02*. Urfahr prope Lentiam: programmate Collegii Petrini, 1902.
―――. *See also* Bernard d'Utrecht.
Endt, Johann, ed. *Adnotationes super Lucanum*. Leipzig: B. G. Teubner, 1909.
Erfurt Commentator (Pseudo-John Scot). *Saeculi noni Auctoris in Boetii Consolationem Philosophiae Commentarius*. Edited by Edmund Taite Silk. Papers and Monographs of the American Academy in Rome, vol. 9. Rome: American Academy in Rome, 1935.
Florentine Commentary on Martianus Capella. Florence, Biblioteca Nazionale Centrale. MS Conventi Soppr. J. 1. 28. Fols. 50r–64v.
―――. [Selections]. Edited by Peter Dronke. In *Fabula: Explorations into the Uses of Myth in Medieval Platonism*, 114–18, 167–83. Mittellateinische Studien und Texte, vol. 9. Leiden and Cologne: E. J. Brill, 1974.
Fulgentius, Fabius Planciades. *Mitologiae*. In *Opera*, edited by Rudolf Helm. 1898. Reprint. Stuttgart: B. G. Teubner, 1970.
―――. *Fulgentius the Mythographer*. Translated by Leslie George Whitbread. Columbus: Ohio State University Press, 1971.
Furness, Horace Howard, ed. *The Variorum Hamlet*. 14th ed. Vol. 1. Philadelphia: Lippincott, 1905.
Gawain Poet. *Sir Gawain and the Green Knight*. Edited by J. R. R. Tolkien and E. V. Gordon. 2d ed. Revised by Norman Davis. Oxford: Clarendon Press, 1968.
Geoffrey, of Monmouth. *History of the Kings of Britain*. Edited and translated by Lewis Thorpe. Hammondsworth, Middlesex, England: Penguin, 1966.
Giovanni, del Virgilio. *Allegorie librorum Ovidii Metamorphoseos a magistro Johanne de Virgilio prosaice ac metrice compilate*. Ed. Fausto Ghisalberti. In "Giovanni del Virgilio espositore delle 'Metamorfosi.' " *Il giornale dantesco*, n.s. 4, 34 (1933): 3–110.

Godman, Peter, ed. *Poetry of the Carolingian Renaissance*. Norman: University of Oklahoma Press, 1985.
Gower, John. *Confessio Amantis*. In *The Complete Works*, edited by G. C. Macaulay. Vol. 2. 1901. Reprint. Grosse Pointe, MI: Scholarly Press, 1968.
———. *The English Works of John Gower*. Edited by G. C. Macaulay. Early English Text Society, 2 vols. 1900. Reprint. London, New York, Toronto: Oxford University Press, 1957.
Gregory the Great. *Moralia. PL* 75: 509–1162.
Guido, da Pisa. *Expositiones et glose super Comediam Dantis or Commentary on Dante's Interno*. Edited by Vincenzo Cioffari. Albany: State University of New York Press, 1974.
Guido, delle Colonne [Guido de Columnis]. *Historia destructionis Troiae*. Edited by Nathaniel Edward Griffin. Cambridge, MA: Medieval Academy of America, 1936.
———. *Historia destructionis Troiae*. Edited and translated by Mary Elizabeth Meek. Bloomington and London: Indiana University Press, 1974.
Guillaume, de Lorris, and Jean de Meun. *Le Roman de la Rose par Guillaume de Lorris et Jean de Meun*. Edited by Ernest Langlois. 5 vols. Société des Anciens Textes Français, vols. 117–21. Paris: Librairie ancienne Honoré Champion, 1914–24.
———. *Le Roman de la Rose*. Edited by Félix Lecoy. Les Classiques français du Moyen Age, 92, 95, 98. Paris: H. Champion, 1970.
———. *The Romance of the Rose*. Translated by Harry W. Robbins. Edited by Charles W. Dunn. New York: E. P. Dutton, 1962.
———. *The Romance of the Rose*. Translated by Charles Dahlberg. Princeton: Princeton University Press, 1971.
Hesiod. *Hesiod, the Homeric Hymns, and Homerica*. Translated by Hugh G. Evelyn-White. Loeb Classical Library. Cambridge, MA: Harvard University Press, 1936.
Holkot [Holcot], Robert. *In librum duodecim prophetas*. Oxford. MS Bodleian 722.
———. *Liber moralizationum historiarum*. In *M. Roberti Holkoth . . . In Librum Sapientiae Regis Salomonis Praelectiones CCXIII*, 705–50. Bale, 1586.
———. *Moralitates*. Venice, 1514, 1586.
———. *Super librum Ecclesiastici*. Venice, 1509.
Hollander, Robert. *The Dartmouth Project on Dante Commentaries: A Data Base*. Dartmouth: Dartmouth College, forthcoming.
Horace. *The Odes and Epodes*. Translated by C. E. Bennett. Cambridge, MA: Harvard University Press, 1914.
Horne, Herbert P., et al., eds. *Nero and Other Plays*. The Mermaid Series, vol. 8. London, 1888.
Hugutio [Huguitio; Uguccione] da Pisa. *Liber derivationum* or *Magnae derivationes*. Oxford, Bodleian Library. MS 376. Florence, Biblioteca Medicea Laurenziana. MS Pluteus XXVII Sinister, Codex 1. Fols. 1r–453v.
Hyginus. *Astronomica*. Edited by Bernard Bunte. Leipzig, 1875.
———. *Fabulae*. Edited by H. J. Rose. Leiden: A. W. Sijthoff, 1934.
———. *The Myths*. Translated and edited by Mary Grant. University of Kansas Publications, Humanistic Studies, no. 34. Lawrence: University of Kansas Publications, 1960.
Isidore, of Seville. *Etymologiarum libri XX*. Edited by W. M. Lindsay. Scriptorum Classicorum Bibliotheca Oxoniensis. 2 vols. Oxford: Clarendon Press, 1911.
John, of Garland. *Integumenta Ovidii: Poemetto Inedito del secolo XIII*. Edited by Fausto Ghisalberti. Testi e documenti inediti o rari, 2. Messina and Milan: Giuseppe Principato, 1933.
———. *Integumenta Ovidii*. Translated by Lester Kruger Born. In "The Integumenta on

the Metamorphoses of Ovid by John of Garland—First cited with Introduction and Translation." Ph.D. diss., University of Chicago, 1929.
John, Scot [Joannes Scottus]. *Annotationes in Marcianum*. Edited by Cora Lutz. 1939. Reprint. New York: Kraus Reprint Co., 1970.
Kulcsár, Péter, ed. *Mythographi Vaticani I et II*. Corpus Christianorum, Series Latina, 91C. Turnholt: Brepols, 1987.
Lactantius Firmianus. *The Divine Institutes, Books 1–7*. Translated by Sister Mary Francis McDonald. The Fathers of the Church, vol. 49. Washington, DC: Catholic University of America Press, 1964.
Lactantius Placidus. *Commentarii in Statii Thebaida et commentarius in Achilleida*. Edited by Richard Jahnke. Vol. 3 of *P. Papinius Statius*. Leipzig, 1898.
———. *Narrationes fabularum Ovidianarum*. Edited by Hugo Magnus. In *P. Ovidii Nasonis Metamorphoseon libri XV et Lactantii Placidi qui dicitur Narrationes fabularum Ovidianarum*. Berlin: Weidmann's, 1914.
Lana Bolognese, Jacopo della. *Comedia de Dante degli Allagherii col commento di Jacopo della Lana Bolognese*. Edited by Luciano Scarabelli. 3 vols. Bologna, 1866–67.
Landino, Cristoforo. *Dante con l'espositione di Cristoforo Landino, e di Alessandro Vellutelli*. Venice, 1564.
———. *Disputationes Camaldulenses*. Edited by Peter Lohe. Istituto Nazionale di Studi sul Rinascimento, Studi e Testi 6. Florence: Sansoni, 1980.
———. *Disputationes Camaldulenses*, Books 3 and 4. Translated by Thomas H. Stahel. In "Cristoforo Landino's Allegorization of the *Aeneid*: Books III and IV of the *Camaldolese Disputations*." Ph.D. diss., Johns Hopkins University, 1968.
Lavinius, Peter. *P. Ovidii Nasonis poete ingeniosissimi Metamorphoseos Libri xv. In eosdem libros Raphaelis Regii luculentissime enarrationes. Neque non Lactintii et Petri Lavinii commentarii non ante impressi*. Venice, 1527.
Lucan. *The Civil War Books I–X*. Translated by J. D. Duff. Loeb Classical Library. London, W. Heinemann; New York, G. P. Putnam's Sons, 1928.
———. *See also* Endt; Usener.
Lucian. *Lucian: in Eight Volumes*. Translated by A. M. Harmon, M. D. Macleod, et al. 8 vols. Loeb Classical Library. 1925. Reprint. Cambridge, MA: Harvard University Press, 1960–67.
Lydgate, John. *The Assembly of Gods*. Edited by O. L. Triggs. Early English Text Society, E.S. 69. London, 1896.
Machaut, Guillaume de. *Oeuvres*. Edited by Ernest Hoepffner. 3 vols. 1908–21. Reprint. New York: Johnson Reprint Co., 1965.
Macrobius, Ambrosius Theodosius. *Macrobius*. 2 vols. Edited by James Willis. Leipzig: B. G. Teubner, 1963.
———. *Commentary on the Dream of Scipio*. Translated by William Harris Stahl. Records of Civilization: Sources and Studies, no. 48. 1952. Reprint. New York and London: Columbia University Press, 1966.
———. *Saturnalia*. In *Macrobius*. Translated by Percival Vaughan Davies. Records of Civilization: Sources and Studies, no. 79. New York and London: Columbia University Press, 1969.
Manegold, von Lautenbach [Lutterbach]. "Explicationes Metamorphoseon Ovidii." Munich, Staatsbibliothek. MS Monacensis Latinus 4610, 144872, 14809.
———. "Explicationes Metamorphosen Ovidii." Edited by Meiser. In "Ueber einen Commentar zu den Metamorphoseon des Ovid." *Sitzungsberichte der philosophisch-philologischen und historischen Classe der Königliche-Bayerische Akademie der Wissenschaften zu München*, 47–89. Munich, 1885.

Map, Walter. *De nugis curialum*. Edited by Montague Rhodes James. Oxford: Clarendon Press, 1914.
Martianus Capella. *Martianus Capella*. Edited by Adolf Dick. Corrected by Jean Préaux. Bibliotheca Scriptorum Graecorum et Romanorum Teubneriana. Stuttgart: B. G. Teubner, 1969.

———. *Martianus Capella and the Seven Liberal Arts*, vol. 2: *The Marriage of Philology and Mercury*. Translated by William Harris Stahl and Richard Johnson with E. L. Burge. New York: Columbia University Press, 1977.

Martianus Capella, Anonymous Commentary on. Cambridge, Corpus Christi Library. MSS 153, 330.

Martin, of Laon (Dunchad). *Glossae in Martianum*. Edited by Cora E. Lutz. Philological Monographs no. 12. Lancaster, PA: American Philological Association, 1944.

Mythographi Vaticani. See Bode; Kulcsár.

Neckam, Alexander. Commentary on *Theodoli Ecloga*. Vatican Library. MS 1479. Fols. 15v–25r.

———. *De naturis rerum*; *De laudibus divinae sapientiae*. Edited by Thomas Wright. Rolls Series, 34. London, 1863.

———. *Super Marcianum de nupciis Mercurii et Philologie* (Books 1 and 2). Oxford, Bodleian Library. MS Digby 211. Fols. 34b–88.

Notker Labeo. *Des teutschen Werke*. Edited by Heinrich Hattemer. In *Denkmahle des Mittelalters. St. Gallens altteutsche Sprachschätze*, vol. 3. St. Gall, 1846.

———, trans. *Boethius de Consolatione Philosophiae*. In *Notkers des deutschen Werke*, edited by E. H. Sehrt and Taylor Starck. Vol. 1, pts. 1–3. Altdeutsche Textbibliothek nos. 32–34. Halle and Saale: Max Niemeyer, 1933–34.

———, trans. *Boethius, "De consolatione Philosophiae," Buch I/II–III*. Edited by Petrus W. Tax. Vol. 1–2, Die Werke Notkers des Deutschen. Tübingen: Max Niemeyer, 1986, 1988.

———, trans. *De nuptiis Philologiae et Mercurii*. In *Notkers des deutschen Werke*, edited by E. H. Sehrt and Taylor Starck. Vol. 2. Altdeutsche Textbibliothek no. 37. Halle and Saale: Max Niemeyer, 1935.

Odo, Picardus. *Liber Theodoli cum commento noviter impressus*. London, 1508.

Osbern, of Gloucester (*Glossarium Osberi*). *Thesaurus novus latinitatis, sive lexicon vetus e membranis nunc primum erutum*. Edited by Angelo Mai. In *Classicorum Auctorum e Vaticanis codicibus editorum*, vol. 8. Rome, 1836.

Ottimo Commentary on the *Divine Comedy*. *L'Ottimo Commento della Divina Commedia testo inedito d'un contemporaneo di Dante citato dagli Accademici della Crusca*. Edited by Alessandro Torri. 3 vols. Pisa, 1827–29.

Overmeyer, Kathleen. "Text, Authorship, and Use of the First Vatican Mythographer." Ph.D. diss., Radcliffe College, 1942.

Ovid [Publius Ovidius Nasonis]. *The Fasti of Ovid*. Edited and translated by Sir James George Frazer. 5 vols. London: W. Heinemann; New York: G. P. Putnam's Sons, 1931.

———. *Heroides and Amores*. Translated by Grant Showerman. Loeb Classical Library. 2d ed. Cambridge, MA: Harvard University Press; London: W. Heinemann, 1977.

———. *Metamorphoses*. Edited and translated by Frank Justus Miller. 2 vols. Loeb Classical Library, 3d ed. Cambridge, MA: Harvard University Press; London: W. Heinemann, 1977.

———. *Metamorphoses*. Translated by Mary M. Innes. Harmondsworth, Middlesex, England: Penguin, 1955.

———. *Metamorphoses*. Translated by Rolfe Humphries. Bloomington and London: Indiana University Press, 1955. Reprint, 1972.

———. *Metamorphoses*. Anonymous Commentary. Copenhagen, Royal Library. MS Fabricius 29.2.

———. *Metamorphoses*. Anonymous Commentary. London, British Library. MS Add. 15733.

———. *Metamorphoses*. Anonymous Commentary. Oxford, Merton College. MS 299.

———. *Metamorphoses*. Anonymous Commentary. Paris, Bibliothèque Nationale. MS lat. 8253.

———. *Metamorphoses*. Anonymous Commentary. Rome, Vatican Library. MS Vat. lat. 1479.

———. *Metamorphoses*. Anonymous Commentary. Rome, Vatican Library. MS Ottoboni 1294.

———. *Metamorphoses*. Anonymous Summary. Vienna, Imperial Library. MS Vindob. 3379.

———. *Tristia and Ex Ponto*. Translated by Arthur Leslie Wheeler. Cambridge, MA: Harvard University Press, 1924.

Ovide moralisé: Poème du commencement du quatorzième siècle. Edited by C. de Boer et al. *Verhandelingen der Koninklijke Akademie van Wetenschappen te Amsterdam. Afdeeling Letterkunde*. Nieuwe Reeks 15 (1915): 1–374; 21 (1920): 1–394; 30 (1931): 1–303; 37 (1936): 1–478; 43 (1938): 1–429. Reprint. 5 vols. Wiesbaden: Martin Sändig, 1966–68.

Papias, the Lombard. *Vocabulista*. Turin: Bottega d'Erasmo, 1966.

Paulus, Diaconus. *Excerpta ex libris Pompeii Festi de significatione verborum*. In *Sexti Pompeii Festi de verborum significatu quae supersunt cum Pauli epitome*, edited by Wallace M. Lindsay. 1913. Reprint. Hildesheim: Teubner, 1965.

Petrarcha, Francesco. *L'Africa*. Edited by Nicola Festa. *Edizione nazionale delle opere di Francesco Petrarcha*, vol. 1. Florence: G. C. Sansoni, 1926.

———. *Africa*. Translated by Thomas G. Bergin and Alice S. Wilson. New Haven and London: Yale University Press, 1977.

———. *Prose*. Edited by G. Martellotti et al. La letteratura italiana. Storia e testi, 7. Milan: R. Ricciardi, 1955.

Plotinus. *Complete Works*. Translated by Kenneth S. Guthrie. 4 vols. in 1. Alpine, NJ: Platonist Press, 1918.

Plutarch. *Lives*. Translated by Bernadotte Perrin. 14 vols. Loeb Classical Library. Cambridge, MA: Harvard University Press, 1914–26.

Pontanus, Jacobus. *Ex P. Ovidii Nasonis Metamorphoseon Libris XV*. 1618. Reprint. New York: Garland, 1976.

Quarles, Francis. *Emblems*. In *Complete Works*, 3 vols., edited by Alexander B. Grosart, 3:41–184. Edinburgh, 1880–81.

Rabanus Maurus. *De diis gentium*. In *De universo libri XXII*, 15.6. In *Opera omnia*. PL 111: 426–36.

Ralph, of Beauvais. *Liber Titan*. London, British Library. MS Add. 16380. Fols. 111r–19v.

———. *Liber Titan*. Bern, Stadtbibliothek. MS 519. Fols. 116r–135v.

Rambaldi da Imola, Benvenuto. *Benevenuti de Rambaldis de Imola Commentum super Dantis Aldigherij Comoediam nunc primum integre in lucem editum*. Edited by William Warren Vernon. Revised by Jacopo Philippo Lacaita. 5 vols. Florence, 1887.

Remigius, of Auxerre. *Commentum in Martianum Capellam libri I–II*, and *II–IX*. Edited by Cora E. Lutz. 2 vols. Leiden: E. J. Brill, 1962, 1965.

———. Mythological Glosses from the Commentary on Boethius. In "The Study of the Consolation of Philosophy in Anglo-Saxon England," edited by Diane K. Bolton. *Archives d'histoire doctrinale et littéraire du Moyen Âge* 44 (1977): 61–78.

Ridewall [Ridevall], John. *Fulgentius metaforalis*. Edited by Hans Liebeschütz. In *Ful-

gentius metaforalis, ein Beitrag zur Geschichte der antiken Mythologie im Mittelalter. Studien der Bibliothek Warburg, no. 4. Leipzig and Berlin: B. G. Teubner, 1926.

———. *Fulgentius metaforalis.* Oxford, Bodeian Library. MS 571.

———. Commentary on *De civitate Dei,* books 1–2, 6–7. Oxford, Corpus Christi Library. MS 186–87.

Sabinus, Georgius. *Metamorphoses seu fabulae poeticae.* 1589. Reprint. New York: Garland, 1976.

Salutati, Coluccio. *De laboribus Herculis.* Edited by B. L. Ullmann. 2 vols. Zurich: Editrice Antenore, 1951.

Sandys, George. *Ovids Metamorphosis Englished, Mythologiz'd, and Represented in Figures.* 1632. Reprint. New York: Garland, 1976.

———. *Ovid's Metamorphosis Englished, Mythologiz'd, and Represented in Figures.* Edited by Karl K. Hulley and Stanley T. Vandersall. Lincoln: University of Nebraska Press, 1970.

Serravalle, Giovanni da. *Fratris Iohannis de Serravalle translatio et comentum totius libri Dantis Aldigherii cum textu italico.* Edited by Fratris Bartholomaei A. Colle. Prato, 1891.

Servius Grammaticus. *Servii Grammatici qui feruntur in Vergilii carmina commentarii.* 3 vols. Edited by Georg Thilo and Hermann Hagen. 1881–87. Reprint. Hildesheim: G. Olms, 1961.

———. *Servianorum in Vergilii carmina commentariorum.* Edited by Edward K. Rand et al. 2 vols. Lancaster, PA: Lancaster Press, 1946.

Shakespeare, William. *The Complete Works.* Edited by Hardin Craig. Glenview, IL: Scott, Foresman and Co., 1961.

———. *The Complete Works.* Edited by Alfred Harbage et al. Baltimore: Penguin, 1969.

Statius, P. Papinus. *Statius.* Translated by J. H. Mozley. 2 vols. 1928. Reprint. London: W. Heinemann; Cambridge, MA: Harvard University Press, 1969.

———. *The Medieval Achilleid of Statius.* Edited by Paul M. Clogan. Leiden: E. J. Brill, 1968.

Suetonius. *Suetonius.* Translated by J. C. Rolfe. 2 vols. Loeb Classical Library. London: W. Heinemann, 1920.

Theodulf, of Orleans. "De libris quos legere solebam." *PL* 105:331–33.

———. *See also* Duemmler; Godman.

Trivet [Trevet], Nicholas. Commentary on Augustine's *De civitate Dei* (Books 11–23) and on Seneca. Oxford, Bodleian Library. MS 292.

———. *Exposicio super librum Boecii consolatione.* Oxford, Bodleian Library. MS Rawlinson G. 187. Fols. 46rff. Rome, Vatican Library. 562 and 563; Reg. lat. 1066; Rossian 358; Ottob. lat. 1671 and 2026.

———. Commentary on Boethius (excerpts). Edited by Charles Jourdain. In "Des Commentaires inédits de Guillaume de Conches et de Nicolas Triveth sur la Consolation de la philosopie de Bòece." *Notices et extraits des manuscrits de la Bibliothèque Impériale et autres bibliothèques* 20.2 (1862): 40–82.

———. *Commento alle "Troades" di Seneca.* Ed. Marco Palma. Temi e Testi, vol. 22. Rome: Edizioni di Storia e Letteratura, 1977.

Usener, Hermann, ed. *Scholia in Lucani Bellum civile.* Part 1: *M. Annaei Lucani Commenta Bernensia.* Leipzig, 1869.

Valerian. *See* Bolzani.

Vatican mythographers. *See* Bode; Kulcsár.

Vendôme, Matthieu de. *Comoedia Lydiae.* In *Poésies inédites du Moyen Age.* Edited by M. Edelstand du Meril. Paris, 1854.

Villena, Enrique de [Henry of Arágon]. *Los doze trabajos de Hércules.* Ed. Margherita

Morreale. Madrid: Real Academia Española Biblioteca Selecta de Clásicos Españoles, 1958.
Vincent, de Beauvais. *Speculum naturale*. Nuremberg, 1483.
Virgil (Vergil). *The Aeneid*. Translated by Frank O. Copley. 2d ed. Indianapolis: Bobbs-Merrill Co., 1975.
———. *Virgil.* Translated by H. Rushton Fairclough. 2 vols. Rev. ed. Cambridge, MA: Harvard University Press; London: W. Heinemann, 1978.
Walleys, Thomas [Waleys; "of Wales"]. Commentary on *De civitate Dei*, books 1-10. Oxford, Bodleian Library. MS 292.
Walsingham, Thomas. *Archana deorum*. Edited by Robert A. van Kluyve. Durham, NC: Duke University Press, 1968.
William, of Conches. Glosses on Boethius. Excerpts in Édouard Jeauneau, "L'Usage de la notion d'*integumentum* à travers les gloses de Guillaume de Conches." *Archives d'histoire doctrinale et littéraire du Moyen Âge* 32 (1957): 35-100.
———. Glosses on Boethius [excerpts]. Edited by J. M. Parent. In *La Doctrine de la Création dans l'École de Chartres: Étude et Textes Publications de l'Institut d'Études Médiévales d'Ottawa*, 115-21. Vol. 8. Paris: J. Vrin; Ottawa: Institut d'Études Médiévales, 1938.
———. *Glosae in Iuvenalem*. Edited by Bradford Wilson. Textes philosophiques du Moyen Âge, 18. Paris: J. Vrin, 1980.
———. *Glosses on the Timaeus.* In *Glosae super Platonem: Texte critique avec introduction, notes et tables*, edited by Edouard Jeauneau. Textes Philosophiques du Moyen Âge, no. 13. Paris: J. Vrin, 1965.
Wright, Thomas, ed. "Appendix to the Latin editions of Aesop's Fables printed in the Fifteenth Century." In *A Selection of Latin Stories, from Manuscripts of the Thirteenth and Fourteenth Centuries: A Contribution to the History of Fiction during the Middle Ages*, vol. 9. London, 1872.

Secondary Works

Allen, Don Cameron. *Mysteriously Meant: The Rediscovery of Pagan Symbolism and Allegorical Interpretation in the Renaissance*. Baltimore and London: Johns Hopkins University Press, 1970.
Allen, Judson Boyce. "The Allegorized Mythography of Johannes Calderia." In *Acta*, 4th International Congress on Neo-Latin Studies at Bologna, Italy, August 1979.
———. "Commentary as Criticism: The Text, Influence, and Literary Theory of the Fulgentius Metaphored of John Ridewall." In *Acta Conventus Neo-Latini Amstelodamensis*, edited by P. Tuynman, G. C. Kuiper, and E. Kessler, 25-47. Munich: Wilhelm Fink Verlag, 1979.
———. *The Ethical Poetic of the Later Middle Ages: A Decorum of Convenient Distinction*. Toronto, Buffalo, London: University of Toronto Press, 1982.
———. *The Friar as Critic: Literary Attitudes in the Later Middle Ages*. Nashville, TN: Vanderbilt University Press, 1971.
———. "The Library of a Classicizer: The Sources of Robert Holkot's Mythographic Learning." In *Arts libéraux et philosophie au Moyen Âge*, 721-29. Montreal: Institut d'Études Médiévales, 1969.
———. "Mythology in the Bible Commentaries and *Moralitates* of Robert Holkot." Ph.D. diss., Johns Hopkins University, 1963.
———, and Theresa Anne Moritz. *A Distinction of Stories: The Medieval Unity of*

Chaucer's Fair Chain of Narratives for Canterbury. Columbus: Ohio State University Press, 1981.

Altman, Leslie. "Christine de Pisan: First Professional Woman of Letters." In *Female Scholars: A Tradition of Learned Women Before 1800*, edited by J. R. Brink, 153–82. New York: New York University Press, 1980.

Alton, D. E. H., and D. E. W. Wormell. "Ovid in the Mediaeval Schoolroom." *Hermathena* 94 (1960): 21–38; 95 (1961): 67–82.

Arrathoon, Leigh A., ed. *Chaucer and the Craft of Fiction.* Rochester, MI: Solaris Press, 1986.

———. "For craft is al, whoso do it kan." In *Chaucer and the Craft of Fiction*, edited by Leigh A. Arrathoon, 241–328.

Avril, François. *Manuscript Painting at the Court of France: The Fourteenth Century (1310–1380).* New York: George Braziller, 1978.

Badel, Pierre-Yves. *Le Roman de la Rose au XIVe siècle: Étude de la réception de l'oeuvre.* Geneva: Droz, 1980.

Baldwin, Ralph. *The Unity of the Canterbury Tales.* Copenhagen: Rosenkilde and Bagger, 1955.

Baker, Herschel. *The Race of Time: Three Lectures on Renaissance Historiography.* Toronto: University of Toronto Press, 1967.

Baldwin, T. W. *William Shakespeare's Small Latine and Lesse Greeke.* 2 vols. Urbana: University of Illinois Press, 1944.

Barkan, Leonard. "Diana and Actaeon: The Myth as Synthesis." *English Literary Renaissance* 10 (1980): 317–59.

Basin, Thomas. *Histoire de Charles VII.* Edited and translated by Charles Samaran. 2 vols. Les Classiques de l'Histoire de France au Moyen Âge, vols. 15, 21. Paris: Les Belles Lettres, 1933, 1944.

Baswell, Christopher. "The Medieval Allegorization of the *Aeneid*: Ms. Cambridge, Peterhouse 158." *Traditio* 41 (1985): 181–237.

Battaglia, Salvatore. "La tradizione di Ovidio nel Medioevo." *Filologia romanza* 6 (1959): 185–224.

Baum, Paull F. "Chaucer's 'Glorious Legende.'" *Modern Language Notes* 60 (1945): 377–81.

Beidler, Peter. "Chaucer's *Merchant's Tale* and the *Decameron*." *Italica* 50 (1973): 266–84.

Benson, Larry, and Theodore Andersson. *The Literary Context of Chaucer's Fabliaux.* Indianapolis: Bobbs-Merrill, 1971.

Bethurum, Dorothy. *See* Loomis, Dorothy Bethurum.

Biagi, Guido. *Le novelle antiche dei codici Panciatichiano-Palatino 138 e Laurenziano-Gaddiano 193.* Florence, 1880.

Bleeth, Kenneth. "The Image of Paradise in the 'Merchant's Tale.'" In *The Learned and the Lewed*, edited by Larry Benson, 45–60. Harvard English Studies 5. Cambridge, MA: Harvard University Press, 1974.

Bloch, R. Howard. *Medieval French Literature and Law.* Berkeley: University of California Press, 1977.

Boitani, Piero, ed. *Chaucer and the Italian Trecento.* Cambridge and London: Cambridge University Press, 1983.

Bolton, Diane K. "Manuscripts and Commentaries on Boethius, *De consolatione Philosophiae* in England in the Middle Ages." B. Litt. thesis, Oxford, 1965.

———. "Remigian Commentaries on the 'Consolation of Philosophy' and their Sources." *Traditio* 33 (1977): 381–94.

———. "The Study of the Consolation of Philosophy in Anglo-Saxon England." *Archives d'histoire doctrinale et littéraire du Moyen Âge* 44 (1977): 33–78.
Bolton, W. F. "The Miller's Tale: An Interpretation." *Mediaeval Studies* 24 (1962): 83–94.
Born, L. K. "The Manuscripts of the *Integumenta* on the *Metamorphoses* of Ovid by John of Garland." *Transactions of the American Philological Association* 60 (1929): 179–99.
Bornstein, Diane. "Chivalry as a Social Code." In *Mirrors of Courtesy*, 47–62. Hamden, CT: Archon Books, 1975.
———, ed. *Ideals for Women in the Works of Christine de Pizan*. Detroit, MI: Consortium for Medieval and Early Modern Studies, 1981.
Bowden, Muriel. *A Commentary on the General Prologue to the Canterbury Tales*. 2d ed. London: Macmillan; New York: Collier Macmillan, 1967.
Bradley, Ritamary. "Backgrounds of the Title *Speculum* in Mediaeval Literature." *Speculum* 29 (1954): 100–15.
Brinkmann, Hennig. "Verhüllung ('integumentum') als literarische Darstellungsform im Mittelalter." In *Der Bergriff der Repraesentatio im Mittelalter: Stellvertretung, Symbol, Zeichen, Bild. Miscellanea Mediaevalia*, vol. 8. Berlin and New York: Walter de Gruyter, 1971.
Brown, Emerson, Jr. "*Hortus Inconclusus:* The Significance of Priapus and Pyramus and Thisbe in the *Merchant's Tale*." *Chaucer Review* 4 (1970): 31–40.
———. "Priapus and the *Parlement of Foulys*." *Studies in Philology* 72 (1975): 258–73.
Brown, Peter. "An Optical Theme in the *Merchant's Tale*." *Studies in the Age of Chaucer* 6 (1984): 231–43.
Brownlee, Kevin. *Poetic Identity in Guillaume de Machaut*. Madison: University of Wisconsin Press, 1984.
Bühler, Curt F., ed. *The Epistle of Othea*. Translated into Middle English by Stephen Scrope. Early English Text Society. London, New York, Toronto: Oxford University Press, 1970.
———. "The *Fleurs de Toutes Vertus* and Christine de Pisan's *L'Épître d'Othéa*." *PMLA* 62 (1947): 32–44.
Burgess, Glyn S. *Contribution à l'étude du vocabulaire précourtois*. Geneva: Droz, 1970.
Bush, Douglas. *Mythology and the Renaissance Tradition in English Poetry*. 1932. Rev. ed. New York: W. W. Norton, 1963.
Campbell, P. G. C. *L'Épître d'Othéa: Étude sur les sources de Christine de Pisan*. Paris: Champion, 1924.
Cerquiglini, Jacqueline. *"Un engin si soutil": Guillaume de Machaut et l'écriture au XIVe siècle*. Paris: Champion, 1985.
———. "Tension sociale et tension d'écriture au XIVème siècle: Les dits de Guillaume de Machaut." In *Littérature et société au Moyen Âge. Actes du Colloque d'Amiens des 5 et 6 mai, 1978*, 111–29. Paris: Champion, 1978.
Chance [Nitzsche], Jane. "Chaucer and Mythology." *The Chaucer Newsletter* 6:2 (Fall 1984): 1, 2.
———. "Creation in Genesis and Nature in Chaucer's *General Prologue*, 1–18." *Papers on Language and Literature* 14 (1978): 459–64. Reprint in *Modern Critical Approaches to Chaucer's 'General Prologue,'* edited by Harold Bloom, 67–71. New York: Chelsea Books, 1988.
———. " 'Disfigured is thy Face': Chaucer's Pardoner and the Protean Shape-Shifter Fals-Semblant (A Response to Britton Harwood)." *Philological Quarterly* 67 (1989): 422–33.
———. *The Genius Figure in Antiquity and the Middle Ages*. New York and London: Columbia University Press, 1975.

———. "The Medieval Sources of Cristoforo Landino's Allegorization of the Judgment of Paris." *Studies in Philology* 81:2 (1984): 45–60.
———. *The Mythographic Chaucer*. Forthcoming.
———. *The Mythographic Tradition in the Middle Ages*. Vol. 1, complete.
———. "The Origins and Development of Medieval Mythography: From Homer to Dante." In *Mapping the Cosmos*, edited by Jane Chance and R. O. Wells, Jr., 35–64, 151–59. Houston, TX: Rice University Press, 1985.
Charney, Maurice. *Style in Hamlet*. Princeton: Princeton University Press, 1969.
Chenu, M.-D. "*Involucrum:* Le mythe selon les théologiens médiévaux." *Archives d'histoire doctrinale et littéraire du Moyen Âge* 30 (1955): 75–79.
———. *Nature, Man, and Society in the Twelfth Century: Essays on New Theological Perspectives in the Latin West*. Selected, edited, and translated by Jerome Taylor and Lester K. Little. Chicago and London: University of Chicago Press, 1968.
Chydenius, Johan. *The Theory of Medieval Symbolism*. Commentationes Humanarum Litterarum, 27.2. Helsinki: Societas Scientiarum Fennica, 1960.
Clogan, Paul M. "Chaucer's Cybele and the *Liber Imaginum Deorum*." *Philological Quarterly* 43 (1964): 272–74.
Colby, Alice. *The Portrait in Twelfth-Century French Literature: An Example of the Stylistic Originality of Chrétien de Troyes*. Geneva: Droz, 1965.
Comparetti, Domenico. *Vergil in the Middle Ages*. Translated from the 2d ed. by E. F. M. Benecke. 1895. Reprint. New York, Leipzig, Paris, London: G. E. Stechert and Co. (Alfred Hafner), 1929.
Cornford, F. M. "The Origin of the Olympic Games." Chapter 7 in *Themis: A Study of the Social Origins of Greek Religion*, by Jane Ellen Harrison, 212–59. 2d ed. Reprint. Cleveland: Meridian-World, 1962.
Costello, Sister Mary Angelica. "The Goddes and God in the Troilus." Ph.D. diss., Fordham University, 1962.
Courcelle, Pierre. *La Consolation de Philosophie dans la tradition littéraire: Antécédents et postérité de Boèce*. Paris: Études Augustiniennes, 1967.
———. "Étude critique sur les commentaires de la Consolation de Boèce (IXe–XVe siècles)." *Archives d'histoire doctrinale et littéraire du Moyen Âge* 14 (1939): 5–140.
Covella, Sister Frances Dolores. "Audience as Determinant of Meaning of the *Troilus*." *Chaucer Review* 2 (1967–68): 235–45.
Coville, A. "France: Armagnacs and Burgundians (1380–1422)." In *Cambridge Medieval History*, vol. 7, edited by J. R. Tanner et al., 368–92. Cambridge: Cambridge University Press, 1958.
Cummings, Hubertis M. "Chaucer's *Prologue*, 1–7." *Modern Language Notes* 37 (1922): 86–90.
Curnow, Maureen Cheney. *See* Christine de Pizan.
Curtius, Ernst Robert. *European Literature and the Latin Middle Ages*. 1948. Translated by Willard Trask. 1953. Reprint. New York and Evanston: Harper and Row, 1963.
Danby, John F. "Eighteen Lines of Chaucer's 'Prologue.' " *Critical Quarterly* 2 (1960): 28–32.
Davis, Natalie Z. "Gender and Genre: Women as Historical Writers, 1400–1820." In *Beyond Their Sex: Learned Women of the European Past*, edited by Patricia H. Labalme, 153–82. New York: New York University Press, 1980.
Davis, Richard Beale. *George Sandys: Poet Adventurer: A Study in Anglo-American Culture in the Seventeenth Century*. New York: Columbia University Press, 1955.
de Boer, Cornelis. "Guillaume de Machaut et l'*Ovide moralisé*." *Romania* 43 (1914): 335–52.

Delaney, Sheila. *Writing Woman: Women Writers and Women in Literature, Medieval to Modern.* New York: Schocken, 1983.

Demats, Paule. *Fabula: Trois études de mythographie antique et médiévale.* Publications Romanes et Françaises, no. 122. Geneva: Droz, 1973.

de Winter, Patrick M. "Christine de Pizan, ses enlumineurs et ses rapports avec le milieu bourguignon." *Actes du 104e congrès national des sociétés savantes (1979),* 335–76. Paris: Bibliothèque Nationale, 1982.

Didron, Julien. "L'Arbre de la Vierge." *Annales archéologigues* 13 (1853): 5–15.

Donaldson, E. Talbot. "The Ending of Chaucer's Troilus." In *Early English and Norse Studies Presented to Hugh Smith in Honour of His Sixtieth Birthday,* edited by Arthur Brown and Peter Foote, 115–30. London: Methuen, 1963.

Donovan, M. J. "The Image of Pluto and Proserpina in the *Merchant's Tale.*" *Philological Quarterly* 36 (1957): 49–60.

Dornbusch, Jean. "Ovid's *Pyramus and Thisbe* and Chrétien's *Chevalier de la Charrette.*" *Romance Philology* 36 (1982): 34–43.

Dressler, Alfred. *Der Einfluss des altfranzösischen Eneas-Romanes auf die altfransösische Litteratur.* Borna-Leipzig: Robert Noske, 1907.

Dronke, Peter. *Fabula: Explorations into the Uses of Myth in Medieval Platonism.* Mittellateinische Studien und Texte, vol. 9. Leiden and Cologne: E. J. Brill, 1974.

Economou, George D. *The Goddess Natura in the Middle Ages.* Cambridge: Harvard University Press, 1972.

Edwards, Robert. "The *Book of the Duchess* and the Beginnings of Chaucer's Narrative." *New Literary History* 13 (1982): 189–204.

Ehrhart, Margaret J. *The Judgment of the Trojan Prince Paris in Medieval Literature.* Philadelphia: University of Pennsylvania Press, 1987.

———. "Machaut's *Dit de la fonteinne amoureuse,* the Choice of Paris, and the Duties of Rulers." *Philological Quarterly* 59 (1980): 119–37.

Eliade, Mircea. *Birth and Rebirth.* Translated by W. Trask. New York: Harper, 1958.

———. *Myth of the Eternal Return.* New York: Pantheon, 1954.

Elliott, Kathleen O., and J. P. Elder. "A Critical Edition of the Vatican Mythographers." *Transactions of the American Philological Association* 78 (1947): 189–207.

Engels, Joseph. "Berchoriana I: Notice bibliographique sur Pierre Bersuire, Supplement au Repertorium Biblicum medii aevi." *Vivarium* 2 (1964): 62–124.

———. "Berchoriana: Les Pseudo-Bersuires." *Vivarium,* 3 (1965): 128–48.

———. "L'Edition critique de l'*Ovidius moralizatus* de Bersuire." *Vivarium* 9 (1971): 19–24.

———. *Études sur l'Ovide Moralisé.* Groningen-Batavia: J. B. Wolters' Uitgevero-Maatschappij, 1945.

———. Introduction to *Reductorium morale, liber XV: Ovidius moralizatus, cap. i, De formis figurisque deorum,* by Pierre Bersuire.

———. "La Letter-dédicace de Bersuire à Pierre de Prés." *Vivarium* 7 (1969): 62–72.

———. "Note complémentaire sur les manuscrits Berchoriens de Worcester." *Vivarium* 7 (1969): 73–78.

———. "Note sur quelques manuscrits mythologiques." *Vivarium* 6 (1968): 102–7.

Erlich, Avi. *Hamlet's Absent Father.* Princeton: Princeton University Press, 1977.

Ferguson, Margaret W., Maureen Quilligan, and Nancy J. Vickers, eds. *Rewriting the Renaissance: The Discourses of Sexual Difference in Early Modern Europe.* Chicago: University of Chicago Press, 1986.

Finkel, Helen R. "The Portrait of Woman in the Works of Christine de Pisan." *Les Bonne Feuilles* 3 (1974): 138–51.

Fleming, John V. *The Roman de la Rose: A Study in Allegory and Iconography.* Princeton: Princeton University Press, 1969.
Fowler, James. "On Medieval Representations of the Months and Seasons." *Archaeologia* 44 (1873): 137-224.
Frank, Robert Worth, Jr. *Chaucer and the Legend of Good Women.* Cambridge, MA: Harvard University Press, 1972.
Frappier, Jean. *Chrétien de Troyes: L'Homme et l'oeuvre.* Paris: Hatier-Bovin, 1957.
———. "Variations sur le thème du miroir de Bernard de Ventadour à Maurice Scève." *Cahiers de l'Association Internationale des Études Francaises* 11 (1959): 134-58.
Freeman, Michelle. "Problems in Romance Composition, Chrétien de Troyes, and *The Romance of the Rose.*" *Romance Philology* 30 (1976): 158-68.
Friedman, John Block. *Orpheus in the Middle Ages.* Cambridge, MA: Harvard University Press, 1970.
Furnivall, F. J., E. Brock, and W. A. Clouston, eds. *Originals and Analogues of Some of Chaucer's Canterbury Tales.* London: The Chaucer Society, 1888.
Fyler, John M. *Chaucer and Ovid.* New Haven and London: Yale University Press, 1979.
Gadol, Joan Kelly. *See* Kelly-Gadol, Joan.
Gaeta, Franco. "L'avventura di Ercole." *Rinascimento* 5 (1954): 227-60.
Galinsky, G. Karl. *The Herakles Theme: The Adaptations of the Hero in Literature from Homer to the Twentieth Century.* Totowa, NJ: Rowman and Littlefield, 1972.
Gardner, Edmund Garratt. *Dante and the Mystics: A Study of the Mystical Aspect of the Divine Comedy and its Relations with Some of its Mediaeval Sources.* New York: Dutton, 1913.
Garrett, Robert Max. " 'Cleopatra the Martyr' and Her Sisters." *JEGP* 22 (1923): 64-74.
Gates, Barbara. " 'A Temple of False Goddis': Cupidity and Mercantile Values in Chaucer's Fruit-Tree Episode." *Neuphilologische Mitteilungen* 77 (1976): 369-75.
Ghisalberti, Fausto. "Arnolfo d'Orleans, un cultore di Ovidio nel sec. XII." *Memorie del Reale Istituto Lombardo di Scienze e Lettere* 24 (1932): 157-234.
———. "Giovanni del Virgilio espositore delle 'Metamorfosi'." *Il giornale Dantesca* 34, n.s. 4 (1933): 3-110.
———. "L'*Ovidius Moralizatus* di Pierre Bersuire." *Studi romanzi* 23 (1933); 5-136.
Gibson, Margaret, ed. *Boethius: His Life, Thought, and Influence.* Oxford: Basil Blackwell, 1981.
Goddard, H. C. "Chaucer's *Legend of Good Women.*" *JEGP* 7.4 (1908): 87-129; 8 (1909): 47-111.
Goldin, Frederick. *The Mirror of Narcissus in the Courtly Love Lyric.* Ithaca: Cornell University Press, 1967.
Gordon, R. K. *The Story of Troilus.* Medieval Academy Reprints for Teaching, 2. Toronto, Buffalo, London: University of Toronto Press, 1978.
Grabes, Herbert. *The Mutable Glass: Mirror-Imagery in Titles and Texts of the Middle Ages and English Renaissance.* Translated by Gordon Collier. Cambridge and New York: Cambridge University Press, 1982.
Grandgent, Charles. *Companion to the Divine Comedy.* Edited by Charles S. Singleton. Cambridge, MA: Harvard University Press, 1975.
Graves, Robert. *The Greek Myths.* 2 vols. Harmondsworth, Middlesex, England: Penguin, 1960.
Green, Richard Hamilton. "Alain de Lille's *De Planctu Naturae.*" *Speculum* 31 (1956): 649-74.
———. "Classical Fable and English Poetry in the Fourteenth Century." In *Critical Approaches to Medieval Literature: Selected Papers from the English Institute, 1958-59,*

edited by Dorothy Bethurum, 110-33. New York: Columbia University Press, 1960.
Grennan, Joseph E. "Aristotelian Ideas in Chaucer's *Troilus.*" *Mediaevalia et Humanistica* 14 (1986): 125-38.
Guichard-Tesson, Françoise. "La *Glose des Echecs amoureux*: Un savoir à tendance laïque: Comment l'interpréter?" *Fifteenth-Century Studies* 10 (1984): 229-59.
Guthrie, Shirley Law. "The *Ecloga Theoduli* in the Middle Ages." Ph.D. diss., Indiana University, 1973.
Guyer, Foster E. "The Influence of Ovid on Chrétien de Troyes." *Romanic Review* 12 (1921): 97-134, 216-47.
Hadot, Pierre. "Le Mythe de Narcisse et son interprétation par Plotin." In *Nouvelle revue de psychoanalyse,* vol. 13: *Narcisses.* Paris: Gallimard, 1976.
Hall, Louis Brewer. "Chaucer and the Dido-and-Aeneas Story." *Medieval Studies* 25 (1963): 148-59.
―――. "The Story of Dido and Aeneas in the Middle Ages." *Dissertation Abstracts* 14 (1954), 2339 (University of Pittsburgh).
Halverson, John. "Aspects of Order in the Knight's Tale." *Studies in Philology* 57 (1960): 606-21.
Hamilton, A. C. "Venus and Adonis." *Studies in English Literature* 1 (1961): 1-15.
Hannay, Margaret Patterson, ed. *Silent But for the Word: Tudor Women as Patrons, Translators, and Writers of Religious Works.* Kent, OH: Kent State University Press, 1985.
Hatinguais, Jacqueline. "Points de vue sur la volunté et le jugement dans l'oeuvre d'un humaniste chartrain (Guillaume de Conches, XIIe siècle)." In *L'Homme et son destin d'après les penseurs du Moyen Âge. Actes du premier congrès international de philosophie médiévale,* 417-29. Louvain: Éditions Nawelaerts; Paris: Beatrice-Nawelaerts, 1960.
Havely, N. R., ed. *Boccaccio—Sources of "Troilus" and the Knight's and Franklin's Tales. Chaucer Studies,* vol. 5. Woodbridge, Suffolk: D. S. Brewer; Totowa, NJ: Rowman and Littlefield, 1980.
Heisig, Karl. "Zur fränkischen Trojanersage." *Zeitschrift für romanische Philologie* 90 (1974): 441-48.
Heitmann, Klaus. "Typen der Deformierung antiker Mythen im Mittelalter: Am Beispiel der Orpheussage." *Romanistisches Jahrbuch* 14 (1963): 45-77.
Henderson, Katherine Usher, and Barbara F. McManus, ed. *Half Humankind: Contexts and Texts of the Controversy about Women in England, 1540-1640.* Urbana: University of Illinois Press, 1985.
Hexter, Ralph J. *Ovid and Medieval Schooling. Studies in Medieval School Commentaries on Ovid's Ars Amatoria, Epistulae ex Ponto, and Epistulae Heriodum.* Münchener Beiträge zur Mediävistik und Renaissance-Forschung. Munich: Arbeo-Gesellschaft, 1986.
Hindman, Sandra L. *Christine de Pizan's "Epistre Othéa": Painting and Politics at the Court of Charles VI.* Studies and Texts, 77. Toronto: Pontifical Institute of Mediaeval Studies, 1986.
Hiscoe, David. "The Earthly, the Heavenly, Separations and St. Paul's 'Thorn' in Chaucer's *Troilus.*" In *Traditions and Innovations: Essays on British Literature of the Middle Ages and Renaissance,* edited by David G. Allen and Robert A. White. University of Delaware Press, forthcoming.
Hoffman, R. L. "Mercury, Argus, and Chaucer's Arcite: *Canterbury Tales* I (A) 1384-90." *Notes and Queries* 210 (1965): 128-29.

———. *Ovid and the Canterbury Tales*. Philadelphia: University of Pennsylvania Press, 1966.

———. "Ovid and Chaucer's Myth of Theseus and Pirithous." *English Language Notes* 2 (1965): 252–57.

———. "Ovid and the Wife of Bath's Tale of Midas." *Notes and Queries* 211 (1966): 48–50.

———. "Ovid's Argus and Chaucer." *Notes and Queries* 210 (1965): 213–16.

———. "Ovid's Priapus in the Merchant's Tale." *English Language Notes* 3 (1966): 169–72.

———. "Pygmalion in the *Physician's Tale*." *American Notes and Queries* 5 (1967): 83–84.

———. "The Wife of Bath as a Student of Ovid." *Notes and Queries* 209 (1964): 287–88.

Hölgen, K. J., "Die 'Nine Worthies.'" *Anglia* 77 (1959): 279–309.

Hollander, Robert. *Boccaccio's Two Venuses*. New York: Columbia University Press, 1977.

———. *The Dartmouth Project on Dante Commentaries: A Data Base*. Dartmouth College, forthcoming.

Holzworth, Jean. "Hugutio's *Derivationes* and Arnulfus' Commentary on Ovid's *Fasti*." *Transactions of the American Philological Association* 73 (1942): 259–76.

———. "An Unpublished Commentary on Ovid's *Fasti* by Arnulfus of Orleans." Ph.D. diss., Bryn Mawr College, 1940.

Hull, Suzanne W. *Chaste, Silent and Obedient: English Books for Women, 1475–1640*. San Marino, CA: Huntington Library, 1982.

Hunt, R. W. "The Deposit of Latin Classics in the Twelfth-Century Renaissance." In *Classical Influence on European Culture AD 500–1500*, edited by R. R. Bolgar, 51–56. Cambridge: Cambridge University Press, 1971.

———. "Studies on Priscian in the Twelfth Century: The School of Ralph of Beauvais." *Mediaeval and Renaissance Studies* 2 (1950): 1–56.

Huppé, Bernard F. *A Reading of the Canterbury Tales*. Rev. ed. Albany: State University of New York Press, 1967.

Ignatius, Mary Ann. "Christine de Pizan's *Epistre Othea*: An Experiment in Literary Form." *Medievalia et Humanistica* 9 (1979): 127–42.

Jeauneau, Édouard. "La Lecture des auteurs classiques à l'école de Chartres durant la première moitié du XIIe siècle. Un témoin privilégié: Les 'Gloses super Macrobium' de Guillaume de Conches." In *Classical Influences on European Culture A.D. 500–1500*, edited by R. R. Bolgar, 95–102. Cambridge: Cambridge University Press, 1971.

———. "L'Usage de la notion d'*integumentum* à travers les gloses de Guillaume de Conches." *Archives d'histoire doctrinale et littéraire du Moyen Âge* 32 (1957): 35–100.

Jones, Ann Rosalind. "Surprising Fame: Renaissance Gender Ideologies and Women's Lyric." In *The Poetics of Gender*, edited by Nancy K. Miller, 74–95. New York: Columbia University Press, 1986.

Jung, Marc-René. *Hercule dans la littérature française du XVIe siècle: De l'Hercule courtois à l'Hercule baroque*. Travaux d'humanisme et Renaissance, no. 79. Geneva: Droz, 1966.

Kamowski, William. "A Suggestion for Emending the Epilogue of *Troilus and Criseyde*." *Chaucer Review* 21 (1987): 405–18.

Kaske, Carol V. "The Dragon's Spark and Sting and the Structure of Red Cross's Dragon Fight: *The Faerie Queene* I.xi–xii." *Studies in Philology* 66 (1969): 609–38.

Kaske, R. E. "*Sapientia et Fortitudo* as the Controlling Theme of *Beowulf.*" *Studies in Philology* 55 (1958): 423-56.

———. "The Summoner's Garleek, Oynons, and eeke Lekes." *MLN* 74 (1959): 481-84.

Keach, William. *Elizabethan Erotic Narratives: Irony and Pathos in the Ovidian Poetry of Shakespeare, Marlowe, and Their Contemporaries.* New Brunswick, NJ: Rutgers University Press, 1977.

Keen, Maurice. *Chivalry.* New Haven: Yale University Press, 1984.

Kelly, Douglas. Review of *Christine de Pizan: A Bibliographical Guide*, by Angus J. Kennedy. *Speculum* 62 (1987): 770-71.

Kelly-Gadol, Joan. "Did Women Have a Renaissance?" In *Becoming Visible: Women in European History*, edited by Renate Bridenthal and Claudia Koonz, 137-64. Boston: Houghton Mifflin, 1977.

———. *Women, History, and Theory.* Chicago: University of Chicago Press, 1984.

Kelso, Ruth. *Doctrine for the Lady of the Renaissance.* Urbana: University of Illinois Press, 1956. Reprint. 1978.

Kermode, Frank. *Shakespeare, Spenser, and Donne.* London: Routledge and Kegan Paul, 1971.

Kirkham, Victoria. "An Allegorically Tempered *Decameron.*" *Italica* 62:1 (1985): 1-23.

Kirkpatrick, Robin. "The Wake of the *Commedia*: Chaucer's *Canterbury Tales* and Boccaccio's *Decameron.*" In *Chaucer and the Italian Trecento*, edited by Pietro Boitani, 201-30. Cambridge: Cambridge University Press, 1983.

Kiser, Lisa J. *Telling Classical Tales: Chaucer and the Legend of Good Women.* Ithaca: Cornell University Press, 1983.

Kittredge, George Lymon. *Chaucer and his Poetry.* 1915. Reprint. Cambridge, MA: Harvard University Press, 1970.

Klibansky, Raymond, Erwin Panofsky, and Fritz Saxl. *Saturn and Melancholy: Studies in the History of Natural Philosophy, Religion, and Art.* London: Thomas Nelson and Sons, 1964.

Klippel, Maria. *Die Darstellung der fränkischen Trojanersage in Geschichtsschreibung und Dichtung vom Mittelalter bis zur Renaissance in Frankreich.* Marburg: Beyer und Hausknecht, 1936.

Knoespel, Kenneth. "From Poetry to Historiography: Ovid's *Metamorphoses* and Seventeenth-Century Historiography." Special Session on Ovid and Renaissance Poetry, MLA Convention. New York, December 28, 1983.

Lacy, Norris J. "Narrative Point of View and the Problem of Erec's Motivation." *Kentucky Romance Quarterly* 18 (1971): 355-62.

Ladner, Gerhart B. "Vegetation Symbolism and the Concept of Renaissance." In *Essays in Honor of Erwin Panofsky*, 2 vols., edited by Millard Meiss, 1:303-22. De Artibus Opuscula, 40. New York: New York University Press, 1961.

Lavin, Irving. "Cephalus and Procris: Underground Transformations." *Journal of the Warburg and Courtauld Institutes* 17 (1954): 260-87.

Levin, Harry. *Shakespeare and the Revolution of the Times, Perspectives and Commentaries.* New York: Oxford University Press, 1976.

Lewis, C. S. *The Allegory of Love.* London, Oxford, New York: Oxford University Press, 1936. Reprint, 1958.

Loomis, Dorothy Bethurum, ed. *Critical Approaches to Medieval Literature: Selected Papers from the English Institute 1958-59.* New York and London: Columbia University Press, 1960. Reprint. 1967.

———. "Saturn in Chaucer's *Knight's Tale.*" In *Chaucer und seine Zeit*, edited by Arno Esch, 149-61. Tübingen: Tübingen University Press, 1968.

———. "The Venus of Alanus de Insulis and the Venus of Chaucer." In *Philological Essays; Studies in Old and Middle English Language and Literature, in Honour of Herbert Dean Meritt*, edited by James L. Rosier, 182–95. The Hague: Mouton, 1970.
Lord, Mary Louise. "Dido as an Example of Chastity: The Influence of Example Literature." *Harvard Library Bulletin*, 17:1; 2 (1969): 22–44, 216–32.
Loukopoulos, Halina D. "Classical Mythology in the Works of Christine de Pisan, with an Edition of 'L'Epistre Othea' from the Manuscript Harley 4431." Ph.D. diss., Wayne State University, 1977.
Lounsburg, Thomas R. *Studies in Chaucer: His Life and Writings*. 3 vols. 1892. Reprint. New York: Russell and Russell, 1962.
Lowes, John L. "The Prologue to the *Legend of Good Women* Considered in its Chronological Relations." *PMLA* 20 (1905): 748–864.
Lubac, Henri de. *Exégèse médiévale*. Paris: Aubier, 1959–64.
Mainzer, Conrad. "John Gower's Use of the 'Mediaeval Ovid' in the *Confessio Amantis*." *Medium Aevum* 41 (1972): 215–29.
———. "A Study of the Sources of the *Confessio Amantis* of John Gower." Ph.D. diss., Oxford University, 1967.
Manitius, Max. *Geschichte der lateinischen Literatur des Mittelalters. Erster Teil. Von Justinian bis zur Mitte des zehnten Jahrhunderts*. 3 vols. In *Handbuch der klassischen Altertums-Wissenschaft*, vol. 9, part 2. Munich: C. H. Beck'sche, 1911–31.
Mathieu-Castellani, Gisele. "Acteon ou la rhétorique du mythe dans la poésie baroque." In *La Mythologie au XVIIe Siècle*. Eleventh Conference of the Centre Meridional de Rencontres sur le XVIIe Siècle (C.M.R. 17), Jan. 1981. Org. Claude Faisant. Nice: C.M.R. 17-Centre National des Lettres et de l'U. E. R., University of Nice, n.d.
McCall, John P. *Chaucer among the Gods: The Poetics of Classical Myth*. University Park and London: Pennsylvania State University Press, 1979.
———. "Classical Myth in Chaucer's *Troilus and Criseyde*: An Aspect of the Classical Tradition in the Middle Ages," Ph.D. diss., Princeton University, 1955.
McCleod, Enid. *The Order of the Rose. The Life and Ideas of Christine de Pizan*. Totowa, NJ: Rowman and Littlefield, 1976.
McGrady, Donald. "Chaucer and the *Decameron* Reconsidered." *Chaucer Review* 12 (1977): 1–26.
Meech, Sanford B. "Chaucer and the *Ovide Moralisé*: A Further Study." *PMLA* 46 (1931): 182–204.
Meiss, Millard. *French Painting in the Time of Jean de Berry: The Limbourgs and Their Contemporaries*. New York: George Braziller, 1974.
Meyer, Paul. "Les Premières compilations françaises d'histoire ancienne." *Romania* 14 (1885): 1–81.
Miller, R. N. "Pandarus and Procne." In *Studies in Medieval Culture*, edited by John R. Sommerfeldt. Kalamazoo: Western Michigan University Press, 1979.
Minnis, Alastair J. *Chaucer and Pagan Antiquity*. Woodbridge, Suffolk: D.S. Brewer; Totowa, NJ: Rowman and Littlefield, 1982.
———. *Medieval Theory of Authorship: Scholastic Literary Attitudes in the Later Middle Ages*. London: Scolar Press, 1984.
———. " 'Moral Gower' and Medieval Literary Theory." In *Gower's 'Confessio Amantis': Responses and Reassessments*, edited by Alastair J. Minnis, 50–78. Cambridge: D. S. Brewer, 1983.
Mirot, Léon. "L'Enlèvement du Dauphin et le premier conflit entre Jean Sans Peur et Louis d'Orléans." Parts 1, 2. *Revue des questions historiques*, n.s. 51 [= o.s. 95] (1914): 329–55; n.s. 52 (1914): 369–94.

Mombello, Gianni. "Per un'edizione critica dell'"Epistre Othea' di Christine de Pizan." Parts 1, 2. *Studi francesi* 8 (1964): 401–17; 9 (1965): 1–12.

———. "Quelques aspects de la pensée politique de Christine de Pizan d'après ses oeuvres publieé." In *Culture politique en France à l'époque de l'humanisme et de la Renaissance*, edited by Franco Simone, 43–153. Turin: Accademia delle Scienza, 1974.

———. *La Tradizione manoscritta dell' "Epistre Othea" di Christine de Pizan*. Memorie dell'Accademia delle Scienze di Torino: Classe di Scienze, Morali, Storiche e Filologiche, Serie 4ª, 15. Turin: Accademia delle Scienze, 1967.

Morgan, Gerald. "The Ending of *Troilus and Criseyde*." *Modern Language Review* 77 (1982): 29–32.

———. "The Significance of the Aubades in *Troilus and Criseyde*." *Yearbook of English Studies* 9 (1979): 221–35.

Moss, Ann. *Poetry and Fable: Studies in Mythological Narrative in Sixteenth-Century France*. Cambridge and New York: Cambridge University Press, 1984.

Munari, Franco. *Ovid im Mittelalter*. Zurich and Stuttgart: Artemis, 1960.

Muscatine, Charles. "Form, Texture, and Meaning in Chaucer's *Knight's Tale*." *PMLA* 65 (1950): 911–29. Reprinted in *Chaucer: Modern Essays in Criticism*, edited by Edward Wagenknecht, 60–82. New York: Oxford University Press, 1959.

Musseter, Sally. "The Education of Enide." *Romanic Review* 73 (1982): 147–66.

Nelson, William. *Fact or Fiction: The Dilemma of the Renaissance Storyteller*. Cambridge, MA: Harvard University Press, 1973.

Nicolini, Elena. "Christina da Pizzano: L'origine e il nome." *Cultura neolatina* 1 (1941): 143–50.

Nightingale [Husemoller], Jeanne A. "Chrétien de Troyes and the Mythographical Tradition: The Couple's Journey." In *King Arthur through the Ages*, 2 vols., edited by Valerie Lagorio. New York: Garland, forthcoming.

———. "Court, Cosmos, and Conjointure: A Study of Chartrian Patterns of Thought in the Imagination of Chrétien de Troyes." Ph.D. diss., Bryn Mawr College, 1985.

Nitzsche, Jane Chance. *See* Chance, Jane.

Nohrnberg, James. *The Analogy of* The Faerie Queene. Princeton: Princeton University Press, 1976.

Nordberg, Michael. *Les Ducs et la royauté: Etudes sur la rivalité des ducs d'Orléans et de Bourgogne 1392–1407*. Studia Historica Upsaliensia, 12. Stockholm: Svenska Bokförlaget, 1964.

North, J. D. *Chaucer's Universe*. Oxford: Clarendon Press, 1988.

———. "'Kalenderes Enlumyned Ben They': Some Astronomical Themes in Chaucer." *Review of English Studies*, n.s. 20 (1969): 129–54, 257–83, 418–44.

Otis, Brooke. "The Argumenta of the So-called Lactantius." *Harvard Studies in Classical Philology* 47 (1936): 131–63.

Ouy, Gilbert, and Christine M. Reno. "Identification des autographes de Christine de Pizan." *Scriptorium* 34 (1980): 221–38.

Panofsky, Dora, and Panofsky, Erwin. *Pandora's Box: The Changing Aspects of a Mythical Symbol*. London: Routledge and Kegan Paul, 1956.

Panofsky, Erwin. *Hercules am Scheidewege und andere antike Bildstoffe in der neueren Kunst*. Studien der Bibliothek Warburg, 18. Leipzig and Berlin: B. G. Teubner, 1930.

———. *The Life and Art of Albrecht Dürer*. 4th ed. Princeton: Princeton University Press, 1955.

———. *Meaning in the Visual Arts*. Garden City, NY: Doubleday, 1955.

———. Preface. In *Reductorium morale, liber XV: Ovidius moralizatus, cap. i: De formis figurisque deorum*, by Pierre Bersuire.

———. *Renaissance and Renascences in Western Art*. Figura, no. 10. Stockholm: Almquist and Wiksell, 1960.

———. *Studies in Iconology: Humanistic Themes in the Art of the Renaissance.* 1939. Reprint. New York: Harper and Row, 1967.

Panofsky, Erwin, and Fritz Saxl. "Classical Mythology in Mediaeval Art." *Metropolitan Museum Studies* 4 (1932–33): 228–80.

Parry, Hugh. "Ovid's *Metamorphoses:* Violence in a Pastoral Landscape." *Transactions and Proceedings of the American Philological Association* 95 (1964): 268–82.

Patch, Howard Rollins. *The Goddess Fortuna in Mediaeval Literature.* 1927. Reprint. New York: Octagon Books, 1967.

Pépin, Jean. *Mythe et allégorie: Les Origines grecques et les contestations Judéo-Chrétiennes.* Paris: Aubier; Editions Montaigne, 1958.

Perella, Nicholas J. *Midday in Italian Literature: Variations on an Archetypal Theme.* Princeton: Princeton University Press, 1979.

Pernoud, Régine. *Christine de Pisan.* Paris: Calmann-Levy, 1982.

Phillips, Margaret Mann. *The 'Adages' of Erasmus: A Study with Translations.* Cambridge: Cambridge University Press, 1964.

Pinet, Marie-Josèphe. *Christine de Pisan: Etude biographique et littéraire.* Paris: Champion, 1927.

Poirion, Daniel. *Le Poète et le prince: L'Evolution du lyrisme courtois de Guillaume de Machaut à Charles d'Orléans.* Paris: Presses Universitaires de France, 1965.

———. *Le Roman de La Rose.* Paris: Flammarion, 1974.

Pratt, Robert A. "Chaucer and the Visconti Libraries." *ELH* 6 (1939): 191–99.

Pulsiano, Phillip. "Redeemed Language and the Ending of *Troilus and Criseyde.*" In *Sign, Sentence, Discourse: Language in Medieval Thought and Literature*, edited by Julian N. Wasserman and Lois Roney, 153–74. New York: Syracuse University Press, 1989.

Quaglio, A. E. *Scienza e mito nel Boccaccio.* Padua: Liviano, 1967.

Quinn, Betty N. "Venus, Chaucer, and Pierre Bersuire." *Speculum* 38 (1963): 479–80.

Raith, Joseph. *Boccaccio in der englischen Literatur von Chaucer bis Painter's Palace of Pleasure.* Schrifftum und Sprache der Angelsachsen, 3. Leipzig: R. Noske, 1936.

Rand, Edward Kennard. *Ovid and his Influence.* 1925. Reprint. New York: Longmans, Green and Co., 1928.

Reiss, Edmund. "Boccaccio in English Culture of the Fourteenth and Fifteenth Centuries." In *Il Boccaccio nella cultura inglese e anglo-americana*, edited by Giuseppe Galigani, 15–26. Atti del Convegno di Studi, Certaldo, 14–19 settembre 1970. Florence: Olschki, 1974

Reno, Christine. "Feminist Aspects of Christine de Pizan's 'Epistre d'Othea a Hector.' " *Studi francesi* 71 (1980): 271–76.

Reynolds, William D. "The *Ovidus Moralizatus* of Petrus Berchorius: An Introduction and Translation." Ph.D. diss., University of Illinois–Urbana, 1971.

Richards, Earl J. "Christine de Pizan and the Question of Feminist Rhetoric." *Teaching Language through Literature* 22 (1983): 15–24.

Rigaud, Rose. *Les Idées féministes de Christine de Pisan.* Neuchatel: Attinger, 1911.

Robertson, D. W., Jr. "The Doctrine of Charity in Medieval Literary Gardens: A Topical Approach through Symbolism and Allegory." *Speculum* 26 (1951): 24–49. Reprinted in *Essays in Medieval Culture*, 22–50. Princeton: Princeton University Press, 1980.

———. "The Concept of Courtly Love as an Impediment to the Understanding of Medieval Texts." In *The Meaning of Courtly Love*, edited by F. X. Newman, 1–18. Albany: State University of New York Press, 1968.

———. *A Preface to Chaucer: Studies in Medieval Perspectives.* 1962. Reprint. Princeton: Princeton University Press, 1969.

———. "Some Medieval Literary Terminology, with Special Reference to Chrétien." *Studies in Philology* 48 (1951): 669–92.

———. "Why the Devil Wears Green." *MLN* 69 (1954): 470–72.

———. "The Wife of Bath and Midas." *Studies in the Age of Chaucer* 6 (1984): 1–20.

Robson, C. A. "Dante's Use in the *Divina Commedia* of the Medieval Allegories on Ovid." In *Centenary Essays on Dante*, by Members of the Oxford University Dante Society, 1–38. Oxford: Clarendon Press, 1965.

Rocca, Luigi. *Di alcuni commenti della Divina Commedia composti nei primi vent'anni dopo la morte di Dante*. Florence: G. C. Sansoni, 1981.

Root, Robert Kilburn, ed. *The Book of Troilus and Criseyde*. Princeton: Princeton University Press, 1926.

Rose, Mary Beth, ed. *Women in the Middle Ages and the Renaissance: Literary and Historical Perspectives*. Syracuse: Syracuse University Press, 1986.

Roseberg, Nathan Francis. "A Literary History of the Legend of the Argonautic Expedition through the Middle Ages." *Dissertation Abstracts* 14 (1954): 2339 (University of Pittsburgh).

Rubin, Deborah. *Ovid's Metamorphoses Englished: George Sandys as Translator and Mythographer*. New York: Garland, 1985.

Russo, Joseph. "Narcissus/Narkissos: The Transfiguration of a Myth." Unpublished, 1977.

Samaran, C., and J. Monfrin. "Pierre Bersuire." *Histoire littéraire de la France* 39 (1962): 1–192.

Sandkühler, Bruno. *Die frühen Dantekommentare und ihr Verhältnis zur mittelalterlichen Kommentartradition*. Münchener romanistische Arbeiten, no. 19. Munich: Mac Hueber, 1967.

Sasso, Luigi. "L'"interpretatio nominis' in Boccaccio." *Studi sul Boccaccio* 12 (1980): 129–74.

Savage, John Joseph H. "Mediaeval Notes on the Sixth *Aeneid* in *Parisinus 7930*." *Speculum* 9 (1934): 204–12.

———. "The Medieval Tradition of Cerberus." *Traditio* 7 (1949–51): 405–10.

Scherer, Margaret. *The Legends of Troy in Art and Literature*. New York: Phaidon, 1974.

Schilling, R. "L'Hercule romain en face de la reforme religieuse d'Auguste." *Revue de philologie*. 3d ser., 16 (1942): 31–57.

Schless, Howard. *Chaucer and Dante: A Revaluation*. Norman, OK: Pilgrim Books, 1984.

———. "Transformations: Chaucer's Use of Italian." In *Writers and their Background: Geoffrey Chaucer*, edited by Derek Brewer, 184–223. Athens: Ohio University Press, 1975.

Schreiber, Earl G. "Venus in the Mythographic Tradition." *JEGP* 74 (1975): 519–35.

Schulenburg, Jane. "Clio's European Daughters: Myopic Modes of Perception." In *The Prism of Sex: Essays in the Sociology of Knowledge*, edited by Julia Sherman and Evelyn Beck, 33–53. Madison: University of Wisconsin Press, 1974.

Seinaert, Edgar. *Les Lais de Marie de France: Du Conte merveilleux à la nouvelle psychologie*. Paris: Champion, 1978.

Seznec, Jean. *The Survival of the Pagan Gods: The Mythological Tradition and its Place in Renaissance Humanism and Art*. Translated by Barbara F. Sessions from the 1940 ed. New York: Harper and Row, 1953. Reprint. Princeton: Princeton University Press, 1972.

Shannon, Edgar Finlay. *Chaucer and the Roman Poets*. Harvard Studies in Comparative Literature, 7. Cambridge, MA: Harvard University Press, 1929.

Shapiro, Barbara J. *Probability and Certainty in Seventeenth-Century England: A Study of the Relationships between Natural Science, Religion, History, Law, and Literature*. Princeton: Princeton University Press, 1983.

Sheps, Walter. "Chaucer's Theseus and the *Knight's Tale*." *Leeds Studies in English* 9 (1976–77): 19–34.

Shoaf, R. A. " 'Certius exemplar sapientis viri': Rhetorical Subversion and Subversive Rhetoric in *Pharsalia* 9." *Philological Quarterly* 57 (1978): 143–54.

———. *Dante, Chaucer, and the Currency of the Word.* Norman, OK: Pilgrim Books, 1983.

Slater, D. A. *Towards a Text of the Metamorphoses of Ovid.* Oxford: Clarendon Press, 1927.

Smalley, Beryl. *English Friars and Antiquity in the Early Fourteenth Century.* Oxford: Basil Blackwell; New York: Barnes and Noble, 1960.

———. "Jean de Hesdin O. Hosp. S. Ioh." *Recherches de théologie ancienne et médiévale* 28 (1961): 283–330.

Solente, Suzanne. *Christine de Pisan.* Paris: Klincksieck, 1961. Reprinted in *Historie littéraire de la France,* 40: 335–422. Paris: Imprimerie Nationale, 1974.

Stallybrass, Peter. "Patriarchal Territories: The Body Enclosed." In *Rewriting the Renaissance: The Discourses of Sexual Difference in Early Modern Europe,* 123–42. *See* Ferguson, Margaret W.

Steadman, John M. "Venus' *citole* in Chaucer's *Knight's Tale* and Berchorius." *Speculum* 34 (1959): 620–24.

———. *Disembodied Laughter: 'Troilus' and the Apotheosis Tradition. A Reexamination of Narrative and Thematic Contexts.* Berkeley, Los Angeles, London: University of California Press, 1972.

———. "Falstaff as Actaeon: A Dramatic Emblem." *Shakespeare Quarterly* 14 (1963): 230–44.

Stock, Brian. *Myth and Science in the Twelfth Century: A Study of Bernard Silvester.* Princeton: Princeton University Press, 1972.

Storm, Melvin. "The Mythological Tradition in Chaucer's *Complaint of Mars.*" *Philological Quarterly* 57 (1978): 323–35.

———. "Troilus, Mars, and Late Medieval Chivalry." *Journal of Medieval and Renaissance Studies* 12 (1982): 45–65.

Tate, Robert B. "Mythology in Spanish Historiography of the Middle Ages and Renaissance." *Hispanic Review,* 22 (1954): 1–18.

Thomas, Antoine. "Guillaume de Machaut et l'*Ovide moralisé.*" *Romania* 41 (1912): 382–400.

Tilley, Morris P. *A Dictionary of the Proverbs in England in the Sixteenth and Seventeenth Centuries: A Collection of the Proverbs Found in English Literature and Dictionaries of the Period.* Ann Arbor: University of Michigan Press, 1950.

Tuve, Rosemond. *Allegorical Imagery: Some Medieval Books and their Posterity.* Princeton: Princeton University Press, 1966.

———. *Elizabethan and Metaphysical Imagery.* Princeton: Princeton University Press, 1947.

———. *Seasons and Months.* Paris: Librairie Universitaire, 1933.

———. "Spring in Chaucer and before Him." *Modern Language Notes* 52 (1937): 9–16.

Twycross, Meg. *The Medieval Anadyomene: A Study in Chaucer's Mythography.* Medium Aevum Monographs, n.s. 1. Oxford: Society for the Study of Mediaeval Languages and Literature, 1972.

Uitti, Karl. "A Propos de Philologie." *Litteratura* 41 (1982): 30–46.

Van Der Bijl, Maria S. "Petrus Berchorius, *Reductorium Morale, liber XV: Ovidius moralizatus, cap. ii.*" *Vivarium* 9 (1971): 25–48.

Van Kluyve, Robert A. Introduction. *Archana deorum.* By Thomas Walsingham.

Vance, Eugene. "Le Combat érotique chez Chrétien de Troyes: De la Figure à la forme." *Poétique* 3 (1972): 544–71.

Vickers, Nancy J. "Diana Described: Scattered Woman and Scattered Rhyme." *Critical Inquiry* 8 (1981): 265–79.
Vinge, Louise. *The Narcissus Theme in Western European Literature up to Early Nineteenth Century*. Lund: Gleerups, 1967.
Vitto, Cindy. "The Figure of the Virtuous Pagan in Middle English Literature." Diss., Rice University, 1985. Reprinted as *The Virtuous Pagan in Middle English Literature: A Study of St. Erkenwald and Piers Plowman*. American Philosophical Society, 1989.
Vivanti, Carrado. "Henry IV, the Gallic Hercules." *Journal of the Warburg and Courtauld Institutes* 30 (1967): 176–97.
von Bezold, Friedrich. *Das Fortleben der antiken Götter im mittelalterlichen Humanismus*. 1922. Reprint. Aalen: Otto Zeller Verlagsbuchhändlung, 1962.
Waith, Eugene M. *The Herculean Hero*. New York: Columbia University Press, 1962.
Wallace, David. "Chaucer and Boccaccio's Early Writings." In *Chaucer and the Italian Trecento*, edited by Pietro Boitani, 141–59. Cambridge: Cambridge University Press, 1983.
Warden, John, ed. *Orpheus: The Metamorphoses of a Myth*. Toronto and London: University of Toronto Press, 1982.
Warner, Marina. *Joan of Arc: The Image of Female Heroism*. New York: Alfred A. Knopf, 1981.
Wentersdorf, Karl P. "Imagery, Structure, and Theme in Chaucer's Merchant's Tale." In *Chaucer and the Craft of Fiction*, edited by Leigh A. Arrathoon, 35–62. Rochester, MI: Solaris Press, 1986.
———. "Theme and Structure in the Merchant's Tale: The Function of the Pluto Episode." *PMLA* 80 (1965): 522–27.
Wetherbee, Winthrop. *Chaucer and the Poets: An Essay on Troilus and Criseyde*. Ithaca and London: Cornell University Press, 1984.
———. *Platonism and Poetry in the Twelfth Century: The Literary Influence of the School of Chartres*. Princeton: Princeton University Press, 1972.
Wheeler, Bonnie. "Dante, Chaucer, and the Ending of *Troilus and Criseyde*." *Philological Quarterly* 61 (1982): 205–23.
Wilkins, Ernest Hatch. "Descriptions of Pagan Divinities from Petrarch to Chaucer." *Speculum* 32 (1957): 511–22.
Willard, Charity Cannon. "Christine de Pizan: The Astrologer's Daughter." In *Mélanges à la mémoire de Franco Simone: France et Italie dans la culture européenne, I, Moyen Âge et Renaissance*, 95–111. Geneva: Slatkine, 1980.
———. *Christine de Pizan: Her Life and Works*. New York: Persea Books, 1984.
Williams, Clem C., Jr. "A Case of Mistaken Identity: Still Another Trojan Narrative in Old French Prose." *Medium Aevum* 53 (1984): 59–72.
Williams, Lynn Flickinger. "The Gods of Love in Ancient and Medieval Literature as Background of John Gower's *Confessio Amantis*." Ph.D. diss., Columbia University, 1967.
Wind, Edgar. " 'Hercules' and 'Orpheus': Two Mock-Heroic Designs by Dürer." *Journal of the Warburg Institute* 2 (1938–39): 206–18.
———. *Pagan Mysteries in the Renaissance*. 1958. Rev. ed. London: Faber and Faber, 1967.
Wisman, Josette A. "Manuscrits et éditions des oeuvres de Christine de Pisan." *Manuscripta* 21 (1977): 144–53.
Witlieb, Bernard L. "Chaucer and the *Ovide Moralisé*." Ph.D. diss., New York University, 1969.
Wittig, Joseph S. "The Aeneas-Dido Allusion in Chrétien's *Erec et Enide*." *Comparative Literature* 22 (1970): 237–53.

Woodbridge, Linda, ed. *Women and the English Renaissance: Literature and the Nature of Womankind, 1540-1620*. Urbana: University of Illinois Press, 1984.

Wüst, Ernst. "Paris." In *Real-Encyclopädie der classischen Altertumswissenschaft*, edited by A. Pauly and G. Wissowa, cols. 1494-1501. Vol. 18, part 4. Waldsee: Alfred Druckenmüller, 1949.

Yenal, Edith. *Christine de Pisan: A Bibliography of Writings by Her and About Her*. Metuchen, NJ: Scarecrow, 1982.

Young, Karl. "Chaucer's Appeal to the Platonic Deity." *Speculum* 19 (1944): 1-13.

Contributors

JUDSON BOYCE ALLEN was professor of medieval English literature at the University of Florida, Gainesville, when he passed away in mid-1985. His books include *The Friar as Critic: Literary Attitudes in the Later Middle Ages* (Vanderbilt University Press, 1971); with Theresa Anne Moritz, *A Distinction of Stories: The Medieval Unity of Chaucer's Fair Chain of Narratives for Canterbury* (Ohio State University Press, 1981); and *The Ethical Poetic of the Later Middle Ages: A Decorum of Convenient Distinction* (University of Toronto Press, 1982). At the time of his death he was at work at two books, on Langland's use of Hugh of St. Cher in *Piers Plowman* and on a psychoanalytic reading of medieval first-person discourses.

JANE CHANCE is professor of English at Rice University, where she has taught since 1973. Author of *The Genius Figure in Antiquity and the Middle Ages* (Columbia University Press, 1975), *Tolkien's Art: A "Mythology for England"* (Macmillan Press Ltd. / St. Martin's Press, 1979), and *Woman as Hero in Old English Literature* (Syracuse University Press, 1986), she has also coedited *Mapping the Cosmos* (Rice University Press, 1985) and *Approaches to Teaching Sir Gawain and the Green Knight* (Modern Language Association, 1986). Her translation of Christine de Pizan's *Epistre Othea* will appear in 1990 in a series she is editing for Focus Information Group entitled the Focus Library of Medieval Women. She has recently completed a new book, *The Mythographic Chaucer*, and the first volume of *The Mythographic Tradition in the Middle Ages*.

GEORGE D. ECONOMOU, professor and department chair of English at the University of Oklahoma, has published many articles on modern and medieval poetry, and has written and edited five books on medieval literature, including *The Goddess Natura in Medieval Literature*. He has also published seven books of poetry and translation. After receiving his Ph.D. from Columbia University in 1967, he taught at the Brooklyn Center of Long Island University for twenty-two years and as visiting faculty at Hunter College and Columbia. He lives in Norman, Oklahoma, and Wellfleet, Massachusetts, with his wife, poet-playwright Rochelle Owens.

MARGARET J. EHRHART is an associate professor of English at Edward Williams College, Fairleigh Dickinson University. She is the author of *The Judgment of the Trojan Prince Paris in Medieval Literature* (University of Pennsylvania Press, 1987), and recipient of a *Choice* "Notable Book" award. She has also published articles on the Old English *Genesis B* and the narrative poetry of Guillaume de Machaut. She is at work on a book on Machaut's narrative poetry, as well as a long-term project on ancient Greece in the medieval imagination.

JUDITH L. KELLOGG received her Ph.D. in comparative literature and medieval studies from the University of California at Berkeley. She is now associate professor of English at the University of Hawaii at Manoa. She holds a special interest in continental backgrounds to Chaucer and has published on the *Chanson de Roland*, Chrétien de Troyes, Chaucer, and Middle English romance.

JEANNE A. NIGHTINGALE received her Ph.D. from Bryn Mawr College in 1985 and was a Charles Phelps Taft Postdoctoral Fellow at the University of Cincinnati in the Department of Romance Languages and Literatures. She is now teaching French at Miami University in Oxford, Ohio. Her dissertation is a study of the patterns of allusion to Latin scholarly poetry found in French courtly romance. Among her publications present and forthcoming are articles on the French quest romances as adventures in interpretation, Chrétien's *Erec et Enide* and Martianus Capella, feminine speaking and poetic resolution in French courtly romance, and, with Sue Farrier (for Garland Press), a *Bibliography of Charlemagne in History, Legend, and Literature*. She is revising her dissertation for publication as a book.

PATRICIA R. ORR, who has taught history at the University of Houston, was recently offered the Clifford Lefton Lawrence award for excellence in the writing of British history for her Rice University dissertation. In that study she investigates women's rights in the king's courts of justice in thirteenth-century England. She has delivered papers at various conferences, on medieval rape, widows' property rights, the King's Peace, trial by jury after the loss of trial by ordeal, and this essay (in different form) on the *Troilus*; she has also reviewed for *Speculum*. She is now working on the origins of the jury and its effect on women as victims of crime.

WILLIAM D. REYNOLDS is professor of English at Hope College. He received his M.A. from Columbia and his Ph.D. from the University of Illinois and has published articles on Pierre Bersuire and *Beowulf* as well as Tolkien, Dorothy L. Sayers, and detective fiction.

DEBORAH D. RUBIN received her Ph.D. from Yale in 1984 and is associate professor of English and Women's Studies at the University of Oklahoma. She has published *Ovid's Metamorphoses Englished: George Sandys as Translator and Mythographer* (Garland, 1985) and is currently working on a book, *Remembering Magdalene Herbert: Four Men's Construction of a Renaissance Woman*.

JANET L. SMARR, associate professor of comparative literature at the University of Illinois, Urbana, is the award-winning translator of *Italian Renaissance Tales* (Solaris Press, 1983) and author of *Boccaccio and Fiammetta: The Narrator as Lover* (University of Illinois Press, 1986) and articles on Italian and English literature from the fourteenth to the seventeenth centuries.

Contributors

THEODORE L. STEINBERG is a professor in the Department of English at the State University College of New York at Fredonia, specializing in medieval and Renaissance literature. He has published on Spenser, Lyle, medieval Hebrew writers like Ibn Gabirol and Yahuda Halevi, and Yiddish literature. At present he is completing a book on Langland's use of biblical literature in *Piers Plowman.*

MELVIN STORM teaches Old and Middle English literature and language at Emporia State University. Of great mythographic interest, among his articles in *Modern Language Quarterly, Philological Quarterly, Journal of Medieval and Renaissance Studies, PMLA,* and *Chaucer Review,* are his studies of the figure of Mars in the poems of Chaucer.

Index

Abelard, Peter, 51
Achilleid: tenth-century scholia on, 10
Achilles: in Chaucer's *House of Fame*, 216; in Christine de Pizan's *Epistre Othea*, 110
Acrisius, 269
Actaeon, 30, 273n.10; in Gower's *Confessio Amantis*, 273n.10; in Ovid's *Metamorphoses*, 29, 263; in Ovid's *Tristia*, 262; in Sandys's *Ovids Metamorphosis Englished*, 29, 258–65, 267, 270, 271
Adanan the Scot (first Vatican mythographer?), 10, 178
Admetus, 87, 91
Adonis, 30; in Shakespeare's *Venus and Adonis*, 28, 235–44
Aegeus, 216
Aeneas, 7, 25, 132, 168–69; in Bernard Silvestris's *Commentum super sex libros Eneidos Virgilii*, 162; in Chaucer's *House of Fame*, 215–16; in Chrétien de Troyes's *Erec et Enide*, 72–75; in Cristoforo Landino, 162
Aeolus, 178, 191n.4
Aesop, 251
Aglauros, 117
Ajax, 110
Alanus de Insulis, 3, 20, 51
 Anticlaudianus: as convergence of allegorical and commentary traditions, 19; Nature in, 14
 De planctu Naturae: Chrétien de Troyes's *Erec et Enide*, parallels with, 53–57; *conjunctura* (use of term), 56; convergence of allegorical and commentary traditions, 14; Faith and Prudentia (allegorical figures) in, 69; Macrobius's influence on, 6, 13; Narcissus, allusion to Ovid's description of, 79n.23; Nature in, 14, 61, 78n.14, 80n.31; poetic images, ambiguity of, 79n.23; Venus in, 235–36
Distinctiones, 201
Albert the Great, 85

Albigensian heresies, 188
Alcathoe, 216, 217
Alceste, 87, 102
Alcione, 116
Alexander Neckam: commentary on *Ecloga Theoduli*, 11; *De naturis rerum*, 9, 79n.29
Alexander the Great, 112
Allegorie Hovidii, 285
Androgeus, 216
Andromache, 116–17
Andromeda, 85, 267
Anima mundi, 13–14. See also World Soul
Anonymous of St. Gall, 10
Antenor, 110
Aphrodite, 265, 268, 274n.16. See also Venus
Apollo, 3, 60; in Bersuire's *De formis figurisque deorum*, 87; in Ovid's *Metamorphoses*, 268; in *Ovidius moralizatus*, 120n.17; in Petrarch's *Africa*, 87; in Ridewall's *Fulgentius moralizatus*, 86
Apollodorus, 274n.16
Apostle's Creed, 103, 107–8, 133, 143
Apuleius, 152n.15, 189–90
Aquinas, St. Thomas, 85, 185
Arachne, 117
Arethusa, 106
Argonauts, 7
Argus, 202, 208–10; in Bersuire's *Ovidius moralizatus*, 91–92
Ariadne, 27, 30; in Chaucer's *Legend of Good Women—Ariadne*, 215–23; in classical source, 220–21
Aristotelian philosophy: influence on Macrobian theory, 16; in Jean de Meun's *Roman de la Rose*, 19
Aristotle, 161; on contemplative life, superiority of, 162; influence of, on empiricism, 19; translations of, influenced Ovid commentary, 11
 Nicomachaean Ethics: as source for Chaucer's *Troilus and Criseyde*, 170
Arnulf of Orleans, 20, 30, 76n.8, 230n.10,

Arnulf of Orleans (*continued*)
  281; Ovid's philosophy of cosmic metamorphosis in, 51; textual history of, 283–85
  Allegoriae super Ovidii Metamorphosin, 76n.10, 84
  commentary on Ovid's *Fasti*, 178
  Glosule super Lucanus, 10, 48, 84
  influence of: on Boccaccio and Chaucer, 192n.6; on Giovanni del Virgilio's *Allegoriae librorum Ovidii*, 85; on *Ovide moralisé*, 96n.8
Arthur, King, 55, 67, 73; as one of Nine Worthies, 112–13
Asser, 10
Astraeus, 178
Atalanta, 258, 265, 270, 274n.16; in Bacon's *De sapientia veterum*, 266–67; in Christine de Pizan's *Epistre Othea*, 116; in Ovid's *Metamorphoses*, 268; in Sandys's *Ovids Metamorphosis Englished*, 266–68
Athamas, 110
Athena, 102, 268. *See also* Minerva; Pallas
Atlas, 88, 252, 266
Augustine: and allegorical principles, 120n.18; quoted by Bersuire, 90; quoted by Christine de Pizan, 142
  Confessions, 212n.17
  De civitate Dei (City of God), 9, 24, 243
  De Genesi ad litteram, 207–8
Augustus, Caesar, 109, 112–23, 114
Aurora, 178

Bacchus, 60, 220; in Bersuire's *De formis figurisque deorum*, 87; in Bersuire's *Ovidius moralizatus*, 91; in Ovid's *Fasti*, 27; in William of Conches, 14
Bacon, Francis
  De sapientia veterum: Atalanta in, 266–67; influence of, on Sandys's *Ovids Metamorphosis Englished*, 272n.4, 273n.10; political reading of myth in, 29
Balbi, Giovanni, 10, 178
Bartholomaeus Anglicus (Anglicanus): *De proprietatibus rerum*, 87, 205, 212n.15
Basin, Thomas, 141
Baudri de Bourgeuil, 10
Bede: *Didascalia genuina*, 191n.3
Belides, 87
Benoit de St. Maure: *Roman de Troie*, 164

Berchorius, Petrus. *See* Bersuire, Pierre
Bernard, St., 90
Bernard de Clairvaux, 51
Bernard d'Utrecht, 11
Bernard Silvestris, 164, 281; Aeneas in, 170; influence of, on Chaucer's *Troilus and Criseyde*, 236; Venus in, 236; and Virgil commentary tradition, 9, 74
  Commentum super sex libros Eneidos Virgilii: Judgment of Paris in, 161–62
  Cosmographia: Macrobius's influence on, 6
Berne Scholiast, 9
Bersuire, Pierre (Petrus Berchorius), 18, 20, 30, 273n.10, 281; and ecclesiastical reform, 18; iconographic and literary gloss traditions, convergence of, in work of, 21; influence of, literary, 93–95; influence of, on visual arts, 92–93; life and career of, 86–87, 87–88; mythographic tradition, place in, 83; sources of, 282; textual history and problems of, 83–84, 284
  Breviarium morale, 87
  Cosmographia, 87
  De formis figurisque deorum, 87–91
  Livy: translation into French of, 87
  Ovidius moralizatus, 25, 83–97, 273n.11; audience of, 125; iconography and mythography blended in, 22; method in, 91–92, 120n.17; *Ovide moralisé*, relation to, 83; purpose of, 88–92; quotations as prooftexts in, 89 90; textual history and problems, 82, 95–96; Zephirus in, 26
  —influence of, 22, 83, 92–97; on Chaucer's *Troilus and Criseyde*, 164, 170; on Christine de Pizan's "Because I have no comfort from Juno," 150; on Christine de Pizan's *Epistre Othea*, 105–8; on Gower's *Confessio Amantis*, 97n.20
  —sources for, 87–88; *Ovide moralisé*, 105, 120n.14; Petrarch's *Africa*, 87
  Reductorium morale, 83, 86, 89, 105, 120n.14; audience of, 89–91; Mercury in, 202–3, 206, 212n.11; Proserpina in, 212n.11; sources for, 87; Zephirus in, 179
Bible, 14
bird imagery: in Shakespeare's *Venus and Adonis*, 240

Index

Boccaccio, Giovanni, 4, 17, 20, 21, 30; Chaucer's use of, 17, 216; lectures of, on Dante's *Inferno*, 185; use of sources in, 200
  Comedia delle ninfe fiorentine: influence of, on Chaucer's *Merchant's Tale*, 210; Mercury in, 204
  Decameron, 20–21; blindness in, 206–10; garden / womb connection in, 201–2; influence of, on Chaucer's *Merchant's Tale*, 26, 199–210; Mercury in, 202–6
  —sources for: *Comoedia Lydiae*, 209; *Roman de la Rose*, 26
  Il Filostrato: influence of, on Chaucer's *Troilus and Criseyde*, 25, 164, 165
  Genealogie deorum gentilium, 21, 25, 27; convergence of epic and commentary traditions in, 12; Mars in, 230n.10; Mercury in, 203–4, 211; Pallas in, 165; Phaedra in, 220; Pluto and Proserpina in, 204; Saturn in, 205–6; Venus in, 230n.10, 236, 238; Zephirus in, 26, 178, 183, 184, 191n.6
  —influence of, 88; on Chaucer's *Merchant's Tale*, 26; on Chaucer's *Troilus and Criseyde*, 162
  —sources for, 178
  Teseida: as source for Chaucer's *Legend of Good Women—Ariadne*, 217, 223
Boethius, 7, 12
  De consolatione Philosophiae, 9, 12–13, 68, 69, 78n.25, 79n.25, 131, 159; Hercules in, 247; translations of, 10, 18; Zephirus in, 179, 181
  —commentaries and glosses on, 10, 11; by Asser, 10; by Nicholas Trivet, 24; by Notker Labeo, 19; Old High German, 18; by Remigius of Auxerre, 10; by University of Paris scholars, 19
  —influence of: on Alanus de Insulis's *De planctu Naturae*, 78n.14; on Chaucer's *General Prologue to the Canterbury Tales*, 179; on Chrétien de Troyes's *Erec et Enide*, 68; on Christine de Pizan's "Because I have no comfort from Juno," 128; on John of Salisbury's *Policraticus*, 76n.10
Bolent, Johannes: *Constructio Ovidii Magni*, 284
Bolzani, Valeriano, 29, 272n.4
Bonaventure, St., 185
Breviari d'amour, 205

Brutus: legend of, 169
Budé: *Institution du prince*, 247

Cacus, 247
Caesar Augustus, 109, 112–13, 114
Calderia, John, 30; *Concordatia*, 285–86; list of works by, 288n.14
Calliope, 181
Callisto, 30, 268, 273n.10; in Ovid's *Metamorphoses*, 29, 263; in Sandys's *Ovids Metamorphosis Englished*, 29, 258–65, 267, 271
cardinal virtues, 103
Cartari, Vincenzo: *Le imagini con la spositione de i dei de gli antichi*, 237–38, 239
Cassandra, 115
Cato: *Distichs*, 284
Cerberus, 7, 86
Ceres, 30, 32n.7, 33n.7; in Christine de Pizan's *Epistre Othea*, 107–8, 115–16; in *Ovide moralisé*, 106–7; in *Ovidius moralizatus*, 105–6; in William of Conches, 14
Ceys, 116
Chain of Being, 68
charity, 103
Charlemagne, 112
Charles V, King of France, 100; as wise king, in Christine de Pizan's *Livre du chemin de long estude*, 147, 149
Charles VI, King of France, 92, 132; Christine de Pizan's *Livre du chemin de long estude* dedicated to, 147, 149; moral laxity at court of, 141–42
Charles of Orleans, 141
Charon, 32n.6
Chartres: Neoplatonist poets of, 51
Chaucer, Geoffrey, 3–4, 16, 17, 18, 21, 23, 24, 25, 30, 31, 244; iconographic description in, Bersuire's influence on, 22; journeys to Italy by, 185; and mythographic tradition, 24–27; use of sources in, 17, 20, 185, 200
  Anelida and Arcite: Theseus in, 215, 225
  Boece: Zephirus in, 179
  Book of the Duchess: Macrobian use of myth in, 177–78; Zephirus in, 26, 180–81, 185
  The Canterbury Tales, 3–4; date, 222–23; Macrobian use of myth in, 177–78; Theseus in, 26

Chaucer, Geoffrey (*continued*)
  Franklin's Tale, 208, 222
  General Prologue: Zephirus in, 177–90
  —sources for, 192n.7; Boethius's *De consolatione Philosophiae*, 179; Dante's *Paradiso*, 26, 189–90
  Knight's Tale: Theseus in, 215, 216, 222–29
  —sources for: Bersuire, 94–95; Boccaccio's *Teseida*, 27, 217, 223; Statius's *Thebaid*, 220
  Manciple's Tale, 3, 4
  Merchant's Tale, 217; blindness in, 206–10; garden/womb connection in, 201–2; Mercury in, 202–6; Pluto and Proserpina in, 203, 204
  —sources for, 211n.9; Boccaccio's *Comedia delle ninfe fiorentine*, 210; Boccacci's *Decameron*, 26, 199–210; Boccaccio's *Genealogie deorum gentilium*, 26; *Comoedia Lydiae*, 209; *novellino* "De caeco et ejus uxore," 209–10; *Roman de la Rose*, 26
  Miller's Tale, 248
  Monk's Tale: Hercules in, 28, 246–47
  Nun's Priest's Tale: Macrobius's influence on, 6
  Parson's Prologue, 3
  Reeve's Tale, 27, 221
  Complaint of Mars, 4, 225
  House of Fame, 169; Bersuire as source for, 94–95; Theseus in, 215–16, 227, 228
  Legend of Good Women: date of, 222–23
  Ariadne: Phaedra in, 217–22; Theseus in, 27, 215–23, 225–29; tone of, 217, 221–22
  —sources for, 216–17, 220–21; Boccaccio's *Teseida*, 217, 223; Ovid's *Heroides*, 218
  Hypsipyle: Hercules in, 28, 247
  Hypermnestra: Zephirus in, 26, 182–83
  Phyllis: Theseus in, 215
  Prologue, 222; Zephirus in, 26, 182
  Parlement of Foules, 4, 237
  Treatise on the Astrolabe, 20
  Troilus and Criseyde, 159–71, 222; date of, 222–34; dedication to Ovid and Virgil, 168–69; Judgment of Paris in, 159–71; Macrobian use of myth in, 177; political issues in, 25; Zephirus in, 26, 181–82
  —sources for, 25; Aristotle's *Nicomachaean Ethics*, 170; Boccaccio's *Genealogie deorum gentilium*, 162; Boccaccio's *Il Filostrato*, 164, 165; Ovid, 170; *Ovide moralisé*, 162–64, 168, 170; *Ovidius moralizatus*, 164, 170; Petrarch's *De viribus illustribus*, 162; Petrarch's Sonnet 88, 164
chevalerie, 140–41; in Christine de Pizan's *Epistre Othea*, 137, 138, 142–44, 148–49; in Guillaume de Machaut's *Dit de la fonteinne amoureuse*, 130–31, 137, Pallas associated with, 146. *See also* chivalric ethics; courtly love
chivalric ethics, 111; association with Pallas of, 146; in Christine de Pizan's *Epistre Othea*, 115, 117, 118, 133, 136–38, 140–41, 142–44, 148–49; in Christine de Pizan's *Livre du chemin de long estude*, 144
Chrétien de Troyes, 18, 23, 25; French, reasons for writing in, 21; myth as vehicle for Neoplatonism in, 21; romance and mythographic traditions, convergence of, in, 19
  Cligès: list of Chrétien's works in, 50, 76n.6
  Erec et Enide, 47–80; Alanus de Insulis's *De planctu Naturae*, parallels with, 53; commentary tradition, use of, 17; courtly love in, 53, 56, 57, 59–60; Erec's motivation in, 67–72; Enide as *femme-image* and *femme-langage*, in, 70–71; Enide compared with Dido and Lavinia in, 73; *integumentum* in, 69–70; Macrobian use of Ovid in, 22; Macrobius, reference to, 49–50; Martianus Capella's *De nuptiis Philologiae et Mercurii*, parallels with, 80n.33; metamorphosis in, 66; mirror symbolism in, 59–63, 65, 69–70; Narcissus, Ovid's description of, parallels with Enide, 60
  —sources for: *Conte d'Erec*, 47; Ovid, 50, 63, 76n.6
  Perceval: influence of, on Guillaume de Lorris, 62
  Philomela: Ovid as source for, 75n.6
Christine de Pizan, 4, 18, 21, 25, 30, 31;

Index   325

courtly love, attitudes about, 100–101; as court poet, 23, 125, 131, 148; father of, court astrologer to Charles V, 145; and feminism, 18, 101–2; French, reasons for writing in, 21; intellectual and social attitudes of, 100–101; Judgment of Paris in, 125–53; life and career of, 100; lyric poetry of, 100; manuscript illuminations in, 24, 120n.20; misogyny, attitudes about, 100–101; myth, political and moral uses of, 21; use of sources in, 17, 20, 125–26, 132
"Because I have no comfort from Juno" (*balade*), 125–26, 126–31, 136, 142, 146–48; Guillaume de Machaut's *Dit de la fonteinne amoureuse* as source for, 146; other sources of, 128–31
Epistre Othea, 100–122, 125, 132–44; audience for, 103, 104, 136, 137, 138–40, 141, 142–44; chivalric ethics in, 115, 117, 118, 133, 136–38, 140–41, 142–44, 148–49; as commentary on Ovid, 20; courtly love in, 117; dedication to Louis of Orleans, 138, 141–42, 150n.11; female prophets in, 109, 112–13, 114, 121n.23; Judgment of Paris in, 23–24, 125–26, 132–44, 148; manuscript illuminations of, 138, 139–40; masculine orientation of, 114; method in, 101–22; misogyny opposed in, 117–18; mythographic, chivalric handbook, and romance traditions blended in, 23, 101–2, 108; popularity of, 101, 118n.3; role of women in, 114–18; structure of, 102–5, 107–8, 108–9, 114, 133, 140, 143; textual history and problems of, 151n.11; time, pagan and Christian, in, 108–9, 112–14; as vernacular imitation of glossed classical texts, 140
—sources, 23, 119n.8, 119n.9, 135–38; Guillaume de Machaut's *Dit de la fonteinne amoureuse*, 143, 153n.24; *Ovide moralisé*, 105, 143; *Ovidius moralizatus*, 105
Livre de la Cité des Dames, 101, 118; feminism in, 121n.30; Sibyls in, 121n.23
Livre de la mutacion de Fortune, 125
Livre du chemin de long estude, 144–49; audience for, 148–49; chivalric ethics

in, 144; debate format of, 147; dedication of, to Charles VI, 144, 149; deities in, astrological and planetary treatment of, 24; French nobility, relation to Trojans, 132–33; Judgment of Paris in, 23–34, 125–26, 144–49; Sibyls in, 121n.23; sources for, 23, 144
Chronos, 32n.6
Cicero: *Somnium Scipionis*, 5, 12, 49, 90
Cité des Dames Master, 138
Claudian: *Epithalamium de nuptiis Honorii Augustii*, 95
Clement of Alexandria: *Pedagogus*, Narcissus in, 78n.18
clergie, 103–31, 140
Comes, Natalis, 29, 30, 271; as source for Sandys's *Ovids Metamorphosis Englished*, 272n.4
  Mythologiae sive explicationum fabularum libri decem: Venus in, 237–38, 239
Comoedia Lydiae, 209, 210n.9, 212n.12
conjointure: Chrétien's use of term, 22, 56
conjunctura: Alanus de Insulis's use of term, 55
Conte d'Erec, 47, 67
Coronis, 3, 4, 274n.19
courtly love: in Chrétien de Troyes's *Erec et Enide*, 22, 56; in Christine de Pizan's *Epistre Othea*, 111, 115, 117; Christine de Pizan's opposition to, 101
courtly love lyric: mirror symbolism in, 57; role of lady in, 72
Creon, 224
Cupid, 7, 19, 117, 184
Cybele, 14, 87, 286
Cypria: Judgment of Paris in, 149n.3; Pallas in, 152n.15

Danae, 268; in Horace's Ode, 16, 269–70; in Lactantius, 269; in Ovid's *Metamorphoses*, 85; in Ridewall's *Fulgentius metaforalis*, 86; in Sandys's *Ovids Metamorphosis Englished*, 269–70
Dante Alighieri, 4, 7, 17, 30, 48, 200, 237; influence on Chaucer of, 17, 185
  Divina Commedia, 9, 11, 12, 20
  Inferno: Boccaccio's lectures on, 185
  Paradiso, 167–68; as source for Chaucer's *General Prologue to the*

Dante Alighieri (*continued*)
    Canterbury Tales, 26, 183, 189–90;
    Zefiro (Zephirus) in, 183, 185
Daphne, 120n.17, 274n.19
Dares the Phrygian: *De excidio Troiae*,
    149n.2
David, 112
de Gonguyon, Jean: *Voeux du paon*, 111
de Hesdin, Jean, 92
deities, planetary, 24, 103, 145–46
Demogorgon, 12
Demophon, 216
de Polo, Damianus, 284–85
Deschamps, Eustace, 4
destiny, planets as: in Christine de Pizan's
    Epistre Othea and *Livre du chemin de
    long estude*, 145–46, 147
Diana, 4, 228; in Bersuire's *De formis fig-
    urisque deorum*, 87, 90–91; in
    Chaucer's *Knight's Tale*, 94; in Chris-
    tine de Pizan's *Epistre Othea*, 103,
    115–16; in Lucian's "Dialogues of the
    Gods," 270; in Petrarch's *Africa*, 87; in
    Sandys's *Ovids Metamorphosis En-
    glished*, 258–65, 270, 273n.10, 274n.16,
    274n.22
Dicta philosophorum, 119n.8
Dido, 7, 73–75; in Chaucer's *House of
    Fame*, 215–16; in Virgil's *Aeneid*, 183;
    and Zephirus, 189
Digby mythography, 9, 10
Discord: in Christine de Pizan's *Epistre
    Othea*, 134, 144; in Guillaume de
    Machaut's *Dit de la fonteinne amour-
    euse* and the *Ovide moralisé*, 136, 139
Dominic, St., 26, 185–89
Dominicans, 185, 187
Donatus: *Ars major*, 284
Dunbar, William, 4, 24
Dürer, Albrecht, 93

Echecs amoureux, 152n.19
Echo, 70; in Chrétien de Troyes's *Erec et
    Enide*, 17; in Ovid's *Metamorphoses*,
    67, 80n.30, 80n.31
Ecloga Theoduli, 7, 284; commentaries on,
    11; commentary on Virgil in, 9; epic
    and commentary traditions, conver-
    gence in, 12
empiricism, 19
Eneas, 73

Epicurean view of Venus, 235
Epistre Master, 138
Erasmus, 28, 247; *Adagia*, 246, 251
Erfurt commentary on Boethius, 10
Eteocles, 224
Etienne de Castel, 100
Eurydice, 274n.15

fable, 3, 57, 88–89
fabula. See fable; *integumentum;
    involucrum*
Faith (allegorical figure): in Alanus de In-
    sulis's *De planctu Naturae*, 69
faith (theological virtue): in Christine de
    Pizan's *Epistre Othea*, 103
fate. *See* destiny
Favonius (alternative name for Zephirus),
    178
feminism, 18, 101–2, 114–18, 121n.30
femme-image: Enide as, in *Erec et Enide*,
    67, 70–71
femme-langage: Enide as, in *Erec et Enide*,
    67, 71
Festus, 10
Ficino, 29, 272n.4
first Vatican mythographer, 9, 10, 30,
    191n.3; possibly Adanan the Scot, 10,
    178; Zephirus in, 26, 178, 183, 191n.4
Flores bibliorum, 119n.9
Fortune, 68, 69, 128
France, mythography in, 21–24
Francio (legendary founder of France), 132
Francis I, King of France, 248
Franciscans, 185
free will vs. destiny, 145–46, 147
Froissart, Jean, 4
Fulgentius, 30, 32n.7, 89, 164, 168, 170;
    Judgment of Paris in, 136, 162–63;
    Ovid, allegorization of, in, 84; Pallas
    in, 152n.15; commentary on Statius by,
    9–10; commentary on Virgil by, 9
—influence of, 10; on Bersuire's *Ovidius
    moralizatus*, 87; on Boccaccio's *Gene-
    alogie deorum gentilium*, 162; on
    Chaucer's *Troilus and Criseyde*, 25
Mitologiae, 230n.10; commentaries on,
    importance of, 11; influence of, 10;
    Judgment of Paris in, 141, 160–61;
    Ridewall's *Fulgentius metaforalis*, 86;

Venus in, 227, 235, 236; Zephyrus in, 183–84

Gallic Hercules, 247–48
garden/womb connection in mythographic and theological texts, 201–2, 207
Gemini, 210; association of, with May, 204; association of, with Mercury, 210; iconographic treatment of, 206
Genius (allegorical figure), 4, 7, 19
Geoffrey of Monmouth, 169
Giovanni del Virgilio, 20, 96n.8, 281, 282, 284, 285; *Allegoriae librorum Ovidii*, 85
Giraldus, 29, 271, 272n.4
Globe Theatre, 254n.8
Glosa ordinaria, 281
Godfrey de Bouillon, 112–13
Goliards, 51
Gorgon, 88
Gower, John, 4
  Confessio Amantis, 4, 24; Actaeon in, 273n.10; Ariadne in, 27; Phaedra in, 220
  —sources for: Bersuire's *Ovidius moralizatus*, 22, 94, 97n.20
Great Chain of Being: as chain of mirrors, in Macrobius, 58
Gregory, St.: *Moralia*, 90, 201, 207–8
Guido delle Colonne: *Historia destructionis Troiae*, 164, 179, 192n.7
Guillaume de Lorris, 3, 22
  Roman de la Rose, 13, 125; description of Narcissus in, 62, 78n.22; romance and mythographic traditions, convergence in, 19; as source for Chaucer, 17
Guillaume de Machaut, 4; and court of Charles V, 135; as court poet, 125; use of *Ovide moralisé* and *Ovidius moralizatus* in, 125
  Dit de la fonteinne amoureuse, 141; audience of, 136, 139, 142; *chevalerie* in, 137–38; Judgment of Paris in, 143, 148
  —influence: on Chaucer's *Book of the Duchess* and *Troilus and Criseyde*, 164–65; on Christine de Pizan's "Because I have no comfort from Juno," 126, 128–31, 146, 148; on Christine de Pizan's *Epistre Othea*, 23, 132, 135–38, 143, 153n.24; on Christine

de Pizan's *Livre du chemin de long estude*, 23, 144
  Remède de fortune, 152n.14

Hades, 87
Hector, 30; in Christine de Pizan's *Epistre Othea*, 23, 103–4, 108–22, 132–44; as one of Nine Worthies, 111; relation of, to French nobility, 102, 121n.24, 132
Helen of Troy, 54, 130, 131, 160–61, 164
Henry IV, King of England and France, 248
Henryson, Robert, 4, 24
Hera, 265, 270
Heracles, 265
Hercules, 7, 28, 30, 258; as allegorical figure for Christ, 246; association of, with Nero, 250–51; in Bersuire's *Ovidius moralizatus*, 91; in Boethius's *De consolatione Philosophiae*, 247; as braggart soldier in New Comedy, 247; in Chaucer's *House of Fame*, 216; in Chaucer's *Legend of Good Women—Hypsipyle*, 247; in Chaucer's *Monk's Tale*, 246–47; in Erasmus's *Adagia*, 246; Globe Theatre, on sign of, 254n.8; in Lucian's *Heracles*, 247; in Macrobius's *Saturnalia*, 247; in Ovid's *Metamorphoses*, 265; in *Roman de la Rose*, 19, 247; in Sandys's *Ovids Metamorphosis Englished*, 265–66, 267, 269; in second Vatican mythographer, 247; in Shakespeare's *Hamlet*, 248–54; in sixteenth-century France, 247–48; in third Vatican mythographer, 247
Hermaphrodite, 235
Hermes, 114, 247
Hesiod, 5, 8; *Theogony*, 191n.4
Hesperides, golden apples of, 265; in Sandys's *Ovids Metamorphosis Englished*, 265
Hildebert de Lavardin, 51
Hippolyte, 224
Hippolytus, 274n.22
Hippomenes, 266, 267, 268, 270
Histoire ancienne jusqu'à César, 128, 149n.2
Hoccleve, Thomas, 4
Holkot, Robert, 24, 30, 282; *Moralitates*, 286

Homer, 8, 48, 74; in Chaucer's *House of Fame*, 169; *Iliad*, Judgment of Paris in, 159; *Odyssey*, 73
Honorius III, Pope, 188
hope (theological virtue), 103
Horace: *Ars Poetica*, 56; Ode, 16, 269–70
horse imagery: in Shakespeare's *Venus and Adonis*, 239
Hugh of St. Victor, 51
Hugutio of Pisa, 9, 10, 192n.6
Hyginus
  Fabulae, 10; Ariadne in, 27, 220; Pallas in, 152n.15; Phaedra in, 220; as source for Chaucer's *Legend of Good Women—Ariadne*, 216; Theseus in, 220
Hymen, 19

illuminations, manuscript: Bersuire's influence on, 22; in Christine de Pizan, 24, 120n.22; in Christine de Pizan's *Epistre Othea*, 138–40
imago mundi, 54
Ino: in Christine de Pizan's *Epistre Othea*, 110–11
Integumenta Ovidii, medieval tradition of, 51–52. *See also* John of Garland
integumentum: in Bernard Silvestris, 14–15; in Chrétien de Troyes's *Erec et Enide*, 70; in Macrobius, 49; in William of Conches, 14–15. *See also involucrum*
involucrum, 14, 49, 54–55. *See also integumentum*
Io, 91–92, 202
Iris, 183
Isabeau of Bavaria, Queen of France, 132, 141
Iseut, 61
Isidore of Seville, 9, 170; quoted in Bersuire's *Ovidius moralizatus*, 90; Zephirus in, 26
  De natura rerum: Zephirus in, 179
  Etymologiae, 10, 210; Mercury in, 202–3
Isis, 115–16
Isocrates, 152n.15
Isolde, 61, 79n.24

Janus, 205
Jason, 247; in Chaucer's *House of Fame*, 216; in Chaucer's *Legend of Good Women—Hypsipyle*, 28; in Christine de Pizan's *Epistre Othea*, 117
Jean de Meun, 3
  Roman de la Rose, 13, 19, 125; Aristotelian philosophy in, 19; Chaucer's use of, 17; Hercules in, 28, 247; *integumentum* in, 15
Jerome, St., 90
Joan of Arc, 100
John of Garland, 11, 20, 281; Zephirus in, 26
  Fulgentius metaforalis, 96n.8
  Integumenta Ovidii, 77n.10, 84; as source for Giovanni del Virgilio's *Allegoriae librorum Ovidii*, 85; Zephirus in, 178
John of Salisbury, 51, 79n.29
  Policraticus: moralizations of Virgil's *Aeneid* in, 9; Narcissus in, 76n.10
John the Good, King of France, 86
Joshua, 112
Judas Maccabaeus, 112
Judgment of Paris: in Boccaccio's *Genealogie deorum gentilium*, 162; in Chaucer's *Troilus and Criseyde*, 159–71; in Christine de Pizan's works, 125–53; in *Cypria*, 149n.3; in Fulgentius, 136, 141, 160–61; goddesses associated with gifts offered in, 127–29, 136, 145–47; in Guillaume de Machaut's *Dit de la fonteinne amoureuse*, 142, 143, 144; in Hyginus's *Fabulae*, 159–60; in *Iliad*, 159; in *Ovide moralisé*, 135–38, 140, 144, 148–49, 162–64
Julius Caesar, 48; as one of Nine Worthies, 112–13
Juno, 30, 125, 162, 259, 260, 263, 268; in Bersuire's *De formis figurisque deorum*, 8, 87, 88; in Bersuire's *Ovidius moralizatus*, 91, 150n.7; in Calderia's *Concordatia*, 286; in Christine de Pizan's "Because I have no comfort from Juno," 126–31, 148; in Christine de Pizan's *Epistre Othea*, 132–44, 146–47; in Christine de Pizan's *Livre du chemin de long estude*, 146–47, 149; in Guillaume de Machaut's *Dit de la fonteinne amoureuse*, 136, 148; and Judgment of Paris, 160–61; in *Ovide moralisé*, 132, 135–36, 141, 163–64; in Ovid's *Metamorphoses*, 80n.30; in Petrarch's *Africa*, 8, 87; in Petrarch's

Index   329

De viribus illustribus, 162; in Ridewall's *Fulgentius metaforalis*, 86; in Virgil's *Aeneid*, 183
Jupiter, 4, 14, 208, 259, 260, 263, 269; in Bersuire's *Ovidius moralizatus*, 91; in Calderia's *Concordatia*, 286; in Christine de Pizan's *Epistre Othea*, 103, 134–35, 144–45; in Christine de Pizan's *Livre du chemin de long estude*, 144–45; in *Ecloga Theoduli*, 13; in Horace's Ode 16, 270; in Ovid's *Metamorphoses*, 85; in Petrarch's *Africa*, 87; in Ridewall's *Fulgentius metaforalis*, 86; in William of Conches, 14
justice: in *Epistre Othea*, 103
Juvenal, 30, 32n.6

Knightliness (personification): in Christine de Pizan's *Livre du chemin de long estude*, 144, 146, 147

Lactantius, 269
Lactantius Firmianus: *Divinae institutiones*, Zephirus in, 177–78, 191n.6
Lactantius Placidus: *Commentarii in Statii Thebaida et commentarius in Achilleida*, 9–10; *Narrationes fabularum Ovidianarum*, 11, 84, 281
Lai of Narcisus, 72; description of Narcissus in, 62, 78n.22
Landino, Cristoforo, 20, 162, 170
Lavinia, 74–75
Lavinius, Peter, 281, 285
Layomon: *Brut*, 169
Leda, 286
Legenda aurea, 188
Legrand, Jacques (Jacobus Magnus): *Introductorium sermocandi*, 92
Leomedon, 104
Libellus de imaginibus deorum: Bersuire's influence on, 88, 93; as possible intermediary source for Chaucer's knowledge of Bersuire, 94–95
liberal arts: Pallas as goddess of, 128–29, 131, 148
Liber albus, 169
literary theory, medieval, 3–31
Lorens, Frère: *Somme le roi*, 133
Louis of Orleans, 137–39, 143; character of, 141; and Christine de Pizan, 132–33; Christine de Pizan's *Epistre Othea* dedicated to, 151n.11
Lucan, 8; *Pharsalia*, 84, 283; scholia and commentaries on, 10–11
Lucian: Hercules in, 28; Pallas in, 152n.15
"Dialogues of the Gods," 270
Heracles: Hercules in, 247, 254n.3
Lydgate, John, 4, 24

Mabonagrin, 51
Macrobius, 30, 31n.1, 31n.3; chain of mirrors in, 66; Great Chain of Being as chain of mirrors in, 58; immoral material excluded by, 13; influence of, on Chrétien de Troyes, 19, 49–50; influence of Aristotelian philosophy on, 16; *involucrum* in, 54–55; *narratio fabulosa* in, 58, 77n.9; Virgil's *Aeneid* as literary *microcosmos* in, 69; William of Conches's reinterpretation of, 14–16
Commentum in Somnium Scipionis: commentary on Virgil in, 9; influence of, on medieval mythography, 5–6; influence of, on Chaucer, 177–78; *integumentum* as valid use of myth, 49; Petrarch's *Africa* as "commentary" on, 12
Saturnalia: commentary on Virgil's *Aeneid* in, 9, 74; Hercules in, 247
Manegold von Lautenbach, 281, 285; "Explicationes Metamorphoseon Ovidii," 11, 19
manuscript illuminations. See illuminations, manuscript
Map, Walter: *De nugis curialium*, 230n.10
Marie de France, 21; *Lais*, 80n.32
Marriage: in Neoplatonism and courtly love traditions, 59
Mars, 4, 32n.7, 223, 225, 226, 228; in Bersuire's *De formis figurisque deorum*, 87; in Boccaccio's *Genealogie deorum gentilium*, 230n.10; in Chaucer's *Knight's Tale*, 94; in Christine de Pizan's *Epistre Othea*, 103, 104; in Petrarch's *Africa*, 87; in William of Conches, 14
Martianus Capella, 12, 30; Chrétien de Troyes's use of, 19
—commentaries on, 10, 11; by Notker Labeo, 19; by Remigius of Auxerre,

Martianus Capella (*continued*)
  10; by University of Paris scholars, 19; Welsh, 18
  De nuptiis Philologiae et Mercurii, 12–13; Favonius (Zephirus) in, 191n.5; parallels with *Erec et Enide* of, 80n.33
Mary, Virgin, 90–91
matière bretonne, 61
Matthew of Vendôme: *Tobias*, 284
May: iconographic models of, 204–5
Medea, 54
Medusa, 267
Mercury, 4, 25, 30, 200, 201; association of, with Gemini, 202; in Bersuire's *De formis figurisque deorum*, 87; in Bersuire's *Ovidius moralizatus*, 91–92; in Bersuire's *Reductorium morale*, 202–3, 206, 212n.11; in Boccaccio's *Comedia delle ninfe fiorentine*, 204, 210; in Boccaccio's *Decameron*, 26, 202–6; in Boccaccio's *Genealogie deorum gentilium*, 203–4, 211n.9; in Chaucer's *Merchant's Tale*, 26, 202–6; in Christine de Pizan's *Epistre Othea*, 103, 117, 134, 144; in Isidore of Seville's *Etymologiae*, 202–3; in Martianus Capella's *De nuptiis Philologiae et Mercurii*, 80n.33; in *Ovide moralisé*, 139; as patron of doctors, 203; as patron of merchants, 203–4; as patron of thieves and deceivers, 202–3; in Petrarch's *Africa*, 87
metamorphosis: in Chrétien de Troyes's *Erec et Enide*, 66
Milton, John: *Paradise Lost*, 243
Minerva, 152n.17; in Bersuire's *De formis figurisque deorum*, 87; in Bersuire's *Ovidius moralizatus*, 91, 150, 164; in Christine de Pizan's *Epistre Othea*, 110, 115, 116; and Judgment of Paris, 160–61; in Petrarch's *Africa*, 87; in Petrarch's *De viribus illustribus*, 162
Minos, 216, 217
Minotaur, 216, 217, 218, 220, 224, 226–27
mirror symbolism: in Chrétien de Troyes's *Erec et Enide*, 56–58, 65, 69–70; in courtly love lyric, 57; in Neoplatonism, 57, 59–60
misogyny, 257–58; Christine de Pizan's opposition to, 100–101, 117–18, 121n.30;
  in Sandys's *Ovids Metamorphosis Englished*, 29, 257–72
Montanus, 263, 265
Morpheus, 4
myth: medieval uses of, 3–31
mythographic tradition: effect of, on rise of vernacular literature, 16–31

Nambroth, 109–10
Narcissus: in Alexander Neckam's *De naturis rerum*, 79n.29; allegorical uses of, in twelfth century, 51; in Chrétien de Troyes's *Erec et Enide*, 17, 47–75; in Clement of Alexandria's *Pedagogus*, 78n.18; courtly lover's relation to, 57; descriptions of, in Old French texts, 61–67, 78n.22; in Neoplatonic tradition, 57–59; in Ovid's *Metamorphoses*, 47–75
narratio fabulosa, 5, 8; in Macrobius, 58, 77n.9
Natura, Nature (personification), 5–6, 7, 16, 49, 56–57, 76n.2; in Alanus de Insulis's *De planctu Naturae*, 19, 53–57, 78n.14, 79n.23, 80n.31, 235–36; in Chaucer's *Parlement of Foules*, 237; classical deities as projections of, in William of Conches, 13–14; as *Natura plangens*, 72
Neoplatonism, 16, 57–59; in Chrétien de Troyes's *Erec et Enide*, 71; dominance in mythographic tradition, 19; myth as vehicle for, 13, 21
Neoplatonist poets of Chartres, 51
Neptune, 86, 87
Nero: association with Hercules, 250–51, 263, 265
Nero (play), 250
Nine Worthies, 111–13
Nobility (personification): in Christine de Pizan's *Livre du chemin de long estude*, 144, 146, 147
Notker Labeo, 10, 19
novellino—"De caeco et ejus uxore": as source for Chaucer's *Merchant's Tale*, 209–10, 211n.9
Numenius, 6, 33n.7

Odysseus, 247
Oenone, 160

Index   331

Olympus, Mount, 145
Orpheus, 5, 7, 274n.15
Osbern of Gloucester, 9, 10
Ovid, 4, 7, 8, 49, 51; Chaucer's *Troilus and Criseyde* dedicated to, 168–69; Pallas in, 152n.15; significance of, in twelfth-century culture, 50; translations of, by Chrétien de Troyes, 50; translations of, by Sandys, 29
—commentary on: in Bersuire's *Ovidius moralizatus*, 22; dominance of mythographic tradition by, 19–20; by Giovanni del Virgilio, 85; influenced by earlier commentaries, 11; influence of, on Renaissance mythography, 7–8; in John of Garland's *Integumenta Ovidii*, 84–85; by Manegold von Lautenbach, 19; by University of Paris scholars, 19
—influence of: on Bersuire, 164; on Chaucer's *Legend of Good Women—Ariadne*, 216; on Chaucer's *Troilus and Criseyde*, 170; on Chrétien de Troyes, 19; on Christine de Pizan's *Epistre Othea*, 133

Amores: Arnulf of Orleans's commentary on, 84
Epistolae ex Ponto, 84
Fasti: Ariadne in, 27, 220; glosses and commentary on, 11, 84; Phaedra in, 220; Theseus in, 220; Zephirus in, 178–79, 191n.6
Heroides: Ariadne in, 27, 220–21; Judgment of Paris in, 160; Phaedra in, 220–21; as source for Chaucer's *Legend of Good Women—Ariadne*, 218; Theseus in, 220–21
Metamorphoses, 83, 105; influence of, on Chrétien de Troyes, 76n.6; influence of, on *Ecloga Theoduli*, 12–13; medieval schools, use in, 5; metamorphosis as resolution in, 66–67; textual history of, 281
—commentaries on, 19–20, 84–86; by Arnulf of Orleans, 11, 48; importance of, 11; in *Ovide moralisé*, 85; textual history of, 281–86; unpublished, 30, 281–86
—mythological figures in: Actaeon, 263; Apollo, 268; Ariadne, 27, 220; Atalanta, 268; Callisto, 263; Diana, 274n.22; Narcissus, 30–48, 60–63; Phaedra, 220; Theseus, 220
Remedia amoris, 84, 284
Tristia, 262
Ovide moralisé, 20, 29–30, 86, 120n.13, 230n.10, 282; audience of, 125, 136, 139, 141, 143; combined with Bersuire's *De formis figurisque deorum*, 87; illustrations of, Bersuire's influence on, 93; sources for, Arnulf of Orleans and John of Garland as, 96n.8; structure of, 85, 143
—influence of: on Bersuire's *De formis figurisque deorum*, 87–88; on Bersuire's *Ovidius moralizatus*, 83, 95, 120n.14; on Chaucer's *Legend of Good Women—Ariadne*, 216; on Chaucer's *Troilus and Criseyde*, 25, 162–64, 168, 170; on Christine de Pizan's "Because I have no comfort from Juno," 128–29; on Christine de Pizan's *Epistre Othea*, 23, 105–8, 132, 135–38, 143–44, 146, 148; on Christine de Pizan's *Livre du chemin de long estude*, 23, 144, 149; on Guillaume de Machaut's *Dit de la fonteinne amoureuse*, 135–36, 142
—mythological figures and events in: Ariadne, 27, 220–21; Judgment of Paris, 140–41, 142–44, 148–49; Pallas, 132, 135–36, 137–38, 140, 141, 144, 165; Paris, 136, 142–43, 148–49; Phaedra, 220; Zephirus, 26, 178

Pallas, 30, 125; in Boccaccio's *Genealogie deorum gentilium*, 165; in Christine de Pizan's "Because I have no comfort from Juno," 148; in Christine de Pizan's *Epistre Othea*, 24, 116, 126–31, 132–44, 146–47; in Christine de Pizan's *Livre du chemin de long estude*, 146–47; eighth sphere of heaven, association with, 168; in Guillaume de Machaut's *Dit de la fonteinne amoureuse*, 135–36, 137, 148; and Judgment of Paris, 160–61; in *Ovide moralisé*, 132, 135–36, 137–38, 140, 141, 144, 165; in Petrarch's *De viribus illustribus*, 165. *See also* Athena; Minerva
Pan, 87
Pandora, 7

Papias the Lombard, 9; *Distinctiones*, 10; *Vocabulista*, Zephirus in, 178
Paris, 7, 30, 125, 162, 258, 265, 268; in Benoit de St. Maure's *Roman de Troiae*, 164; in Chaucer's *House of Fame*, 216; in Chaucer's *Troilus and Criseyde*, 159-71; in Christine de Pizan's "Because I have no comfort from Juno," 126-31; in Christine de Pizan's *Epistre Othea*, 132-44, 144-45, 148-49; in Christine de Pizan's *Livre du chemin de long estude*, 144-45, 146-47; in Guido delle Colonne's *Historia Troiana*, 164; in Guillaume de Machaut's *Dit de la fonteinne amoureuse*, 136, 137-38, 148-49; in *Ovide moralisé*, 136, 142-43, 148-49
Paris, University of, 17, 19; and Macrobian literary theory, 13
Pasiphae, 117, 217, 227
Paulus Diaconus, 10
Pegasus, 115
Peleus and Thetis, wedding of, 125; in Bersuire's *De formis figurisque deorum*, 87; in Christine de Pizan's *Epistre Othea*, 134, 143; in Christine de Pizan's *Livre du chemin de long estude*, 145-46
Penthesilea, 116
Perseus, 258, 265, 267, 269; in Bersuire's *De formis figurisque deorum*, 88; in *Ovide moralisé*, 85; in Ridewall's *Fulgentius metaforalis*, 86; in Sandys's *Ovids Metamorphosis Englished*, 266, 269
Pervigilium Veneris, 192n.7
Petrarch, 4, 17, 170; Bersuire's acquaintance with, 86, 282
Africa: as commentary on Macrobius, 12; deities in, 87; as source for Bersuire's *Ovidius moralizatus*, 22, 87
De viribus illustribus: Pallas in, 165; as source for Chaucer's *Troilus and Criseyde*, 162
Sonnet 88: as source for Chaucer's *Troilus and Criseyde*, 25, 164
Phaedra, 27, 30, 220-21; in Chaucer's *Legend of Good Women—Ariadne*, 217-22
Phillipe of Vitry, 87
Phoebe, 117. See also Diana
Phoebus, 181. See also Apollo

Pierre des Pres, Cardinal, 86
planets, as deities: in Christine de Pizan, 103, 145
Plato, 5, 31n.1, 32-58
Phaedrus: horse imagery in, 237; mirror imagery in, 58
Republic, 5
Timaeus, 30, 31n.3
Pliny, 90, 192n.6
Plotinus: interpretation of Homer in, 74; Narcissus in, 57-59; nature in, 58
Plutarch: Ariadne in, 27; as source for Chaucer's *Legend of Good Women—Ariadne*, 216
Lives: Theseus and Ariadne in, 220
Pluto, 4, 30, 33n.7; in Bersuire's *De formis figurisque deorum*, 87; in Bersuire's *Ovidius moralizatus*, 91; in Boccaccio's *Genealogie deorum gentilium*, 204; in Chaucer's *Merchant's Tale*, 203, 204; in *Ovide moralisé*, 106; in *Ovidius moralizatus*, 106; in Petrarch's *Africa*, 87; in Ridewall's *Fulgentius metaforalis*, 86; in William of Conches, 14
Poimandres, 57
Polibetes, 110
Polydectes, 269
Polynices, 224
Polyxena, 110
Pontanus, Jacobus, 29, 271, 272n.4
Priapus, 4
Priscian, 285
Proserpina, 4, 30, 33n.7, 241; in Bersuire's *Ovidius moralizatus*, 105-6; in Bersuire's *Reductorium morale*, 212n.11; in Boccaccio's *Genealogie deorum gentilium*, 204; in Chaucer's *Merchant's Tale*, 203, 204; in Christine de Pizan's *Epistre Othea*, 107-8; in *Ovide moralisé*, 106-7; in Ridewall's *Fulgentius metaforalis*, 86; in William of Conches, 14
Prudencia: in Alanus de Insulis's *De planctu Naturae*, 69; in Ridewall's *Fulgentius metaforalis*, 86
Pseudo-John Scot, 10
Pseudo-Lactantius Placidus, 281, 282
Psyche: connection with Zephirus, 189; in Fulgentius's *Mitologiae*, 183-84
Pythagoras, 76n.2

Pythagorean Y, 162

Quadrivium, 56

Rabanus Maurus: *De universo*, Zephirus in, 184–85; influence on Bersuire's *Ovidius moralizatus*, 87, 90
Raison. *See* Reason
Ralph of Beauvais, 30; *Liber Titan*, 11, 283
Reason (personification): in Christine de Pizan's *Livre du chemin de long estude*, 144, 145, 147; in Jean de Meun's *Roman de la Rose*, 15–16
Reflection (personification): in Christine de Pizan's *Livre du chemin de long estude*, 144
Remigius of Auxerre, 30; commentary of, on Martianus Capella, 10; commentary of, on Virgil's *Aeneid*, 9; possibly second Vatican mythographer, 10
Riches (personification): in Christine de Pizan's *Livre du chemin de long estude*, 144, 146, 147
Ridewall, John, 20, 30; as Franciscan, 85; iconography in, 24, 35
  Fulgentius metaforalis, 286; Augustinian psychology in, 20; textual history of, 285
  —influence of, 85–86; on Bersuire's *De formis figurisque deorum*, 87; on Bersuire's *Ovidius moralizatus*, 90, 95
  —sources, 85–86; *Liber imaginum deorum*, 86
Roman de la Rose, 201. *See also* Guillaume de Lorris; Jean de Meun

Sabinus, 29; as source for Sandys's *Ovids Metamorphosis Englished*, 272n.4
Salmacis, 235
Salutati, Coluccio: *De laboribus Herculis*, 12
Sandys, George, 18, 30
  Ovids Metamorphosis Englished, 29; misogyny in, 18, 257–72; sexuality in, 260–61, 263, 265, 271; sources of, 272n.4; style and structure of, 271–72; uses of myth in, 259–72
  —mythological figures in: Actaeon, 267, 270, 271; Atalanta, 266–68; Callisto, 267, 271; Danae, 269–70; Diana, 270, 274n.22; Hercules, 267, 269; Perseus, 266, 269
Saturn, 4, 7, 200, 209, 212n.14; in Bersuire's *De formis figurisque deorum*, 87; in Bersuire's *Ovidius moralizatus*, 91; in Boccaccio's *Decameron*, 26; in Boccaccio's *Genealogie deorum gentilium*, 205–6; in Calderia's *Concordatia*, 286; in Chaucer's *Merchant's Tale*, 26; in Christine de Pizan's *Epistre Othea*, 103; in *Ecloga Theoduli*, 13; in glosses on Juvenal, 31n.6; in Petrarch's *Africa*, 87; in Ridewall's *Fulgentius metaforalis*, 86; in William of Conches, 14
Scaliger, 29, 272n.4
schools and universities, medieval: and mythography, 6–7, 8
Scylla, 216, 217
second Vatican mythographer (Remigius of Auxerre?) 9, 30, 164, 230n.10; Demogorgon in, 12; Fulgentius as source for, 161; Hercules in, 247; identified as Remigius of Auxerre, 10, 178; as source for Chaucer's *Troilus and Criseyde*, 25; Zephirus in, 26
Secreta secretorum, 192n.7
Segward, John, 284
Semele, 14, 274n.19
Seneca: commentaries on, 9, 24; quotations from, in Bersuire, 90
Servius, 10, 13; commentary on Virgil's *Aeneid*, 9, 12, 88–89, 140, 191n.3, 191n.4
sexuality: in Boccaccio's *Genealogie deorum gentilium*, 236, in Chaucer's *Parlement of Foules*, 237; connection with Venus, 236–39; in Genesis, 243; in Milton's *Paradise Lost*, 243; in Sandys's *Ovids Metamorphosis Englished*, 260–61, 263, 264–65, 269–70, 271–72; in Shakespeare's *Venus and Adonis*, 237, 238–44; in Spenser's *Epithalamion*, 240
Shakespeare, William, 9, 17, 18, 21; Hercules in, 248; and mythographic tradition, 27–28; use of sources by, 17
  Antony and Cleopatra: Hercules in, 248
  Hamlet: Hercules in, 28, 248–54
  King John, 251

Shakespeare, William (*continued*)
  Midsummer Night's Dream: Hercules in, 28, 248
  Venus and Adonis: bird imagery in, 240; horse imagery in, 239; humor in, 237, 239, 243–44; sexuality in 237, 238–44; sources of, 27–28, 235; Venus in, 235–44
Sibyls: in Christine de Pizan's works, 109, 114, 121n.23
Sins, Deadly: in Christine de Pizan's *Epistre Othea*, 103, 133, 143
Sir Gawain and the Green Knight, 26, 180
Sir Orfeo, 24
Solinus, 90
Song of Songs, 201
speculum caducis: Natura as, in Alanus de Insulis's *De planctu Naturae*, 54, 62, 78n.23
Spenser, Edmund, 28; sexuality in, 240
Statius, 9, 30; commentaries and glosses on, 9–10, 11
  Thebaid, 285; scholia on, 191n.3; as source for Chaucer's *Knight's Tale* and *Legend of Good Women—Ariadne*, 220
Stoicism, 183, 193n.10; dominance of, in mythographic tradition, 19; view of Venus in, 235
Suetonius, 250, 254n.6
summa tradition, 133
Syrinx, 274n.19

Tacitus, 263
Ten Commandments: in *Epistre Othea*, 103, 133, 143
Temperance (personification): in Christine de Pizan's *Epistre Othea*, 103
Tethys, 259
Theatres, War of, 252
Themis, 266
Theodulf of Orleans, 11, 84
theological virtues, three: in Christine de Pizan's *Epistre Othea*, 103, 116
Theseus, 30; in Chaucer's *Anelida and Arcite*, 215, 225; in Chaucer's *House of Fame*, 27, 215–16, 227, 228; in Chaucer's *Knight's Tale*, 27, 215, 216, 222–29; in Chaucer's *Legend of Good Women—Ariadne*, 27, 215–23, 225–29; in Chaucer's *Legend of Good Women—Phyllis*, 215–16; in Hyginus's *Fabulae*, 220; in Ovid's *Fasti*, 220; in Ovid's *Heroides*, 220–21; in Ovid's *Metamorphoses*, 220; in Plutarch's *Lives*, 220; in Statius's *Thebaid*, 220; in Virgil's *Aeneid*, 220
Thetis and Peleus, wedding of, 125; in Bersuire's *De formis figurisque deorum*, 87; in Christine de Pizan's *Epistre Othea*, 134, 143; in Christine de Pizan's *Livre du chemin de long estude*, 145–46
third Vatican mythographer (Albericus of London or Alexander Neckam?), 9, 30, 230n.10; identity of, 10–11
  Liber imaginum deorum: Hercules in, 247; influence of, on Bersuire's *Ovidius moralizatus*, 87; influence of, on Ridewall's *Fulgentius metaforalis*, 86; Venus in, 227
Thomas à Becket, St.: in Chaucer's *General Prologue to the Canterbury Tales*, 26; connection with Zephirus of, 189
Thomas de Pizan (Christine de Pizan's father), 100, 145
Thomas Hibernicus: *Manipulus florum*, 119n.9
Thomyris, 116
time, pagan and Christian: in Christine de Pizan's *Epistre Othea*, 108–9
Titans, 178
Triptolomous, 30; in Bersuire's *Ovidius moralizatus*, 106; in Christine de Pizan's *Epistre Othea*, 107
Tristan and Isolde, legend of, 79n.24
Trivet, Nicholas, 24, 284
trivium, 56
Trojan war, 125, 160–61, 164–65; in Christine de Pizan's *Epistre Othea*, 110–11

Ulysses, 59

Vatican commentaries on Boethius, 10
Vatican mythographers. *See* first, second, and third Vatican mythographers
velamen figmentorum, 5–6
Venus, 4, 7, 30, 32n.7, 125, 160–61, 162, 181, 225, 226–28, 273n.10; in Alanus de Insulis's *De planctu Naturae*, 13, 19, 235–36; in Benoit de St. Maure's

Roman de Troiae, 164; in Bernard Silvestris, 236; in Bersuire's *De formis figurisque deorum*, 87; bifurcation of, 236–38; in Boccaccio's *Genealogie deorum gentilium*, 27–28, 230n.10, 236, 238; in Cartari's *Le imagini con la spositione de i dei gli antichi*, 237–38, 239; in Chaucer's *House of Fame*, 94–95, 215–16; in Chaucer's *Knight's Tale*, 94–95; in Chaucer's *Parlement of Foules*, 27–28, 237; in Chaucer's *Troilus and Criseyde*, 25, 159, 167; in Christine de Pizan's "Because I have no comfort from Juno," 126–31; in Christine de Pizan's *Epistre Othea*, 103, 117, 126, 134–37, 144–45, 146–47; in Christine de Pizan's *Livre du chemin de long estude*, 126, 144–45, 145–46, 147; in Comes's *Mythologiae sive explicationum fabularum libri decem*, 237–38, 259; Epicurean view of, 235; in Fulgentius's *Mitologiae*, 227, 235, 236; in Guido delle Colonne's *Historia Troiana*, 164; iconographic depiction of, Bersuire's influence on, 93; in Machaut's *Dit de la fonteinne amoureuse*, 135–36; in *Ovide moralisé*, 135–36, 141, 142, 163–64; in Petrarch's *Africa*, 87; in Petrarch's *De viribus illustribus*, 162; in Shakespeare's *Venus and Adonis*, 235–44; as single figure with dual aspect, 237–38; Stoic view of, 235; in third Vatican mythographer, 227; in William of Conches, 14. *See also* Aphrodite

vernacular literature, rise of: effect of mythographic tradition on, 16–31

vernacular poetics: in Latin commentary tradition, 20–21

vices, seven: in Christine de Pizan's *Epistre Othea*, 133, 143

Vincent of Beauvais: *Speculum naturale*, 192n.7, 207, 210

Virgil, 7, 8, 20; Ariadne in, 27; Chaucer's *Troilus and Criseyde* dedicated to, 168–69; commentaries on, 9, 11, 12; popularity and significance of, in twelfth century, 51; as source for Chaucer's *House of Fame*, 169

Aeneid, 5, 22, 30, 140; Ariadne and Theseus in, 220; Chrétien de Troyes's allusions to, in *Erec et Enide*, 73–74; Damianus de Polo's commentary on, 285; Dante's *Divina commedia* as commentary on, 12; first Vatican mythographer's quotations from, 183; as literary *microcosmos* in Macrobius, 69; Zephirus in, 189–90

Eclogues, 11

Virgin Mary, 90–91

virtues, seven: in Christine de Pizan's *Epistre Othea*, 133, 143

Vives, 29, 272n.4

Vulcan, 226; in Bersuire's *De formis figurisque deorum*, 87, 88; in Petrarch's *Africa*, 87

Vulgate Bible: quotations from, in Christine de Pizan's *Epistre Othea*, 102

Walsingham, Thomas, 30
Archana deorum, 25; Bersuire's influence on, 22, 92

Walter of Châtillon, 284

White Stag, 67

William of Conches, 6, 30, 33n.7; commentary of, on Boethius, 10; commentary of, on Macrobius, 14–16, 177; commentary of, on Plato's *Timaeus*, 10, 31n.3; commentary of, on Virgil's *Aeneid*, 9; Natura or World Soul in, 13–14

Wisdom (personification): in Christine de Pizan's *Livre du chemin de long estude*, 144, 146, 147

World Soul, 16, 193n.10; classical deities as projections of, in William of Conches, 13–14; linked with Zephirus, 183. *See also* Anima mundi

Zephirus, 26, 30; in Apuleius, 189–90; in Arnulf of Orleans, 178; in Bede's *Didascalia genuina*, 191n.3; in Bersuire's *Reductorium morale*, 179; in Boccaccio's *Genealogie deorum gentilium*, 178, 183, 184, 191n.6; in Boethius's *De consolatione Philosophiae*, 179, 181, 188; in Chaucer's *Book of the Duchess*, 180–81, 185; in Chaucer's *General Prologue to the Canterbury Tales*, 177–90; in Chaucer's *Legend of Good Women—Hypermnestra*, 182–83; in Chaucer's *Legend of Good*

Zephirus (*continued*)
    Women—Prologue, 182; in Chaucer's *Troilus and Criseyde*, 181–82; in Dante's *Paradiso*, 183, 185–89; in first Vatican mythographer, 26, 178, 183, 191; in Fulgentius's *Mitologiae*, 183–84; in Giovanni Balbi's *Catholicon*, 178; in Guido delle Colonne's *Historia destructionis Troiae*, 179; in Isidore of Seville's *De natura rerum*, 179; in John of Garland's *Integumenta Ovidii*, 178; in Lactantius Firmianus's *Divinae institutiones*, 178–79, 191n.6; in Martianus Capella's *De nuptiis Philologiae et Mercurii*, 191n.5; in Ovid's *Fasti*, 178–79, 191n.6; in *Ovide moralisé*, 178; in Papias the Lombard's *Vocabulista*, 178; in Pliny's *Natural History*, 192n.6; in Rabanus Maurus's *De universo*, 184–85; in second Vatican mythographer, 178; in Virgil's *Aeneid*, 189–90

Zeus, 269, 270. *See also* Jupiter